D1095544

AVIATION IN THE CINEMA

by
Stephen Pendo

The Scarecrow Press, Inc.
Metuchen, N.J., and London
1985

All photographs included in this book are courtesy of the Lester Glassner collection.

Quotations from The Complete Directory to Prime-Time Network TV Shows, 1946-Present, by Tim Brooks and Earle Marsh, copyright © 1979 by Tim Brooks and Earle Marsh, are reprinted by permission of Ballantine Books, a division of Random House, Inc.

Quotations from Locklear: The Man Who Walked on Wings, by Art Ronnie, copyright © 1973 by A. S. Barnes & Co., Inc., are reprinted by permission of Oak Tree Publications, Inc.

Quotations from Stunt Flying in the Movies, by Jim and Maxine Greenwood, copyright © 1982 by Tab Books, Inc., are reprinted by permission of Tab Books, Inc., Blue Ridge Summit, Pa. 17214.

Excerpt from HOLLYWOOD PILOT by Don Dwiggins. Copyright © 1967 by Don Dwiggins. Reprinted by permission of Doubleday & Company, Inc.

Excerpt from LEGION OF THE LAFAYETTE by Arch Whitehouse. Copyright © 1962 by Arch Whitehouse. Reprinted by permission of Doubleday & Company. Inc.

Library of Congress Cataloging in Publication Data

Pendo, Stephen, 1947–
    Aviation in the cinema.

    Bibliography: p.
    Includes index.
    1. Flight in motion pictures. 2. World War, 1914-1918--Motion pictures and the war. 3. World War, 1939-1945--Motion pictures and the war. 4. Korean War, 1950-1953--Motion pictures and the war. I. Title.
PN1995.9.F58P46   1985   791.43'09'09356   84-14169
ISBN 0-8108-1746-2

To Eleanor

CONTENTS

INTRODUCTION

A character in THE GREAT WALDO PEPPER summarizes flying by observing that things are simple in the sky. For the filmmakers who produced the films discussed in this book, life has been anything but simple. The complexity, expense, and risk involved in making a major aviation picture would seem to discourage anyone. But if, as Orson Welles suggested, a movie studio is the largest toy train layout in the world, then certainly an aviation movie is the ultimate model airplane experience. It's not hard to translate the image of a ten-year-old zooming and diving a toy airplane into Howard Hughes orchestrating dozens of full-scale planes in a mammoth dogfight sequence.

Perhaps this is what sets aviation films apart from other genres. The filmmakers have often been pilots and aviation enthusiasts who cared deeply about their subject. They certainly haven't gone into aviation filmmaking for the money. Only one airplane film, AIRPORT, ever became a "block-busting" movie. In terms of box office receipts there are simply no STAR WARS, GONE WITH THE WIND, or RAIDERS OF THE LOST ARK among aviation pictures, though not for the lack of large production budgets. But the filmmakers' love of flying has often proved the genre's greatest weakness. So much attention has been lavished on aircraft that story and characters have suffered. THE BATTLE OF BRITAIN serves as an excellent example of an elaborately planned and meticulously executed film that falls flat because of its script. As we shall see, the best aviation films combine a good story with exciting aviation sequences for greatest possible impact.

This book deals with feature motion pictures, made-for-television films, and television series that feature some aspect of aviation. It does not cover individual episodes of non-aviation television series that featured aviation. Nor does it discuss science fiction films, either those that portray futuristic airplanes, such as THE SHAPE OF THINGS TO COME, or movies exclusively devoted to space travel, like MAROONED.

The story of the men who filmed, and sometimes died, in Hollywood skies is an exciting one. It is the equal of the story of any other film genre, although it has long been neglected by cinematic scholars.

CHAPTER 1

ACTION IN THE CLOUDS

Coincidentally, the motion picture and the airplane share the same "birthday." In the fall of 1903, Edwin S. Porter, working for Thomas Edison, produced THE GREAT TRAIN ROBBERY. Motion pictures had existed since the 1890s, but generally they were limited to short segments of film showing moving objects, or they were filmed plays, in which the camera remained fixed as though the viewer were seated watching a play. But to photograph THE GREAT TRAIN ROBBERY, which many film historians regard as the first "story" film, Porter placed the camera in different locations. When he edited the segments of film together, his movie told a complete story through the creative use of film.

Pioneers of a different sort labored on other projects. The Wright brothers spent many hours in their bicycle shop making wind tunnel tests of airfoil designs. And, on December 17, 1903, they did what no other men had done: fly a heavier-than-air craft under its own power. As in Porter's case Wilbur and Orville Wright's work was based on the successes and failures of people who had preceded them, as well as their own innovative thinking. But the similarity between the development of the motion picture and the airplane ends with the closing of 1903.

After THE GREAT TRAIN ROBBERY movies quickly became longer and better. They were cheap to produce and inexpensive to view. Audiences, eager to see anything on film, crammed the mushrooming nickelodeons. These people made motion pictures a mass entertainment medium. The airplane, however, followed a different course of development.

For many years after the Wrights, aviation remained the province of a select group of scientists, inventors, and

1

enthusiasts rich and/or interested enough to participate in it. This in no way belittles these individuals' accomplishments. While many early filmmakers concerned themselves with making money rather than art, the early aviation pioneers invested their time, money, and even lives to further aviation. The general public, though, remained unaffected. Even after World War I, aviation had not yet become a part of everyday life. The differences in the development of motion pictures and aviation are illustrated by the fact that, by the end of World War I, virtually all major filmic devices and techniques had been attempted (e.g., color, sound, wide screen, moving camera, crosscutting) while most major aviation advances still lay in the future. Not until the 1920s did the public begin to experience widespread effects of aviation, with the establishment of regular mail and passenger service. And not until the 1930s did aviation match the motion picture's impact on society.

The decade following the Wright brothers' first flight contained few aviation films. Jim and Maxine Greenwood, in STUNT FLYING IN THE MOVIES, cite 1908 as the date of the first successful films of planes. During this period, aviation in the cinema consisted either of documentary recordings of early flying experiments (including those not only of the Wright brothers but of more unorthodox, and less successful, inventors) or of pictures of aircraft in non-aviation films. Not until the beginning of World War I did the aviation film genre become established.

Early filmmakers experienced a basic problem making airplane movies: they didn't know what to do with the planes. Aviation was a young science; how to make an effective aviation film was a skill not yet mastered. As a result, many early airplane movies (until WINGS in 1927) were simply standard melodramas of the period with an aircraft or two thrown in. Most plots could have been filmed without any airplanes at all, but aircraft were a novelty and even people who didn't have barnstormers swooping into their hayfield on a summer's afternoon could participate in aerial stunts, wrapped in the darkness of the local cinema. After sound came to the movies, the melodramas became the "B" movies that often filled the bottom half of double bills, but these films remained a staple of the aviation film genre into the age of television.

Three films released in 1914-15 set the pattern for the

melodramas that would follow. MARRIAGE BY AEROPLANE,
shown in January 1914, was a French production adapted
by the Gaumont Company to an American setting by appro-
priate English subtitles. Everything else about the picture,
of course, remained decidedly French. The simple plot depicts a young girl who wants to marry against her father's
wishes. She runs away with her lover in an airplane, returns, and is forgiven. AN AERIAL REVENGE (1915), an
Italian film, featured a mid-air collision when two of the picture's principals staged an aerial duel. DIZZY HEIGHTS
AND DARING HEARTS (1915), a Triangle-Keystone comedy,
told of two foreign airplane buyers who come to the United
States. Their rivalry formed the basis for the two-reel picture.

Although the war in Europe didn't spawn a large number of aviation films, the increased interest in aviation by
the war's end encouraged the use of airplanes in melodramatic films. Art Ronnie stated:

> Aware that the public was demanding more and
> more thrills in motion pictures, producers were turn-
> ing to the airplane for added sensations. It wasn't
> that airplanes hadn't been used before. But now
> they were bigger and faster and able to do more
> things than they could ever do before. Whether
> the stunt had anything to do with the plot was im-
> material. The idea was to get people into the the-
> atres. One minor serial queen, Ruth Clifford, was
> so anxious to play in an aerial epic that she begged
> producers **for a "scenario with action in the clouds."**
> She finally got her chance the following year with
> THE INVISIBLE RAY.[1]

Of course, using airplanes solely for thrills did not neces-
sarily mean more or better aviation films, but it did help to
produce a climate in which more serious efforts could be
made, as well as providing movie-making practice for pilots
and aerial cameramen. The importance of this experience
was crucial, for the lyrical and breathtaking aerial sequence
in such films as WINGS would not have been possible had
the filmmakers not trained on many lesser aviation films.

Interestingly, film producers saw not only the value
of aviation in films, but also the value of aviation in general.

Near the end of 1918 Cecil B. DeMille built DeMille Fields
Numbers 1 and 2 in Los Angeles. By May 1919 DeMille had
only five Curtiss Jennies, but he formed the Mercury Aviation Company and scheduled flights for May 11, making it
the second scheduled commercial airline passenger service
in the world. (An aviator in Florida in 1914 set up the first
passenger service.) In September 1919 DeMille opened Field
Number 3 just north of Pasadena and rented his planes and
facilities to other studios. Others followed DeMille's lead.
Syd Chaplin, Charlie's brother, opened Chaplin Aerodrome
in Los Angeles and Thomas Ince started Ince Field in Culver
City.

In their quest for ever more daring stunts in aerial
films, filmmakers teamed the master of illusion, Harry Houdini,
with an airplane. For his first full-length feature film,
Houdini selected THE GRIM GAME, produced by the Famous
Players-Lasky company, shot at DeMille Field Number 2, and
released in September 1919. Houdini wanted to thrill his
fans with a mid-air plane change and, **supposedly scorning**
the use of a stunt man, was to hang by a rope and drop
into the cockpit of a plane flying below. When it came time
to perform the stunt, however, a sudden gust of wind pushed
the Curtiss Jennies together, and the landing gear of the
upper plane collided with the lower one's top wing. The
planes spun earthward while the camera plane carrying di-
rector/cameraman Irvin Willat followed them. The aircraft
separated two hundred feet up and came to earth with no
one seriously injured, although one plane came to rest upside down. The film's script was rewritten to include the
incident. Houdini offered $1,000 to anyone who could prove
the sequence had been faked. The sequence was real enough,
but **it was Robert E. Kennedy,** a stunt flier recently discharged from the air service, who risked his life on the rope,
not Houdini.

The most famous, flamboyant, and short-lived of the
early stunt flier/actors was Ormer Locklear. Great fanfare
had accompanied the release of Locklear's first film, THE
GREAT AIR ROBBERY (1919) **(discussed in** Chapter 3),
so it became natural that the next major aviation film would
be a Locklear one. Universal Studios, producers of THE
GREAT AIR ROBBERY, had second thoughts about Locklear,
however, and decided not to produce another film starring
the aviator. Thus Locklear signed a contract with the Fox

studio and promised that THE SKYWAYMAN "... would be 'the most daring [picture] ever filmed.'"[2] Among the production crew was Jules Furthman, a noted screenwriter who would do JET PILOT and several excellent non-aviation films.

THE SKYWAYMAN's plot concerns a Lafayette Escadrille ace, Norman Locke (Locklear), who loses his memory before the end of World War I. He becomes involved with the Czar's niece, who's carrying the Russian crown jewels. The jewels are stolen by her companions but, after many adventures, it turns out that the whole affair was a ruse to help Locke recover his memory.

In order to minimize risk the filmmakers planned to use optical effects for most stunts. Locklear's only air transfer would take place when the flier went from a plane to a train and back again to the plane. Many stunts called for a nighttime setting; because of this, panchromatic film would be used. This allowed shooting night scenes in daylight if a red filter was placed over the lens. Locklear protested at this type of shooting. He got permission to perform the film's last scene, a near-fatal spin, at night, provided it was the last sequence filmed. The sequence, however, had already been done with models.

Filming of THE SKYWAYMAN started on June 11, 1920. Generally the production went well, despite Locklear's increasing depression. At one point Locklear narrowly avoided a potentially bad accident. The script called for the flier to knock over a balsa wood church steeple with the Jenny's wing tip. The prop men, however, constructed the steeple out of sturdy wood. Fortunately for Locklear, the structure had been sawed half-way through and ropes had been attached to facilitate the steeple's collapse. Locklear only damaged the Jenny's wing tip, and did not crash.

Another problem developed during the plane-train-plane stunt. Locklear made the transfer from the Jenny to the moving train without trouble but, because of the 100° heat and the 1,500-foot altitude, the plane couldn't easily lift Locklear off the train. It took several attempts to complete the stunt. That left the spin at the film's end as the only uncompleted aerial sequence.

The climactic tailspin had all the elements of disaster.

Locklear was depressed because Fox hadn't renewed his contract. He would therefore have to go on another barnstorming tour, something he liked less and less as time went on. In addition, although Locklear was married, he was in love with actress Viola Dana. Conflicting emotions about the two women nagged him. Perhaps this was why the pilot reportedly had a feeling he might die soon and shouldn't fly that evening. And, of course, the night flying was unnecessary because of the previous model shots, and, if live-action became necessary, the flying could have been done in the daytime.

Workers placed five spotlights around DeMille Field 2. By observing the lights, Locklear could maintain correct positioning if he flew ninety degrees to their beams. The light men had strict orders to turn the lights off when Locklear's spin reached five hundred feet. He would then pull out of his dive. Although it made Locklear's Jenny thirty pounds heavier, his plane had been whitewashed for greater contrast. Locklear took off at 9:40 p.m., August 2, 1920, with his long-time flying partner, Skeets Elliott. A large crowd had gathered to watch the stunt, including Howard Hawks, who would direct many aviation films, Richard Arlen, who would act in airplane pictures, and stunt pilot Leo Nomis. After about fifteen minutes of stunting, Locklear signaled his readiness for the tailspin. The fliers ignited five magnesium flares on each wing. Locklear leveled off at 2,000 feet and began the spin. The spotlights never shut off, and Locklear never pulled out. He and Elliott died in the spectacular crash. Stunt pilot Dick Grace described the ghastly scene: "'... the sky was covered with red. Everything for blocks around was illuminated. The ship had fallen into the sludge pool of an oil well. Everything was on fire--the pool, the gasoline, the ship.'"[3] Uncertainty remains as to whether the lights blinded Locklear or whether the flares severed his aileron control cables. Whatever the reason, Locklear and Elliott have the tragic distinction of being the first professional stunt pilots killed while filming a picture.

Fox rushed finished prints of the film to the theatres before Locklear's fame had a chance to dim; and the film premiered on September 12 at the Superba Theatre in Los Angeles. Fox used an ad campaign similar to the one developed for THE GREAT AIR ROBBERY, including model displays and exhibition flights. And the studio did not let the public forget that they had a chance to see Locklear's fatal crash.

Unlike Locklear's, Al Wilson's film career spanned more than ten years, and he acted in more films than any other professional pilot. Besides starring in several aerial westerns, discussed later, Wilson appeared in many other films featuring barnstorming stunts and melodramatic plots. In THE CLOUD RIDER (1925), he played an aviator and a Secret Service agent who has his plane sabotaged by a drug smuggler, who loosens a wheel. But a girl takes up the plane instead. When the wheel falls off in mid-air, the aviator straps a spare to his back, makes a mid-air plane change, and attaches the new wheel. Further aerial action included a plane crash in the ocean. (Stunt pilots Frank Clarke and Frank Tomick also appeared in the film.)

FLYIN' THRU (1925) starred Wilson as a World War I veteran who barnstorms around the country and eventually leaps from his plane to a car to catch the villain. THREE MILES UP (1927) featured the pilot as a former ace forced into crime and then trying to escape his situation. Wilson jumped from one plane to another by lassoing one aircraft and swinging on the rope. In SKYHIGH (or SKY-HIGH) SAUNDERS (1927) he played twin brothers, one an aerial smuggler and the other a member of the U.S. border patrol. Wilson kills his outlaw brother in aerial combat, takes his place, and breaks up the gang, even marrying the brother's former girl friend. Wilson wrote THE AIR PATROL (1928), as well as starring in the film. Here Wilson battled diamond smugglers and an almost non-existent plot. He starred in WON IN THE CLOUDS (1928) and repeated wing walking stunts he'd done for a previous picture, THE PHANTOM RIDER (1928). THE CLOUD DODGER (1928), concerned an elopement and a fight on an airplane. THE SKY SKIDDER (1929) returned him to the screen in a story about a super aviation fuel that could power a plane for 1,000 miles on a single pint. The aerial stunts featured a parachute jump, a faked plane change, and the pick-up of the heroine from a car by the hero on a ladder hanging from a plane. Like many other film personalities, Wilson didn't **survive** the transition to sound, and his acting career ended with the silent cinema. He continued to fly, however, in and out of movies, until a 1932 crash took his life.

Numerous other films of the 1920s repeated the stories and stunts of Wilson's films. THE GIRL FROM GOD'S COUNTRY (1921) depicted, among other things, a millionaire airplane manufacturer, "solidified gasoline," and a transpacific flight contest. THE BOOTLEGGERS (1922) had a Navy aviator rescuing his sweetheart from the clutches of a lecherous bootlegger. WITH WINGS OUTSPREAD (1922) dealt with two U.S. Army fliers sent to Havana to subdue bandits. WHITE MAN (1924) had an aviator and an English lady stranded in the jungle when the flier breaks a propeller on landing. The pilot is called "white man" and is worshiped as a god. The only noteworthy aspect of the film is that it had Clark Gable in a supporting role. BACK TO LIFE (1925) offered the audience a World War I French aviator, given up for dead, who winds up in an airplane factory.

In THE KISS BARRIER (1925), a former World War I pilot becomes a playwright. In THE ADVENTUROUS SEX (1925), a man's love for his airplane sends his girl friend into the arms of a cad. When her reputation is endangered, she jumps into the waters above Niagara Falls. Her original boy friend swims out to her and they climb to safety on a rope ladder hanging from a plane. PARADISE (1926) concerned a stunt pilot who is given the deed to a tropical island by his father. In THE HIGH FLYER (9126), a war veteran had difficulty hanging on to the plans for a new airplane. In MARRIAGE (1927), an inventor finds romance when he crash-lands his plane on a girl's land. THE BROADWAY DRIFTER (1927) featured a disowned wealthy playboy who gets work in an airplane factory and makes possible the happy ending with his aerial exploits.

PUBLICITY MADNESS (1927) told of a man who puts up $10,000 as a publicity stunt to give to the first pilot who flies the Pacific to Australia. When Lindbergh makes his flight, the hero realizes someone may actually win the money. To save his company, he makes the flight himself. A HERO FOR A NIGHT (1927) involved high jinks over a transatlantic flight unwittingly sponsored by a soap manufacturer. AFLAME IN THE SKIES (1927), from a story by Mary Roberts Rinehart, had two aviators experimenting with a luminous smoke screen in the New Mexican desert. They come to the aid of a rich old landowner when one of them calls for help by skywriting. SHIELD OF HONOR (1927) dealt with a police aviator chasing diamond thieves. A society debutante is chosen to christen the first airplane to be used by the Los Angeles Police Department. She falls in love with the pilot and becomes involved with jewel thieves. After a daring robbery the bandits escape by plane and train and the aviator sets out in pursuit, resulting in some interesting night flying shots. DARING DEEDS (1928) concerned an airplane race. ACROSS THE PACIFIC (1928) mixed amnesia and airplanes. Two brothers love their father's secretary. She marries Hugh, one of the brothers, but he is shot down in France during the war and loses his memory. Eight years later the secretary, after a visit to France, agrees to marry the other brother. Meanwhile, Hugh returns to America and while test flying for his father's company, regains his memory. He crashes and is taken to an asylum. He escapes, steals an experimental transatlantic plane, and flies to France to be with his family.

VIRGIN LIPS (1928) offered adventure with an American aviator hired by business interests to protect them from a bandit leader. FLYING LUCK (1928), with Jean Arthur, had Monty Banks as an airplane enthusiast who takes correspondence school flying lessons and subsequently wins an air polo match for the Army. FLYING ROMEOS (1928) had two barbers becoming involved in aviation because the girl they love likes flying. THE SKY RANGER (1928), a 32-minute short adapted from the Russ Farrell flying stories in American Boy magazine, dealt with the U.S. air patrol on the Mexican border. Gangsters, airplanes, and a death ray figured in the plot of CODE OF THE AIR (1928). THE SKY RIDER (1929) starred a dog, Champ. THE AIR CIRCUS (1928) was probably the first aviation film with dialogue (fifteen minutes' worth).

THE JAZZ SINGER (1927) had shown that sound could be a powerful audience attraction and by 1928 synchronous sound was being used in airplane films. THE AIR CIRCUS featured Dick Grace and was the first aviation film directed by Howard Hawks, who co-directed with Lew Seller. The story concerned two youths, Buddy Blake and Speed Dolittle, who are fascinated by planes and build a glider. Against Mrs. Blake's wishes, Buddy and Speed join the Pacific School of Aviation. Buddy crashes trying to avoid Speed's plane and, although only slightly injured, loses his nerve. Mrs. Blake, in one of the dialogue scenes, visits her son and makes him promise not to fly again. Speed and his girl

friend, also a pilot, take off in a plane which loses its landing gear. Buddy takes up a plane to warn them, they parachute to safety, and Buddy's confidence is restored.

CAPTAIN SWAGGER (1928) had Captain Swagger (Rod
La Rocque), an American flier in the French aviation service,
shooting down a German ace in World War I but landing behind the German lines to pull him out of the burning plane.
The German lets Swagger escape back to his own lines. Ten
years later, Swagger, who has become a cafe dancer, meets
up with the German, who has become a stick-up man in New
York. The film offered all this to the audience in sound.

THE FLYING MARINE (1929), a seventy per cent dialogue picture starring Ben Lyon and Jason Robards, Sr., had
nothing to do with the military. As in CONQUEST (1929),
its major aerial action consisted of a couple of crashes. THE
FLYING FOOL (1929), an all-dialogue film, concerned two
brothers, one a stunt pilot called the Flying Fool who tries
to keep the other brother from falling for his girl. Noted
cameraman Arthur Miller lensed the film. Somerset Maugham's
stage play formed the basis of the all-dialogue THE SACRED
FLAME (1929), the story of an aviator, crippled on his wedding day, who is put out of his misery by his mother. DANCE
HALL (1929) (also all dialogue) told of the involvement of
a dancehall hostess with an aviator. The Polish STAR SQUAD-
RON (GWIAZDZISTA ESKADRA) (1930) was based on a screenplay by Polish pilot and author Janusz Meissner and directed
by Leopold Buczkowski.

Aerial Westerns

Of all the early melodramatic aviation films, none was
more popular than the aerial western. These films substituted planes for horses but retained the traditional western
elements. Instead of jumping from horse to horse, the hero
jumped from plane to plane. Bandits, who once lay in wait
for the stage, now lurked in the clouds, waiting to pounce
on a valuable air mail shipment or attack the hero. The
western clichés remained the same, and little, if any, attempt was made to use aviation as anything but a gimmick
to bring the audience into the theatre.

Among the aerial westerns were the following: MAID

OF THE WEST (1921), with Frank Clarke; AFTER YOUR OWN
HEART (1921), with Tom Mix; A COWBOY ACE (1921); THE
VENGEANCE TRAIL (1921); SKY HIGH (1922), with Tom
Mix; HEADIN' WEST (1922), featuring Hoot Gibson; A WEST-
ERN DEMON (1922); UNSEEING EYES (1923), with Tom Mix;
EYES OF THE FOREST (1923), with Dick Grace flying in
this Tom Mix story of a forest ranger pilot; THE AIR HAWK
(1924), with Al Wilson and featuring a mid-air leap between
planes; RECKLESS COURAGE (1925); TRIPLE ACTION (1925);
LIGHTNING (1927); SILVER VALLEY (1927), with Tom Mix
as a cowboy airplane builder; THE YOUNG WHIRLWIND (1928);
THE FLYING BUCKAROO (1928); THE PHANTOM FLYER (1928),
with Al Wilson as a border patrol aviator who helps a home-
steading family against a cattle owner; THE BIG HOP (1929),
with stunt pilot Dick Grace; UNTAMED JUSTICE (1929), involving the robbery of an air mail pilot; THE AMAZING VAGA-
BOND (1929), with a stunt flier character, cowboy star Bob
Steele, sent to a lumber camp by his father; THE WINGED
HORSEMEN (1929), with Hoot Gibson as a flying Texas Ranger; WINGS OF ADVENTURE (1930), about an aviator and
his mechanic being captured by Mexican rebels; THE SKY
RAIDERS (1931); THE SKY SPIDER (1931), about air mail
bandits; AIR HOSTESS (1934); and SPEED WINGS (1934), a
Tim McCoy picture that featured three plane crashes and
a chase between a plane and a train. The aerial western
died in the middle 1930s, a victim of more contemporary themes,
particularly the spy and saboteur plots that would soon spring
from World War II. Occasionally a film like COWBOY IN THE
CLOUDS (1944), which told of a rancher who helps the Civil
Air Patrol when it is criticized by the richest man in the
state, revived the aerial western theme until the subgenre
found new life in the television series SKY KING.

SKY KING began as a radio show and ran from 1946
to 1954. In 1951 it became a half-hour TV series that lasted
until 1954. Kirby Grant played Sky King, an Arizona rancher
who was also a pilot. He flew his twin-engined Cessna, The
Songbird, against the bad guys from his Flying Crown Ranch.
Grant, and Gloria Winters, who played his niece Penny, were
licensed pilots in real life.

THE WHIRLYBIRDS (1956-1959) also used the aerial
western theme. This syndicated TV show starred Ken Tobey
and Craig Hill as two free-lance helicopter pilots operating
in Southern California. On occasion, one of the heroes

would leap from the helicopter to pull an escaping villain off his horse.

By the early 1930s, a concern for the veterans of World War I became evident. THE LAST FLIGHT (1931) was the first aviation film to examine what happened to wounded fliers after the war. The First National Picture was based on a John Monk Saunders story entitled "Nikki and Her War Birds" that was originally published in Liberty magazine. Next it became a novel, Single Lady, and then a play, Nikki (both the novel and the play also came out in 1931). Saunders wrote the screenplay which told of four American fliers (Richard Barthelmess, Johnny Mack Brown, David Manners, and Elliott Nugent), either physically or emotionally wounded, and their adventures after the war's end with Nikki (Helen Chandler). Directed by William Dieterle, a German directing his first English-speaking picture, THE LAST FLIGHT was an unspectacular affair (early flying scenes came from THE DAWN PATROL) but it did touch on the problems faced by pilots scarred by the war.

Melodramatic aviation films of the early 1930s used plots indistinguishable from those of the late 1920s, in spite of the addition of sound. The introduction of sound had surprisingly little effect on aviation films although it made certain other types of films extremely popular. Detective films, for example, required long dialogue sequences to explain the plot. Musicals are another example. But airplane films, merely adding the sounds of roaring machines and barking machine guns, were little different from silent films.

THE FLYING FOOL (1931), a British effort, featured jewel robbers, an airplane-auto chase, and an aerial crash into an airfield observation tower. L'AVIATEUR (THE AVIATOR, 1931) was a Warner Brothers picture made in French and with a partially French cast and crew. Douglas Fairbanks, Jr. starred in the picture which featured some stunt flying. LOVE AFFAIR (1932) starred Humphrey Bogart as an airplane engine inventor who falls in love with a spoiled heiress (Dorothy Mackaill). She loses her money but plans to marry a wealthy man so that Bogart can finish his invention. Bogart refuses, and Mackaill backs out of her marriage and tries to kill herself by flying a plane. Bogart saves her. The cheaply-made AIR DEVILS (1932) told of two friendly aviators who formerly fought against each other during the war and now fly mock air duels for a carnival. When the German tries to rob the kid brother (who is flying a payroll) of the American, the American intervenes and both aviators are killed. A Hungarian film, FLYING GOLD (A REPULO ARANY, 1932), also released in a French version entitled ROULETABILLE AVIATEUR, told of the robbery of a gold shipment being sent to Hungary by the Bank of France by air.

China provided the setting for WAR CORRESPONDENT (1932). Correspondent Ralph Graves broadcasts to the world the details of an air fight, which a man known as General Chang wins. Chang turns out to be an American seeking to make a profit out of the war. He has little love for the correspondent and denounces him over the radio. But eventually the newsman proves his courage when he and the aviator rescue the girl they both love from the Chinese villain.

The Swedish VAGABOND OF THE AIR (LUFTENS VAGA-BOND, 1933) was the first film from that country to deal with flying. A seaplane lands on a lake to rescue an injured hiker. The hiker is an old flame of one of the two seaplane pilots (played by Albin Ahrenberg) who now finds himself in competition with the other pilot for the girl's affections. He loses and eventually dies in a crash while on a polar expedition. Ahrenberg was a real-life pilot who tried unsuccessfully to make regular flights to the U.S. in 1929. He later flew on trips around Sweden promoting aviation.

PARACHUTE JUMPER (1934) starred Douglas Fairbanks Jr., Frank McHugh, and Bette Davis. Fairbanks and McHugh play a couple of flying Marines who get their discharges and turn to parachute jumping, eventually becoming involved with gangsters. The aviation scenes, particularly the crash scenes, are effectively done. Noted pilot Paul Mantz did the stunt flying. SOLDIERS OF THE STORM (1934) was a routine border patrol film about a flier sent to break a ring which is smuggling drugs and aliens into the U.S. from Mexico. The picture featured a car-plane crash. FLYING DEVILS (1934) starred Ralph Bellamy as the head of Speed Hardy's Flying Circus. Bellamy's wife falls in love with a boy (Eric Linden) with whom she does a double parachute jump. Bellamy sets out to murder Linden, but Linden's brother, Bruce Cabot, crashes head on into Bellamy to save the boy. SKYWAY (1934), a comedy drama released by Monogram, offered the

aviation viewer little in the way of excitement. HAPPY LAND-
ING (1934), another Monogram adventure, dealt with the U.S.
border patrol. Crooks position a seaplane over an ocean liner
and threaten to drop a bomb on it unless the captain hands
over money to an accomplice aboard ship and drops him overboard for the seaplane to pick him up. The film had Noah
Beery in one of the roles.

A picture in a lighter vein was BRIGHT EYES (1934),
starring Shirley Temple as the darling of an aviation field.
The chief aerial event came when James Dunn was forced to
bail out of an airplane with Temple in his arms.

The Warner Brothers' MURDER IN THE CLOUDS (1934)
was stronger on flying than on plot, and concerned a secret
formula for high explosives which the government was trying
to transport from the West Coast to Washington. Lyle Talbot
played Three-Star Bob Halsey, a pilot whose reckless stunts
have gotten him into trouble but whose flying skill causes
him to be chosen to fly the formula and the scientist who developed it to Washington. The picture featured several stunts,
including a machine gun battle in which one plane is shot down,
a mid-air explosion, and an aerial kidnapping.

FLIERS (1935) was a Russian film set in a civil aviation
school. It had the usual American film elements; two fliers
in love with the same girl, also training to be a pilot, and
the conflict between a bold, reckless flier and the more conservative chief of the school. Naturally, this trend toward
individualism was a lot less desirable in a communist film.
Another Russian film, MEN ON WINGS (1935), contained un-
exciting flying scenes. It told of a flying school and how
its commander, a fanatical stunt flier, falls into disgrace and
loses his love interest, a lady pilot, after stunting a plane
against orders and crashing it. Like FLIERS, it extolled the
virtue of discipline.

STORM OVER THE ANDES (1935) starred Jack Holt as
an aviator flying for Bolivia in a fictitious war with Paraguay,
inspired by the 1932-1935 conflict. The story was co-adapted
by Frank Wead. Holt falls in love with the wife (unknown to
him) of his commanding officer. He eventually saves the officer from the jungle after a crash, steals a plane from the
enemy, bombs an ammunition dump, and captures the Para-
guayan ace, El Zorro, "the fox who flies like an eagle." The

film was remade in 1939 in a Spanish-language version called
WINGS OVER THE CHACO. It had the same director but
some cast changes.

DEATH FLIES EAST (1935) involved a mystery on a
transcontinental plane with one character, played by Conrad
Nagel, who is entrusted to deliver a secret armament formula
to the Secretary of the Navy in Washington. In THE SKY
PARADE (1936) Jimmie Allen played himself in a story of
three war heroes who leave barnstorming for commercial aviation and perfect a robot plane. The 13-chapter serial ACE
DRUMMOND (1936) featured John King and Noah Beery, Jr.
in a story about a criminal organization's efforts to sabotage
a worldwide clipper air service. LOVE ON THE RUN (1936)
starred Clark Gable and Franchot Tone as rival foreign correspondents for New York newspapers. Gable unmasks a
stratosphere flier as a spy and leads an heiress (Joan Crawford) around Europe. Paul Mantz did the stunt flying.
DEATH IN THE SKY (1937) (also called PILOT X) was a very
bad, quickly made melodrama about a murder-bent ex-war pilot; it used much stock airplane footage. THE MAN WHO
FOUND HIMSELF (1937), based on Wings of Mercy by Alice F.
Curtis, was another quickly-made film designed for the bottom half of a double bill. The New York Times summed it up
by saying: "... the operating room takes to the air--for no
other reason except, presumably, that things were getting
too easy for patients on the ground."[4]

FLIGHT FROM GLORY (1937) starred Chester Morris in
a story about misfit pilots who have been banned from flying
in the U.S. and have come to South America to fly supplies
from a supply base to various mines. They live in bad conditions and fly old airplanes, and fatalities are common. Love
interest comes with the wife of a new pilot (Van Heflin) to the
group, and Morris falls in love with her. Onslow Stevens
played the manager who's more concerned with his planes than
his pilots.

RIDING ON AIR (1937) was a Joe E. Brown picture
about a newspaper man in a small town who goes up with a
pilot and has an air battle with smugglers. CRIMINALS OF
THE AIR (1937) dealt with the border patrol's efforts to stop
an alien smuggling ring along the Mexican border. The border patrol agent's cover is a "honeymoon express" which hops
over the border for quick marriages. Rita Hayworth did a

dancing number which caused <u>Variety</u> to speculate that "...
she seems to have possibilities for straight talking roles."[5]
In REPORTED MISSING (1937) an airplane bandit caused airliner crashes and robbed passengers. The uninspired Canadian serial, MYSTERIOUS PILOT (1937), consisting of 15 episodes of 33 minutes each, told of flying Canadian Mounties.
The film had the famous stuntman Yakima Canutt in one role.

In WITHOUT ORDERS (1938) a flashy stunt pilot (Vin-
ton Hayworth), the spoiled son of an airline tycoon, and a
down-to-earth transport pilot (Robert Armstrong) are both
in love with the same girl (Sally Eilers). She falls for the
stunt pilot, but realizes her mistake when he panics in a
crisis and the transport pilot talks down the plane she's in
by radio. HAPPY LANDING (1938) featured Don Ameche and
Cesar Romero as transatlantic aviators on their way to Paris
who end up in Norway. Sonja Henie starred in this vehicle
for her ice skating talents. The French film L'ESPOIR (1938),
made by André Malraux, dealt with the Spanish Civil War.

FLIGHT INTO NOWHERE (1938) starred Jack Holt as the
head of an American airline planning to introduce a run down
the western coast of South America. An irresponsible pilot
crashes in the jungle and Holt rescues him. SKY GIANT
(1938) was an RKO film climaxing in an around-the-world
flight over Alaska and Russia. Set in the training school
operated by Trans-World Airways, it told of the school's
commander (borrowed from the Army), Harry Carey; a veteran pilot, Richard Dix; Carey's son, Chester Morris; and a
girl who falls in love with Morris, Joan Fontaine, but who
also likes Dix.

A Warner Brothers film, SECRET SERVICE OF THE AIR
(1939), starred Ronald Reagan and was based on material collected by H. W. Moran, former head of the U.S. Secret Service. It had an old plot, dealing with the smuggling of aliens
across the border. WINGS OVER AFRICA (1939) was a minor
British production about an airplane expedition to Africa to
locate a fortune in diamonds. The film made use of newsreel
photography taken by Mr. and Mrs. Martin Johnson on their
trip to Africa in the early 1930s.

PIRATES OF THE SKIES (1939) was a low-budget actioner about an ex-commercial record-holding aviator who joins
the state police air service and battles against a gang of rob-

bers who use airplanes for their getaway. ETERNALLY YOURS (1939) had little aviation footage and featured both David Niven, as a magician who does a parachute escape trick, and the flying of Mantz and Frank Clarke.

A film that featured some canyon flying was LEGION OF LOST FLYERS (1939), about a group of fliers (one played by Richard Arlen) operating out of an independent airport in the Alaskan wilderness. Arlen spends much of the time clearing himself of suspicion concerning a crash which killed several people (he supposedly bailed out). The Russian FIGHTER PLANES (ISTREBITELI, 1939) featured a romantic triangle.

Spies Aloft

By the end of the 1930s aerial spies took over where the aerial bandits of the 1920s left off. Political tensions of the 1930s foreshadowed war clouds on the horizon, and it was obvious that aviation would have an enormous impact in any future war. Plane designs and aircraft data became prime technological secrets to be guarded and spied on. Filmmakers were quick to pick up on this theme. Although it contains no flying scenes, Alfred Hitchcock's THE 39 STEPS (1935) was one of the first such films. The plans for a new plane are stolen and a Canadian (Robert Donat) in London is drawn into the plot. He races with time to stop the spies before the specifications can be smuggled out of England. Twentieth Century-Fox's CRACK-UP (1937) starred Peter Lorre and Brian Donlevy in a story about a spy ring, the theft of valuable blueprints, and the crash of a transport plane in the Atlantic. FLIGHT TO FAME (1938), produced by Columbia, involved a death ray used to destroy planes.

The next aerial spy picture was a Columbia picture produced in Britain, CLOUDS OVER EUROPE (1939) (also called Q PLANES). The film, one of the best aviation spy pictures because it didn't take itself too seriously, told of a gang of enemy agents stationed on a trawler. They use a radio beam to disable the radios and ignitions of four new army test aircraft, and then pick them up after they have come down in the ocean. According to Time, such a radio beam was possible: "... such a ray was reported working three years ago by Marconi at distances up to 25 feet. Another such ray, rigged up by a radio ham in Wisconsin, was last year reported gobbled up by the U.S. War Department."[6] The film served as a showcase for Ralph Richardson's talents. He played a Scotland Yard inspector who is the only one to suspect the real cause of the crashes.

FLYING G-MEN (1939) was a Columbia serial (18 minutes per episode) that Variety best summed up: "Planes smash, plans disappear and spies strike at the nation's defense, bringing four flying G-men into the picture. Plenty of flying, fights, and narrow squeaks to keep a full quota of interest for the kids."[7] SPIES OF THE AIR (1939) was a British production set in a secret airplane factory where a test pilot (Barry K. Barnes) is involved with selling plans of a secret aircraft to a foreign government.

TRAPPED IN THE SKY (1939) starred Jack Holt as a U.S. Army flier who goes under cover. The Columbia production told of foreign agents who sabotage the test of a high-speed noiseless airplane so that the Army will reject the aircraft, thus allowing them to gain the rights to the plane. Ronald Reagan starred in MURDER IN THE AIR (1940), a Warners picture in which he chases a gang of spies that possesses an "inertia projector" which disables electric current at the source. The device is used to disable the villains' plane. SKY MURDER (1940) had Walter Pidgeon playing detective Nick Carter in the third film of the Nick Carter series. Here Carter battles foreign agents and becomes involved in a murder on a flight to New York. Not to be outdone by Nick Carter, Charlie Chan tackled aviation spies in MURDER OVER NEW YORK (1940). Chan (Sidney Toler) exposes the spy ring's leader during the test flight of a new bomber in which the suspects are riding over New York. JOE SMITH, AMERICAN (1942) starred Robert Young as a factory worker kidnapped and returned by enemy agents who are after a new bomb sight.

Four Tailspin Tommy adventures, based on Hal Forrest's newspaper comic strip, were released in 1939. These featured John Trent playing the hero and Milburn Stone as Tommy's friend. In MYSTERY PLANE, spies go after a new bombing device invented by Tommy and his friend. Aerial footage included Army bombing tests from 30,000 feet and an aerial battle between Tommy and the villain. STUNT PILOT dealt with movie making and concerned a film company working out of an airport near Hollywood. Trouble brews during the filming of a dogfight sequence when somebody replaces the blanks in Tommy's plane's gun with real bullets. Tommy shoots down another pilot and thus faces a murder charge. Most of the aerial footage was HELL'S ANGELS material. In SKY PATROL a test border patrol made up of cadets under the leadership of Tommy goes after smugglers. The film also featured Jackie Coogan. And in DANGER FLIGHT Tommy interests a boy in model airplane building. This leads to the creation of a sky-writing model plane which enables the boy to find Tommy after a plane crash.

The year 1940 opened with YUKON FLIGHT, a minor film with songs about Mounties chasing after the crooked operators of a flying freight service from the Yukon gold fields. The Russian BRAVERY (MUZJESTRO, 1940) told of a pilot capturing a foreign spy. THE MARINES FLY HIGH (1940) was a minor RKO picture set "in a conveniently anonymous Central American republic, roughly divided into United States Marines, bandits and Lucille Ball...."[8] The film starred Richard Dix and Chester Morris as two Marine aviators after a guerrilla leader. MEN AGAINST THE SKY (1940) was an airplane construction picture with the screenplay by Nathanael West from a story by John Twist. It starred Richard Dix as a famous flier who ends up as a drunken stunt pilot flying at county fairs. When his sister goes to work in the design section of an airplane factory, Dix helps her in designing a plane that is accepted by the Government, which gives the company a big contract. The airplane shots were model ones.

MERCY PLANE (1940) dealt with the theft of a hospital aircraft by a gang of "hot plane" thieves. A flier, Speed Leslie (James Dunn) is forced out of a race when his engine is tampered with. The flier's rival (Frances Gifford), who is the sister of the gang's leader, wins the race. When the hospital plane, which is equipped with secret devices and can land in a small area, is stolen, Dunn is suspected because he was the test pilot; as a result he's grounded. Gifford gets Dunn a job in her brother's airplane factory, not realizing what he's up to. Dunn learns the truth, stops the brother, and recovers the hospital plane.

GIVE US WINGS (1940) starred the Dead End Kids in a sometimes unintentional Universal comedy. The Kids learn aircraft mechanics in a WPA project and take flying lessons.

Their lack of schooling keeps them out of most flying because they can't meet the Civil Aeronautics Authority's scholastic requirements. They go to work for a crop duster who has outmoded planes, but are shown the error of flying for the crop duster when the planes prove unsafe. FLYING WILD (1941) pitted the Dead End Kids against saboteurs in an airplane factory. JUNIOR G-MEN OF THE AIR (1942) was a Universal serial involving the Kids battling spies/saboteurs when the Kids become fliers.

THE GREAT PLANE ROBBERY (1940, originally titled KEEP HIM ALIVE) was a poor Jack Holt adventure with the star playing an insurance investigator assigned to protect a racketeer who is released from prison three months before his $500,000 life insurance policy is due to expire. His old cronies want the racketeer killed, and they hijack the airliner carrying Holt and the gangster.

CHARTER PILOT (1940) starred Lloyd Nolan as a charter pilot who is the subject of a radio series written by his girl friend, Lynn Bari. Nolan agrees to give up flying for Bari's sake but can't refuse a charter job in Honduras flying ore out of inaccessible gold mines. He's menaced by a saboteur working for a ring which wants the gold-flying job. Bari has come to Honduras and the climax comes when Nolan fights the saboteur on board a plane while Bari broadcasts the play-by-play. The film contained only two flying scenes.

POWER DIVE (1941) was a Paramount release starring Richard Arlen. The story told of two brothers, a test pilot and a design engineer, both in love with the same girl. The girl's blind father develops a plastic-material ship which Arlen successfully test-flies for the Army. A power dive of the plane climaxes the picture. At the time of the filming, Arlen was operating a training school for private fliers outside Hollywood. Variety called the film "... good program entertainment, taking full advantage of present interest in aviation and national preparedness."[9] It was the first in a series of Richard Arlen aviation films made by independent producers William Pine and William C. Thomas.

FORCED LANDING (1941) was the second Richard Arlen aviation film produced by Pine and Thomas. Arlen played an ex-airline pilot who joins the army of an island country. A confrontation with the country's air corps head over Eva Gabor (in her first film appearance) forces Arlen into flying for the country's civil airline. The forced landing of Arlen's payroll flight puts him and Gabor in the hands of bandits. But Arlen flies the bandit leader's son to a hospital, delivers the payroll to the mine, and defeats the villain, the air corps head, in a dogfight.

FLYING BLIND (1941) was the third film in the series. Here Arlen played a flier operating a honeymoon air service from Los Angeles to Las Vegas. He becomes involved with spies who are out to steal a new transformer designed for American fighter planes. During the film he becomes involved in a fast-paced aerial ride, a forced landing, and an emergency take-off forced by a brush fire.

EMERGENCY LANDING (1941) was a weak affair starring Forrest Tucker as a test pilot involved with a radio-controlled aircraft developed by a desert airline flier. The crash of the plane sends them both into hiding, which is upset by a madcap heiress. A subplot involved an airplane building tycoon whose plant is troubled by enemy agents. Variety felt the film's major asset was sex appeal: "... the director made the most of the s.a. possibilities at hand. Miss Brent takes a makeshift shower, and Miss Hughes warms up the screen in shorts and sweaters."[10]

The Spanish Civil War had served as a "warm-up" for World War II. SQUADRON (ESCUADRILLA, 1941) was a Spanish film about Nationalist fliers. Two pilots come into conflict when they fall in love with the same girl. The woman, educated abroad, doesn't understand the political situation, but she finally realizes why the Nationalists need to fight. The film contained some actual combat footage.

By 1942, World War II was in full swing. Most aviation pictures dealt with some aspect of combat flying, and only a few films made during the war tackled other themes. CANAL ZONE (1942) was a cliché-ridden effort starring Chester Morris as a trainer of pilots who ferry bombers across the South Atlantic to Africa. FLIGHT LIEUTENANT (1942, originally titled HE'S MY OLD MAN) was an equally poor Columbia film. It told of a pilot (Pat O'Brien) who is disgraced when he crashes his plane, killing his co-pilot. He goes to Dutch Guiana, leaving his son (Glenn Ford) to be raised as an aviation cadet. O'Brien returns to the country as a private in the U.S. Army. He vindicates himself by substituting for his son on a crucial test flight and when the plane crashes he is killed. The film featured a Brown Racer. The aerial shots were unconvincing.

THE FOREST RANGERS (1942), a Technicolor film from Paramount, was directed by George Marshall and starred Fred MacMurray, Paulette Goddard, and Susan Hayward in a story about the U.S. Forest Service's aerial patrol. They use airplanes for spotting fires and for parachuting in the men and equipment to fight them. The aerial shots were done with miniatures mounted on an elaborate boom constructed by Ivyl Burks which allowed the planes to simulate all the maneuvers of a real plane without the difficulty and risks of trying to shoot the action at an actual forest fire.

BOMBAY CLIPPER (1942) was a routine story about a reporter, spies, and $4,000,000 of Indian diamonds for Britain's war effort on board a clipper flight from Bombay to Singapore. The spies hijack the plane but the reporter gets the best of them. ARMY SURGEON (1942), a poor production about an Army nurse (Jane Wyatt), recalls her WWI experiences with a doctor, whom she loves, and the flier who loves her. The aerial footage consisted of stock shots from HELL'S ANGELS.

SKY DOGS (HIMMELHUNDE, 1942) told of a Hitler Youth Group member (Carl Raddatz) who wins a sailplane competition with a plane he wasn't supposed to borrow. He learns the importance of Nazi discipline, however, and will now make a fine Luftwaffe pilot.

PRINCESS O'ROURKE (1943) starred Robert Cummings as a DC-3 pilot who falls in love with a woman (Olivia de Havilland) who he thinks is a penniless refugee. She is, in fact, an exiled princess. THE SKY'S THE LIMIT (1943) starred Fred Astaire as a Flying Tiger on an eight-day leave in New York, while ADVENTURES OF THE FLYING CADETS (1943), a children's serial, dealt with four cadets at a flying school. NORTHERN PURSUIT (1943) was directed by Raoul Walsh and starred Errol Flynn as a Mountie trying to stop a German aviator sent to Canada on a sabotage mission.

The German film YOUNG EAGLES (JUNGLE ADLER, 1944) told of the headstrong son of an airplane manufacturer

who learns discipline both in the Hitler Youth flying division
and in his father's factory. ESCAPE IN THE DESERT (1945)
was a minor Warners film about a young Dutch flier (Philip
Dorn) who captures an escaped Nazi in the Arizona desert.
The picture was based on the play, The Petrified Forest,
filmed in 1936 under that title by Warner Bros. and starring
Humphrey Bogart.

When World War II ended, "B" aviation film makers returned to the standard themes of the 1930s. JOHNNY COMES
FLYING HOME (1946) had a little of everything from prop-
driven planes to jets. The Twentieth Century-Fox film dealt
with the efforts of three discharged fliers to establish a
freight line with no more than a C-47 and their knowledge
of flying. The partners fight mounting debts with vigor,
even going so far as to steal their impounded plane to rescue a possible customer. Still facing bankruptcy, one of the
trio agrees to test dive a new jet for a large salary. Another
partner takes his place and the test is a success. On the
whole, the film and its flying sequences were unimaginative.

JUNGLE FLIGHT (1947) is the story of a freight line
flying equipment and ore for a mining company in a Latin
American country. The line is operated by two partners,
one of whom is killed while trying to increase profits by flying an overloaded plane. The film is peopled with stock
characters including a girl on the run from her husband; he,
in turn, is on the run from the police.

HIGH BARBAREE (1947) told of a World War II PBY
pilot (Van Johnson) whose plane is damaged and forced down.
While Johnson and a companion float in the plane awaiting rescue, Johnson tells of his boyhood, which was heavily influenced by his seafaring uncle (Thomas Mitchell) and the uncle's tales of a magical island called High Barbaree. As the
two men in the plane weaken from lack of food and water,
Johnson realizes the plane is drifting toward the supposed
location of High Barbaree. The island isn't there, but Johnson's life is saved by his strong determination to visit High
Barbaree, which has given him the will to live.

In SAIGON (1948) Alan Ladd played an ex-Army Air
Force hero who becomes involved in espionage. He and two
buddies fly Veronica Lake and a suitcase of stolen money
from Shanghai to Indochina.

Alan Ladd flies from Shanghai with a cargo of money and Veronica Lake, in SAIGON (1948).

DAREDEVILS OF THE CLOUDS (1948) was a tedious story of a large airline that wished to destroy a smaller competitor, Polar Airways. Trans-Global Airlines plants a spy in the Polar ranks to gather information to put them out of business. The problems are resolved and the film ends happily, for both the characters and the viewer. The aerial sequences are routine.

Charlie Chan returned to the air in 1949 in SKY DRAGON, the last and worst of the Chan films. A murder is committed on board a plane coming into San Francisco while the passengers are unconscious from drugged coffee. Twenty-five thousand dollars are at stake and Charlie Chan (Roland Winters) is sent to investigate. The film concludes with a re-enactment of the murder. SKY LINER (1949) dealt with a transcontinental flight on which are traveling, among others, a spy and the FBI agent who is after him. The film had some exciting moments but its greatest asset was that the aerial shots provided good advertisements for TWA's Constellations.

Polish director Leopold Buczkowski made a sailplane story, FIRST SOLO (PIERWSZU START), in 1950. He followed it with THE PILOT MARESZ AFFAIR (WA PILOT A MARESZA) (originally called BLUE TRAILS, NIEBIESKIE DROGI) in 1955.

CROSSWINDS (1951) had a plane with a cargo of gold crashing in New Guinea and touching off a search made dangerous by crooks and headhunters. JET JOB (1952) had test pilot Joe Novak (Stanley Clements) working for Sam Bentley (John Litel) and refusing to follow Bentley's orders when testing a new jet plane. He's fired and goes to work for Bentley's rival, Tom Powers. There is a crash and Novak is grounded because of Powers' false testimony. Novak then kidnaps Bentley's new test pilot and takes up a new jet to demonstrate it to the Army. The test is a success and Novak gets his old job back.

THUNDER IN THE EAST (1952) starred Alan Ladd as an adventurer with an airplane for hire. He becomes involved in running guns to the Indian state of Ghandahar. The ruling maharajah is fighting rebels and Ladd's guns are for sale to the side who will pay the most. Ladd finds that all the British are trying to leave the war-torn state and he charges double for seats on his plane. His aircraft is wrecked, however, and when another comes it can only take seven people to safety. Experiencing a change of heart, Ladd stays to fight the rebels. Romance is provided in the person of a blind English girl (Deborah Kerr).

A YANK IN INDOCHINA (1952) told of two Americans flying supplies to the French and South Vietnamese in Indochina. They are captured, escape, and eventually lead the French in a successful air attack on the Viet Minh guerrillas. This was one of the first films to allude to the growing involvement in Vietnam. ARCTIC FLIGHT (1952) is about an Alaskan bush pilot (Wayne Morris) who takes on a passenger (Alan Hale, Jr.) who claims to be hunting polar bears. He is, however, a Communist spy using the plane to take pictures for the Russians. Morris finds out but has trouble

convincing other people that Hale is a spy. He finally succeeds, and Hale is stopped before he can pass on the information. The movie was made on location near the Arctic circle. Dull as the film was, it was still better than WINGS
OF DANGER (1952), a British film with Zachary Scott as an
airline pilot mixed up in a smuggling web or counterfeiting
ring, depending on how one interprets the vague plot.

Czechoslovakian director Cenek Duba filmed WINGED
VICTORY (VITEZNA KRIDLA, 1952) about gliding. He also
made SIX O'CLOCK AT THE AIRPORT (V6 DANO NA LETIS-
TI, 1958) and THE AIRPORT IS CLOSED (LETISTE NEPRI-
JIMA, 1959).

THE NET (1953), also called PROJECT X-7, was a
British film about the testing of a new jet plane, the X-7.
A Communist agent infiltrates the base and makes an unsuccessful attempt to steal the plane. FLIGHT TO TANGIER
(1953) told of a frantic search for a large sum of money
aboard a crashed plane. A poor effort, its only distinction
is that it was the first aviation film to be photographed in
Technicolor 3-D.

OUT OF THE CLOUDS (1955) was a documentary-style
British film dealing with the daily workings of the London
Airport, with a ridiculous romance thrown in. Anthony Steel
plays a gambling pilot and Robert Beatty a pilot waiting to
be declared fit to fly again. The only aerial excitement is
talking down a plane in a dense fog. I'VE LIVED BEFORE
(1956) told the story of an airline pilot who thinks he's a
World War I flier who was shot down.

MAN IN THE SKY (1957) was a British film with Jack
Hawkins playing a test pilot given the task of demonstrating
a new rocket-powered transport plane. The entire future of
the company he works for is tied up in this one aircraft, so
a successful test flight is vital for both himself and the company. In the air, one engine catches fire and the passengers
and the rest of the crew bail out. He stubbornly refuses to
obey orders to ditch in the Irish Sea and flies the plane until he has burned up enough fuel to allow him to make a safe
landing. He brings the plane down intact and wins the contract for his company.

DESTINATION 60,000 (1957) was a miserable film with

stock flying shots, supplied by Douglas Aircraft. Colonel
Ed Buckley (Preston Foster) is a plane manufacturer who is
having troubles with his latest experimental jet. His crack
test pilot (Pat Conway) fails in the first flight attempt. His
second pilot (Denver Pyle) is seriously injured. Buckley
elects to take up the third prototype and nearly blacks out,
but is brought back to consciousness by Conway barking
commands over the intercom. TAMMY AND THE BACHELOR
(1957) had Debbie Reynolds nursing pilot Leslie Nielsen back
to health after a plane crash.

An East German film, THE BAT SQUADRON (GESCH-
WADER FLEDERMAUS, 1958) told of American civilian aircraft
aiding the French in Vietnam, carrying medical supplies and
military stores. The hero of the film finally deserts to the
North Vietnamese. Polish director Hubert Drapella's TOWARD
THE GODS (PREZECIWKU BOGOM, 1961), a psychological
story of modern aviation, was apparently so bad that it ruined the director's career.

HERE COME THE JETS (1959) tells of an alcoholic Korean war hero (Steve Brodie) who is dragged out of the gut-
ter by an aircraft manufacturer (John Doucette) and put to
work test-flying Doucette's new airliner. Brodie cracks up
in a flight simulator, proving he can't handle a plane in
flight. But he gets control of himself in time to test the
airplane. In the West German REBEL FLIGHT TO CUBA
(1960) an airline pilot is expelled by the government of
Santo Quinto.

TROUBLE IN THE SKY (1961), also called CONE OF
SILENCE, was a British effort modeled to some extent on
BREAKING THROUGH THE SOUND BARRIER. Bernard Lee
plays an aging commercial pilot involved in an unusual accident while taking off a new jet transport plane. He shoul-
ders all the blame for the crash and continues his flying du-
ties. When he is killed in another take-off accident, his
daughter (Elizabeth Seal) proves the crashes were due to a
design flaw and not to her father's incompetence.

STATION SIX-SAHARA (1964), a British film, was
about a group of men at a desert oasis whose lives are dis-
rupted when a pilot and his sexy wife crash land nearby.

FLIGHT FROM ASHIYA (1964), a Japanese-American

production, deals with three members of an air-sea rescue team sent to aid a small group of survivors shipwrecked by a typhoon in the North China Sea. These members of the U.S. Army's Air Rescue Corps are Sergeant Mike Takashima (Yul Brynner), a Japanese-Polish rescueman, Colonel Glenn Stevenson (Richard Widmark), a neurotic who hates the Japanese, and Lieutenant John Gregg (George Chakiris), who is full of self-recrimination. These men's personal problems are told in flashbacks: Takashima had a tragic affair with a Moslem woman; Stevenson went through a bad war-time experience with a woman war correspondent; and Gregg blames himself for lives lost in an avalanche rescue. Their mutual problem in the film is whether or not to land in a choppy sea to pick up Japanese survivors floating on a life raft. The film is generally poor, with an over-abundance of flashbacks.

THE CARPETBAGGERS (1964) starred George Peppard as a Howard Hughes-type millionaire airplane builder who became a movie maker. The film, based on a Harold Robbins book, featured Frank Tallman's stunt flying.

THE LIFT (1965) was a dismal British film. Shot in and around London at a cost of $60,000, it tells of a young man who tries to convince a tycoon to use his plane for business purposes. He becomes involved with the tycoon's two daughters, seduces both of them, and then returns to an earlier girl friend.

LOST COMMAND (1966), a moderately good film, tells of a group of French paratroopers, among them Anthony Quinn, Alain Delon, and George Segal, and their adventures, first in Indochina and then in strife-torn Algeria. Most of the action takes place on the ground and it is one of the few aviation films to mention the Vietnam war. LT. ROBIN CRUSOE, U.S.N. (1966) told of the adventures of a Navy pilot (Dick Van Dyke) who drifts onto a deserted island.

DEVIL'S ANGEL (1968) starred Ty Harden as an American pilot recruited by a Latin American revolutionary to rescue the ex-president of his country from the current dictator.

SOME GIRLS DO (1969), a British picture, pitted Bulldog Drummond (Richard Johnson) against a villain out to sabotage Britain's supersonic transport program.

SOLE SURVIVOR (1969) was a made-for-TV movie about
a B-25 discovered in the desert many years after it crashed
in World War II. The navigator (Richard Basehart) bailed
out against orders while the rest of the crew flew on until
the plane ran out of fuel and crashed. The ghosts of the
crew haunt Basehart when he comes to the crash site with
an investigating team. SOLE SURVIVOR was based on the
legend of the Lady Be Good, a B-24 that disappeared on
April 4, 1943 and crashed in the Libyan desert. British
geologists looking for oil found the plane in May 1959. The
water jugs in the aircraft were full and it had its full complement of ammunition, but the geologists could find no trace
of the nine-man crew. "The Air Force labeled the discovery
'one of the greatest mysteries in aviation history.'"[11] The
story had previously formed the basis for a TWILIGHT ZONE
episode. The movie was filmed on El Mirage Dry Lake. A
B-25J once used by the Air Guard served as the wreck.

The MOVIE MURDERER (1970) was a made-for-TV film
directed by Boris Sagal, dealing with an arsonist who torches
airliners. When he is accidentaly filmed, he tries to recover
the movies and destroy them.

THIS IS A HIJACK (1973) was a minor affair about the
kidnapping of a wealthy industrialist by hijacking his plane.
In CHARLEY VARRICK (1973), Walter Matthau played a crop
duster stunt pilot turned small town bank robber who accidently steals Mafia money. Knowing the mob won't rest until they kill him, Matthau concocts an elaborate ruse to escape which hinges on Matthau's ability to flip his PT-17
Stearman on its back while taxiing. BIRDS OF PREY (1973)
starred David Janssen in a TV movie about a traffic-helicopter
pilot who witnesses a bank robbery and becomes involved.
DELIVER US FROM EVIL (1973), another made-for-TV movie
directed by Boris Sagal, was about five men on a camping
trip who kill a skyjacker and fight over his $600,000.

THE DISAPPEARANCE OF FLIGHT 412 (1974) starred
Glenn Ford in a made-for-TV movie about an Air Force
cover-up of two missing aircraft. SKY HEIST (1975) was a
TV film that dealt with airborne police trying to stop a gold
bullion robbery. SKY RAIDERS (1976) featured James Co-
burn, Susannah York, and Robert Culp in a tale of a political kidnapping. The film offered spectacular hang-gliding
sequences and a Greek setting.

VICTORY AT ENTEBBE (1976) and RAID ON ENTEBBE (1977) were television movies dealing with the startling July 4, 1976 airborne Israeli commando raid on Entebbe, Uganda, and OPERATION THUNDERBOLT (1977) was an Israeli-made feature film dealing with the same subject.

SOLO (1978), a combined Australian-New Zealand production, tells of a flying fire ranger (Vincent Gil). Gil daily flies over New Zealand's forest, finding companionship with a man who lives seven months of the year in a fire control tower. A pretty girl disturbs their relationship. TERROR OUT OF THE SKY (1978) told of a free-lance pilot struggling to defeat an attack of savage bees. SERGEANT MATLOVICH VS. THE U.S. AIR FORCE (1978) tackled the sensitive theme of a gay airman's battle to stay in the service.

CAPRICORN ONE (1978) depicted a fake mission to Mars. The three astronauts involved (James Brolin, O. J. Simpson, and Sam Waterson) at first cooperate in the elaborate hoax, but then realize that only their deaths will assure the scheme's absolute success. They escape in a Lear Jet but crash in the desert. A scruffy pilot (Telly Savalas) flying a Stearman and a newsman (Elliott Gould) pick up Brolin, who clings to the wing of the plane through some elaborate stunts as the Stearman is chased by the villains in two Hughes 500C turbine helicopters.

Frank Tallman flew the Stearman through Red Rock Canyon in California for forty flying hours over a three-week period, and he labeled the flying job one of his most dangerous. The climactic crash scene of the two helicopters slamming into a cliff was effectively done with radio-controlled model helicopters.

THE PILOT (1979) starred and was directed by real-life aviator Cliff Robertson and told of a commercial pilot who risks the lives of his passengers and crew because of his addiction to alcohol. He refuses to take time off from flying to dry out because he needs both the drinking and the flying to sustain him. His DC-8 crashes taking off, but it is the fault of a pilot sent to watch Robertson, not Robertson himself.

THE PURSUIT OF D. B. COOPER (1981) was a poor film about the 1971 hijacker of a Boeing 727 who bailed out over the state of Washington with $200,000 and was never seen again. The film went through numerous script changes, several directors, and a hastily patched-together ending. THE FLYING MACHINE (LETALOTO, 1981) was a Bulgarian picture set against the Balkan Wars of 1912-1913 and told of a shepherd boy, who, awed at his first sight of an airplane, builds a plane of his own to help his people win the war. He meets a tragic end, however, when his countrymen think he's a deserter.

RACE TO THE YANKEE ZEPHYR (1981) was a made-for-TV movie about good guys and bad guys trying to recover $50 million in gold that went down when a DC-3 was wrecked in World War II. PACIFIC BANANA (1981), an Australian film, concerned a young airline pilot with an impotence problem, even though he has great sex appeal. THE SURVIVOR (1981) was another Australian film, directed by actor David Hemmings, and dealt with a pilot (Robert Powell) who returns from the dead to get revenge on the villain who planted a bomb on his airliner. MODERN PROBLEMS (1981) featured Chevy Chase as an air traffic controller with telekinetic powers.

FIREFOX (1982) starred Clint Eastwood as a veteran suffering from delayed stress syndrome who's drafted by the U.S. government into stealing the hottest Russian fighter, the Firefox. It is a surprisingly grim film, with little levity to break up the tension. The special effects of Eastwood flying the plane at the picture's end are reminiscent of STAR WARS. These sequences were done with a computerized model airplane system that effectively simulated flying conditions.

HIGH ROAD TO CHINA (1983), set in 1920, starred Tom Selleck as O'Malley, a boozing World War I pilot hired by an heiress (Bess Armstrong) to find her father before he's declared legally dead, twelve days hence. The pair, along with O'Malley's mechanic (Jack Weston), fly from Istanbul to Afghanistan and then to Nepal, with O'Malley and the heiress tracking down her father in China. The film is notable mainly for its aviation sequences, for it lacks character and plot development. Made on location in Yugoslavia, it has lyrical aviation sequences. Five Belgian-designed, French-built Stampe biplanes were restored to flying condition for the picture. Two planes were used throughout most of the film, with the others serving as backups.

BLUE THUNDER (1983) starred Roy Scheider as a police

helicopter pilot recovering from a nervous breakdown, brought on in part by his interaction with his sadistic commanding officer in Vietnam (Malcolm McDowell). By accident, Scheider is given the job of testing a new helicopter, nicknamed Blue Thunder, designed by McDowell. It's equipped with the latest surveillance devices and is heavily armed. Scheider discovers the helicopter has a sinister purpose: deadly crowd control. To prove its effectiveness, McDowell and some government officials plan to incite riots and then use Blue Thunder to quell them. Schedier's attempt to break up the plan results in a thrilling helicopter dogfight between him and McDowell. McDowell is killed, and the plot is exposed. Although the plot and character development in BLUE THUNDER leave something to be desired, the helicopter stunts are truly amazing. Done with a combination of real helicopters and radio-controlled models, the action is among the best to be found in any recent aviation film.

The movie inspired two 1984 television series devoted to attack helicopters: BLUE THUNDER and AIRWOLF. The television version of BLUE THUNDER used not only the helicopter from the film, but scenes from the film as well. This ABC series starring James Farentino was canceled after only three months. AIRWOLF, on the other hand, combined the helicopter from BLUE THUNDER with Clint Eastwood's character from FIREFOX to come up with the story of Stringfellow Hawke (Jan-Michael Vincent), a reclusive ace pilot who plays the cello and has stolen Airwolf, a super-sophisticated combat helicopter developed by the Firm, a CIA-style organization headed by Archangel (Alex Cord). In the two-hour pilot for the series, the developer of Airwolf steals it and takes it to Libya. Archangel recruits Hawke and his friend Dominic Santini (Ernest Borgnine) to get it back. After the mission, however, Hawke hangs onto the Airwolf. The price for its return is that the government find Hawke's brother, a prisoner-of-war still in Vietnam. This task is beyond even Archangel's capability, but he is able to persuade Hawke to take Airwolf on selected missions. The series was played very seriously, but came across as good-natured adventure. The flying sequences were well staged, if a bit unbelievable, with Airwolf routinely tangling with MIGs and always shooting them down.

THE AIRSHIP (1983), an East German film, is based on a true story about a man who grows up at the turn of the century and is fascinated with flying. He becomes a merchant in Spain and builds an airfield that is eventually used by the Condor Legion during the Spanish Civil War. Returning to Germany to protest against the Nazis, he is thrown into a madhouse for the rest of his life.

DEAL OF THE CENTURY (1983) starred Chevy Chase in a dismal comedy about an independent arms dealer who stumbles into the sale of a remote-controlled pilotless drone to a Latin American dictator. The "Peacemaker," as the drone is called, is unfortunately as unperfected as it is sophisticated. The British AERODROME (1983) was based on a 1941 novel by Rex Warner. This BBC Television production starred Peter Firth and told of an Air Force base being built near a peaceful English village. The Air Force gradually takes over the village by enforcing its own rules and absorbing the villagers. The depiction of this Fascist-style Air Force is an unusual one for an aviation film.

With the exception of SKY KING few melodramatic aviation TV shows have been successful. RIPCORD, a half-hour syndicated show, ran from 1961 to 1963 and featured two adventurers who ran a skydiving business. The series featured the stunts of Howard Curtiss, a pilot and skydiver who was killed with another parachutist in a 1979 accident. THE BOB CUMMINGS SHOW starred Cummings as an adventurer who was both a charter pilot and amateur detective. When operating near his California base Cummings used a car that had attachable wings to turn it into a plane. Cummings flew in real life and Frank Tallman did much of the flying for the series. The show debuted in October 1961 and lasted but one season. CHOPPER ONE (1974) had an even shorter life: the series about two police helicopter pilots survived only six months. SPENCER'S PILOTS (1976), though, takes the prize for the shortest-lived TV aviation melodrama. The story of a small charter airline in Southern California was grounded after two months.

Two television series have dealt with former members of the Flying Tigers. MAJOR DELL CONWAY OF THE FLYING TIGERS (1951) was a half-hour show that had Major Dell Conway (played by Eric Fleming and then by Ed Peck) found Flying Tiger Airlines on the West Coast after World War II. There was such an airline (as well as the present-day one) and the producer, "Gen" Genovese, had been a pilot in China during the war. TALES OF THE GOLD MONKEY debuted in the fall of 1982 after a rocky start and was canceled after one season. The script called for a particular kind of dog, and a replacement had to be found after the first one died. The series featured a Grumman Goose, and a replacement for that, too, had to be located after the first one sank while being ferried from Alaska. The central character, clearly inspired by Indiana Jones from RAIDERS OF THE LOST ARK, was that of a free-lance charter pilot operating "somewhere in the South Pacific" in 1938. Although the Goose was authentic, little else about the series had much relation to reality, because the story had the hero flying for the Flying Tigers in China more than three years before they were formed in 1941!

Twilight Zone

In addition to the above-mentioned aviation TV series, many non-airplane series have broadcast episodes featuring aviation. While it would be virtually impossible to discuss each one of these, four from the anthology series THE TWILIGHT ZONE stand out. "The Last Flight," broadcast in February 1960, told of a World War I flight lieutenant (Kenneth Haigh) who runs away from a dogfight in 1917 and becomes lost in a cloud. He emerges to land at an American airfield in France in the present day. While being questioned by authorities, he learns that the man he left to die in the dogfight survived and saved hundreds of lives in World War II. The lieutenant realizes he must return to save his companion at the cost of his own life. He escapes from the MPs and flies his Nieuport back into the cloud. The drama was filmed at Norton Air Force Base in San Bernardino, California. Frank Tallman supplied and flew the Nieuport, which he credited as being in more World War I films than any other airplane.

" 'King Nine' Will Not Return" was also broadcast in 1960, as part of THE TWILIGHT ZONE's second season. It was based on the legend of the Lady Be Good. In 1943 Captain James Embry (Robert Cummings) comes to next to the wreckage of his B-25, the King Nine. He can remember crashing with his fellow crew members, but can recall nothing more. He looks around for the crew and finds the grave of one, mirages of them all, and a jet aircraft flying above

him. He can't make sense of the situation and collapses.
When he wakes up this time, it is 1960 and he's in a hospital
bed. It seems he was sick in 1943 and missed the flight of
King Nine. A newspaper story that the plane has been found
unleashes his enormous guilt. That explains everything, except for the sand in his shoes. "'King Nine' Will Not Return"
was shot in the desert near Lone Pine, California. A surplus
B-25 was picked up from the Air Force for $2,500, taken
apart, flown to the shooting site, and put back together.
The cast and crews were transported to the location by a
DC-3.

"The Odyssey of Flight 33," first shown on February
24, 1961, told of a 707 passenger plane, Global Flight 33,
flying from London to New York. It picks up a freak tail
wind that propels it through a time barrier back to the age
of dinosaurs. The crew realize that the only way they can
get back to their own time is to fly back into the tail wind.
They are sent forward in time, but to the 1939 New York
World's Fair. The episode ends as the plane, low on fuel,
is about to make one more try to return to the present. The
episode was filmed in an American Airlines 707 passenger
cabin mock-up that the company had used for stewardess
training.

The fourth TWILIGHT ZONE episode about aviation,
"Nightmare at 20,000 Feet," was shown in 1963, and redone
as one of the four episodes of the 1983 movie THE TWILIGHT
ZONE. William Shatner played a man just released from a
sanitarium after recovering from a nervous breakdown. On
the flight home, he sees, or thinks he sees, a creature trying to sabotage the wing. Every time he calls someone to
look at it, the gremlin disappears. In desperation he finally
grabs the pistol from a policeman, opens the emergency door,
and shoots the gremlin off the wing. He is taken off the
plane in a strait jacket, but the visible damage to the plane's
exterior assures him he's not going mad. Shooting of the
episode involved great difficulty. The interior of a passenger plane with the left wing attached was suspended over a
large tank, used to hold the water from the rain that was
supposed to be falling outside the plane. The actor playing
the gremlin was suspended on a wire as smoke was blown by
him to simulate clouds. Any hitch in this complicated set-up
meant the scene had to be redone.

Airborne Humor

　　　　Some of the melodramatic pictures discussed here have
been so bad as to be unintentionally funny. A few of these
films, however, were intended to be humorous, and a small
number of deliberate aviation comedies have been produced.
The most popular premise for such films is that of placing a
totally inexperienced pilot in the cockpit and depicting his
wild flying antics as he tries to keep the plane under control. The first aviation comedy, in fact, used this theme.
GOING UP (1923) featured a good deal of aviation action.
GOING UP began as a Broadway musical before being made
into a film. The plot had Robert Street (Douglas McLean)
writing a very successful book, Going Up, about an aviator.
Trouble is, Street has a fear of airplanes and has never
flown in his life. For a publicity stunt, the publisher tricks
Street into a plane which ground loops on take-off. Street
is slightly injured and goes to a resort where he falls in
love with a girl who believes he's a great aviator. A French
ace comes to the hotel and also falls in love with the girl.
Street finds himself forced into a flying duel with the Frenchman. Street takes a crash course in flying, takes to the air,
and performs incredible stunts while trying to control the
plane. The antics suitably impress the French flier and the
umpires in a blimp, and Street wins the match. GOING UP
contains some interesting flying scenes, such as Street going
through a railroad tunnel, but these shots are intercut with
poorly-done close-ups of McLean in the cockpit. The film
was remade in 1930 as THE AVIATOR (1930), starring Edward
Everett Horton as the reluctant aviator who manages an incredible series of air stunts.

　　　　GROUNDS FOR DIVORCE (1925) had a man force his
lover's husband to give the lady a divorce by taking the husband through some dangerous airplane stunts. PAJAMAS
(1927), a romantic comedy, had as its chief aviation interest
an airplane crash near Lake Louise, in the Canadian Rockies,
where the picture was shot. THE LITTLE WILDCAT (1928)
involved an American ace and an airplane factory promoter in
an aerial elopement. THE MAN AND THE MOMENT (1929) was
a tame comedy directed by George Fitzmaurice and involved
yachts and a couple of crashes.

　　　　GOING WILD (1931) was an aviation comedy with a
theme similar to THE AVIATOR's. Joe E. Brown played an

aviator who claims to have shot down one plane less than Rickenbacker but who, in fact, has never been up in a plane. When he does go aloft with a girl who knows as little about flying as he does, the stage is set for some fancy stunt flying, which filled out the picture's last ten minutes.

HIGH FLYERS (1937) was a comedy about two goof-off aviators (Bert Wheeler and Robert Woolsey) who get involved with smugglers. THE FLYING DEUCES (1939) had Stan Laurel and Oliver Hardy involved in a climactic wild airplane ride, with the aerial photography done by Elmer Dyer.

IT'S IN THE AIR (1940) was a British picture starring the comic George Formby. The slapstick picture has Formby mistaken for an RAF flier and climaxes in a stunt flying episode when the inexperienced Formby takes a plane aloft.

Freelance aviator Jimmy Cagney with his friend Stuart Erwin in THE BRIDE CAME C.O.D. (1941).

Warner Brothers' THE BRIDE CAME C.O.D. (1941) starred James Cagney and Bette Davis and was originally scheduled as a vehicle for Ann Sheridan. Cagney plays a man hired to deliver a young heiress to her father by airmail (at $10 per pound) to prevent her marrying a band leader. His plane crashes in the desert, the two hole up with an eccentric man in a ghost town, and Davis falls in love with Cagney. Mantz flew his P-12 in the film, with Dyer photographing. As a joke, Mantz buzzed the filming location upside down just as a rain squall happened to hit. When asked by a spectator why he flew that way, Mantz replied that he always flew upside down when it rained.

KEEP 'EM FLYING (1941) was a routine Abbott and Costello picture involving the pair in high jinks at a fictional flight training school. Ralph Cader directed the flying scenes,

Bud Abbott and Lou Costello play with dynamite in KEEP 'EM FLYING (1941).

which involved Mantz. Elmer Dyer did the aerial photography.

QUAX, DER BRUCHPILOT (1941) was a rare German comedy about a travel agency clerk, nicknamed Quax (Heinz Ruhmann), who wins free flying lessons at a flight school. He is expelled from the school because he lacks discipline, but realizes he must become a flier to win back the affections of his girl. His professional handling of a balloon earns him another chance at the flying school, where he proves he has become a mature pilot. He ends up as a flying instructor at the school. A sequel to the film, QUAX IN FAHRT (also known as QUAX IN AFRIKA), was made in 1945. This time instructor Quax became involved in flying adventures in Africa.

FATHER TAKES THE AIR (1951) has a woman take over a flying school when the owner is recalled to service. Her father and the town mayor help her out and relive their WWI flying days. A bank robber charters a plane with the two old timers as pilots. They run out of gas and the robber is captured.

SKY HIGH (1952) was a comedy that had Sid Melton as a stupid GI who looks like a saboteur out to steal the secrets of a new plane. Through sheer stupidity he helps an Intelligence officer catch the villain and break up the gang.

ALL THE WAY BOYS (1973) was a mediocre Italian comedy starring Terence Hill and Bud Spencer as two adventurers flying a Jenny in South America.

Surprisingly, the most spectacular comedy aviation stunt didn't occur in an airplane film but in the slapstick comedy IT'S A MAD, MAD, MAD, MAD, WORLD (1962). Buddy Hackett and Mickey Rooney play the unlucky people trapped in a plane with the pilot unconscious. After some hair-raising flying, Frank Tallman crashed his Beechcraft through a balsa wood and styrofoam billboard placed on a hill. He flew through it perfectly, with only a few feet to spare on each wing tip. The collision damaged the windshield and knocked out one engine, but Tallman managed to land safely.

Tallman's flying in IT'S A MAD, MAD, MAD, MAD WORLD summarizes the essential quality about aviation melodramas: if there's anything good in the picture, chances are it's the stunt flying. The plot lines and character development in most of these films are marginal, and makers of these films have usually not done much to advance the art of the aviation film. But some of them provide unique views of old airplanes, and many of the aerial stunts are just as thrilling as they were when the films were made.

CHAPTER 2

STUNT PILOTS

It takes a special breed of pilot to fly for motion pictures. Part daredevil and part aeronautical engineer, such
men and women have a unique sense of purpose. Movie
stunts are, after all, not "necessary." Whether a film has a
particular stunt or not is relatively unimportant when compared to, say, combat flying. Yet stunt pilots risk their
lives to give audiences a thrill and to challenge themselves.
Some of the world's most skilled aviators have done their
best flying for motion pictures.

Jim and Maxine Greenwood, in Stunt Flying in the Movies, credit Commodore J. Stuart Blackton as the first movie
stunt flier. Blackton had been one of the cameramen who
filmed the San Juan Hill charge in 1898, and he went on to
found the Vitagraph Studios in New York. Blackton took to
flying for his own films about 1910, and received a life membership in the Aero Club of America (the National Aeronautical Association) for cinema aviation work.

By the end of World War I, stunt fliers had begun to
congregate in the rapidly growing city that was Hollywood.
Surprisingly, none of these early pilots had flown in combat
in the war, although many learned flying in the Army. Typical of these was Frank Tomick. Tomick was born in Austria
on September 8, 1897 and came to America with his parents
in 1910. He worked as a mining engineer and then joined
the Army. He tried to enlist in the Signal Corps so that he
could learn to fly, but had to settle for the Third Infantry. He finally got into the Aero Squadron, flying forest
fire and border patrols. He left the Army in 1920 to fly for
films after he had met another flier, Frank Clarke. During
World War II he ferried bombers for the Army Air Force. He
worked as a sound recorder after he quit flying in 1948 and
died in 1966 at the age of 69.

41

Frank Clarke had been a cowboy before he learned to fly in 1918. He quickly became one of the most famous fliers in Hollywood. He flew a Cannuck off the top of a ten-story building under construction in Los Angeles for the film STRANGER THAN FICTION (1921) and quickly became known for his practical jokes. He often carried a pet rattlesnake named Pedro in the cockpit with him. Jim Greenwood best summed up Clarke's career:

> Few of Frank Clarke's peers would dispute that he was the best. He created a number of intricate and spectacular stunts for both aviation movies and flying exhibitions.... And despite his mischievous pranks off screen, Clarke's leadership and example in [the Association of Motion Picture Pilots] activities were largely responsible for bringing about the highest standards of professionalism in motion picture flying. [1]

It was Al Wilson who taught Cecil B. DeMille to fly in 1917. Wilson, an innovator of many barnstorming stunts, formed the Wilson Aviation Company in 1919 and worked with Garland Lincoln, DeMille, and Ralph Newcomb. The firm eventually became DeMille's Mercury Aviation Company. Wilson appeared in more aviation films in the 1920s than any other flier.

Garland Lincoln learned to fly in the Army Air Service in 1918. He met Frank Clarke in 1920 and left the Army to fly for films. He left Wilson Aviation in 1921 to barnstorm, but soon returned to films. He owned many World War I planes and when these had been worn out he designed and built the LF-1 series of planes, which became known as "Garland Lincolns" and often doubled for Nieuports. He trained pilots and ferried bombers in World War II and left the service in 1946.

As good as these pilots were, the one who captured the most attention after World War I was Ormer Locklear. (For the definitive biography of Locklear, see Locklear, The Man Who Walked on Wings, by Art Ronnie, A. S. Barnes, 1973.) Locklear was born on October 28, 1891, in Texas. In 1910 he saw his first barnstorming planes in Fort Worth, and his interest in aviation grew with Calbraith Perry Rodgers' 1911 transcontinental flight. Risking his life appealed

to the Texan, and Locklear built gliders and engaged in motorcycle stunts. He enlisted in the United States Air Service
on October 25, 1917, but his fascination with aviation went
beyond mere flying. He began to wing-walk. On November
8, 1918 he made the first mid-air transfer between two planes.
After his May 5, 1919 discharge, Locklear barnstormed around
the country doing stunts that few dared try. He earned a
national reputation that brought him to the attention of Hollywood. Thus, on July 4, 1919, Carl Laemmle, head of the Universal film company, announced that Locklear had been hired
to appear in a film that would feature his daredevil stunts.
Locklear's flamboyant nature made him a natural for the Hollywood lifestyle, and he felt at home with the filmmakers.

Locklear used the Curtiss JN-4 "Jenny" (or "Cannuck,"
as the Canadian version was called) for his stunts. Indeed,
the Jenny served as the principal plane not only for barnstormers but also for aviation filmmakers in the 1920s. Almost 7,000 Jennies were built during World War I, for anywhere between $5,000 and $7,000 each. After the war, the
Government sold them as surplus for $2,000 apiece, but the
price soon dropped to about $400 a plane, something the
barnstormers could afford. The Jenny's multitude of wires
and struts, coupled with its slow speed and stable responses,
made it the perfect plane for stunting.

Locklear appeared in only two films and his flying career lasted only 16 months, but he brought a notoriety to
aviation films that had been lacking. For the first time,
films were made and advertised on the premise that the public would go to see a particular stunt flier, rather than an
established movie star.

In spite of all their publicity, Locklear's films were a
long way from good aviation movies. THE GREAT AIR ROB-
BERY and THE SKYWAYMAN didn't attempt to capture the
"feel" of aviation. If Locklear had lived, it's doubtful he
would have had a long career as an aviation movie star.
Neither film made a great deal of money and two studios had
failed to renew his contract. But his two pictures did con-
tribute significantly to aviation film development. As Carl
Laemmle stated: "'Locklear's films marked the beginning of
a regular and extensive use of airplanes by movie companies.'"[2]

Locklear was also responsible for bringing one of Hollywood's most famous pilots, Dick Grace, into films. Grace had been a Navy aviator in World War I and became a barnstormer after the war. He came to Hollywood when Locklear told him of the opportunities for good pilots. He took stunting jobs which included jumping from ships' yardarms, leaping from a burning five-story building into a net, and working with lions in a Ruth Roland serial. Grace quickly became the king of plane crashing. He once bragged he never landed a plane intact, and he broke more than 80 bones crashing for movies. He wrote several airplane movies; and he flew 44 combat missions as a bomber pilot in Europe in World War II. He died in 1965 at the age of 67.

By the first half of the 1920s, aviation films had increased in number to the point where they could supply a reasonable amount of work for stunt fliers. To meet this demand, a group of stunt pilots organized the Thirteen Black Cats (or Black 13) in Los Angeles in 1924. (The original membership of 13 was later expanded.) The group consisted of Reginald Denny, a mid-twenties movie star; Arthur C. Goebel, winner of the 1927 Dole air race to Hawaii; Sanford "Sam" Greenwall, well-known at the time as a daring newsreel cameraman; Al Johnson, William "Wild Billy" Lind, Frank Lockhart, Ronald "Bon" MacDougall, William "Spider" Matlock, Herd McClellan, Ken Nichols, Paul Richter, Jr., Bill Stapp, Burdette Fuller, Jack Frye, Jerry Tabnac, Gladys Ingle, and Ivan "Bugs" Unger. Denny was largely an honorary member because his studio forbade him to fly. Dick Grace was not a member.

Calling themselves "the world's greatest stuntmen--the only flyers who will do anything for a fixed price," the group outfitted themselves in black sweaters, the front of which sported a large white circle with a vicious-looking cat and the number "13" in its center. The Black 13, which barnstormed when film work was not available, offered the following price list:

Blow up ship in mid-air (pilot leaves by parachute)	$1,500
Ship spins down to crash (smoke pots included for fire)	$1,200
Crash ship (will fly into trees, side of house--anything)	$1,200

Fight between two stuntmen on upper wing
   with one man being knocked off $225

Two-man parachute jump with one parachute $180

Plane to train, auto; motorcycle to plane;
   speedboat to plane; delayed parachute jump $150

Upside down aerial stunts $100

Regular parachute jump $80

Ship spins down on fire (does not crash) $50

For roughly the next decade, members of the Thirteen Black Cats stunted their way across the movie screens of America.

During the 1920s, new pilots joined the stunt flying ranks. Florence "Pancho" Barnes learned to fly in 1928, and in 1929 flew in the first transcontinental women's air race, the "Powder Puff Derby." In 1930 she set a new speed record for women that bested Amelia Earhart's time. She came by her aviation interest naturally, for her paternal grandfather had commanded the Union Army's observation balloons in the Civil War. She was instrumental in organizing the stunt fliers, and her ranch near Edwards Air Force Base, the Happy Bottom Riding Club, became such a favorite watering hole for test pilots that she and it were portrayed in the 1983 film about the Mercury 7 astronauts, THE RIGHT STUFF. She died in 1975.

By the end of the 1920s, Hollywood stunt flying had become a major business. The production of Howard Hughes' HELL'S ANGELS had two indirect effects on the movie stunt fliers. The first was the disbandonment of the Black 13. The death of Al Johnson convinced the other members, especially Spider Matlock, that they **should quit the stunt business**. They felt they had already been at it too long, and that to continue would mean death. So the movies' first stunt flying organization passed into history.

The second effect concerned the Motion Picture Pilots Association (or the Association of Motion Picture Pilots). The MPPA had been formed by Pancho Barnes in the interest of fair play, to ensure that stunt pilots who often risked their lives for little pay got a fair deal from the studios, since no other organization then existed to look out for the fliers' needs. The charter members of the MPPA were Frank Clarke, Leo Nomis, Ira Reed, Al Wilson, Pancho Barnes, Roy Wilson, E. H. Robinson, Dick Grace, Frank Tomick, Tave Wilson, Dick Renaldi,

Jack Rand, Clinton Herberger, Bob Blair, Howard **Batt, Earl** Gordon, Oliver Le Boutiller, and Garland Lincoln. (None of the Black 13 became members of the Association.) The **numerous aviation films of the late 1920s** provided virtually unlimited employment for stunt pilots. HELL'S ANGELS alone gave them two years of steady work. With so many pilots working and in demand, an organization like the MPPA became necessary. The Association was dedicated to professional standards in movie flying and fair wages for its fliers. It received its charter from the Airline Pilots Association in 1931. While it did protect the pilots' interests, it also presented problems.

The MPPA became a tight organization, demanding high rates for its members. Not only this, the studios often had to pay for poor flying. For example, if the pilots were out of camera range or if weather or mechanical problems forced a flight to be canceled, the pilots still drew salary. In addition, the MPPA was a closed shop operation: to be a member a pilot had to fly in the movies; to fly in the movies he had to have an MPPA card. This made it virtually impossible for a newcomer to break into the movie stunt flying business. In spite of its power, however, the MPPA was not a unified body. The pilots fought among themselves for the best jobs and were often jealous of other members.

It was this group of fliers that faced Paul Mantz when he came to Hollywood in 1930. Mantz is Hollywood's most famous stunt pilot, and during his 35-year movie flying career he did more to advance the art of the aviation film flying than any other individual. (For a biography of Mantz, see Hollywood Pilot by Don **Dwiggins, Modern** Literary Editions, 1967.)

Mantz was born on August 2, 1903 in Alameda, California. His first introduction to aviation came when he saw Lincoln Beachey fly his Lincoln Beachey Special in March 1915, and die when the plane crashed. Mantz took his first flying lesson on his sixteenth birthday at the Redwood City, California airport, paying for the lesson with the $50 he had earned driving a hearse for the local undertaker during the 1919 flu epidemic at $5 a body. But Mantz's flying instructor was killed and he forgot about flying for five years, taking a trip around the world in 1921.

Mantz met world flier Lieutenant Leigh Wade in 1924 and the aviator introduced him to other pilots. Lindbergh's 1927 flight inspired Mantz to enlist in the Army Air Corps and he was inducted into the Army on October 27, 1927. He trained at March Field but was expelled the day before graduation for buzzing a train.

Mantz became the West Coast distributor for the Fleet airplane in 1930, all the while eyeing the riches the pilots in Hollywood were accumulating. But to be a Hollywood flier, Mantz had to get into the powerful Motion Picture Pilots Association. To attract headlines, Mantz set a new world's record by doing 46 consecutive outside loops. Mantz headed for Hollywood with the idea that his new world's record would give him an edge. He also thought that the studios would be happy to see a unified, reliable movie stunt flying organization to replace the MPPA, if only he could find the money to set one up.

Mantz learned all he could about movie stunt flying, but he faced stiff opposition getting into the MPPA. His chief foe was MPPA president Frank Clarke, perhaps because Clarke recognized that this newcomer would soon challenge Clarke's authority. When Mantz had the $10 fee to join, Clarke quickly raised the fee to $100. To get film flying experience, the other requirement for membership, Mantz was forced to take flying jobs no one else would undertake.

Mantz's first movie job was to earn the $100 fee. He was to fly low past a camera on the ground with a stuntman on the wing for a film based on the life of Red Grange, THE GALLOPING GHOST. Mantz soon found out why no other movie stunt pilot would take the job. With stuntman Bobby Rose on the top wing of his Stearman, Mantz flew down a Hollywood Hills' canyon toward the camera crew. A tall sycamore tree lay directly in Mantz's path, and when he tried to bank around it, nothing happened. Rose's body canceled out the effect of the ailerons. Mantz dove the plane to the ground and hauled back on the stick as the wheels hit the ground. He bounced through the tree's top branches. It was a close call, but Mantz had both his membership fee and his movie flying experience. He was now a member of the MPPA.

Mantz set out to build his Hollywood flying service. He got space at the United Airport in Burbank and opened United

Air Services, Limited. Although he had only three planes, other fliers who parked their planes there made them available for Mantz's movie flying, thus expanding the size of his "air force." But the studios did not beat a path to Mantz's hanger door, so he sent a brochure to every producer he could think of. It read:

> We claim to be the first organization that has combined business with the rental of ships to the motion picture industry. We fully appreciate the cost of delays and have a highly trained crew at our end of the production to facilitate speed. Frank Clarke and all the boys of the Motion Picture Pilots Association make their headquarters here. We also have a great deal of material for making crashes. [3]

The other pilots did hang around the hanger, but they didn't work for Mantz. But by taking a dangerous job for which Clarke recommended him, for AIR MAIL (discussed later), Mantz gradually became more sought after by the studios.

The resentment between Mantz and Clarke continued to grow through the 1930s, but gradually Mantz began to replace Clarke as the most sought after pilot. For all of the twenties, cameraman Elmer Dyer refused to fly with any other camera plane pilot but Clarke because of the pilot's skill in getting the camera in the best position to film a sequence. But soon Dyer was flying with Mantz, the superior of Clarke as a camera plane pilot. Dyer stated:

> Paul had more of a feel for what his plane was doing than any man I ever flew with.... The nice thing was that when he flew me for camera he could fly his airplane and at the same time concentrate on the action, angle, and distance. It's quite a trick to fly a camera ship. You have to know all the time where the lens is looking; you can't just fly right on past your action, or the poor guy in back will end up shooting the tail or wingtip. [4]

By 1931, United Air Services was going rapidly, as Mantz subsidized its development with charter work. Mantz acquired new planes, among them a Lockheed Vega NC 48M which would become the Honeymoon Express, and soon had pilots like Howard Batt, Ace Braguinier, Speed Nolta,

Frank Tomick, Dick **Renaldi,** Tex Rankin, and Pancho Barnes doing occasional work for him. Frank Clarke, Leo Nomis, and Roy Wilson divided up whatever flying was not done by United Air Services. Mantz charged higher prices than before, $50 a day plus $250 per week for regular movie flying and another $150 for Mantz as aerial director, but the studios were happy to pay, for Mantz delivered dependable service that helped to avoid costly production delays.

Throughout the 1930s and 1940s Mantz became the undisputed leader of Hollywood fliers, and there seemed to be few non-film aspects of aviation in which he wasn't involved. He teamed with Clarke and Howard Batt, and they flew at airshows billed as the Hollywood Trio. Mantz helped Amelia Earhart prepare for her around-the-world flight, and was scheduled to be her co-pilot until a movie commitment interfered. He was **grieved** and appalled to learn that her death was caused in part by her not heeding some of his advice. He joined the Army during World War II and made many training films. After the war, Mantz bought 75 B-17s, 228 B-24s, 90 P-40s and 31 P-47s, as well as over 50 other aircraft including B-25s, Marauders, Mustangs, and Airacobras for $55,000. These aircraft had cost over $117,000,000 to produce and the aviation gasoline in their tanks was worth well over $45,000.

By the 1950s, a new flier came to Hollywood to challenge Mantz. Frank Tallman was born in 1919, the son of a Navy flier. Tallman learned to fly in 1938 and during World War II served as a naval flight instructor at Pensacola. After the war, he worked for CBS and flew at airshows. He started collecting vintage aircraft and went into movie stunt flying. Instead of a repeat of the Clarke versus Mantz scenario, Mantz and Tallman teamed up in 1961 to form Tallmantz Aviation. They specialized in providing planes for films and established the Movieland of the Air Museum at the Orange County Airport in Santa Ana, California to display and rent historic aircraft.

Mantz was killed in 1965, and Jim Greenwood summed up Mantz's career: by the time of his death "... Mantz had piled up some 25,000 hours as a pilot; he had pulled off impossible stunts in more than 250 movies."[5]

At the time of Mantz's death, Tallman had suffered a

knee injury while pushing his son's go-cart. The wound became infected and the leg had to be amputated above the knee.
It is a testament to Tallman's fortitude that within a year of
the accident he had returned to flying, as fully FAA-qualified
as he had been before, and by the end of his career he had
flown more than 500 types of aircraft.

The majority of the great stunt fliers died as they
lived: in their planes. Locklear spun into the ground while
filming THE SKYWAYMAN. Al Wilson died in a mid-air collision at the National Air Races in Cleveland in 1932. Frank
Clarke died in a freak accident on a visit to Frank Tomick.
Ever the joker, Clarke planned to drop a sack of manure as
he swooped over Tomick's house. The manure sack slid in
the plane, jamming the controls, and Clarke and a passenger
died in the crash. The event so unnerved Tomick that he
never flew again. Mantz met his death when the makeshift
"Phoenix" crashed while filming THE FLIGHT OF THE PHOE-
NIX. And Tallman died in 1978 when his Piper Aztec slammed
into a California mountain in poor weather.

After Tallman's death, ex-Navy flier Frank Pine (who
had gone to work for Mantz in 1959) took over Tallmantz Aviation. Other fliers, too, helped fill the void left by Tallman's death. James Appleby retired from the Air Force in
1963 and joined Tallmantz. In 1972 he and his wife formed
Antique Aero, Ltd, which specialized in building full-scale
replicas of World War I planes. James Gavin flew in Korea
and got into films in 1959 while flying a helicopter for the
U.S. Forest Service where THE MISFITS was being filmed.
Director John Huston needed aerial shots of the wild horses
and Gavin got the job. Hal Needham, co-founder of Stunts
Unlimited, worked in films doing wing-walking and parachute
jumps and has become the director of many Burt Reynolds
stunt-oriented movies. Clay Lacy, a United Air Lines pilot,
formed Clay Lacy Aviation and specializes in aerial photography with a specially equipped Learjet. He has been a president of the Professional Race Pilots Association and has flown
for more than 50 made-for-TV movies and feature films.

Stunt Flying Films

With all the thrills and glamor associated with stunt
flying, it is only natural that Hollywood would have tackled

the subject in films. THE LOST SQUADRON (1932) was the first picture to deal with the stunt pilots who flew for the movies. (Another 1932 film based on a Dick Grace story, LUCKY DEVILS, also dealt with stunt men.) THE LOST SQUADRON was based on a Liberty magazine story by Dick Grace and told of three pilots, Captain Gibson (Richard Dix), Red (Joel McCrea), and Woody (Robert Armstrong), who have just returned from the war. Gibson finds his girl friend, Follette Marsh (Mary Astor), has married another man. Red discovers that if he takes his old job back, an elderly man will be fired. And Woody learns that his business partner has disappeared with all their money.

Woody heads for Hollywood, and when Gibson and Red also arrive they discover their pal all dressed up at a movie premiere. He's making good money flying for motion pictures ($50 a flight) and convinces his friends to join him. Gibson and Red go to work for Woody's director, the autocratic Arnold von Furst (Erich von Stroheim). Von Furst makes sure his pictures carry the ultimate aerial thrill to the audience, whatever the risk to the pilots. In true Hollywood fashion, Gibson's ex-girl friend has married von Furst, and the director, jealous of the affection that still exists between the two, puts acid on the control wires of Gibson's plane. But Woody takes the plane up and is killed in the crash. Gibson and Red learn the truth, and Red shoots von Furst. To save his pal, Gibson takes von Furst's body aloft. He deliberately crashes the plane and thereby saves Red, although Gibson is killed.

THE LOST SQUADRON was made during the transition period between the regimes of William Le Baron and David O. Selznick at RKO. When Selznick came in, he examined the pictures awaiting release at the studio. He ordered this film back into production, and his improvements helped make it a critical and popular success. Critics praised both the acting and the stunt flying, the latter done by Dick Grace, Art Gobel, Leo Nomis, and Frank Clarke. As if to bitterly underscore the dangers of movie stunt flying, Leo Nomis had already been dead a month (killed while flying for SKY BRIDE) when THE LOST SQUADRON was released.

SKY BRIDE (1932) told about a reckless barnstorming pilot, Speed Condon (Richard Arlen), who causes a fellow pilot's death and vows never to fly again. He goes to work

in an airplane factory and staves off attempts by the leader
of the barnstorming troup (Jack Oakie) to get him to go up
in the air. But later, the young nephew of the dead flier,
who likes to experiment with makeshift parachutes, is carried
aloft on a plane's landing gear and Condon has to rescue him.

SKY BRIDE spelled death for Leo Nomis, who had flown
in aviation films for over ten years. Nomis was born in Iowa
in 1894. He was in the air service in World War I and flew
as a barnstormer, doing parachute jumps at state fairs. In
1929 he tried unsuccessfully, with Maurice Morrison, to set a
refueling endurance flight record at Culver City, California,
quitting after more than forty hours in the air. He was also
a member of the Army Reserve Flying Corps.

The flier's death came while doing a spin, the same
kind of stunt that killed Locklear. Nomis had gone through
the stunt with Earl Gordon and Captain E. H. Robinson several times before. The director asked for one more scene,
and for some reason Nomis never recovered from the spin.
His plane crashed directly into the ground, driving the engine eight feet into the earth. Only a few weeks earlier,
Nomis had been injured when he drove a race car for THE
CROWD ROARS, and perhaps this injury contributed to his
inability to regain control of the plane.

Other stunt fliers besides Americans have appeared on
the screen. The German film FLIEGENDE SCHATTEN (FLY-
ING SHADOWS, 1932) was an account of an expedition to cen-
tral Africa and it featured the famous German flier, Ernst
Udet. The picture showed Udet stunting, flying over the
Mediterranean, over the pyramids, and down the Nile. The
Central African footage shows Udet hunting animals by plane
and flying low over vast herds of animals (hence the title).
An unfortunate attempt at romance was made through the in-
clusion of a lady aviator who follows Udet's route.

The picture is most notable for the presence of Udet.
Udet was the second most successful German ace of World
War I (after von Richthofen) and therefore the most successful German flier to survive the war. After the war, Udet
became a stunt pilot, explorer, and hunter, and journeyed
to America where he participated in air shows and races,
making friends among the American pilots. (Udet served as
the model for the flier Ernst Kessler in THE GREAT WALDO

PEPPER.) Besides FLYING SHADOWS, he appeared in at least three other German films. THE WHITE HELL OF PITZ PALU (1930) and AVALANCHE (1932) were Alpine adventures, while S.O.S. ICEBERG (1933) was an Arctic adventure with Rod La Rocque. Each of these three films starred actress Leni Riefenstahl, who later went on to become one of the major filmmakers in Hitler's Germany. At the start of World War II, Udet was made second in command of the Luftwaffe. But he was ill-suited to the desk job and when he got blamed for Goering's blunders, he committed suicide (in June 1941).

THE TARNISHED ANGELS (1957) is the only film devoted to pylon racing. Adapted from William Faulkner's novel Pylon, the movie investigates the personalities of a group of air circus fliers in the early 1930s. The aerial show route has taken them to New Orleans at Mardi Gras time. The

Dorothy Malone tries to stop an argument between her husband, Robert Stack, and his mechanic, Jack Carson, in THE TARNISHED ANGELS (1957).

group is led by Roger Schumann (Robert Stack), a speed
flier and WWI ace. His wife, Laverne (Dorothy Malone), is
a trick parachutist. The third member of the team is the
mechanic, Jiggs (Jack Carson), who is in love with Laverne.
This trio arouses the interest of a hard-drinking reporter,
Burke Devlin (Rock Hudson), and he hangs around them collecting material for his newspaper. Roger is so devoted to
flying that he sells his wife to Matt Ord (Robert Middleton)
for the use of a plane. This disturbs Devlin, as he is becoming attached to Laverne. While flying the pylon event,
Roger realizes that for the first time in his life he can do
some good, so he kills himself by crashing in a lake after
rounding a pylon. He has sacrificed himself so that Laverne
can have a better life. The picture avoids the usual happy
ending, for Laverne leaves New Orleans and Devlin at the
end of the movie.

None of the characters in the film is ever able to
achieve what he strives for. The pilots are always chasing
the illusive aerial race victory and seldom achieving it. Laverne is never able to raise herself above the status of an
object to be bought and sold (Roger won her in a dice game).
And Devlin, on what he thinks is a big and meaningful story,
is fired from the newspaper. A poor film it is; however, it
is acknowledged by many, including Faulkner himself, to be
the best screen adaption of a Faulkner story.

THE GYPSY MOTHS (1969) had Burt Lancaster, Gene
Hackman, and Scott Wilson as a trio of barnstorming sky divers. This time they are performing in a small mid-western
town, Bridgeville, on the Fourth of July weekend. Their
major problems concern their fears about jumping and Lancaster's brief romance with a Kansas housewife (Deborah
Kerr). The picture is totally a lackluster affair. Lancaster
is killed off early in the film and the only scenes of any interest are the sky-diving shots. The movie begins and ends
with some good skydiving footage, a lot of which was shot
by a cameraman who jumped with the parachutists. The picture also gives some insight into how the men prepare for
their jumps.

ACE ELI AND RODGER OF THE SKIES (1973) was based
on a Steven Spielberg story. The film told of a father-and-
son (Cliff Robertson and Eric Shea) barnstorming team of the
1920s. The film was a pet project of Robertson's, whose

fascination with airplanes made a Standard J-1 the real star
of the picture. Except for some of Frank Tallman's flying,
the film is a miserable affair that deservedly sat on the studio
shelf a long time.

SKY HIGH (1974) was a documentary on airborne sports.
It featured skydiving and air races held at Cape May, New
Jersey, Reno, San Diego, and Mojave.

One of the best films dealing with stunt flying in or
out of movies is THE GREAT WALDO PEPPER (1975). Robert
Redford played Pepper, a natural-born flier who arrived in
France too late to see combat in World War I. Now it is the
1920s, and he barnstorms his way around the Midwest, telling false stories about how his life was spared by the great
German ace, Ernst Kessler. Pepper puts his barnstorming
money into the development of a plane, designed and built
by his friend, with which he hopes to do the outside loop,
"the last great stunt." Out of economic necessity, Pepper
teams up with a rival barnstormer, Axel Olsson (Bo Sven-
son), and they develop a wing-walking act and join a Flying
Circus. When Olsson's girl friend falls to her death from a
plane while doing a publicity stunt, Pepper and Olsson are
grounded by Pepper's war-time commander, who now works
for the C.A.A. Afraid that someone else will do an outside
loop before he can fly again, Pepper lets his friend attempt
the stunt in the newly-designed plane. The plane crashes;
and Pepper is forced to knock his friend unconscious when
the unfeeling crowd ignites gasoline from the leaking plane.
Pepper's friend burns to death. Incensed, Pepper buzzes
the crowd until he crashes. The C.A.A. permanently grounds
him.

Pepper makes his way to Hollywood, where Olsson has
found work as a stunt man. When Pepper learns that a studio is looking for two fliers for a World War I picture, he
convinces Olsson that they should apply for the jobs. The
picture turns out to be a re-enactment of the aerial battle
Pepper bragged about, and his hero, Ernst Kessler (Bo
Brundin), is technical advisor. Kessler is 40 and balding,
the opposite of the traditional dashing image of a World War I
ace. Pepper has great rapport with Kessler, and finds him
all that he expected. During the filming of the final dogfight
sequence, Pepper and Kessler attack each other for real,
testing their flying skill by each trying to ram the other's

plane. Pepper "wins" the dogfight, and Kessler salutes him, a gesture that had made Kessler famous during the war. With the C.A.A. waiting for him on the ground, Pepper flies his Sopwith Camel off into the clouds.

Frank Tallman supervised the flying sequences that included two Standards, two Jennies, a Fokker Triplane, three Tiger Moths, a DeHavilland Chipmunk (modified to look like a period aircraft), a French Stampe, and a replica Sopwith Camel built from scratch. The planes were usually trucked to the shooting locations because it was too dangerous to fly them over long distances. Original Hispano-Suiza engines were used in the J-1 Standards.

The flying team consisted of Tallman, Ralph **Wiggins** (a 63-year-old wing walker who disdained the use of a parachute), Frank Pine, Jim Appleby, and Art Scholl. Tallman naturally undertook the most difficult stunts himself. In one sequence, the script called for Pepper to fly down a town's main street. The filmmakers had to get permission from the FAA, bury all the power lines and phone cables along the route, and evacuate an area of several blocks (the people in the street were stuntmen). Tallman had only a couple of feet between wing tips and street light poles, but he successfully completed the stunt. In another scene, Olsson has to ditch in a pond after Pepper loosens the wheels on his plane. Tallman took off a Jenny that had small casters attached to the axle to enable him to land the plane even though it appeared not to have wheels. For the watery crash, a Tiger Moth was modified to look like a Jenny. Tallman deftly set it down in the pond, but he had scuba gear in the plane just in case!

As in WINGS nearly 50 years before, the actors in THE GREAT WALDO PEPPER took to the sky. For the very dangerous stunts, Tallman wore a rubber mask on the mouth and chin to make him look like Redford. But for the "routine" shots, Redford exposed himself to a good deal of risk. For the shots of Redford standing on the top wing, the actor stood on the back end of an L-1 observation plane at 3,000 feet while Tallman made passes in a Standard 224. Bo Brundin, playing Kessler, as well as Edward Herrmann, also flew.

Like many films before it, THE GREAT WALDO PEPPER had some accidents. A Garland Lincoln Nieuport was destroyed when Frank Pine tried to land it too soon after a

heavy rain. Fortunately, the pilot was unhurt. Tallman
narrowly escaped injury when he missed balsa booths in the
fairground crash scene and hit solid 9 × 9 posts. Another
time, however, he wasn't so lucky. He was landing a Nieuport when the rudder pedal broke off at 400 feet. He
crashed through some high tension wires and was hospitalized for a month. Tallman cracked two vertebrae and split
open his scalp on the windshield, a wound that required 55
stitches. It was the worst crash of his movie career and
film production was shut down.

In THE GREAT WALDO PEPPER, director George Roy
Hill (a World War II Marine Corps pilot) and screen writer
William Goldman created a loving tribute to aviation, an age
when life was simpler, and the notion that some men are little boys who never grow up. The flying is some of the best
to be found in any aviation film. Pepper has an adventurous
nature, and he can't understand that the days of unsuper-
vised barnstorming are coming to a close. When Newt explains the new regulations to Pepper, he says: "If I study
real hard you think I'll pass, Newt? You gonna license the
clouds, the rain, you gonna make highways up in the sky
for us all to follow?" Yes, replies Newt, all that and more
is coming. It isn't only Pepper who feels trapped by the
new way. The character of Ernst Kessler was based on the
German World War I ace, Ernst Udet. Udet committed suicide in 1941; and the Kessler character finds life in the 1920s
difficult. In the sky, alone, life is simple. On the ground
it is much more difficult, a fact Pepper knows all too well.

In spite of its many strong points, THE GREAT WALDO
PEPPER earned mixed reviews. The chief criticism leveled
against it was the abrupt shift in tone. The first third of
the film is light-hearted; when Olsson's girl friend suddenly
falls to her death, barnstorming isn't fun any more. This
transition is made in a few seconds, and it disconcerted many
viewers. If taken as a story of a man who gets to live out
his daydreams, the movie has a lot to offer. Some critics
felt that the plot needed more to make the movie memorable.
But for people who enjoy flying films, THE GREAT WALDO
PEPPER is a "must see."

A somewhat different approach to the subject of barnstorming was taken by NOTHING BY CHANCE (1975), a documentary about a modern-day re-creation of olden-day barn-

stormers' adventures. Written by Richard Bach and based on his book of the same title, the film featured Bach, Jack Brown, Chris Cagle, Steve McPherson, Spense Nelson, Glenn Norman, and Steve Young doing the flying in the midwest. The excellent aerial scenes were photographed by Fleming Olsen and the picture provided a unique look at the barnstorming lifestyle.

CLOUD DANCER (1980) featured David Carradine in a story set against the world of aerobatic air show flying. Although the film featured a number of the world's best aerobatic pilots, including Charlie Hillard and Tom Poberezny, a substantial budget, numerous flying sequences, and planes that included a P-51 and a Pitts S-1, the picture was so bad that it never went into wide distribution. Here is a classic example of how good stunt flying cannot save an otherwise poor film.

A much better look at the world of stunting came in STUNT MAN (1980). Although not an aviation film, it did feature some interesting flying sequences as a satanic director, played by Peter O'Toole, manipulates everyone around him in his efforts to make a World War I movie. Things are never what they seem in STUNT MAN; the film is a classic exercise in filmmaking as an illusion.

Throughout aviation cinema history, it is the stunt fliers that have set aviation films apart from all other movies. A special breed, they have often sacrificed their lives to give an audience thrills. It is fortunate that most of these films survive; and their efforts can be enjoyed now as much as when these stunt pilots owned the sky.

CHAPTER 3

PAR AVION

The first popular aviation film sub-genre was not, as one might expect, World War I. In spite of the thrilling aviation events of that war, the public was in no mood for combat pictures in 1919. But the air mail--that was another story. Air mail pilots had taken the place of World War I aviators in the public's imagination. Regular service began in 1918, and by 1924 'round-the-clock transcontinental service was the rule. Flying unreliable machines with few instruments in all kinds of weather, these fliers set new standards for aviation determination and daring. Early aviation filmmakers, however, often ignored the real hazards of mail flying, and focused their attention on aerial bandit plots, making the first air mail movies nothing more than westerns with wings. It took the decade of the 1920s for the airmail film to mature into a more serious depiction of the perils encountered by air mail pilots.

The first star of an air mail film was none other than Ormer Locklear. According to Carl Laemmle, Locklear's first film, THE GREAT AIR ROBBERY (originally titled CASSIDY OF THE AIR LANES), was to be "... the most amazing and unbelievable photodrama of all time."[1] Universal planned to spend $250,000 on the picture, the **largest aviation film budget up to that time. Ideas for** the movie included wireless communication aboard the planes and "a spectacular pony express style mail exchange ... at night with magnesium flares attached to the plane's wings. [THE GREAT AIR ROBBERY] would make all **other pictures 'look like** milk and water.' "[2]

Elmer Dyer assisted the head cameraman, Milton Moore. Dyer would go on to become the top aerial film photographer (with work on HELL'S ANGELS and WAKE ISLAND, among others), frequently teaming up with Paul Mantz.

If THE GREAT AIR ROBBERY's production aspects seem spectacular, its plot wasn't. Locklear played Larry Cassidy, the Air Mail Service's best pilot. Cassidy's exploits battling the Death's Head Squadron, which was bent on stealing $20,000 in gold from an air mail shipment, served mainly as a showcase for Locklear's stunting.

Filming took place on DeMille Field Number 1. It was the first movie made there, and DeMille modestly made the most of it by painting "CB" on the hangers and fuselages and rudders of some planes. The cameramen photographed aerial close-ups by placing the Jennies on wooden platforms, but no aerial stunts were faked. The shooting ended on August 2, 1919.

THE GREAT AIR ROBBERY premiered at the Superba Theatre in Los Angeles on December 28, 1919, accompanied by an extensive advertising campaign. The studio sent Locklear on a two-month personal appearance tour to promote the film. The Curtiss Airplane company loaned airplanes, engines, and miniatures for the advertising. Air shows promoted the movie and model airplane contests with $50 prizes were staged in many cities. A Minneapolis department store used its entire fourth floor for a model airplane display. And, of course, the advertising copy was appropriately superlative. For all the publicity, however, the film was only a moderate box-office success.

TRAPPED IN THE AIR (1922) repeated the theme of THE GREAT AIR ROBBERY: a gang of crooks are out to steal $100,000 from an air mail pouch.

THE AIR MAIL (1925) proved to be the first serious film dealing with the U.S. Air Mail Service. The plot had Russ Kane (Warner Baxter) joining the Air Mail Service with the intention of robbing the first valuable air mail shipment that comes his way. His experiences while undergoing training in Reno, however, so enthuse him with the spirit of the mail corps that he changes his mind. Forced down in a blizzard, Kane meets a girl and her father in a ghost town. While trying to deliver some medicine to the girl's father, Kane is attacked by air mail robbers. Kane is forced down, but wins the ensuing gun battle.

Byron Morgan, a flier himself, wrote THE AIR MAIL.

To find out exactly what the air mail pilots encountered in
their flights, Morgan went along on an air mail run between
Salt Lake City and San Francisco. The route consisted of
three legs: Salt Lake City to Elko, Elko to Reno, and Reno
to San Francisco. Among the hazards facing the airmen were
the lofty Ruby Mountains, a section of the route where there
was no place to make an emergency landing during one hour
of flying time, and frequent fog in San Francisco. Even after Morgan's flight experience, however, air mail outlaws
posed the chief danger in his story.

THE SKY RAIDER (1925) was released at almost the
same time as THE AIR MAIL. This picture featured Captain
Charles Nungesser, a French ace who had 43 victories by
the end of World War I, playing himself, chasing after an air
mail robber in the United States. The film proved to be
quite popular and Nungesser, like Bert Hall before him, made
personal appearances at showings of the film. Nungesser also had Bert Hall's sense of flair, and he sometimes arrived
for dawn patrols in World War I dressed in a tuxedo and with
a girl draped on his arm. He had mixed success in his aviation career after the war, and disappeared while trying to
fly the Atlantic in 1927.

WIDE OPEN, starring Dick Grace, led off 1927. The
story of airplane engine design, two rival engineers, an air
mail pilot, and an air race gave the audiences many thrills.
WOLVES OF THE AIR (1927) also dealt with the building of
an airplane. A World War I veteran returns to find his father's plane factory in the hands of crooks. He builds a
plane to enter in a race with the villains for a government
air mail contract. When the hero gets wounded, his girl
friend flies the plane herself. Most of the picture's aerial
stunts were faked.

Four other films in 1927 dealt with the Postal Service,
which, if one were to believe filmmakers, seemed threatened
with extinction by air mail bandits. FLYING HIGH, with its
story of a society woman and her husband as air mail thieves,
offered the viewers several elaborate and exciting air stunts
as the pilot-hero drove off the air mail bandits and later parachuted into their camp to capture them. The main faults of
the film were its poor plot and badly done ground sequences.
In addition, the picture ended anticlimactically, because the
previous aerial stunts were more exciting than the final scene

in which the hero rescues his sweetheart from the bandit's plane. THE FLYING MAIL showcased the talents of Al Wilson and Frank Tomick. Wilson played an air mail flier framed by crooks. He jumped from a motorcycle to a ladder suspended from a plane, fought a hand-to-hand battle on the plane's wing, and made a two-man, one-parachute drop --all, as a title in the film clearly stated, with no double or trick photography. More violent action characterized THE GREAT MAIL ROBBERY, in which government agents using an airplane and tear gas fought off robbers. PIRATES OF THE SKY was the least exciting of the four. It told of a amateur criminologist enlisted by the U.S. Secret Service to solve air mail robberies and had two main action sequences: a mid-air change of planes and a drop from a plane into a hay stack.

AIR MAIL PILOT (1928) was a cheaply made film. Air mail robbers strike and the hero goes after them. He jumps from his plane to theirs (the heroine flies his plane) and engages in hand-to-hand battle on the wings of the robbers' plane. He parachutes safely to earth when the robbers' plane crashes into his, and the heroine also jumps safely. The film blended actual stunting with trick photography, and some of the shots of air mail planes landing and taking off were filmed at a real air mail airport.

THE AIR LEGION (1928) had a young stunt flier (Ben Lyon) joining the air mail service. On his first job, he panics in a storm and cracks up the plane, but later redeems himself. Although the picture was a minor effort, it is notable that this air mail film concentrated on the very real danger of air mail flying--the weather--rather than on aerial robbery.

The next major aviation film was AIR MAIL (1932), the first of a new breed of major air mail pictures. Gone were the aerial bandits of the 1920s; now more realistic hazards of air mail flying would dominate the screen. AIR MAIL, directed by John Ford, one of America's best directors, written by Dale Van Ecery and Frank Wead, and photographed by Karl Freund and Elmer Dyer, depicted the operations of an air mail service. (Wead and Ford would become great friends, leading to Ford's film biography of Wead.) One of the pilots, Duke Talbot (Pat O'Brien), is a show-off flier and is also romancing the wife of a fellow pilot. This affair

rouses the ire of the head of the operation, Mike Miller
(Ralph Bellamy), who runs the Desert Station, an airfield in
the Rocky Mountains. When the husband of the wayward
wife is killed in a violent snowstorm, Duke refuses to take
the mail through, electing instead to go off with the wife.
So the mail flight falls to Mike, even though he suffers from
eye trouble. Mike crashes in the mountains and is badly
injured. No plane can land and rescue him, and the other
pilots give up. But Duke looks upon this as a challenge.
Jilting the girl, he does some dangerous flying among the
mountains and manages to set the plane down, although the
right wing and undercarriage are damaged. He gets Mike
into the plane and takes off. But the plane begins to fall
apart in the air and Duke dumps Mike out of the craft, allowing him to parachute to safety. Duke crash-lands the
plane and is injured.

Although this story is no dramatic masterpiece, it is
set against the day-to-day workings of an air mail service,
and this, along with the excellent stunt flying, is the strong
point of the picture. To quote one reviewer: "Picture is a
fund of interesting atmosphere about the air mail service,
impressing the auditor as authentic to the last detail. It is
full of technical touches of an air mail depot routine."[3]

AIR MAIL was the picture that gave Paul Mantz the
opportunity he needed to become an established movie stunt
flier. By 1932 Mantz had joined the MPPA and established
United Air Services, but he wasn't getting the important
movie stunt flying jobs. Interestingly, his opportunity was
provided by his arch rival, Frank Clarke:

> One afternoon the phone [rang] and Mantz dove for
> it. It was Frank Clarke.
> "There's a job up at Bishop nobody wants, Paul,"
> Clarke said. "Will you take it?"
> "Why not?" he yelled. "What do I have to do, fly
> through a hangar?"
> There was a long silence. "How did you know?"[4]

Naturally, Mantz wondered why no one else wanted the
job. The flier soon found out the two problems with the
task. Bishop, California lay in the head of Owens Valley at
the beginning of the Sierra Nevada mountains. When cold
winds off the mountain slopes mixed with the hot desert air,

turbulence was created. Then, too, the Bishop Airport hangar was only forty feet wide, five feet wider than Mantz's Stearman. But Mantz's career as a movie stunt flier depended on this job, so he went ahead. As he circled in preparation for the stunt, Mantz could see the turbulent winds blow dust around the airport. When he headed toward the hangar at near-ground level the wind buffeted his plane. A cloud of dust obscured his vision and when it cleared he could see he was off course. He quickly corrected and went perfectly through the hangar, earning welcome praise and more movie jobs. Sometimes, it is more interesting to discover what's not put in movies than what is included. The most critical time for the U.S. air mail came in 1934. In 1927 the Post Office handed the flying chores to private contractors, but in 1934 a Senate committee determined that these contracts had been illegally let. President Roosevelt then canceled the contracts, with the understanding that the Army would fly the mail. Army pilots, however, were trained to fly in daytime in good weather and lacked the experience and planes of the professional mail pilots. In the first week after the Army took over, six pilots died. After three weeks, ten pilots had been killed. Public outcry resulted in the contracts being reinstated. While this controversy had excellent possibilities for the movies, no films have been made on the subject.

NIGHT FLIGHT (1934) dealt with conventional themes. Produced by David O. Selznick for MGM, the film featured John Barrymore, Helen Hayes, Clark Gable, Lionel Barrymore, Robert Montgomery, and Myrna Loy, as well as Elmer Dyer and Charles Marshall doing the aerial photography and Mantz doing the stunt flying. The picture was based on a novel by the French air mail pilot, Antoine de Saint-Exupery, and told of the efforts to establish night flights in South America over the Andes. (Interestingly, Howard Hawks' classic air mail picture, ONLY ANGELS HAVE WINGS, would also be set in South America.) Lights on a large map of South America show Barrymore the positions of various planes, some of which have been lost in fog, blown out to sea, or lost when their crews parachuted to their deaths in the water. Barrymore is of "the mail must go through" school, although the wife of one pilot complains about risking men's lives so that someone in Paris can receive his mail on Tuesday instead of Thursday. But, in the end, one of these planes turns out to be carrying a desperately needed serum from Santiago to Buenos Aires.

NIGHT FLIGHT provided Mantz with one of his most dangerous experiences. Mantz had developed special camera mounts and cowlings to protect the cameras from the freezing wind. His Stearman camera ship, NR 4099, had a special inboard camera mount and heaters, and Mantz's ingenuity helped him win the NIGHT FLIGHT contract. Mantz and Dyer flew to Denver to shoot Rocky Mountain scenes which would double for the Andes. After waiting two weeks, the weather turned favorable and they flew over a canyon at 12,000 feet. But they hit a down draft and dropped 2,000 feet in a few seconds. The force was so severe that it broke Dyer's still camera, pushed his feet through the flooring, and loosened eight large bolts which held the aerial camera to the plane.

NIGHT FLIGHT also involved one of the greatest cloud chases in the history of film. Mantz and Dyer went looking for a black squall line for Herb White and Ivan Unger, one of the original Black 13, to parachute through (so their white canopies would look dramatic against a black background) when Clark Gable and Robert Montgomery were supposed to jump from a plane over the Andes. Mantz found what they wanted near Denver, but it meant climbing to 22,000 feet without oxygen. White and Unger passed out and had to be hospitalized. The weather had cleared by the time they recovered. A call to the Weather Bureau revealed a squall line headed for El Paso. They flew to Texas but were too late, as they were in Omaha a few days later. They went to Kansas, Missouri, **New** Mexico, Arizona, and Nevada and still didn't find what they wanted. Mantz returned to his wife in Burbank after an absence of two months, only to leave immediately to catch a squall moving right over United Airport. Mantz and Dyer finally got their footage.

The next air mail movie was AIR HAWKS (1935), a film in which Wiley Post put in a brief appearance playing himself. The story concerned two rival airlines after air mail contracts. One firm goes beyond the bounds of fair play and uses a death ray to destroy the rival's planes. (The use of a death ray against planes was a popular device in aviation melodramas of the 1930s.) FLIGHT AT MIDNIGHT (1939) was a Republic film about a mail pilot, an airline hostess, and a landing field supervisor. The film had **Roscoe Turner playing himself.** **The New York Times** summed up the film by asking: "... couldn't something be done about providing filmgoers with their own anti-aircraft batteries to

Jean Arthur patches up Cary Grant after she has shot him
to stop him flying a dangerous mail run in ONLY ANGELS
HAVE WINGS (1939). Thomas Mitchell (center) observes
closely.

to bring down ... such menaces to commercial aviation movies
as 'Flight at Midnight'..?"[5]

Howard Hawks' ONLY ANGELS HAVE WINGS (1939) climaxed two decades of air mail film images, conventions, and
situations. Criticized by some aviation enthusiasts because
of its sometimes unrealistic flying sequences, the film nevertheless stands out as a classic airplane movie. Written by
Jules Furthman from an original story by Hawks and photographed by Elmer Dyer and Joseph Walker, the film centered
around the character of Geoff Carter (Cary Grant) who runs
an air mail service in the South American coastal town of
Barranca for the service's owner, the Dutchman (Sig Ruman).
The only way inland by air from Barranca is through a high
mountain pass, where an observer is stationed who radios the

weather conditions back to the mail service's airstrip. Unknown to Carter's pilots, the Dutchman must maintain a regular air service for six months or lose an important air mail
contract. Into this group comes Bonnie Lee (Jean Arthur),
on her way by boat to Panama. One flier, Joe (Noah Beery,
Jr.) loses his life in a plane crash trying to keep a date
with her, but she stays in Barranca, becoming ever more
attached to Carter. A replacement flier, Bat McPherson
(Richard Barthelmess, in his first film role in three years),
turns out to be the man who bailed out of a plane and left
the brother of another air mail flier, Kidd Dabb (Thomas
Mitchell), to die. McPherson is also married to Judith (Rita
Hayworth), Carter's former girl friend. McPherson is given
flying jobs no one else will take and eventually redeems himself, although Dabb, Carter's friend, is killed. Carter and
Bonnie Lee fall in love.

The film explores the nearness to death that these
fliers feel. When Joe is killed trying to keep his date with
Bonnie Lee, he is ostensibly forgotten. When a steak comes
that Joe had ordered, Carter goes to eat it and Bonnie Lee
says, "That was Joe's." Carter quickly replies, "Who's
Joe?" And when Bonnie Lee says it was her fault that Joe
died, Carter says, "Sure it was your fault. You were going to have dinner with him, the Dutchman hired him, I
sent him up on schedule, the fog came in, a tree got in the
way. All your fault."

To serve as a setting for the film, a 270-foot by 350-
foot section of Barranca was built on the Columbia back lot
in the San Fernando Valley. Numerous animals were used
to dress the set, including monkeys, water buffalo, and sea
gulls. An excavation dug to simulate Barranca harbor was
filled with sea water to keep the gulls happy.

The flying sequences were a combination of adequate
model work and stunt flying, the latter including a scene in
which a windshield breaks off, knocking Grant unconscious,
and a flight onto and off a mesa, where Barthelmess has
landed to pick up an injured man. This latter stunt cost
Mantz his Honeymoon Express Vega. Mantz was taking off
the mesa at St. George, Utah, when his wheel hit a soft
spot and the plane went on one wing and then on its nose,
splitting the fuselage. (Mantz would continue the Honeymoon Express service in a Lockheed Orion.)

ONLY ANGELS HAVE WINGS proved to be the quintessential air mail film, summing up the themes, action sequences,
and clichés of a quarter-century of air mail pictures. Only
two mail films followed it, and one was an anachronism.

BLAZE OF NOON was released in the early spring of
1947. The major problem with this Paramount picture was
that it was fifteen years after its time, for it was very similar in style to the air mail films of the early thirties. The
plot deals with four flying brothers, the Mcdonalds, who
leave carnival stunt flying for a newly-formed air mail company, Mercury Air Lines. At the same time, Colin McDonald
(William Holden) falls in love with and marries Lucille (Anne
Baxter). As the film progresses, the youngest brother dies
while trying to land in the fog, another brother is crippled
in a crash, Porkie (William Bendix) is grounded, and finally
Colin is killed in a crash.

Besides having some more-or-less realistic characters
(the head of the company, Howard DeSilva, refuses to become too friendly with the pilots because "it's a risky business"), BLAZE OF NOON examines the problem of women who
are involved with fliers. Lucille's troubles with Colin's love
for planes is an interesting aspect of the film. She won't let
him give up flying because she knows he won't be happy on
the ground. The result of her insisting that Colin fly is a
constant series of sacrifices with which she must learn to
live. For example, as she is about to show him her wedding
dress, news of a new turn-and-bank indicator comes and the
brothers dash off for the field. And Colin passes up the
quiet dinner for two they planned so he can eat with his
brothers and their mechanic. But Lucille has Colin's baby
just before he is killed, leaving a part of Colin with her.

The aerial sequences of the Pitcairn biplanes, used to
carry the mail in the late twenties and early thirties, were
photographed by Thomas Tutwiler. Mantz served as chief
pilot and aerial supervisor. Mantz engaged in some spectacular flying for the film, notably air circus stunting at the
film's beginning, buzzing a train, and flying under the
Brooklyn bridge. In an effort to publicize the movie, Mantz
flew from coast to coast in the 1946 Bendix race in a blood-
red P-51 called Blaze of Noon, in six hours, seven minutes,
and five seconds, breaking a transcontinental record for
single-engine propeller-driven aircraft.

Three of the four flying brothers--Sterling Hayden, William Holden, and Sonny Tufts--with Anne Baxter in BLAZE OF NOON (1947).

BLAZE OF NOON ended the air mail film genre until 1984, when MGM/UA began shooting THE AVIATOR, a movie about the early days of air mail flying based on the novel by Ernest K. Gann. Starring Christopher Reeve and Rosanna Arquette, the film is currently in production. While many aspects of aviation have continued to interest filmmakers years after the events have passed, the glamor of flying the mail faded quickly when regularly scheduled airlines took over the routes. As the early mail pilots disappeared from view, so too did air mail films, but the ones that were made captured forever much of the courage, excitement, and sheer luck that were so much a part of the air mail pioneers.

CHAPTER 4

POUR LE MERITE

Canvas falcons. Knights of the air. Balloon busters.
The Flying Circus. World War I created new synonyms for
pilots. The war started friendly enough, with enemy aviators often waving to each other as they flew reconnaissance.
But it quickly became obvious that the key to victory lay in
control of the skies. Fliers began to take pot shots at each
other with pistols, rifles, shotguns. One Frenchman claimed
a German threw a brick at him. Spandaus, Vickers, and
Lewises took the place of bricks and side arms. The machine guns chopped planes and pilots to pieces. It was a
deadly war, and the average life of a fighter pilot on the
Western Front was three weeks. But to shell-shocked soldiers and war-weary civilians, the aviators were the only
noble things about the Great War. Chivalry wasn't dead.
Maybe civilization wasn't dying, after all.

WARFARE IN THE SKIES (1914) was released at the
start of World War I. A Vitagraph two-reeler, the fictional
film was based on the European situation in 1914. As in
other war films of the day, however, mythical countries
served as protagonists to avoid antagonizing viewers.

The plot concerns a Federalist army general's son,
Lawrence, who is an aviator. He and a flying Count are
both in love with an American girl. The Count deserts to
the Revolutionists to get even with Lawrence for winning
the girl. The Count bombs the Federalists and Lawrence
crashes his plane into the Count's to stop him (this is before warplanes were armed). Lawrence is captured and
learns that his sweetheart faces a firing squad for being a
spy. He rescues her by swooping down in an airplane just
in time and they fly off toward home.

Only two other non-zeppelin aviation war films were

70

made during the First World War. BRITAIN'S FAR FLUNG
BATTLE LINE (1918) showed straight documentary footage
of British sea and land planes. A ROMANCE OF THE AIR
(1917), based on Lieutenant Bert Hall's book, In the Air,
was the second film. The picture remains one of the very
few to feature a World War I flier playing himself, and it
dealt with Hall's experiences in the Lafayette Escadrille.
The plot has Hall involved with a woman, Edith Day, and
they both eventually escape from German lines after he is
shot down.

Hall was one of the Lafayette Escadrille's charter members and a real life character. He claimed to have fought
in the Turkish-Bulgarian War of 1912 and to have served
with Lord Kitchener's army. He served in France as a pilot
in 1915 and 1916 and left France in January 1917 for Ru-
mania or Russia, finally ending up in the United States.
When A ROMANCE OF THE AIR opened in New York, Hall
made personal appearances at the theatre to promote the
film; there he modestly stated that he had been decorated
by the Czar only four days before the revolution. Hall's
American wife divorced him in 1921, but he wasn't lonely.
"At ceremonies dedicating the postwar monument to the Lafayette Escadrille near Paris in 1928, three women claiming
to be Mrs. Bert Hall showed up to occupy the same seat."[1]
Hall tried to sell the Nationalist Chinese non-existent planes
in the 1930s and eventually went to prison in the United
States for another China swindle. During World War II, he
set up a toy company that made balsa wood models of V-2
rockets. Hall died in 1948.

Hall's career had a surprising and far-reaching effect
on the aviation film genre, as Arch Whitehouse noted:

> Following his death, his tangled domestic life was
> revealed. A Hollywood syndicate ... planned to film
> a complete documentary of the Lafayette Escadrille,
> and to do this the producers had to obtain clearances
> from all concerned.
> In coming up against Hall's background--and one
> or two others who also served in that organization--
> it was obvious that it would be impossible to "clear"
> most of Bert's adventures, since in one form or an-
> other they had been parceled out to [his] survivors.
> This is one of the chief reasons why no motion pic-
> ture producer has been able to present a complete

and full history of the Lafayette Escadrille: too
many survivors with delusions of importance concerning their rights in the presentation of such a history.[2]

Ten years elapsed between A ROMANCE OF THE AIR
and the next World War I aviation film, but it was worth the
wait. WINGS (1927) did for the aviation film what Lindbergh's
flight did for aviation. Bigger and more spectacular than
any airplane film before it, WINGS captured the public's
imagination and started a whole cycle of major aviation movies. In a sense, WINGS is the first true aviation film. Its
makers had a genuine feeling for the men and planes that
fought and died in the skies of Europe.

After World War I, the war film disappeared. Audiences had just gone through the most horrible conflict ever
to plague mankind, and they had no wish to be reminded of
it. Thus World War I films remained box-office poison until
King Vidor's THE BIG PARADE in 1925. This film, along the
WHAT PRICE GLORY (1926), demonstrated that the public
would go to see war films. And these two films inspired
writer John Monk Saunders to lobby for the production of a
major aviation film. Saunders went on to become the fore-
most aviation film writer during the next several years.

Saunders, born in 1898, was a Rhodes scholar who
also attended the U.S. School of Military Aeronautics in
Berkeley, California. He served as a second lieutenant in
the Signal Corps' aviation section during World War I. After the war, he worked for The Los Angeles Times, The
New York Tribune, and American magazine. He married his
second wife, Fay Wray (of KING KONG fame), in 1927 and
they divorced in 1939. In March 1940, Saunders was found
hanged in a closet in Fort Myers, Florida.

One of Saunders' stories formed the basis of Josef von
Sternberg's DOCKS OF NEW YORK and Saunders was introduced to Jesse Lasky, Paramount Picture's second in command and producer on THE GRIM GAME. Saunders argued
that a picture based on the World War I exploits of pilots in
France could be as popular as THE BIG PARADE and WHAT
PRICE GLORY. Saunders' arguments and Lasky's desire to
produce a road show film for 1927 resulted in the go-ahead
signal for WINGS. Saunders was hired to produce an original story and to serve as an advisor during filming. Louis

P. Lighton and his wife, Hope Loring, were told to do a screenplay from Saunders' original idea, and Lighton became producer. (Lucien Hubbard, a maker of Zane Grey films, later replaced Lighton in this capacity.)

B. P. Schulberg, Paramount's production chief, suggested William Wellman, a young director who had been assigned low-budget films, as ideal for WINGS because Wellman was the only director in Hollywood who had flown in the war. Wellman had joined the Norton House Ambulance Corps. This got him to Paris where he enlisted in the section of the French Foreign Legion attached to the French Air Corps, which got him into the Lafayette Flying Corps. He joined the Chat-Noir, the Black Cat Group, at 19 and was sent to Luneville. For his efforts, the French awarded him the Crois de Guerre with four palms, and he got credit for three planes shot down. Wellman returned home, joined the American Air Corps, and

Buddy Rogers has accidentally killed his best friend, Richard Arlen, at the conclusion of WINGS (1927).

spent the war's last six weeks with them. While in San Diego, Wellman met some Hollywood people, among them Douglas Fairbanks, and he would visit Fairbanks by flying to the actor's house in a Spad. Wellman tried his hand at acting, and then, finding himself a dismal actor, went into directing. When Schulberg suggested him as WINGS' director, Wellman had just made YOU NEVER KNOW WOMEN, with Florence Vidor and Clive Brook. The film's success no doubt helped give Schulberg confidence in Wellman, who would go on to become one of the cinema's two most prolific aviation film directors (the other is Howard Hawks).

Saunders convinced Lasky that the film could only be made with the cooperation of the War Department. The War Department agreed to supply planes, troops, pilots, shooting sites, and other equipment, including tanks, trucks, explosives, and artillery. The combined worth of the War Department's assistance fell in the neighborhood of $16,000,000. (The previous year Congress had authorized a five-year expansion program, the Air Corps Act of 1926, aimed at enlarging the Army's flying force by some 16,000 men. The government certainly saw WINGS as excellent recruitment vehicle.) So many planes were used, in fact, that had the continental United States been attacked the Army would have been hard pressed to muster enough aircraft for defense. Kelly Field, San Antonio, Texas, was selected as the filming location. Pilots came from Selfridge Field, Michigan, Crissy Field, California, and Langley Field, Virginia. From Scott Field, Illinois came balloons their officers, and crews.

Often, the better the aviation sequences in a film, the weaker the plot. WINGS proved no exception. It had the plot of a typical Twenties melodrama, causing Mordaunt Hall of The New York Times to remark: "... the story ... is a conventional narrative that serves its purpose as a background for remarkable scenes in the air."[3]

Johnny Powell (Charles "Buddy" Rogers) loves Sylvia Lewis (Jobyna Ralston). She, however, is in love with Powell's best friend, David Armstrong (Richard Arlen), who loves her. Powell is oblivious to their love and to the fact that a tomboy, Clara Preston (Clara Bow), loves him. Powell and Armstrong enlist in the Army Air Service when war breaks out and they are assigned to the 39th Aero Squadron of the First Pursuit Group at Toul, France. On leave in Paris,

Powell gets drunk and is taken to his hotel room by Clara, who has joined the Motor Corps. He doesn't recognize her and it looks to his buddies as though he has spent the night with one of "those girls."

Powell finds out about David and Sylvia and becomes a changed man. He flies like a demon, heedless of his own safety. Powell and Armstrong go after some German balloons, with Powell attacking while Armstrong keeps a lookout. Powell ignores express orders to keep an eye on his friend and Armstrong is shot down and captured. He later escapes, steals a German plane, and flies it back to his own lines. Powell, not realizing who's in the plane, shoots Armstrong down and kills him. Powell learns that Clara loves him and returns home a sadder but wiser man.

The aviation scenes, of course, make WINGS great. Harry Perry, who shot the aviation footage in THE BROKEN WING, served as chief cameraman and made over fifty flights in the camera planes. Moving planes need to be photographed against a background, so Wellman waited almost a month for clouds. (Howard Hughes would experience the same problem while making HELL'S ANGELS.) Ironically, later on, when Wellman needed sunlight to shoot the land battle scene, the filming location was socked in. Wellman saw what he thought was a break in the clouds and started the cameras rolling. He shot the battle in the three and one half minutes of sunlight that occurred before the clouds closed in solidly for three weeks.

The filmmakers mounted cameras, including Eymos, Akeleys, and Mitchells, in every conceivable location on the planes. Some were mounted behind the pilot, shooting forward; some in front of the pilot, shooting backward. Other cameras rested on the landing gear. Some of these were remote-controlled, electrically operated by the pilot who pushed a button in the cockpit.

Never before had such a large group of pilots been assembled for a motion picture. Many top stunt pilots of the day, including Dick Grace and Frank Tomick, flew in the film. Grace had the unhappy distinction of being the only stuntman hurt while making WINGS.

The airplanes assembled for WINGS comprised the

largest movie "air force" up to that time. Tomick went around the country buying surplus aircraft. Most planes were not of the World War I variety, but a few Spads (including one that Tomick paid $3,500 for) and Fokkers did make their way into the picture. Other planes included Thomas-Morse MB-3s, Curtiss P-1s, DeHavilland 4s, Vought VE-7s, and Martin MB-2 bombers. The Fokker D-VIIs that appeared in the film were modified Travel Air 4000s, often used in aviation films and called "Wichita Fokkers." The D.H.4s served as the principal camera planes, but the Martin MB-2s were also used in that capacity, though to a lesser extent.

In WINGS, not only the pilots flew; Charles "Buddy" Rogers and Richard Arlen went aloft as well. Arlen's flying career in and out of movies spanned 50 years. He was born on September 1, 1900. His interest in aviation began early, and he saw Lincoln **Beachey fly.** He ran away from home in 1917 to join the Royal Flying Corps in Winnipeg, Canada. The Corps sent him to Toronto to learn aeronautics. Arlen did not see action in World War I and was discharged from the R.F.C. in 1919. He drifted to Hollywood where he worked as a film developer and a delivery boy before becoming an actor. In 1940 Arlen and Dick Probert formed Arlen-Probert Aviation at Van Nuys Metropolitan Airport. Flier-actors based their planes there, including Robert Taylor, Jimmy Stewart, Andy Devine, Wallace Beery, and Robert Cummings. Wayne Morris, an actor who shot down seven Japanese planes in World War II, learned to fly there. During World War II, Arlen-Probert became a center for the Civilian Pilot Training Program. Buddy Rogers was also a flier, and he became a Navy test pilot in World War II.

In WINGS, both actors would go up in a two-seat air-**craft,** sometimes sitting in the rear cockpit with the camera shooting aft over the head of the pilot in the front cockpit. At other times, they would be in the front cockpit and the camera would shoot forward over the head of the pilot in the rear cockpit. There were dangers for the actors. On occasion they would go as high as 11,000 feet, without goggles or a windshield, and have to try to act into the automatic camera while stinging wind and sleet hit their faces. On one of Arlen's flights, his Vought proved too fast for U.S. Army pilot Thad Johnson's P-1 pursuit plane, which was to attack Arlen's. Arlen's plane had to go so slowly that Arlen was afraid Johnson would clip his tail. Ironically, Johnson died about a year later when his plane's tail was clipped.

The stunt pilots, too, faced problems. Frank Tomick ran into danger when his D-VII was supposed to be attacked by anti-aircraft fire. Small bombs dropped by another plane simulated exploding shell bursts. Tomick flew at 2,000 feet, while the "bombing" aircraft flew at 5,000 feet. The bombs were supposed to explode above and below Tomick, but they burst right on top of him, destroying his aileron control cables. He barely landed safely. Dick Grace also had trouble flying a baby Spad. The plane had its cockpit modified with heavy steel tubing so it wouldn't collapse, and Grace strapped himself in with a special harness he'd designed. He crashed the ship safely, as arranged, only seventeen feet from the camera, and then discovered that a cedar log had pushed through the plane aft of the cockpit, less than a foot from his head. But on another occasion Grace wasn't so lucky. When he crashed a Fokker D-VII the heavy landing gear struts failed to give way. His head went through the instrument panel and he broke his neck in three places, temporarily putting himself out of action.

One unusual aspect of WINGS' production concerned the use of Robert Nichols, an English poet, as an advisor for three months during filming. The filmmakers hired Nichols to give WINGS "poetry of motion," and one scene where the poet's services paid off was when Powell and Armstrong set off for their first patrol over German lines. Up to this time, no planes had been shown in the picture, and Wellman wanted some dramatic way of introducing the aircraft. Nichols conceived the idea of lining the flying field background with a row of French poplars (actually dressed up telephone poles). The planes took off in front of the trees, which cast long shadows, giving rhythm to the shot.

Not all of WINGS' action was confined to the air, for the filmmakers recreated the battle of St. Mihiel. The Second Infantry Division's engineers, based at Fort Sam Houston, built a $300,000 simulated battleground near old Camp Stanley. The site had a five-square-mile area to allow sweeping shots of the battlefield, troop columns, and gun emplacements. Restaging the battle involved using 5,000 men from the Second Division, which had fought in the actual battle. A 100-foot tower was constructed overlooking the field, and twenty-one cameras, both in the air and on the ground, photographed the action. As the troops advanced, explosive charges in the ground were set off from a detonation keyboard. In the middle of all this, Dick Grace crashed a real Spad S. VII into No Man's Land. This battle sequence has been favorably compared to the classic battle shots in THE BIG PARADE and ALL QUIET ON THE WESTERN FRONT. (An attempt to recreate this same kind of ground action in THE BLUE MAX was far less successful.)

Gary Cooper had a minor role in WINGS. He was so nervous before a short scene with Richard Arlen and Buddy Rogers that he couldn't stop eating chocolates, but he made a good impression and started off his career.

The $2,000,000 picture, which took over a year to complete, had its preview in San Antonio in the spring of 1927. Its fourteen reels were cut to 12,000 feet for the New York opening in August, and some additional cutting took place later.

Although Wellman had successfully completed WINGS, all was not harmonious between him and Paramount. The studio paid Wellman $250 a week to make the most expensive picture in Paramount's history, up to that time, but his contract ran out during filming. Taking the advice of his agent, Myron Selznick, Wellman finished the rest of WINGS at a leisurely pace, in spite of Paramount's pressure to hurry. Wellman was not even invited to the film's New York opening, but the studio's feelings quickly changed after the picture proved a hit. During all this time, however, Wellman had not received a cent from Paramount, a fact only discovered by the studio when B. P. Schulberg offered Wellman LEGION OF THE CONDEMNED to direct.

WINGS, dedicated to all fliers, opened in New York on August 12, 1927 at the Criterion Theatre. Workers decorated the theatre's lobby with seventeen paintings of famous aviators, forming an "aviation hall of fame." Commander Richard E. Byrd attended the premiere and was reportedly favorably impressed.

Interestingly, WINGS premiered in wide screen, sound, and color. Many of the aviation scenes used Magnascope, a process that made the picture twice the usual size. Vertical notches were cut in the film near the sprocket holes. These moved a lever which operated a complicated device behind the screen. This device contained musical instruments, emphasizing drums, and assorted other devices to produce the sound of airplane engines and machine gun fire at the right time. (This "sound system" was shipped from city to city in a special box car during road show screenings of the picture.) Color was introduced both by tinting some scenes blue, yellow, or red, and by hand painting machine gun bursts and flames from burning planes directly onto the film. Since the negative could not be so colored, this frame-by-frame painting had to be done with every positive print.

WINGS found great audience acceptance and, in 1928, won the first Academy Award ever given for Best Picture of the Year. The picture's popularity has endured throughout the years, prompting Paramount to make an abortive attempt to re-release it in 1969.

WINGS was the first of two giant steps for the aviation film. Never before had aviation sequences been done so brilliantly, and they set standards for future films. To this day, the drama and magic of some of the flying shots has never been bettered. The shot, for instance, of a shotdown plane slowly spinning toward the distant ground conveys a dramatic sense of how far a dying aviator has to fall before he reaches his final resting place. WINGS' drawback was its plot: it would take another World War I aviation film, THE DAWN PATROL, to raise the level of aviation film stories.

Naturally, the remaining aviation films of 1927 could not match WINGS. HARD BOILED HAGGERTY (1927), a comedy-drama, starred Milton Sills as an American World War I ace who becomes involved with twin sisters. He spent more time in Paris than in the air.

NOW WE'RE IN THE AIR (1927) starred Wallace Beery and Raymond Hatton. These two scheme to get their Scottish grandfather's money. The grandfather is an old airplane lover who tries to become a flier in the war. Beery and Hatton become involved with aircraft and a runaway balloon. The film consisted partly of leftover footage from WINGS.

DOG OF THE REGIMENT (1927) told of an American
flying ace shot down behind the German lines, where he
falls in love with a nurse who owns a dog played by Rin-
Tin-Tin. Supposedly based on Rin-Tin-Tin's life, the film
is the only aviation movie inspired by a dog's biography.
THE LONE EAGLE (1927), one of the period's cheapest films,
dealt with a young flier attached to the Royal Flying Corps.
His guns jam on a flight and his comrades think him a coward. When a German ace issues a challenge for an aerial
duel to avenge the death of his brother, who has been shot
down, the American wins the draw for the honor of fighting
the German. He is shot down, but parachutes to safety and
takes off in an unarmed plane for another crack at the German. He clips the enemy's wing tip with his landing gear
and wins the duel.

The first major aviation film after WINGS was LEGION
OF THE CONDEMNED (1928). B. P. Schulberg offered the
directorship of the picture to Wellman after WINGS' success,
an action which amused Wellman because he had been the one
to suggest that LEGION OF THE CONDEMNED be made into a
picture in the first place.

John Monk Saunders and Jean de Limur wrote the story.
Limur had been in the French army and had brought down
three German and four Austrian planes in one battle, an action that earned him the Croix de Guerre with seven palms.
The story deals with several aviators who, for one reason or
another, have lost the desire to live. Gary Cooper and Fay
Wray starred, with some footage shot for WINGS being incor-
porated into the film.

Cooper played Gale Price, a newspaper reporter. He
meets and falls in love with Christine (Wray), but his spirits
are dashed when he finds her in the arms of a German at a
party in that country's Washington embassy. He is inconsol-
able and goes to France to fly in the Legion of Doomed Men.
(This is told in a flashback.) Cooper draws an assignment
to land a spy behind the German lines and finds out that the
spy is Christine, which explains her actions in Washington.
Cooper goes back to pick her up ten days later and is captured. Just as he and Christine are about to be shot, his
squadron mates come to the rescue. The chief aerial scenes
involve attacking a train (originally shot for WINGS), the
landing of the spy, and the bombing of the German firing
squad at the end.

Their problems over, Gary Cooper and Colleen Moore face a happy life together in LILAC TIME (1928).

LILAC TIME (1928), the next major aviation film, was released almost exactly a year after WINGS. LILAC TIME, a First National picture, remains second only to WINGS as an elaborate aerial film of the decade. Directed by George Fitz-maurice, the picture came from a 1917 play of the same title written by Jane Crowl, who starred in its Broadway presentation, and Jane Murfin. Willis Goldback and Carey Wilson adapted Lilac Time to the screen and changed its ground action sequences to aerial combat ones.

The story concerns Jeannine (Colleen Moore, at the height of her popularity), a French girl who serves as a mascot to a group of British fliers stationed near her house.

She falls in love with Philip Blythe (Gary Cooper), a replacement flier, and he returns her affection. When the squadron goes on a big mission against the Germans (they are told by their commander not to return as long as there are any German planes in the air), Blythe is shot down by the "Red Ace" and crashes near the field. Badly wounded, he is saved by Jeannine, who gets him to an ambulance. They become separated, however, and Jeannine searches the hospitals for him. She finds him, but Blythe's father, who disapproves of their love, tells her Blythe is dead. She leaves, heartbroken. Blythe, however, who knows some lilacs came from her, signals from his hospital window and they are reunited.

Of all the aviation films of the period, LILAC TIME stands out as one of the most sentimental, a factor which a New York Times reviewer found discomforting: "The trouble with the picture lies in its sentiment. War has been made a vehicle for love, and hatred has turned into a pathetic combination of virtues."[4] The proliferation of lilacs also bothered many critics.

Dick Grace, recovered from his WINGS injury, formed a group of pilots called the Buzzards, and they did many of LILAC TIME's stunts. (To qualify for membership in the Buzzards each pilot had to stay on Grace's tail during an hour of low-level stunting. Out of seven who qualified, five eventually died in crashes.) By this time Grace had been in twenty-seven crashes, nineteen of them intentional, for the motion picture cameras. Another flier, Charles Stoffer, won the draw for the honor of crashing a plane between two closely-spaced trees. The major aerial battle, using converted Wacos, involved sixteen dogfighting aircraft, three camera ships, and one observation plane. The chief aerial photographer, Alvin Knechtel, used aircraft camera mountings like those developed for WINGS, shooting at many different angles. Filming took place in the mountains between Santa Ana and Capistrano, California, and on a section of studio lot battlefield. LILAC TIME's stuntmen did not suffer so much as a minor injury during filming.

Like WINGS, LILAC TIME attempted to make use of behind-the-screen sound effects, although these were less elaborate than those on the earlier picture, and color. Explosions or the effect of aircraft hitting the ground were accomplished with a stage play device used to simulate

lightning bolts. Running engines were recorded on a phono-
graph record. An attempt to color the Red Ace's plane by
painting it red on LILAC TIME's positive print met with limited success.

It is interesting to note that LILAC TIME seems to be
the first aviation film to include some figure representing
Germany's Manfred von Richthofen, one of World War I's
greatest heroes and the leading ace of the war, with 80 kills.
Von Richthofen came to represent the typical German air ace
and would become a major figure in aviation films, whether
as some character modeled on the flier or an actor playing
von Richthofen himself.

European filmmakers had not forgotten the war. A
French film, THE LAST FLIGHT (1929), told of a flier on
leave in Paris falling for a girl he later discovers to be his
best friend's wife. Later, mortally wounded, he confesses
to his friend, who forgives him before he dies. The film
had poor air action consisting of newsreel footage and faked
air combat shots. Variety described THE LAST FLIGHT as
"perhaps the last atrocity of the late lamented war."[5]

In September 1929 Germany released RICHTHOFEN (THE
RED KNIGHT OF THE AIR), the first picture that attempted
to capitalize on the ace's reputation. The movie has so little
to do with Richthofen that the actor playing Baron von Richthofen is listed last in the credits! The filmmakers faked
most of the aerial material, although the picture did feature
at least four real planes: a Fokker triplane, a DH-9, an Albatross DV, and a Nieuport 17. The film ended with newsreel shots of Richthofen's post-war Berlin state funeral.

THE SKY HAWK (1929) was one of the first sound aviation films. Based on Llewellyn Hughes' magazine story "A
Chap Called Bardell," it told of a young British flier falsely
accused of having crashed his plane to get out of serving in
France. Partially crippled, he is confined to a wheel chair,
but manages, with a friend's help, to build a plane out of
several wrecks. When a zeppelin bombs London, he takes
his plane aloft and shoots the airship down, proving his
courage.

The film's highlight came in the 30-minute zeppelin
bombing sequence at the film's end. Ralph Hammeras built

a model airship and recreated parts of London in miniature. Studio-made clouds and fog enshrouded the set and the filmmakers photographed the bombing of London in an old U.S. Army balloon hanger in Arcadia, California. By the time THE SKY HAWK went into production in the latter part of 1929, Howard Hughes' HELL'S ANGELS had been in production for about two years. One scene in that picture was a zeppelin raid, and it already had been filmed in that same balloon hanger. It is probable, therefore, that the zeppelin sequence in THE SKY HAWK was an attempt to upstage HELL'S ANGELS.

THE SKY HAWK created something of a controversy when shown in Britain. The British, after all, had been the ones who bore the brunt of the actual zeppelin raids, and some Englishmen thought they should not have to depend on an American import to depict these raids on film. British producers argued that they would be happy to make aviation films, but the government would not provide any assistance to aviation film makers, whether their topic was civilian or military aviation. The producers also claimed that Royal Air Force pilots were not allowed to participate in movies. While the British government's position was in reality not this extreme, it is obvious that they didn't see the recruitment value in aviation films as clearly as the U.S. military flying organizations did.

YOUNG EAGLES (1930), based on two short stories by Elliott White Springs, "The One Who Was Clever" and "Sky High," was William Wellman's next film. It starred Charles "Buddy" Rogers, Jean Arthur, and Paul Lukas in a story about an American pilot (Rogers), a German pilot (Lukas), and an American spy (Arthur). Featuring a couple of interesting dogfight scenes (some of the aerial shots were from WINGS), it mirrored the political climate of the times by presenting the German in a sympathetic light. Wellman, however, didn't like the way the picture was edited and got a release from his contract.

To discuss the next aviation picture, it is necessary to return to 1927, shortly after the release of WINGS. One of WINGS' most avid fans was a new filmmaker, Howard Hughes. But Hughes didn't sit through the picture many times just to be awed by it; he watched WINGS closely because he was going to make something better. In his opinion, he would make the ultimate aerial film.

Howard Hughes, Jr., was born on Christmas Eve, 1905, in Houston, Texas. Both his parents were dead by the time he was twenty, and he inherited the Hughes Tool Company, which his father had founded. The company produced tools and dies used in the oil-drilling industry and, with no supervision from young Howard, it turned out steady and hefty profits. Hollywood beckoned the rich, young, attractive Hughes. He wasted no time in getting into the moviemaking business.

Hughes' first picture was SWELL HOGAN (1925). Made at a cost of $100,000, the picture proved to be such a disaster that it was never released. Better luck awaited Hughes on his next picture, EVERYBODY'S ACTING (1926), made with money from the Caddo Rock Drill Bit Company, a subsidiary of Hughes Tool. Hughes set up the Caddo Corporation as a filmmaking company and EVERYBODY'S ACTING made a tidy profit. The next film, TWO ARABIAN KNIGHTS (1927), earned the Academy Award for its director, Lewis Milestone (who shared the award with Frank Borzage), and made a one hundred per cent profit. Following this film came THE RACKET, also directed by Milestone, which became a popular gangster film of the period. Hughes now felt himself ready for his great aviation movie, HELL'S ANGELS.

Hughes assembled a production team made up of Marshall Neilan, Harry Behn, and Luther Reed. Neilan, who directed EVERYBODY'S ACTING, contributed a short plot outline. Behn worked on the story's continuity and Hughes contributed his own ideas. Reed, an aviation buff and the first aviation editor of the New York Herald, was loaned by Paramount as director. To star, Hughes acquired the services of James Hall from Paramount, Ben Lyon from First National, and a Norwegian actress, Greta Nissen.

Shooting of the dramatic sequences began on October 31, 1927 at the old Metropolitan Studios. By January 1928 the dramatic scenes had been completed at a cost of $400,000. Hughes' methods of filming did not sit well with the cast and crew. For example, the first scene to be shot was supposed to take place on a rainy, muddy London night. Since it was night and actually raining on the London street built on the studio lot, Hughes decided to film the sequence exactly as it was written: at night and in the rain rather than with sprinklers and simulated night photography. The wet actors

The dogfight sequence from HELL'S ANGELS (1930)

and technicians cursed throughout the night, but their com-
plaints made no impression on Hughes. Hughes was just as
particular on the sound stage, demanding endless retakes,
and one grand ball sequence took more than a week to shoot.
But for Hughes the story existed merely as an excuse for
the aviation sequences. When work did begin on the airplane shots, Hughes felt he could film them better than Reed.
Reed quit and Hughes became director. While the dramatic
shots had been in production, work had begun on collecting
the planes for the air epic.

Hughes set out to gather all the old aircraft he could
find. He spent $562,000 acquiring and rebuilding 87 fighters
and bombers (37 of them genuine war-time plane combat
planes) that included Fokker D-VIIs, Avros, Snipes, Sopwith

Camels, DeHavillands, and S.E. 5s. Thomas-Morse Scouts,
Travel Air 2000s, and Wichita Fokkers were among the planes
substituting for the above warbirds in the long shots. As
he had done with WINGS, Frank Tomick traveled around the
world collecting old aircraft. Hughes badly wanted a real
German Gotha bomber. There were no Gothas left in exist-
ence, so Hughes had to make do with a Sikorsky S-29 purchased from speed pilot Colonel Roscoe Turner, who was to
fly the plane from New York to Los Angeles and pilot it for
the bombing sequences.

To handle his airplanes, Hughes built or modified several airfields at a cost of $389,000 (which included rental of
some aircraft). A field at Inglewood became the British flying school, the Caddo Field (named after the film company)
at Van Nuys served as the main base of operations, and a
field at Chatsworth became the German air base. Other
fields were located at Santa Cruz, Encino, Ryan Field in
San Diego, March Field in Riverside, and Oakland Airport--
used, in spite of its distance from Los Angeles, as a base
for the large-scale dogfight sequence because of its handy
clouds.

To fly in the picture, Hughes, who did not ask the
Army Air Corps for the assistance they had given WINGS,
hired virtually all the available stunt pilots. The only major movie stunt flier who was not in the picture was Dick
Grace, who was already occupied with LILAC TIME, THE
AIR CIRCUS, and THE BIG HOP. Frank Clarke, who played
von Breun, was made chief pilot. Frank Tomick (von Richthofen in the silent version of HELL'S ANGELS), Al Wilson,
Al Johnson, Leo Nomis, George Cooper, C. K. "Phil" Phillips, Roy Wilson (as Baldy), Garland Lincoln, and Ross
Cooke were among the other pilots. (Contrary to some
sources, Paul Mantz did not fly in the film.) At first
Hughes tried to get away with hiring novice pilots at ten
dollars a day, but when they cracked up three planes he
knew he needed the professional pilots who went for $200
a week. One hundred and thirty-seven aviators and a similar number of mechanics were hired for the film. The total cost of the actors and fliers involved in the flying scenes
was $754,000. In all, over $400,000 went for the salaries of
mechanics, technicians, cameramen, cutters, etc. who worked
on the aviation scenes.

To photograph the picture, thirty-five cameramen were recruited, twenty-six of them aerial photographers. Harry Perry served as the chief aerial cameraman and was assisted by numerous men in camera planes, including Elmer Dyer.

Hughes lavished attention on the aerial sequences. He spent hours diagramming the planes' movements and then made three-dimensional models of the aircraft's flight paths, using model planes, to study camera angles. He gave the pilots lengthy instructions and then stated he would be flying the camera plane and give hand-signaled directions. But when it came time to film, there were no clouds. Without clouds, there wasn't a suitable background against which the planes could be photographed; the audience had no point of reference against which it could compare the speed and direction of the aircraft. (Wellman had this same problem on WINGS.) So Hughes initiated an intensive cloud search. When a weather report promised clouds in some part of Southern California, Hughes would take his men and planes there a day early to be ready for the next day's shooting. In October 1928 he sent nearly 100 people, including 40 pilots and their aircraft, to Oakland, where they waited for four months until cinematic clouds appeared. The pilots spent so much time waiting for clouds that eventually a sign reading "'Today's War Postponed: No Clouds'" appeared. Ironically, after HELL'S ANGELS was released, one reviewer complained about the inartistic use of clouds!

Hughes insisted on absolute realism and went to great lengths to get it. No trick photography was involved in the dogfight sequence and the only models used were two twelve-foot D-VIIs, which collided in mid-air and fell in a ball of flame. Frank Clarke and Roy Wilson had automatic cameras with cockpit control switches mounted on their planes. Hughes went to even greater lengths with Frank Tomick, who played von Richthofen in the silent version. Tomick was to fly around looking for stragglers while a cameraman, with an Akeley camera strapped to the wing, recorded his facial expression. But no matter what expression Tomick used, Hughes wasn't satisfied; it took four months before the millionaire found an expression he liked.

As in WINGS, the actors also went aloft, making it unnecessary to fake shots of the stars in the air. When Roscoe Turner flew the "Gotha" bomber from inside the fuselage, both

Ben Lyon and James Hall were clearly visible in the open cockpits. Lyon stood in the observer's well, held in by only two thin straps connected to a leather belt around his waist. In all Lyon flew a total of 75 hours; Hall, 65.

If the action shots were realistic, the color schemes and some of the aircraft weren't the genuine article. Tomick, as Richthofen, flew an all-black Fokker D-VII with straight Latin crosses. (Actually, the D-VII was not introduced until the time of Richthofen's death.) The other Fokkers in the dogfight sequence (16 in all, including Tomick's Fokker, five real Fokkers and nine Travel Air 2000s) were painted flat black with different types of white striping to distinguish them from the other aircraft. The most elaborately painted Fokker was Frank Clarke's. His plane was featured in the dogfight sequence, and it had white serpentine strips on most of the wings and fuselage. Except for Tomick's plane, all the other German planes had oversized Maltese crosses with white borders. These were somewhat inaccurate, because they had been used only on a very few early Fokker D-VIIs. They were, however, more theatrical than the plain Latin crosses. The wheels of the Fokkers were also inaccurate. Almost none of the actual aircraft used during the war flew with uncovered wire wheels. But the bare bicycle-looking wheels were good showmanship and they contrasted with the fabric-covered wheels of the S.E. 5s. (Some of the Camels in the picture also had uncovered wire wheels.)

The planes described above appeared in one of the most exciting dogfight sequences ever filmed. Lasting 22 minutes and involving 31 planes, the dogfight featured the Gotha's bombing of an ammunition dump. A large-scale miniature of the dump was built, and a high tower constructed on which to place the camera. The dump virtually exploded into the camera. The most spectacular section of the dogfight is when the 31 planes come together in combat. Army fliers who viewed the picture had never been asked to do such dangerous flying and were amazed that no mid-air collisions had occurred.

The aerial filming, however, was not without accidents and one of the first happened to Hughes himself. Not yet an experienced pilot (he had taken his first flying lessons from the Black 13), he decided to fly a rotary-engined

Thomas-Morse **Scout**. In rotary-engined aircraft, the crankshaft remains fixed while the engine rotates around it, creating a terrific amount of torque. A plea to keep his nose high was lost on Hughes and he took off in a climbing right hand turn. The torque of the engine pulled the plane into the ground. Hughes emerged with minor bruises and a bleeding nose. Several aviators went to the wreck and one of them asked Hughes how his right arm was. When Hughes asked the flier why he wasn't concerned about Hughes' nose, the flier replied that Hughes signed the checks with his right hand.

Hughes was the butt of other jokes. The millionaire would ride around the airfields on his motorcycle while the pilots good-naturedly threw cow chips at him. Hughes had the habit of starting each day with a visit **to a flimsy privy** built on the field. One morning, just after Hughes closed the door, a pilot in a DeHavilland two-seater parked behind the privy started the engine. The prop wash blew the door open and Hughes emerged struggling with his trousers, seconds ahead of the privy's collapse.

Other events were not so humorous. Al Johnson narrowly escaped death when his plane's wing scraped the ground in a low tight turn. George Cooper barely missed a hanger and destroyed the S.E. 5 when he was flying on location in Santa Paula, California. Al Wilson was nearly killed when the propeller of his Fokker D-VII suddenly fell off over the center of Hollywood. Wilson bailed out in the dense fog and prayed. He landed safely on the roof of a house near Hollywood Boulevard, while the D-VII buried itself in the back yard of Joe Schenck, a motion picture mogul. (Ironically, this was only two blocks from Grauman's Chinese Theatre where HELL'S ANGELS would premiere.) Schenck and his actress wife Norma Talmadge left the plane where it crashed for years afterward as a joke. **Roscoe** Turner, who had flown the Sikorsky from New York without incident, was within sight of Hollywood over the mountains near San Bernardino when he lost control of the plane. It went into a spin and pulled out only at the last moment. Later, two, large, expensive Mitchell cameras were supposed to be used photographing the Sikorsky taking off. The plane was to taxi directly up to the Mitchells, where barriers would prevent it from actually taking off. The wheels lifted off and they, along with the propellers, destroyed the cameras.

Harry Perry and a mechanic in the plane's nose were almost
killed by two different sections of broken propeller. The
Sikorsky crashed into a bean field and needed a week's repair job. Hughes was playing golf when a phone call in-
formed him of the incident. Hughes said he would be out
after he finished the game. (Hughes was, in fact, quite
proud of the fact that his film was to have a "Gotha" and
he jealously guarded the secret. Elmer Dyer was nearly
fired when Hughes caught him shooting stills of the Sikorsky for later publicity release.)

Unfortunately, not all of the film's accidents proved
non-fatal. HELL'S ANGELS, in fact, holds the record for
the most aerial stuntmen killed during the production of an
aviation film. Three people died during shooting and one
doing non-film stunts. Al Johnson died ferrying an old Hall
Scott Standard from Grand Central Airport in Glendale to
Mines Field in Inglewood. He took off from the Glendale airport in a cross wind and the engine quit. He tried to bank
the plane for a dead-stick landing but hit the high tension
wires at the field's edge, was burned, and died 18 hours
later. C. K. "Phil" Phillips was to fly an S.E. 5 from Hollywood to the location site. He took off, got lost, and ran
out of gas looking for a place to land. He, too, tried a
dead-stick landing and was killed. Another pilot, an ex-
barnstormer, took a plane off to do a stunt to show off for
the film crew. He was to dive straight down and pull out at
the last minute. He didn't. The last accident took the life
of mechanic Phil Jones. The story called for the twin-engine
Gotha to tailspin into the ground after being shot up by the
hero's plane. No pilot was anxious to take on this task. The
chances of pulling out of the spin, for anyone other than
Roscoe Turner, who flew the plane in all the dogfight and
bombing sequences and wouldn't do this stunt, were rather
poor. Dick Grace was contacted and offered $250. He said
he would do it, but only for $10,000. He told Frank Clarke
if he didn't make it, they could collect $10,000 for Grace's
estate. Clarke refused. Finally Al Wilson agreed to do it.
Because Wilson couldn't operate the called-for tail smoke,
Phil Jones agreed to ride in the tail and set off the smoke
pots. If Wilson couldn't pull out, both men were to parachute to safety. Tomick flew the DeHaviland camera plane
and had a good view of the disaster. At 7,000 feet Wilson
signaled the camera planes and put the Sikorsky into a spin.
Jones ignited the smoke pots. Wilson tried and failed to pull

out at the agreed altitude. The wing fabric began to rip
away and an engine cowl tore loose. Wilson yelled for Jones
to jump and did the same, parachuting to safety. The plane
leveled out near the ground and crashed into an orchard.
Perhaps Jones didn't hear Wilson, or was knocked unconscious during the dive, or thought Wilson could control the
plane. An inquest didn't find the answer; and Wilson earned
the ire of his fellow pilots for the incident.

There are two major sequences in HELL'S ANGELS.
The first, a dogfight between the British and the Germans;
the second, an exciting zeppelin sequence, done with models.
Characteristically, Hughes wanted to buy a full-sized airship
and modify it to look like a zeppelin. His technical advisors
talked him out of it, saying they could get better results
with a large model. Hughes hired Dr. K. Arnstein, who had
been a former executive with the Zeppelin company in Germany, as technical advisor. Two 60-foot models (one for
protection in case anything happened to the first) were constructed. The special effects came under the direction of
E. Roy Davidson. Hughes rented an old U.S. Army balloon
hangar in Arcadia, California. A full-scale section of the
interior of the airship, as well as catwalks and rigging, was
constructed in one corner of the hangar. Technicians installed heavy steel cable so that the zeppelin, mounted on a
trolley, could move in any direction. Cameras were set up
at points around the hangar to photograph the action, including one under a glass plate directly below the airship to
shoot the zeppelin's fiery descent.

Close-ups of the pilots were done with the actors placed
in mock cockpits. Long shots of the planes attacking the
zeppelin were accomplished with models. Clouds were produced by chemicals in a huge tank built on the hangar's
floor. The zeppelin was moved on its trolley through the
clouds against a black background, while the model planes
were carefully moved on suspended wires. Filmmakers staged
the airship's demise by double exposure. First, the model
air plane attacking the airship was filmed at high camera
speed while it swung by a wire in front of a black velour
background. Then the film was rewound and the zeppelin
photographed. The evening before the zeppelin's burn-up
was to be photographed, a workman accidently hit the wrong
switch and the $100,000 kerosene-soaked model went up in
flames. Fortunately, the back-up model was available. The
total cost of the zeppelin: about $460,000.

At last Hughes completed HELL'S ANGELS, at a cost of more than $2,000,000. The picture's premiere took place in March, 1929 at a theatre in Los Angeles. Hughes sat in the theatre carefully monitoring the audience's reaction, which was as silent as the film itself (the picture did contain a few synchronized sound effects). Between the release of WINGS and the premiere of HELL'S ANGELS, sound had revolutionized the movies. Now the public wanted "100% all-talking," and Hughes quickly realized any silent picture, even an epic, was doomed to failure. He decided to re-make HELL'S ANGELS.

For anyone but Howard Hughes, a re-make of HELL'S ANGELS would have been out of the question. But Hughes would not become a $2,000,000 failure, even if he had to gamble another $2,000,000 to avoid it. Besides, Hughes had his own supply of money; he was not bound by the budget restrictions of a studio or other financial backers. So HELL'S ANGELS went back into production.

Fortunately, Hughes could salvage all of the aviation sequences simply by adding a sound track to the airplane footage. To do this he hired Pancho Barnes who, in her red Travel Air Mystery S, spent a whole day flying around a red balloon tethered 1,000 feet high over Caddo Field with a sound recorder hung below it. Every sound stage in the valley shut down because of the noise, but Hughes got his aerial battle sounds. Putting sound into the zeppelin sequence wasn't so easy. When these scenes had been shot, the actors had adlibbed in German and no one could remember what they said. So Julius Schroeder, a German, and writer Joseph Moncure March ran the film through a Moviola. Schroeder tried to read the actors' lips and deduce what they had said. March then figured out what the actors should be saying for the new sound version, while Schroeder thought of a way to say lines in German that would match the actors' lip movements. The new dialogue was then synched to the film.

Hughes assembled a cast and crew to re-shoot the dramatic sequences, which could not be saved by dubbing. The key cast members returned. Ben Lyon and James Hall could satisfactorily make the transition to sound, but Greta Nissen, who supposedly played an British girl, could speak little English, and even that was with a thick Norwegian accent. Hughes dropped her. He interviewed several unknown actresses for the part--unknown because Hughes couldn't afford a big star's salary and because he did not want to direct such a star in his first talking picture. He finally chose an actress introduced to him by Ben Lyon. Jean Harlow passed her screen test, signed a $125-a-week contract, and Hughes developed her into the girl with the platinum blonde hair.

A new crew gathered. Hughes hired James Whale to direct the dialogue sequences. (Whale went on to become a famous horror film director.) Joseph Moncure March had earlier been lent to Hughes by MGM to write the dialogue and a new story. All the old silent story, including the ground part featuring Frank Tomick as Richthofen, was eliminated except for the scene where Hall shoots Lyon, who is about to give information to the Germans. Howard Estabrook was hired to do some work on the story and to do the final continuity.

The new story concerned two American brothers attending Oxford: Monty (Ben Lyon) and Roy Rutledge (James Hall). They have made friends with a fellow student, Karl (John Darrow), and are in Germany visiting him. Karl loves both England and Germany. Monty, unlike Roy, is unconcerned about the imminent war, concentrating instead on the wife of Colonel Von Kranz. Monty runs from a duel with the Colonel and Roy takes his place, sustaining a flesh wound.

When war comes Roy joins the Royal Flying Corps; so does Monty, although reluctantly. **They complete training and** while waiting to be sent to France attend a charity ball (shot in two-color Technicolor with 1,000 extras). Roy's new fiancée, Helen (Jean Harlow), shows an interest in Monty and takes him to her apartment. She asks him, in a famous line, "Would you be shocked if I got into something more comfortable?" He isn't and she does. Fade out.

Fade in. Through a large cloud formation a zeppelin appears, on its way to bomb London's Trafalgar Square at night. Aboard is Karl, who still feels a close affinity for England. Karl is lowered in an observation car to direct the bombing, but knowingly gives a **false** position, and the bombs fall harmlessly in Hyde Park. Four British night fighters are sent up, including a two-seater with Roy and Monty. To eliminate weight, the airship captain cuts loose the observation car, sending Karl to his death.

The British fighters gain on the zeppelin, so most of
its crew members jump overboard to lessen the load. The
airship is now under heavy attack, and it shoots down three
planes, among them Roy and Monty's, which force-lands in a
field. When the fourth British pilot's guns jam, he rams the
zeppelin, setting it on fire. (Many of these events really
occurred, but not at the same time.)

Roy and Monty, now in France, volunteer to fly a captured German Gotha bomber to bomb an ammunition dump.
They make it over the lines and arrive at the target just as
Richthofen's squadron enters the area. Roy and Monty attack the dump, which of course alerts the Germans. A German pilot, Von Bruen (Frank Clarke), attacks the bomber.
It looks hopeless until Roy and Monty's squadron, in white
S.E. 5s and Camels led by Baldy (Roy Wilson), comes to
their rescue. A massive dogfight ensues.

Von Bruen still wants the bomber and goes after it,
after having broken contact to dogfight. Baldy attacks Von
Bruen and, to identify himself to the brothers, rips off his
helmet and goggles and yells, "Goddammit, it's me!" (This
profanity created a furor, but it remained in the film during
its first run.) After a fierce fight, Baldy shoots down Von
Bruen. But Richthofen has been watching all this from a
higher altitude. He dives, makes a quick climb, and attacks
the Gotha from beneath, sending it down in flames. Roy and
Monty survive the crash but are taken prisoner.

The brothers are interrogated by Von Kranz, who
rightly suspects that the ammunition dump bombing was part
of something larger (an advance by the Sixth British Bri-
gade). He threatens the brothers with death, and Monty
cracks. To prevent him from telling everything, Roy bor-
rows a Luger with one bullet from a German officer. Roy
says he will talk, but first he must shoot Monty so that
Monty won't be able to tell anyone Roy is a traitor. Roy
shoots his brother, refuses to talk, and is executed.

The film's final scene, the advance of the Sixth Bri-
gade, was shot on December 7, 1929. Involving 1,700 extras, the scene was almost an afterthought, for it lasted
only 30 seconds and was filmed from one static camera angle.
But at last the shooting of HELL'S ANGELS ended. Not the
coming of sound nor the stock market crash (which dampened

Hughes Tool Company profits) had been able to stop it. The editing and other post-filming tasks took several months, and the picture was finished in April 1930.

Several statistics not yet cited are worth mentioning. Production of the film cost $3,866,475, excluding editing, sound dubbing, and publicity. Thus the total cost of the film rose to over $4,000,000, a cost matched previously in film history only once (by the trouble-plagued BEN HUR of 1926). The cost for negatives and development of the 2,254,750 feet of film used was $225,475. Since the final print ran about 13,000 feet, more than 99 per cent of the film shot for HELL'S ANGELS was not used. About $328,000 went for non-flying actors' salaries, and $220,000 for the crew who filmed the dramatic sequences. In all, the aviation sequences cost $2,113,000, excluding film cost, and the pilots flew approximately 227,000 miles during the filming of the air battles.

HELL'S ANGELS premiered on June 7, 1930 at Grauman's Chinese Theatre in Los Angeles. The numerous stage and screen personalities attending had the honor of holding the first $11 tickets ever issued for a Hollywood movie premiere. The outside crowd numbered about 1,300,000. Frank Clarke's Fokker D-VII stood outside the theatre, painted in a reverse scheme of white background and black striping. The premiere was highlighted by the on-stage introduction of Roscoe Turner and his pet lion cub, Gilmore. Only an hour before, Turner had landed in Los Angeles after completing a record-breaking flight from New York. After a long wait, the picture premiered. The audience sat enthralled. At one point during the dogfight, the projectionist placed a red filter over the lens and the audience cheered. When the film ended, the audience gave a standing ovation.

HELL'S ANGELS broke attendance records at Grauman's Chinese and ran for nineteen weeks to full houses. It became the first film to open simultaneously at two New York theatres, the Criterion and the Gaiety.

Initial critical reaction lavished praised on the aerial sequences. The plot fared less well, with criticism ranging from total panning of the film's story to guarded acceptance of it. The critics really did not know how to assess the importance of the film. They agreed that it was exciting and

had audience appeal, but could not see how Hughes could
even recover his money, let alone make a profit from it.
HELL'S ANGELS went on to play in theatres around the
world for the next 20 years, earning Hughes $8,000,000,
double his investment.

Germany's reaction to HELL'S ANGELS was indicative
of the political climate facing World War I films in the 1930s.
Germany was a powerful force, and film producers weren't
anxious to antagonize a potentially large German audience.
(Ironically, this same situation existed after World War II.
The U.S. government was anxious to be on friendly terms
with our new ally. Filmmakers reflected this position by in-
forming the movie-going public that only a few crazed Nazis,
not the German public, were responsible for World War II.)
Germany at first made no official protest, but let it be known
that they found the film anti-German. In June 1931, the
Federation of German Motion Picture Theatre Owners called
the New York Times demanding that United Artists withdraw
the picture from world-wide distribution because the " 'anti-
German picture is derogatory to the reputation of the German people.' "[6] The cable went on to state if the picture
was not withdrawn "... the federation would take retaliatory
steps 'which have proved effective in other instances.' "[7] In
August 1931 the German government tried and failed to get
the film banned in Czechoslovakia. In February 1932, the
film was shown in Istanbul, and the Turkish government, under pressure from the Germans, cut the final scene where
the brothers are killed.

Controversy over the film again surfaced in 1936 when
a writer, Richard Barry, sued the makers of HELL'S ANGELS,
claiming the story had been plagiarized from two short stories copyrighted in 1911 and 1922. Hughes maintained the
idea had originated in a conversation held in a Havana bar in
1916. A federal judge dismissed the suit. An appeal took
the suit to the Supreme Court in 1939, but the Court refused to hear it.

HELL'S ANGELS is a testament to Hughes' genius for
handling large numbers of men and planes. Although WINGS
is certainly the better of the two films, the lavishness of
HELL'S ANGELS became a standard for epic aviation movies.

Scarcely a month after the release of HELL'S ANGELS,

Richard Barthelmess and "A" Flight in the 1930 version of
THE DAWN PATROL.

the next major aviation film, THE DAWN PATROL (1930),
premiered. Howard Hawks, one of the great aviation filmmakers, directed the picture. Hawks was a natural for the
aviation film genre. Many of his films, no matter what their
background subject, really center on the relationships between men in a small, select group. Thus a group of aviators formed the perfect nucleus for a Hawks film. Many
aviation directors, like Howard Hughes, made aviation films
about planes; Hawks made films about pilots. Hawks' aviation films, therefore, often tend to have more depth than
other films with more elaborate production values. Hawks
made the quintessential aviation story film. In addition, the
women in Hawks' films are of such a special type that there
is a class of heroine known as the "Hawksian woman." These
are women who can survive in a man's world. Hawks' films
tend to be effective treatments of men and women involved
with airplanes.

Howard Hawks was born in 1896. He served as a second lieutenant in the U.S. Army Air Service in World War I,
but did not go overseas. He began in films in 1918, first
serving as a writer and editor and then moving into the director's chair. Hawks' specialties were action-adventure pictures and mad-cap comedies. THE AIR CIRCUS was his first
aviation film and THE DAWN PATROL his first sound picture.

THE DAWN PATROL, a First National Picture, was
based on an eleven-page story outline by John Monk Saunders entitled "The Flight Commander." (When THE DAWN PA-
TROL was remade in 1938, as discussed later, the title of
the 1930 version was changed to FLIGHT COMMANDER, an
action that had led to some confusion, since some sources re-
fer to the original version under its second name.) Hawks
and Seton I. Miller produced the screenplay from Saunders'
outline, with Dan Totheroh helping with the dialogue.

The story tells of England's Royal Flying Corps' 59th
Squadron. Faced with stiff opposition from the Germans and
their superior aircraft, the squadron commander, Major Brand
(Neil Hamilton) is forced to send many of his fliers to their
deaths. Finally only a few expert veterans are left, including Flight Commander Dick Courtney (Richard Barthelmess)
and his best friend, Douglas Scott (Douglas Fairbanks, Jr.).
Against explicit orders, Courtney and Scott stage a devastating raid against a German aerodrome. They bomb the airfield, strafe it, and shoot down German planes one by one
as they try to take off.

Back at base, Brand receives his promotion and transfer orders just as he is balling Courtney out, and takes sat-
isfaction from the fact that the rash flier, who will take
Brand's place as commander, will now receive a taste of responsibility; Courtney has previously called Brand a butcher
for sending men out to die. Courtney, however, soon cracks
under the strain of having to send men to their deaths and
begins to drink. His friendship with Scott dissolves when
Courtney sends Scott's younger brother out on his first
patrol and the man is killed.

Scott volunteers for a suicidal bombing mission 60 kilo-
meters behind German lines. Unable to stand the strain any
longer and wishing to atone for Scott's brother's death,
Courtney gets Scott drunk and takes his place. He bombs
an arsenal, a supply depot, and a railroad junction and

engages in combat with the German ace, von Richter, before being shot down and killed. Scott then assumes the unenviable task of squadron commander.

THE DAWN PATROL used a few authentic Nieuports, but most of the aircraft featured were Thomas-Morse Scouts. Other aircraft included a Travel Air D-4, a Hisso Standard, and Boeing Cs, built as seaplanes but fitted with landing gear. The aerodrome exteriors were photographed in the San Fernando Valley. Fred Jackman had charge of the realistic special effects while Elmer Dyer was the principal aerial photographer. On occasion, Hawks flew the camera plane himself.

Much of the stunt flying for the expertly performed airplane shots was done by Frank Tomick, who had left the HELL'S ANGELS crew after the flying scenes were shot but before the completion of the film, because he had become dissatisfied with Hughes' method of filmmaking. As usual, there were some close calls for the fliers and actors. The most serious incident occurred during the airfield bombing sequence. Tomick, in a German aircraft taxiing for take-off, was supposed to jump out of the plane at a predetermined spot. The plane would continue rolling until it was blown up by a planted charge just as another stunt pilot, Robbie Robinson, flew over dropping a dummy bomb. But the special effects man exploded the charge too soon. Tomick just barely had time to dive for cover but Robinson wasn't so lucky. He flew right into the blast, which blew the plane 100 feet higher into the air. The tail surfaces were blown away and the wing covering shredded. Fortunately, Robinson was able to land the plane, which cartwheeled as one wing dug into the ground. Neither Tomick nor Robinson ever found out which demolition man was responsible for their near disaster.

Nor were the actors completely safe. Because dust on the field prevented cameramen getting a clear shot of Richard Barthelmess in an aircraft, it was necessary to hoist the plane on wires 25 feet high. The plane was then rocked with ropes to simulate flight while the camera was placed in position at the same height. Barthelmess was supposed to show surprise, and when one of the wires broke he thought it had been planned. It hadn't, and Barthelmess could have been seriously injured.

Hawks not only had the usual production problems associated with a film; he also encountered another one: Howard Hughes. Filming of THE DAWN PATROL began just as production on HELL'S ANGELS was drawing to a close, and Hughes became upset when he discovered that another airplane movie was being made. Hughes tried to get a script of THE DAWN PATROL, sent spies to the set, and attempted to sign fliers to exclusive contracts in order to prevent them going the way of Tomick and working for Hawks. (The pilots ended up signing exclusive contracts with both Hughes and Hawks, giving them more work than they could handle.) On one occasion, Hughes, fearing that Hawks was trying to finish THE DAWN PATROL and get it into release before HELL'S ANGELS came out, confronted Hawks directly. Hughes complained that Hawks had a scene where a wounded aviator spits up blood. That scene was already in HELL'S ANGELS and Hughes demanded that Hawks take it out. Hawks replied that it was a perfectly natural thing for a wounded pilot to do, and it would stay. Hawks would later work for Hughes, as director on the film SCARFACE (1932), but only after Hughes agreed to give him a free hand.

First National had little faith in THE DAWN PATROL, so they simply released it in July 1930 without a lot of publicity or fanfare. In addition, the studio executives were unhappy with the way Hawks had handled the film's dialogue, saying it was "'not dramatic' and 'flat.'"[8] Hawks said, "'No one [among the studio executives] liked the film because none of the characters cried or screamed.'"[9] The studio erred in its assessment, however, and the film was successful at the box office.

THE DAWN PATROL represents a significant step in the development of the aviation film. As the aviation film became more popular, the flying sequences improved, culminating in the thrilling air battles in WINGS and HELL'S ANGELS. But during all this time, the plot of airplane pictures progressed little. The plot of HELL'S ANGELS was scarcely better than that of THE SKYWAYMAN, made ten years before. THE DAWN PATROL changed this. Instead of concentrating on a romantic triangle (WINGS) or a lilac-carrying squadron mascot (LILAC TIME), for instance, it attempted to treat the problems faced by fliers on the Western Front. Flying was no longer glamorous; now it was a dangerous business from which few returned. The picture even reflects the anti-war sentiment expressed in such films as ALL QUIET ON THE WESTERN FRONT, by depicting the endless and useless process of men being sent out to die.

Unlike previous aerial war films, THE DAWN PATROL has no traditional heroes, and the pilots are caught in a situation from which they cannot escape. The pilots' real enemy isn't the Germans, but war itself. Young, inexperienced pilots die quickly; some are shot down on their first mission. In a bitterly ironic situation, the older, more experienced veterans survive combat, only to be promoted eventually to squadron commander, a job far worse than aerial combat. The lucky ones, like Major Brand, last long enough to get a promotion, but others, like Courtney, crack. And even Brand will always bear the scars.

WINGS, HELL'S ANGELS, and THE DAWN PATROL insured that the 1930s would be a rich decade for World War I aviation films. Besides sparking the public's interest in such pictures, these three films established a rich library of aviation footage. Sometimes the sequences were used to good advantage; most times they weren't. In one film, because of mixing sequences from various films, Ben Lyon shoots himself down! Also, stunt pilots objected to the use of such scenes, because it meant that they often didn't have to be hired to make an aviation film. Still, many aviation pictures of the 1930s might not have been made if this stock flying footage hadn't been available, and the public eagerly supported these films.

BODY AND SOUL, released in the spring of 1931, was adapted from the stage play Squadrons by E. W. Springs and A. E. Thomas, and featured Humphrey Bogart (in one of his first films) and Charles Farrell as two American pilots attached to a British squadron. Bogart is killed while attacking a German balloon, and Farrell ends up romancing Bogart's young widow. Also in the cast was Myrna Loy. The feminine lead was played by Elissa Landi, a European actress making her film debut.

HEARTBREAK (1931) had a different setting. Based on a story by Llewellyn Hughes, this Fox picture transferred the air action from France to Italy. Charles Farrell plays John Merrick, an American aviator and former U.S. Embassy worker in Vienna, transferred from France to Italy.

Humphrey Bogart (in cockpit) is fated to die quickly in
BODY AND SOUL (1931).

He falls in love with an Austrian countess. When he learns
that a deadly Austrian ace, Captain Wolke, is over the Italian lines, Merrick rises to do battle. (When the film was
shown at the Roxy Theatre in New York, this portion of the
aerial action was displayed on a large screen.) Merrick
shoots the enemy plane down, only to discover that he has
killed the Countess' brother, who borrowed the plane from
Wolke. Merrick is so upset that he refuses to fly in combat again and steals a plane to fly to the countess and tell
her what happened. He is court-martialed and sent to prison for the rest of the war. But the war soon ends and the
Countess forgives him.

A Howard Hughes comedy, COCK OF THE AIR, started
off 1932. The film starred Chester Morris as an American
pilot in love with a French actress, played by Billie Dove.

The film, which contained little air action, was not a success.
Hughes followed up COCK OF THE AIR with SKY DEVILS
(1932), another comedy. The picture was based on a story
by Joseph Moncure March and featured Spencer Tracy, William Boyd, and George Cooper as Allied aviators whose crazy
antics are not in the least interfered with by the war. The
picture contained parts of the dogfight and ammunition bombing sequences from HELL'S ANGELS, as well as some other
aviation footage. Both of these pictures apparently underwent cuts by the censors.

THE WHITE SISTER (1934), a re-make of a 1923 film,
told of a woman (Helen Hayes) who becomes a nun when she
believes her Italian lover (Clark Gable) shot down. She later
discovers he's alive, but she cannot break her vows. Some
of the aerial footage was from HELL'S ANGELS.

TODAY WE LIVE (1934) also used footage from HELL'S
ANGELS. Directed by Howard Hawks, the picture was the
first to be based on a William Faulkner work (the short story
"Turn About") and the first film on which Hawks and Faulkner worked together. Joan Crawford plays a girl in love
with Claude Hope (Robert Young). She soon falls for an
American aviator, Richard Bogard (Gary Cooper), but when
she hears Bogard is dead she returns to Hope. Bogard,
however, turns up and Hope and his brother, sailors in the
British Navy, convince Bogard that torpedo boat fighting is
just as exciting as the aerial kind. Hope is blinded in an
attack and when he learns that Crawford stays with him mainly out of pity and really loves Bogard, he and his brother go
to their deaths attacking an enemy ship before Bogard can
attack it suicidally by plane. TODAY WE LIVE is not one of
Hawks' best films. Designed by MGM (the picture is the only
MGM film Hawks ever directed all the way through) as a starring vehicle for Joan Crawford, the picture falters partly because she wasn't quite up to playing the masculine-type woman usually found in a Hawks film.

FORGOTTEN MEN (1934), a collection of World War I
combat footage, gave a chronological presentation of the war.
Of interest to aviation fans are shots of Richthofen's flying
circus and a zeppelin raid on England. CAPTURED (1934),
on the other hand, dealt with a German POW camp located
near a flying field. The noise of the planes not only woke
the prisoners but also reminded them of their captivity.

THE EAGLE AND THE HAWK (1934) was a better-than-average picture, written by John Monk Saunders and starring Fredric March, Cary Grant, Jack Oakie, and Carole Lombard. March played an expert flier who loses several observers but is not injured himself. The strain of losing the young men so needlessly and the futility of war takes its toll, and March eventually shoots himself. To save March's honor, although he had mocked his sentimentality, Grant loads the body into a plane, takes it up, shoots the body full of holes with a machine gun and crashes, giving March a hero's death. The aviation footage chiefly came from WINGS, THE DAWN PATROL, and newsreels. One crash was from LILAC TIME.

ACE OF ACES (1934) was based on a John Monk Saunders story, "Bird of Prey." Richard Dix played a sculptor whose pacifist leanings are mistaken for cowardice by his girl friend. Dix is forced into war, joins Ralph Bellamy's squadron, and becomes a ruthless ace.

CRIMSON ROMANCE (1934) gave the aviation audience a little more to enjoy. The World War I picture dealt with two American fliers, played by Ben Lyon and James Bush, who join the German air force, only to find themselves fighting against the American army at a later date. Lyon changes sides, but German-born Bush, who left America because of anti-German sentiment, does not and is killed. Lyon survives the war, marries a German girl, and visits Bush's German-American mother in the U.S.; she closes the picture with a pacifist sermon. The picture featured Erich von Stroheim in a minor role. Some of the aerial footage was newly-shot for the picture and some came from Howard Hughes' shots. This resulted in the interesting occurrence of Lyon, flying a British plane in the new footage, shooting at himself in a "Gotha" bomber in the old footage. He scores a "kill" on himself!

HELL IN THE HEAVENS (1934) was a picture based on the play The Ace by Herman Rossman. Warner Baxter starred in this routinely plotted picture which had him as an American in a French squadron who sets out to get the German ace, the Baron. Romance was provided in the form of Conchita Montenegro, who played the daughter of a woman in whose house the fliers are billeted (as in LILAC TIME). When the final confrontation between Baxter and the ace comes, Baxter's guns jam and he rams the enemy's plane.

They crash, but both survive and they toast each other. The picture was merely a rehash of material that had been done before.

SUZY (1936), based on Herbert Gorman's novel (which was toned down to please censors), starred Jean Harlow, Franchot Tone, and Cary Grant. Harlow, as Suzy, marries an Irish airplane inventor, Tone, on the eve of World War I, only to have him shot by a mysterious woman. Harlow leaves London for Paris and there meets and marries a French ace, Grant. Tone turns up alive, the woman who shot him is exposed as a spy, and Grant is killed in combat, after having an affair with the spy. The cast list includes an interesting entry: the character of Gaston, actually a goat, is played by George Spelvin, the name actors use when they don't use their real names. SUZY's aerial footage came from HELL'S ANGELS.

THE WOMAN I LOVE (1937) was the first picture Anatole Litvak directed in the United States. The RKO film, based on the 1924 novel by Joseph Kessel, L'Equipage (The Crew), had been made twice before in France under that title: in 1928 and again in 1935, with Litvak directing the 1935 version, which was released in the U.S. under the title FLIGHT INTO DARKNESS in 1938. The story told of a French pilot--Paul Muni in THE WOMAN I LOVE version--and his observer, Louis Hayward, who both love Muni's wife, Miriam Hopkins. Hayward is killed in an air battle and a wounded Muni is nursed by Hopkins. Muni does not let on that he knows Hopkins' feelings for Hayward. (Charles Vanel, Jean-Pierre Aumont, and Annabella played the roles in the 1935 version.) The 1935 version used footage from the 1928 film, and THE WOMAN I LOVE in turn used footage from the 1935 picture.

One day Mantz's secretary told him about the filming of THE WOMAN I LOVE and that Litvak had brought his own stunt pilots from Paris and wasn't going to use MPPA pilots. Incensed, Mantz called RKO and found out where Litvak was shooting. The next morning he flew to the site and did deck-level stunts that sent everyone to the ground. Litvak was so impressed that he hired Mantz.

Although it contains no aviation sequences, the GRAND ILLUSION (1938) rates mention here. The picture is French director Jean Renoir's classic about the grand illusion of war and of a dying age of chivalry. The picture deals with a German POW camp in World War I and the opening scenes are about aviators. Erich von Stroheim plays a German pilot who shoots down a French plane. He invites the pilot and officer observer to lunch. As they are sitting down to eat, a wreath honoring a dead French flier, which is to be dropped over the French lines, is brought out. Von Stroheim apologizes for the untimely coincidence. The idea of chivalry in the air was already dead by the time the GRAND ILLUSION was filmed, killed by the viciousness of the Spanish Civil War.

Warner Brothers remade THE DAWN PATROL in 1938. The original was now retitled FLIGHT COMMANDER. This

Errol Flynn prepares to take off in the 1938 re-make of THE DAWN PATROL.

new version starred Errol Flynn (Courtney), Basil Rathbone (Major Brand), David Niven (Scott), and Donald Crisp (Phipps), and was directed by Edmund Goulding. It closely followed the original, although the dialogue was revised by Seton I. Miller and Goulding. The remake proved as good as, if not better than the 1930 version, and it was enthusiastically received by the critics. The New York Times called it "... a thrilling, exciting, and heroic film...."[10]

All of the aviation footage from the 1930 DAWN PATROL was used, with close-ups of Flynn et al. being inserted. Some new footage was shot using Nieuport 28s. The film featured an all-male, all-British cast of 67 actors. Completion of the picture was rushed because five members of the cast, Basil Rathbone, Donald Crisp, David Niven, Melville Cooper, and Michael Brooke, were officers in the reserve and the trouble in Europe meant that they might be called up for duty. (A proposed 1961 re-make by Jack Webb never materialized.)

THE DAWN PATROL (and another picture) was launched in a $100,000 Warners' advertising campaign in newspapers and magazines. It proved to be the last major World War I aviation film for twenty years, as the exciting aerial action of World War II became the focus for aviation filmmakers.

THE STORY OF VERNON AND IRENE CASTLE (RKO, 1939) starred Fred Astaire and Ginger Rogers as the famous dance team of the title. The film told the story of their careers from 1911 until Vernon's death in 1918. Vernon served in the Canadian Royal Flying Corps in World War I (the film contains some World War I aerial footage) but was killed in a training accident in Texas. Irene Castle, a silent film star, served as technical advisor on the film. The film was shot in the San Fernando Valley and it was the last picture for Astaire and Rogers under that contract for RKO.

In January 1940 HELL'S ANGELS was reissued. The distribution rights were obtained by Astor Pictures and they cut the film from 119 minutes to 90 minutes, added color to the zeppelin sequences, and added a six-minute prologue called "Wings Over the World," dealing with the history of aviation from the Wright Brothers to the present.

THE FLYING DUTCHMAN (DE VLIEGENDE HOLLANDER,

An unusual perspective shot of Fred Astaire in THE STORY
OF VERNON AND IRENE CASTLE (1939).

1957) was a Netherlands film, the first to be made in that country in two years. Depicting the early aviation efforts in Holland and Germany of Anthony Fokker, it is almost totally devoid of action.

LAFAYETTE ESCADRILLE (1958) was the first World War I film in 20 years. Directed by the most prolific of aviation film directors, William Wellman (who again teamed up with cameraman William Clothier), the movie is abysmally poor. The project was originally titled C'EST LA GUERRE but Jack Warner, the studio head, changed the title and the story. Wellman violently disagreed with Warner and left the studio before LAFAYETTE ESCADRILLE was completed. Wellman never made another picture.

The plot has Thad Walker (Tab Hunter) leaving home to join the Escadrille after another dose of his father's strict discipline (which of course leaves mental scars). Before training begins he meets and falls in love with a French prostitute (Etchika Choureau). His undying love causes her to mend her ways and she gets a morally honest job as a night streetcar conductress. Back at the flying field, the men are being trained by a French officer who doesn't speak English. He literally pushes Thad too far and Thad knocks him to the ground (he's really hitting his father, for he later tells David Janssen, "I finally took a poke at my old man."). His buddies break him out of the stockade and he escapes to Paris and his girl. On the way he fights with a French soldier over the soldier's coat, and Thad gets cut in the face and wounded in the chest. He stays with the girl but is unable to go out in the streets after his wounds heal because the police are after him. He eventually gets hired as a pimp ("the only work a deserter can do") by his girl's former madam. He tells his story to a sympathetic American general who gets him reinstated in the Escadrille. He gets married in a church (they were earlier informally married in her room to keep the censors happy).

The aerial sequences are few and far between; and often they have no connection with the rest of the action. The only dogfight scene came from MEN WITH WINGS, and that was 20 years old. It is only on the ground that the film has some exciting plane shots. The novice pilots begin their training by learning to handle the "Penguin," an old Blériot monoplane with a clipped wing. The pilots are placed in these

Novice pilot Tab Hunter in LAFAYETTE ESCADRILLE (1958).

planes, which cannot fly, and are told to taxi to learn how to steer the plane in a straight line. Their first efforts usually resulted in the Penguins dashing madly across the field in every direction.

In 1965 MGM announced production plans for A TIME FOR GLORY, "... the first motion picture of the 1960s to 'recognize America's new interest in the exploits of World War I's great flying aces.'"[11] Although this film was never made, World War I aces did become the subject of a major motion picture the following year.

THE BLUE MAX (1966) was the first World War I aviation movie filmed in Cinemascope and color. It is 1918 and ex-infantryman Bruno Stachel (George Peppard) has become a pilot in the German air force. His hero is von Richthofen and his goal is to win the Blue Max, the decoration awarded to fliers who down 20 Allied planes. (Frederick the Great designed the medal, which bore the inscription "Pour Le Mérite" because French was the language of the Prussian court. Awarded for valor in battle, the decoration was nicknamed for Max Immelman, the great German pilot, and in reality was awarded to pilots who downed eight enemy airplanes.) The other fliers dislike Stachel because he is a peasant and because he is determined to win the medal. One pilot, Willi von Klugerman (Jeremy Kemp), takes an interest in Stachel and begins to fly with him. Stachel's first air victory cannot be confirmed, even though he searches for hours trying to locate the wreckage. The next time up, he wounds the gunner of a British observation plane and forces the pilot to head toward the German airfield. The gunner regains consciousness, forcing Stachel to shoot down the plane. The other pilots feel he did this to show off and the squadron commander, Heidemann (Karl Michael Vogler), plans to take official action. He is talked out of this by Count von Klugerman (James Mason), who sees in Stachel a hero for the people. Richthofen and the other aces are aristocrats and, therefore, not people the peasants can identify with.

The Count begins to build Stachel into a national hero. As Stachel's score grows, so too does he score with Kaeti (Ursula Andress), the Count's wife and Willi's mistress. The rivalry between Willi and Stachel comes to a head when they try to prove who's the better flier by stunting their triplanes. Willi is killed and Stachel claims two kills Willi made before he died. Everyone suspects Stachel, but can't prove anything. With nineteen planes to his credit, Stachel gets three more kills and wins the Blue Max. In Berlin to receive the medal, he is slated to test-fly a new German monoplane. The Count learns that Kaeti has told an officer Stachel didn't really shoot down the two planes and there is going to be an official investigation. Horrified that Stachel will disgrace the officer corps, the Count lets Stachel fly the unsafe monoplane. The plane crashes and Stachel dies a national hero.

Nine authentic planes were built at a cost of $250,000 for the film and included two British **S.E.-5s (built by the** Miles Organization), two German Pfalz D-IIIs (built in England, one by Douglas Bianchi and one by Peter Hillwood), two Fokker triplanes (built by John Bitz of Munich), and three Fokker D-VIIs (built by Claude Rousseau of France). Not all of the planes were authentic, for some Tiger Moths were painted with German lozenge camouflage and a redesigned Moth was used as a British R.E. 8 observation plane. THE BLUE MAX was the first film to depict von Richthofen (who is in a brief sequence) in the correct aircraft, a triplane. Previous films showed him in an accurate or fake Fokker D-VII, which was not put into wide service until the time of his death.

Aerial cameramen Skeets Kelly and Elmo Williams worked on the picture, and Tom Squire directed the flying scenes. Peppard had learned to fly, piloted several of the planes appearing in the film, and flew a Learjet on a promotional tour for the studio.

The film was made in Ireland, with the area around Dublin used as the setting for 20th Century-Fox's recreation of the Second Battle of the Somme in 1918. Over 1,000 troops of the Eastern Command of the Irish Army spent two weeks refighting one of World War I's bloodiest battles. Trenches were dug and a bombed-out village street was built for the strafing sequences. The aerodrome shots were filmed on a specially built mile-long runway and another existing field.

More than any other mainstream aviation film, THE BLUE MAX emphasized sex. The National **Catholic** Office for Motion Pictures gave the film a B rating (morally objectional in part or all) because of the two love-making sequences between George Peppard and Ursula Andress. Pictures appeared in Playboy showing what Fox touted as "the most sensational love scenes ever screened." Some of these scenes didn't make it into the release print, and the sex seems tame when compared to more daring contemporary films.

THE BLUE MAX's major problem is the inability of the scriptwriters to clearly delineate Peppard's character. The film was based on a novel, The Jew with the Blue Max by Jack D. Hunter, but the conflict in the film occurs not because of Stachel's religion, but because he's not an aristocrat. The film was made at a period in motion picture history when the "anti-hero" was becoming popular, a hero devoid of the usual positive character traits. The filmmakers wanted Stachel to be a nasty fellow, but couldn't let go of enough positive characteristics. The character is, therefore, inconsistent and unconvincing.

Director Blake Edwards' DARLING LILI (1970) cost $20,000,000, and combined musical numbers with dogfights. Julie Andrews plays Lili Smith, a German spy sent to get military secrets out of an American air ace, Major William Larrabee (Rock Hudson). Andrews is a music hall entertainer who collects British military information for her superior, Kurt Von Ruger (Jeremy Kemp). The Germans want information about the activities of Eagle Squadron and its commander, Larrabee. Andrews alternately sings and romances Larrabee throughout the picture, while he alternates between flying missions and responding to her advances. She doesn't learn anything from him but has fun trying. The flying scenes don't have much relationship to the rest of the film.

Most of the planes used in the picture, which served as S.E.-5as, were three-quarter-scale Currie Wots made by Slingsby, the English sailplane builders. They were powered by 100-horsepower Lycoming engines and differed from the real S.E.-5s only in that they had operating ailerons only on the top wing. There's some good stunt flying in the picture, for one of the characters, T.C. (Lance Percival), can't seem to get the hang of flying and demolishes several planes in spectacular "landing" attempts. Besides the planes, the film featured 39 vintage automobiles, leased from a Ghent, Belgium collector.

Don Stroud plays Captain Roy Brown, the man who shot down von Richthofen, in VON RICHTHOFEN AND BROWN (1971).

VON RICHTHOFEN AND BROWN (1971, also called THE RED BARON) used the planes from DARLING LILI (and some from THE BLUE MAX) to depict a much grimmer war. Directed by horror film maker Roger Corman, the movie supposedly reveals the characters of the two titled men and tells of their actions up to the time of their fatal meeting. The film cuts back and forth between them. Richthofen (John Philip Law) is the gentleman, the aristocrat. To him, hunting enemy airplanes is no different from hunting wild game. To kill is the important thing and this is the essence of the hunt. But the killing must be done in a gentlemanly manner. He's cool and self-assured. Capt. Roy Brown (Don Stroud) of RFC 209 squadron, on the other hand, is a Canadian wheat farmer and therefore a commoner. To him war is an ugly business to be fought in any way that keeps him alive. He lacks the coolness of Richthofen and also the good health (Brown has an ulcer). He becomes an outcast

from his fellow pilots when he refuses to drink a toast to the
Germans. As the film progresses, however, Brown's views
become adopted by the rest of the squadron. After the Germans strafe the British field, in retaliation for the British
strafing theirs, the war no longer becomes the exclusive
province of the pilots. When the field is attacked civilians
get killed, and this is ungentlemanly. By the end of the
film the gentleman aristocrat von Richthofen is dead and the
commoner Brown is alive.

The idea for the film arose at the same time THE BLUE
MAX was going into production. Corman thought von Richthofen was the "knight" and wanted to do a film about him.
But United Artists thought a film dealing only with von
Richthofen was "too much of a German picture," so they and
Corman agreed to add Brown. Corman said: "Their contest
marks the end of an era.... Also we found that when children build model planes today they buy more World War I kits
than they do World War II. Many young people can tell you
the names and exploits of the pilots of World War I, but nobody knows anything about the great pilots of World War II."[12]

Because the film's budget was only one million dollars,
all the aerial sequences were carefully planned in advance using the story-board technique. While this economy helped
make the aerial sequences interesting, they couldn't save the
picture. The film fails primarily because actors Law and
Stroud give wooden performances, failing to generate any
interest in their characters. VON RICHTHOFEN AND BROWN
is, in fact, one of the dullest World War I movies ever made.

The film is also technically, and probably historically,
inaccurate. The picture has Brown flying an S.E.-5a, not a
Sopwith Camel. Thorough research has led some historians
to conclude that von Richthofen was shot down by Australian infantrymen, not by Brown. The movie also perpetuates
the popular myth that von Richthofen was killed by one bullet and his plane landed intact, when, in fact, he had been
hit several times and his plane suffered damage to the lower
wing when it impacted the ground. Von Richthofen's triplane
carries an incorrect color scheme, for there were no white
areas on it on the day he died.

The picture was filmed in Ireland with the S.E.-5s from
DARLING LILI and planes from THE BLUE MAX. The Fokker

D-VII, built for THE BLUE MAX and powered by English Gypsy Queen engines, was underpowered and twice as heavy as the 1917 version. A Belgian Stampe biplane (playing a British two-seater in BLUE MAX) served as a German Pfaltz.

ACES HIGH (1976) had good aerial photography by Gerry Fisher but a standard World War I story based on R. C. Sheriff's 1929 play, Journey's End. Air Commodore Alan Wheeler and Group Captain Dennis David served as technical advisors. The British film features Malcolm McDowell, Christopher Plummer, and Simon Ward and focuses on a new pilot Stephen Croft (Peter Firth) and his disillusioned squadron leader John Gresham (McDowell). Croft has idolized Gresham since boyhood, but Gresham is not thrilled to have Croft assigned to him. Gresham has become an alcoholic. He is also attracted to Croft's sister. Croft has several harrowing experiences, crash-landing on one mission and flying a tough reconnaissance flight on another. But soon he ends up like most of the new pilots: dead, having lasted only nine days at the front. It is the loss of such young pilots that has driven Gresham to drink.

THE KID WHO COULDN'T MISS (1983) was a Canadian documentary on the second highest scoring Allied ace of the war: William Avery "Billy" Bishop. The film tells its story in an unusual manner: it cuts back and forth from narrated documentary footage to the performance of a stage play, "Billy Bishop Goes to War," in which the actor playing Bishop reminisces and reflects on his career. Bishop joined 21 Squadron of the RAF in the fall of 1915 as an observer. He became a pilot in 1917 and went on to down 72 enemy planes. He was awarded the Victoria Cross, served in World War II, and died in 1956.

THE KID WHO COULDN'T MISS is an odd mixture of filmic styles and accurate and inaccurate information. The movie paints Bishop as something less than a hero, a man who may have cheated in reporting the number of planes he shot down and whose battle action for which the V.C. was awarded may never have happened at all! The movie's most glaring historical error comes in its reporting on Richthofen. The film claims Richthofen was seriously wounded in the head after his eightieth victory, returned to combat too soon, and was shot down in 1917! Richthofen, in fact, was wounded after his 58th kill in 1917, returned to flying, and shot down another 22 planes before his death in April 1918.

THE KID WHO COULDN'T MISS fails on a number of levels. The intercutting of the stage play and documentary footage doesn't work and it makes the rhythm choppy. Ironically, much of the "documentary" footage is obviously from fictional World War I aviation films. (There are, however, some interesting shots of Guyemer, Nungesser, Ball, Bishop, and Richthofen.)

The picture is interesting for its portrayal of a fighter pilot's life. Because of the design of the engines, the fliers often got a lot of castor oil in their lungs, a malady known simply as "the condition." And Bishop summed up the stress on a fighter pilot: "I fly with a bottle of Milk of Magnesia and a bottle of gin. If one doesn't work the other will."

Perhaps no other aviation films better captured the romance and tragedy of fliers at war than those about World War I. Many of the images and attitudes associated with combat pilots grew out of this sub-genre. Numerous films dealing with World War II reworked the themes of pilot individualism and bravery found in WINGS and THE DAWN PATROL. The romance and tragedy of the first combat aviators linger on.

CHAPTER 5

THE PIONEERS

Civilian aviators occupy a curious place in cinematic aviation. Although the Wright brothers flew the first airplane and individuals like Lindbergh, Wiley Post, Amelia Earhart, and Howard Hughes blazed trails across the world's skies, they have generally received scant attention from filmmakers. Perhaps that's because it is relatively easy to make a war aviation film; the excitement is already built-in. But stories of civilian aviation don't often have intrinsic drama. For all the Wright brothers' fame, for example, it's difficult to make a powerful film about them. And so, only occasionally has the cinema produced noteworthy films chronicling the efforts of civilian pioneers.

Aviation filmmakers have used three techniques when dealing with civilian aviators. The first is the unembellished documentary, and often movie film has been shot on flying expeditions with the intent of editing it later into a feature film. Pseudo-documentaries have recreated the events depicted, sometimes with the actual fliers starring in the films. Some fiction films, on the other hand, have been loosely based on the exploits of particular pilots, or have been composites of some aspect of civilian aviation: starting an airline or test piloting, for example.

One of the first attempts to document civilian aviation came in 1927. FLIGHT COMMANDER (1927) was an uninspired British attempt to capitalize on Sir Alan Cobham's 1926 world flight by casting the flier as himself. A more successful documentary, THE FLIGHT OF THE SOUTHERN CROSS (1929, also known as THE FOUR HUMAN EAGLES), told of a Fokker Trimotor, called the Southern Cross, and its May 31 to June 9, 1928 flight from Oakland, California to Australia by way of Hawaii and the Fiji Islands. The

119

plane's flight commander, Captain Charles E. Kingsford-Smith, and the relief pilot, Captain Charles T. P. Ulm, served as the in-flight photographers. (Their story was filmed again in 1947.)

WITH BYRD AT THE SOUTH POLE (1930), a documentary released by Paramount, matter-of-factly presented the Byrd expedition. The picture was edited from 160,000 feet of film taken by the explorers. The high point, of course, was Byrd's 1,600-mile non-stop polar flight, the aerial photography of that journey being done by Harold June. The picture had dubbed-in music and a narration sequence by Floyd Gibbons supplemented the polar flight scenes. The picture was well received in America, but some British accused Paramount "... of vulgarizing the South Pole" with the studio's editing techniques.[1]

HEROES OF THE ARCTIC (1935) was a Russian documentary which told of the rescue by air of the crew of the Soviet exploration ship Chelyuskin, which was crushed by ice and sank while trying to sail east across the Arctic Ocean to Alaska. The 104 surviving crew members established a station on the ice field, radioed for help, and prepared a place for planes to land. The film was effective Soviet propaganda.

The Swiss WINGS OVER ETHIOPIA (1935) was partly a travelogue and partly a promotional tool for a newly-formed Swiss-African airline. The film had nothing to distinguish it, but Mussolini's invasion of Ethiopia made it a valuable commercial property.

CHINA CLIPPER (1936), a Warner Bros. release, was written by Frank Wead, starred Pat O'Brien, and featured Humphrey Bogart in a supporting role. The picture traced the rise of transoceanic flight from Lindbergh's solo to the transpacific flight of the "China Clipper." The film was done with the cooperation of Pan American Airways and although it dispensed with many aviation film clichés, it also eliminated most of the excitement. O'Brien, as Dave Logan, forms Trans-Ocean Airlines and runs a mail and passenger service in the Caribbean. He begins an expansion program that eventually leads to the flight of the Clipper. The film was based to some extent on the history of Pan American, but most of the real-life drama that went with the forming

Two scenes from CHINA CLIPPER (1936). At top, Pat O'Brien as the airline executive. Below, locals welcome the transpacific plane.

of the airline was omitted. The movie shows an airline being formed by the tireless effort of one man dedicated to the idea of building a transoceanic passenger plane. The major struggles of Pan American, however, took place not in the skies but in the lobbying halls of Washington, D.C. Although the U.S. government encouraged domestic airline competition in the 1930s, it discouraged competition for international routes. The government felt that a single strong overseas airline had the best chance of competing with the nationalized airlines of Britain, France, and Germany. As a result, Pan American received contracts for overseas routes even though it wasn't always the lowest bidder. The smaller airlines were squeezed out, leaving Pan Am with the foreign routes. None of this political struggle appears in the film.

The flying shots for CHINA CLIPPER were either newsreel footage, model shots, or new footage expressly for the picture. Mantz and Dyer shot some of the latter. One day they flew above clouds over San Francisco getting shots of the real Clipper. Mantz desended through the clouds, but by this time the ceiling had dropped to sea level. He went lower and lower until he finally had to fly under the San Francisco-Oakland Bay Bridge to avoid hitting it.

THE FLYING DOCTOR (1935) was a lackluster Australian picture about the Flying Medical Association in that country, made with the help of Gaumont-British.

One of the first aviation films of 1936 was the British production, CONQUEST OF THE SKY, which dealt with the history of flight from 57 A.D. to the present (the film was updated and re-issued in 1944). The film was from a John Monk Saunders story and was co-directed by **five directors,** among them Saunders and Zoltan Korda.

ATLANTIC FLIGHT (1937) was a Monogram picture made to capitalize on the round-trip transatlantic flights of Dick Merrill. The plot was not the best and Variety said, "It bristles with cinematic clichés and manages to come to life only when it follows the path of Merrill's actual career. And although the flyer is a distressing actor, only his presence saves the production from being absolute trash."[2] The plot concerned two rival airplane owners and a flight to London and back within 48 hours to pick up a serum. The air-

plane footage consisted largely of newsreel shots of an air
meet and studio-made shots.

Unlike Locklear, Merrill was reluctant to star in films.
(His co-pilot, John Lambie, was also in the picture.) Merrill said: "'I felt embarrassed from the day the contract was
signed until the picture was finished. I was ready to de-
cline Monogram's offer, but a friend talked me into it.'"[3]
Merrill also specified in his contract that he wouldn't do any
kissing on the screen and that he would be a consultant on
the aerial sequences. The result was that the director, William Nigh, discarded the original script after the first couple
of days of shooting. Also unlike Locklear, Merrill did little
flying for the cameras; just a few take-offs and landings.
The shots of Merrill and Lambie over the ocean were done in
a Condor cabin in the studio.

The German film LOST IN THE CLOUDS (ZIEL IN DEN
WÖLKEN, 1938) told of the early days of aviation. A young
army officer, Walter von Suhr (Albert Matterstock), in 1909
sees great potential in aviation and resigns his commission to
become a flier. His girl friend supports his decision but his
father threatens to disinherit him. Walter is able to convince
his father of his love for flying; and the army welcomes him
back to lead the newly-formed squadron in his old regiment.

TEST PILOT (1938) was the next major aviation film.
Frank Wead wrote the story and the stars were Clark Gable,
Myrna Loy, and Spencer Tracy. Gable played a test pilot
who is forced down in a Kansas wheat field during a transcontinental speed trial when his oil pump gives out. He
meets Myrna Loy, who immediately falls in love with him, and
they are married. Loy then finds out what it's like being
married to a test pilot and her nerves start to go under the
strain of Gable's daily risking of his life. The film ends
happily, however, when Gable's employer, Lionel Barrymore,
decides that Gable will work on the ground from now on.

The story is only average, but the flying enthralled
the critics. The film opened with a note that "the hazards
of test pilots have no relationship to passenger flight" and
the film gave thanks to the U.S. Army. The aerial action,
some of it done by Mantz but much of it accomplished with
miniatures, includes a plane breaking apart in a dive and
Gable bailing out, the crash of a tri-motor bomber out for

Clark Gable as the veteran pilot in TEST PILOT (1938).

an altitude record in which Tracy is killed, and a Cleveland
pylon air race with Gable going for the $10,000 prize. His
engine catches fire, but he goes the last 16 miles to win as
another plane crashes. Featured are a Seversky P-35, a
Harlow PJC-2, a Ryan ST, and early versions of the B-17.
The final crash is a DC-2 drone made up to look like a B-17.
In the formation flying the filmmakers had the cooperation of
the Army air service. The New Republic called the plane
shots "... the most terrific air scenes ever taken or
faked...."[4]

TEST PILOT may have been inspired by the career of
James H. Collins, a test pilot who wrote a book, Test Pilot,
and who was killed while testing a Grumman fighter, leaving
a wife and two children. His widow, however, thought the
picture was more than inspired by her husband's career, and
she sued the filmmakers for plagiarizing her husband's book.

MEN WITH WINGS (1938) was the biggest aviation film
since HELL'S ANGELS. Directed by William "Wild Bill" Wellman and written by Robert Carson, the Paramount picture
told the story of aviation from the Wright brothers' flight up
to the present (1938) day, set against the story of two fliers, Scott Barnes (Ray Milland) a serious, science-oriented
pilot, and Pat Falconer (Fred MacMurray), a World War I ace
and flying soldier of fortune. The picture was the first
aviation film to be shot in Technicolor. Because of this,
every scrap of aerial footage had to be shot expressly for
the film because no stock Technicolor aviation footage existed. Wellman was virtually given a free hand in shooting
the film and worked on a 180-day schedule. He used 60
planes, 25 pilots, and 40 mechanics.

Naturally, Mantz was hired to do the **stunt work**.
Working for Mantz as supervisor for the aerial photography
was W. Howard Greene, whose two aerial cinematographers,
Charles Marshall and Wilford Cline, ran the two 350-pound
three-film Technicolor cameras mounted in Mantz's Travel
Air and Stearman camera planes. These cameras were placed
on mounts designed by Mantz and could move up and down
and swivel 180 degrees.

Wellman used several methods to direct the aerial action. Sometimes he would lie flat on his back looking through
binoculars and directing the pilots by radio. For more

Building an airplane in MEN WITH WINGS (1938)

complicated shots, he would have pictures of the Van Nuys area drawn and mark the plane's courses and where they were to perform what maneuvers. For scenes to be shot at distant locations, sometimes as far as 50 miles away, Wellman would call the pilots and cameramen together and, using a blackboard and model aircraft, explain what he wanted. The pilots and cameramen would then fly to the location and perform the stunts.

For Wellman, the making of MEN WITH WINGS was hard work. Shooting started on May 9, 1938 and Wellman explained:

> From then on, it was airplanes and fliers and the heartening stink of burning oil and the roar of motors. About the middle of the picture I found I had lost fifteen pounds, was living on crackers and milk, and had developed a full head of gray hair. I worked fifteen hours a day and couldn't sleep when I got home. No matter where I was, I yelled at the top of my voice ... I could always hear those motors![5]

As was now common, the filmmakers had to go searching for clouds. (No history of a major aviation film, in fact, seems complete unless there is a good cloud-hunting story to go with it.) It took two months to get all the cloud scenes. Every morning, Wellman's manager would phone the radio stations, airports, and the observatories at Mt. Wilson and Palomar to learn if any clouds were nearby. If things were "go," the manager would phone the cast and crew at 6 a.m., and they'd be loaded onto buses and sent to the proper location, sometimes as much as 75 miles away.

Among the planes used in the film were two powered gliders built from 1904 blueprints, a Curtiss pusher biplane constructed from 1910 plans, Fokker D-VIIs, DeHavilland Liberties, a Spad VII, a **Pfalz** D-XII, a Nieuport 28 C.I., Thomas-Morse Scouts, Boeing 247s, Boeing P-12Es, and an S.E. 5. Pilots got $50 a day. Only four pilots on MEN WITH WINGS had flown in HELL'S ANGELS; the rest were dead or retired. Travel Airs or Wichita Fokkers were also used and some shots of the planes were done with the planes hung on wires.

In four months of flying, with up to fifteen planes in the air simultaneously, there was only one minor accident, when Dick **Renaldi's** Fokker ran out of gas and he nosed over on landing in an asparagus patch. But Mantz did have some close calls, both involving Frank Clarke. Tension between the two men ran high on the set, because Clarke had gone from being one of the top men on HELL'S ANGELS to being just another pilot. One day, flying over Metropolitan Airport, Clarke dived a Fokker on cue from 3000 feet and Mantz took his Stearman with a remote Technicolor camera mounted on the top wing down after him. Clarke dove at full throttle in an open invitation for Mantz to try to keep up with him. As Mantz closed on the Fokker, Clarke released gallons of red chemical smoke spray that went right into Mantz's face. Mantz was blinded and Clarke looked back into the camera and laughed. Both planes pulled out at about 500 feet, and back on the ground Clarke, unconvincingly, apologized. A few days later, Mantz, in a Nieuport, and Clarke, in the Fokker, were crossing the San Fernando Valley at 2000 feet in front of a camera plane. Mantz was supposed to lock wings with the Fokker and force the plane to land after both planes' guns had becomed jammed. Mantz moved into position and Clarke brought his wing down so hard that it drove a control horn on the Nieuport's top wing into the Fokker and stuck there, locking both planes. Neither could free his plane, so they had to land together, with the camera plane catching it all. They made a perfect landing, and the only damage was a hole in the Fokker's wing.

Although it looked as though Mantz had lost a Lockheed Vega named "Miss Patricia" when Fred MacMurray supposedly overshot Roosevelt Field and crashed into the Atlantic, this was really a process shot.

Paramount launched a $20,000 newspaper campaign for MEN WITH WINGS. Critics praised the aviation footage, but not the story. As Time put it: "Were the narrative, the writing and the acting in MEN WITH WINGS up to the same standard [as the photography] it would rank as one of the best pictures ever made. Unfortunately, they do not."[6] The New York Times stated: "A dramatic history of aviation remains to be written for the screen."[7]

Up to now, the armed forces had usually cooperated with the aviation filmmakers with little trouble. But on MEN WITH WINGS the Army put its foot down. On the front page of The New York Times, May 29, 1938, Section 2, it was reported that Paramount had been told to rewrite the last twenty pages of dialogue, eliminating any pacifist sentiments, as a condition of using Army planes and equipment in the picture. Specifically, the Army objected to the use of eighteen planes in a Spanish Civil War sequence (MEN WITH WINGS, by the way, was one of the very few aviation films to mention to Spanish Civil War and the Sino-Japanese War) because "It is against the policy of the War Department to furnish personnel and equipment to represent foreign military forces." (Ironically, thirty years later the USS Lexington would serve as the aircraft carrier from which Japanese planes in TORA! TORA! TORA! would take off to bomb Pearl Harbor.) In addition, neither side in the Spanish Civil War could use U.S. planes except in violation of the Neutrality Act, and "It would be inappropriate for the United States Army to cooperate in making a picture that would indicate that this law was being openly violated." Also, the Army didn't like scenes that indicated that captured American pilots in Spain were being executed: "... the American Army should not lend itself to the propagation of atrocity stories, whether true or false."

But the clincher came in scenes 335 to 342.   The Army said:

> These scenes tend to reflect on American manu-
> facturers of military aircraft by intimating that they
> have a callous disregard for human life and care only
> for profit....   For the Army to cooperate in making
> a picture which placed them in a false light might be
> resented. [8]

These scenes obviously did not make any statements about
the Army, but the Army did have them censored, so that the
heroine does not talk an inventor out of using his genius to
develop a super bomber and "... a general denunciation of
war is avoided." [9]

THE FLYING IRISHMAN (1939) told the story of Douglas "Wrong Way" Corrigan's flight from New York to Ireland
of July 1939 when, ostensibly at least, he was headed to Los
Angeles.   Corrigan was paid in excess of $100,000 for the
rights to his autobiography, and the film told his life story
from the time Corrigan was nine.   Corrigan made a point of
not letting Hollywood go to his head when he went there to
play himself in the picture.   He was thirty-five minutes late
for one appointment because his 1928 car had broken down
and he felt he couldn't afford a cab.   And on a visit to Henry
Ford, he refused to pick any one of Ford's cars because he
didn't want to be obliged to anyone.   When Corrigan arrived
in Hollywood in November 1938 to start work on the picture,
Variety gave him only a two-line mention, so the producers
sent out press agents to be sure the papers gave Corrigan
more coverage.

20,000 MEN A YEAR (1939) starred Randolph Scott in
a tale about the Civilian Pilot Training Program.   The film
had some interesting flying by Mantz and included a bail-out
over the Grand Canyon by a cadet.   Scott flies in to rescue
him, but another pilot has to fly the plane and its passengers
out of the Canyon to safety.

The Russian film WINGS OF VICTORY (1940, also
called VALERI CHKALOV) was the story of Valeri Chkalov,
the man who led the first transpolar flight from Moscow to
Vancouver, Washington in a single-engined NO25 monoplane.
Chkalov was a crack test pilot personally recognized by

Stalin, who advised him to be more careful because his life was valuable to Soviet aviation. The film was done in a documentary style, but omitted the crash of a test plane that took Chkalov's life.

CAPTAIN EDDIE (1945) (called THE STORY OF EDDIE RICKENBACKER in England) was a romanticized, watered-down biography of Eddie Rickenbacker. Produced by Twentieth Century-Fox, the picture's history stretched back to 1941, when Rickenbacker and producer Winfield Sheehan decided to film Rickenbacker's life while the pilot was convalescing from injuries received in a Georgia plane crash. But it wasn't until 1943, and after Rickenbacker had ditched a B-17 into the Pacific and spent weeks floating on a raft, that Rickenbacker, Sheehan, and Fox came to terms on the production of a movie called THE STORY OF EDDIE RICKEN-BACKER. Sheehan said: "... the picture will in no way deal with capital, labor, or politics. 'It will be ... the story of an American, who, through the showing of his own experiences, wishes to drive home to the youth of the land the opportunities the country offers those willing to work for them.'"[10]

The film begins in 1942 with Rickenbacker (Fred Mac-Murray) and his companions crashing in the ocean. A remark about machines gets Rickenbacker to thinking about his life-long relationship with them and the film flashes back to Columbus, Ohio, around 1910. Rickenbacker made primitive attempts to fly and tinkered with automobiles. From there on, much of the film is concerned with Rickenbacker's romance with his future wife (Lynn Bari) and his cars. Rickenbacker's WWI experiences with the 94th Squadron, the First Pursuit Group, where he totaled 26 kills to become the greatest American ace of the war, were quickly covered and Rickenbacker's post-World War I experiences were almost completely excluded.

Just as William Wellman had been the first person to direct a major aviation picture after World War I, so too was he the first to direct a major aviation film after the Second World War. The film was GALLANT JOURNEY (1946), which he also co-wrote and produced for Columbia.

As if to shun wartime aviation as much as possible, Wellman made a film as far removed, in time and subject

matter, from war as he could. He went back to the very beginning of heavier-than-air flight, choosing for his subject
the life of John J. Montgomery. Montgomery, an aviation pioneer, is credited as being the first to make a heavier-than-
air controlled flight (in 1883). The $1,300,000 film follows
Montgomery from his boyhood flying efforts to his death. It
begins with a boy flying a radio-controlled model plane which
is shot out of the air by another boy. An old man, Jim Montgomery (Charlie Ruggles), breaks up the resulting fight,
shows the boys a monument to Montgomery, and tells them
the story of the aviation pioneer. The film then plunges into
a mushy story of Montgomery (Glenn Ford), who, as a boy,
is interested only in flying. Everyone except the girl who
loves him (Janet Blair) thinks he's crazy. While conducting
his early experiments, Montgomery discovers that he suffers
from vertigo and can no longer fly. His girl friend enlists
the aid of a circus performer, who does a trapeze act while
suspended from a balloon, as a pilot for Montgomery. Montgomery's glider is pulled aloft by the balloon and the trapeze
artist disengages the balloon and flies to earth. One day the
balloon fails to release and the trapeze artist is killed. A
priest at Santa Clara College, where Montgomery has been
building his planes, consoles him. Montgomery marries the
girl and eventually is killed when he insists on flying despite his illness.

The movie was conceived by the San Diego Junior
Chamber of Commerce, which was paid $25,000 for the screen
rights to the Montgomery biography. Out of this, the Chamber of Commerce set up a scholarship **fund** and erected a
$10,000 monument to Montgomery on the spot on Otay Mesa
from which Montgomery launched his first successful flight
of 600 feet. At about the same time, a monument to Montgomery was also erected in Santa Clara. To further publicize Montgomery's efforts, Wellman made the film. Wellman
said he expected the film " 'to cause a controversial bomb-
shell in the aeronautics world.' "[11] Whatever can be said
about the picture, that statement is not part of it.

GALLANT JOURNEY suffers in many areas. The dialogue never rises above the trivial and the acting is only
mediocre. But the main flaw is that the subject, as Wellman
treats it, is not suitable for a feature-length film because it
lacks drama. The viewer never really gets interested in
Montgomery, and really doesn't care if he flies or not.

GALLANT JOURNEY's major asset is the aerial footage. Of this, the shot of the glider descending after being released from the balloon stands out. Wellman described this **sequence as the most anxious** of his career. The balloon was to rise to 4,000 feet, the altitude at which the glider was to be released. On the first try, the balloon escaped, delaying production for a week. The second time the balloon rose to 16,000 feet before the pilot, Paul Tuntland, was able to unjam the balloon gas-release valve. The balloon settled to the proper altitude and Tuntland made the flight that was captured on film.

Eleven reproductions of Montgomery's three gliders were built in 60 days by the Radioplane Company of Van Nuys, California. Paul Tuntland and Don Stevens alternated as pilots. By test-flying the planes they located several defects, and the gliders used in the film became a slight compromise between authenticity and flying stability. The gliders flew so well that they received CAA licenses as experimental models. Gliders were also produced in miniature to provide the models on which Montgomery tested his designs.

The anti-war film sentiment was still strong in 1947-- so strong in fact that Columbia made special efforts to insure that its next aviation picture, PACIFIC ADVENTURER (1947), would not be thought of as a war film. The studio exercised care in the film's advertising, describing the picture as "'... the true story of Sir Charles Kingsforth Smith, one of the greatest heroes of our time.'"[12] In large type under the title were the words: "'not a war picture.'"[13] The film dealt with the man who was lost while trying to set a speed record from London to Australia in 1935.

PACIFIC ADVENTURER follows the life of Smith (Ron Randell) from his discharge after WWI to his death. A documentary style is used to show his 'round Australia flight and his Pacific crossing in his plane, the Lockheed-Altair "Lady Southern Cross." He tries to start his own domestic airline and, to win a British mail contract, attempts his fatal flight. The picture fails to capture the color of Smith's life, for much more could have been done with his 1927 flight from California to Sydney and the flight he made in 1930 from London to New York, the first of its kind. Romance is provided by a woman who becomes Smith's wife. In keeping with the documentary style, newsreel footage is used but it's obviously a cost-saving measure. The flight sequences consist mainly of showing the Lady Southern Cross being buffeted by the elements.

ARCTIC FURY (1949) was the true story of Thomas Barlow, a flying doctor in Alaska. When an epidemic breaks out in a remote village, Barlow must fly there even though he's having engine trouble. The engine gives out and he crashes into an iceberg while trying to land his plane. For three months he fights for survival until, in a terrifying sequence, he is rescued from a pack of starving dogs. The story is told mainly by a narrator and is restrained and effective.

WINGED STARS (ZVEZDY NUKRYLJACK, 1950) told of training Russian civilian pilots.

The British produced the first outstanding jet film, BREAKING THROUGH THE SOUND BARRIER (1952, released in England as THE SOUND BARRIER). An excellent film, the picture combines good aerial action and a strong plot while conveying the sense of riding in a supersonic aircraft. John Ridgefield (Ralph Richardson, whose character is modeled on that of Geoffrey DeHavilland) is an airman who has become obsessed with the idea of flying faster than sound. He begins to manufacture supersonic planes and enlists his son to help him, although the young Ridgefield really doesn't want to fly. On his first solo test flight the son is killed. This causes the estrangement of his daughter Susan (Ann Todd) who bitterly condemns her wealthy father for her brother's death. Her husband (Nigel Patrick) also flies for Ridgefield and is killed when he crashes on the first attempt to penetrate the sound barrier. This doesn't stop Ridgefield from trying to achieve his goal, however, and when he finally succeeds he is reconciled with his daughter and her newborn son.

The story by Terence Rattigan grew out of a notebook director David Lean made while gathering information for the film. Lean wanted to make an adventure picture and became intrigued with a newspaper story reporting the breakup of a plane that had been flying faster than sound. Interested in the invisible sound barrier, he talked with jet plane designers and manufacturers and flew with the jet test pilots.

Ralph Richardson and Nigel Patrick observe the technology that will help shatter the sound barrier, in BREAKING THE SOUND BARRIER (1952).

His efforts produced a three-hundred-page notebook of jet
aircraft information. He turned this over to Rattigan who
wrote a plot to accompany the technical details. The result
was a superb plot blended with excellent technical materials.

The film contains brilliant aerial photography. The
movie opens with a Spitfire cavorting above the English
Channel. It is almost destroyed as it goes into a power
dive and encounters shock waves. The movie then leads
to the present efforts to fly faster than sound.

Much of the aerial footage takes the viewer's breath
away, as long, sleek jets climb and dive, leaving various
vapor trails, or seeming to stand still in the high-altitude
clouds. Along with the conventional shots of the aircraft
there is some unusual creative camera work. To illustrate
the passage of a plane, Lean shows only the wheat in a
field being bent by air currents produced by the unseen
jet. He cuts effectively from a burning plane to an open
grave and from a wartime airfield to the noisy jets flying
above a rusty anti-aircraft installation.

The aerial shots culminate in a beautiful sequence in
which Nigel Patrick and Ann Todd, on a jet flight to Cairo,
are over the English Channel and can see the coasts of
France, Belgium, and Holland, with the Alps glimmering to
the east. Even the cockpit shots are very good, with the
test pilots in G suits and goggles framed by the plexiglass
and sky background.

The jet aircraft were supplied by Vickers, DeHavilland,
and other English manufacturers. Whether it's a Vickers
Supermarine 535 Swift diving from 40,000 feet or just a plane
being rolled out of a hanger, the airplane shots in this film
are always interesting. Here, Lean effectively adds to the
visuals by the skillful use of sound. The jet noises range
from a healthy roar to an almost unearthly whine. The
sound that announces the passing of a jet through the sound
barrier is one of the most effective in the whole picture.
The film, which was made in cooperation with the Society of
British Aircraft Constructors, strikes a perfect balance between the metal strain of the plane crashing through the
sound barrier and the mental strain of the characters waiting on the ground while this is being accomplished.

Thirty years after Charles Lindbergh's historic flight Hollywood recreated the exciting events of 1927 in THE SPIRIT OF ST. LOUIS (1957), one of the truly outstanding aviation pictures. It is a detailed aviation film, for it follows the conception, design and flight history of an airplane.

In the Garden City Hotel on Long Island Lindbergh (Jimmy Stewart) speculates on the next day's transatlantic flight and recalls some of his past flying experiences. On May 20, 1927 he makes a hair-raising takeoff in the overloaded plane from a muddy Roosevelt Field. The spectators tense as he barely clears some electrical wires and is on his way. He flies to Newfoundland and then begins the Atlantic crossing. On route he recalls his early life and the events leading up to the flight (told in flashbacks). He almost ditches in the ocean when his wings ice up, but he dives toward the water and the ice breaks off. He makes it to the Irish coast only three miles off course and heads for Paris, where he lands to a tremendous welcome at Le Bourget Field. Tired by his 33-hour and 20-minute flight, Lindberg fondly looks at the plane that got him safely across the Atlantic.

From **takeoff, the director, Billy Wilder, captures the** interest of the audience and holds it. The flashbacks and bits of business, like the housefly over Newfoundland or the discovery of the St. Christopher medal in the plane, keep the audience from being bored.

The **filmmakers paid Mantz $83,853.45 for two re-** built Standard biplanes; and Warners built three replicas of the Spirit. Two of these were constructed by Joe Pfeifer, and one was built for Stewart, a World War II bomber wing commander who flew it in the film. (In 1967 Frank Tallman flew one of these replicas up the Seine to commemorate the 40th anniversary of the flight.) Each of these planes cost over three times as much as the $10,580 original built at the Ryan aircraft plant in Santa Monica, California. The "Spirit" used in filming was fitted with six camera mounts, each camera automatically recording Stewart's actions in the cockpit. The in-flight shots were done by Mantz in his B-25 camera plane, The Smasher, and by a cameraman aboard a smaller, slower plane. Mantz's pilot, Jim Thompson, flew the Spirit for some shots and logged 132 hours in front of the camera. These shots often called for much ingenuity. For example, the Spirit's wing was coated with sugar to make it appear that ice was building up on the leading edge. Le Bourget field had changed too much to be used, so a smaller French field doubled for it. Roosevelt Field had also changed, and this setting had to be reconstructed at Santa Maria, California. (The film was flipped over to make it seem that Lindbergh was flying east instead of west.)

Ever on the alert to promote the movie, Warners' publicity department hired private detectives to find the girl who gave Lindbergh a compact mirror he needed for the instrument panel. After much futile work, they found a picture of her giving Lindbergh the mirror and this identified her as Mrs. Loma Oliver, Jr.

The Swiss SOS GLACIER PILOT (SOS GLETSCHER-PILOT, 1959) cost $175,000 and dealt with the exploits of the guides and glacier pilots who risk their lives to save trapped mountaineers. The film succeeds to a fair degree in capturing the perils of this type of rescue work. The movie starts out rather haphazardly but finds itself in the second half, which is given over to a documentary style treatment of rescue operations. A party of mountaineers, with various personal problems, accidently becomes trapped on a glacier, some of them being killed outright and others injured. The glacier pilots come to the rescue and save some of them. The picture was shot in three months at altitudes of 11,000 to 14,000 feet. The chief pilot was an actual Swiss glacier pilot, Hermann Geiger.

CONQUERERS OF THE SKY (IM POKORIAESTA NEBO, also called MASTERS OF THE SKY, 1962) was a Russian picture examining the work of the test pilot who pioneered the first Soviet jet plane. The film follows the plane from the drawing board to final testing and stresses the important contributions made by the Soviet pilot. The film, directed by Tatiana Liosnova, won first prize at a 1963 French aviation film festival.

CLEAR SKY (TJISTOJENEBO, 1962) dealt with a famous test pilot, Alexsej Astachov (Jevgeni Urbanski), reported killed in World War II. He's been captured by the Germans, however, and when he returns home after the war he's accused of being a traitor and not allowed to fly. He is rehabilitated, though, and once more sits in the cockpit. DEATH LOOP (V METRVOJ PETLE, 1963) dealt with Soviet aviation pioneers, particularly Serge Utotikin.

In the summer of 1965, the first of the high budget aviation epics of the 1960s was released. THOSE MAGNIFI-CENT MEN IN THEIR FLYING MACHINES, OR, HOW I FLEW FROM LONDON TO PARIS IN 25 HOURS AND 11 MINUTES is an enjoyable film about the early days of flying. In 1910 a rich newspaper owner, Lord Rawnsley (Robert Morley) agrees to sponsor an air race from London to Paris, with the first prize being 1,000 pounds. (This situation was in-spired by the 1,000-pound prize offered by the London Daily Mail in 1909 to the first person to fly the English Channel. Louis Blériot won it.) The race attracts a group of magnifi-cent men: proper Englishman Richard Mays (James Fox); an emotional Italian, Count Emilio Ponticelli (Alberto Sordi); a brash American, Orvil Newton (Stuart Whitman); a romantic Frenchman, Pierre Dubois (Jean-Pierre Cassel); a very mili-tary German, Colonel Manfred von Holstein (Gert Frobe); an inscrutable Japanese, Yamamoto (Yujiro Ishihara); and the villain of the film, Sir Percy Ware-Armitage (Terry-Thomas). The film is also a race by the American and the Englishman for the hand of Lord Rawnsley's daughter (Sarah Miles). Besides the usual perils of early flying, all the contestants have to deal with the dastardly doings of Sir Percy, who is determined to win by any means. Through accidents or Sir Percy's handiwork the group is reduced to three contestants by the time it reaches Paris: the Frenchman, the American, and the Englishman. The Frenchman's plane catches fire while he is rounding the Eiffel Tower and the American sac-rifices his chance to win by going to his rescue. The Eng-lishman wins, but the American gets the girl.

Comic situations are developed throughout the movie that make good use of planes. The Germans and the French fight a duel using blunderbusses and balloons (this is based on an actual duel fought during the Franco-Prussian War of 1870); the Italian gets in the way and is shot down. Sir Percy crashes on top of a train and the plane's wings are sheared off when the train goes through a tunnel. The Ger-man Colonel's pilot is put out of action and the Colonel has to fly the plane while trying to read the instruction book, with humorous results. One plane goes out of control on the airfield, starting a chase worthy of the Keystone cops.

THOSE MAGNIFICENT MEN IN THEIR FLYING MA-CHINES came about when Jack Davies, the associate pro-ducer, was looking over some old newsreel footage of early

Two scenes from THOSE MAGNIFICENT MEN IN THEIR FLY-
ING MACHINES (1965). At top, Terry-Thomas finds horse-
drawn transportation frustrating. Below, Gert Frobe comes
to grief in the ocean.

airplanes. He and the director, Ken Annakin (an RAF flier in World War II), came up with a story about an early air race. Nine months were required for a small English construction company to build the 25 planes used in the film. Six of these were flyable, seven were for ground use, and twelve were two copies of each flyable plane, one to serve as a back-up aircraft in case of accidents and the other to be pulled apart for close-ups. The aircraft represented many types of early planes and included (as flying aircraft) a Bristol Box-Kite, an Eardly-Billings biplane, an Antoinette monoplane, a Blériot, an Avro triplane, and a French Demoiselle. The ground-bound aircraft were a Passat Ornithopter, a Walton Edwards Rhomboidal, a Picat Dubreuil, a **Deperdusson**, a Lee Richards Annular, a Dixon Nipper, and a Philips Multiplane. All these aircraft were powered by Volkswagen or Rolls Royce engines (for the larger ones). These provided the same horsepower as the original engines, for motors of greater power would have torn the planes apart. Built from original drawings in air archives in London and Paris, the planes averaged a 20-30-foot wing span, 85 horsepower, a top speed of 65 miles per hour, a flying time of one hour, a ceiling of several hundred feet, and they couldn't fly in anything stronger than a 10-15 mph breeze.

The movie makers encountered special problems trying to film the aerial sequences. Many times the weather refused to cooperate. Because the aircraft were so fragile, both the British and French authorities refused permission for them to fly over populated areas. For this reason the shot of the fliers circling the Eiffel Tower had to be done with models. An airfield that was undisturbed by modern civilization had to be found. Most of the flying scenes were shot at the Booker Air Field (Brookley Aerodrome in the film) in High Wycombe, an abandoned RAF base being used as a training center 50 miles from London.

Douglas Bianchi, Joan Hughes, John **Crewdson**, and Peter Hillwood, a former supersonic test pilot, were among the people who helped build and fly the planes. Miss Hughes proved her worth when it came time to fly the Demoiselle. This plane had been built from drawings in the Musée de l'Air in Paris, but it wouldn't fly. It was discovered that the original builder weighed only 110 pounds and the replica's builder, Douglas Bianchi, was 72 pounds too heavy for it. Since Miss Hughes was the right weight, she was able to get the plane in the air. The planes had no radios, and flag signals had to be used to inform the pilots when a retake was necessary. The aerial scenes were photographed by helicopter; and 289 technicians and 200 performers were used in the film.

The road show picture did not, as expected, cause a boom in plastic model airplanes of the period. The toy manufacturers felt that such models would be too hard to build.

OCTOBER WINGS (KRYLIA OKTIABRIA, 1967) was a Russian documentary about a 1966 air show in Moscow. PEOPLE OF THE SKY (LJUDI ZEMLI I NEBRA, 1969) was a biography of the Russian pilot Serge Garnajev.

Surprisingly, it wasn't until 1978 that a feature-length film was made dealing with the Wright Brothers. THE WINDS OF KITTY HAWK, an NBC television movie, amply demonstrated the problems with producing an exciting story about the Wrights. Although accurate replicas of the Wrights' aircraft were built and well photographed, even the characters of Glenn Curtiss and Alexander Graham Bell couldn't liven up the film. The historical facts were altered in a vain attempt to improve the story, and the actors playing Wilbur (Michael Moriarty) and Orville (David Hoffman) were so wooden that they made the picture almost unwatchable.

Cliff Robertson flew in and narrated A PLACE OF DREAMS, a 1979 PBS television show originating from the National Air and Space Museum on the history of flight. The NASM was also involved in another film. One of the most effective aviation movies ever made is not a commercial film, but the National Air and Space Museum's 30-minute history of flight, TO FLY. This, along with the Museum's FLYER, expertly conveys the true "feel" of aviation to the movie-goer.

Civilian aviators have been among the most difficult of aviation film subjects. At their worst, such films have been overly sentimental, like GALLANT JOURNEY, or just plain dull, as in the case of THE WINDS OF KITTY HAWK. But a few films, like THE SPIRIT OF ST. LOUIS and BREAKING THROUGH THE SOUND BARRIER, have been effective in involving the viewer with aviation pioneers on a personal level. Successes like these have resulted in moving, exciting film experiences.

CHAPTER 6

THE POWDER PUFF DERBY

"Ought women to aviate?" asked the <u>Detroit Free Press</u>
in 1911. Most men of the period didn't think so. Women were
too frail to operate a plane's controls, too unintelligent to understand what they were doing, and prone to panic in the
slightest emergency. But in spite of public disapproval and
financial problems, many women did learn to fly. It wasn't
long before women like Viola Gentry, Amy Johnson, and
Amelia Earhart captured world headlines and put to rest the
idea that no woman could match a male pilot.

Early filmmakers quickly capitalized on the female flier
theme. The comedy FLYING PAT (1920), for example, had a
husband who wanted his wife to develop a career. She choos-
es aviation and gets into trouble when her flying instructor
pays too much attention to her. THE SPEED GIRL (1921), on
the other hand, featured Bebe Daniels as 20-year-old Betty
Lee, a movie stunt girl who uses airplanes and motorcycles.

STRANGER THAN FICTION (1921), a First National
picture with Frank Clarke, had Katherine MacDonald as a
society girl filmmaker. She and her boyfriend, Dick, become involved with criminals who try to escape by airplane.
Dick battles the chief outlaw in the crook's plane, which
catches fire and dives. MacDonald, in her own plane,
throws Dick a parachute and picks him up as he floats down.
The film concluded by revealing that this action had really
been staged for a film being made by MacDonald. Apparently the filmmakers changed their intent while making the film,
for there is satirical comedy in the titles but not in the visuals. A combination of studio close-ups of the heroine and
her plane and aerial stunts done for the newsreel camera
made up the flying scenes. The crash of the criminals' aircraft included scenes shot from a camera placed on the diving plane.

ONE WEEK OF LOVE (1922), a Selznick picture, concerned a spoiled society girl who stakes her marriage on the outcome of an airplane race. Her lover wins, but she crashes and bandits capture her.

In DOLLAR DOWN (1925), a woman aviator saves the day for both her boyfriend and her father by keeping a crook up in an airplane while the option on some valuable property runs out.

BORN TO LOVE (1931) had a female aviator (Constance Bennett) involved with World War I romance.

In CHRISTOPHER STRONG (1933), Katharine Hepburn, in an early starring role, played Lady Cynthia Darrington, a round-the-world pilot who falls in love with Sir Christopher Strong. Hepburn promises to give up flying but when she becomes pregnant she commits suicide by flying to 30,000 feet and removing her oxygen mask so that she loses control of the plane.

The German film RIVALS OF THE AIR (RIVALEN DER LUFT, 1933) had Hanna Reitsch stunt-flying in a story with a heroine (Hilde Gebuhr) who is a glider pilot. She and her boyfriend (Claus Clausen) become passionately interested in gliding. After some romantic entanglements, they rediscover each other; and the boyfriend eventually wins a gliding competition. Reitsch began her aviation career as a record-setting glider pilot; she went on to become a test pilot for the Luftwaffe and eventually flew almost every type of German airplane, including the explosive Me 163 and the manned version of the V1.

WINGS IN THE DARK (1935) offered something a little different. Myrna Loy played a stunt pilot who barnstorms for a living. She talks Cary Grant, an aviator blinded in an accident just before he is about to fly to Paris, into writing airplane stories. He dictates them to her, but instead of sending them in she keeps them and pays him out of her own pocket. Grant is also working on a new invention for blind flying (no pun intended): an instrument panel for the sightless. But Grant's plane is taken away from him just before the panel is perfected and when Grant finds out what Loy has been doing, he sends her away. Angry, Loy decides to fly from Moscow to Paris and set a new world's record in the process. After flying across Russia, Europe, and the Atlantic Ocean, she becomes lost in a fog over Boston. Grant breaks into Roosevelt Field, steals a plane, and guides her safely down. Not wishing to be a burden, he plans to fly off but Loy smashes into him as they are landing, shocking his nervous system and restoring his sight in the process. Only in Hollywood!

FLYING HOSTESS (1936), a Universal Picture, was the first film to deal extensively with the training of air hostesses. As passenger ridership grew in the 1930s, European airlines recruited men to serve as stewards on airliners. American airlines, however, hired women nurses, and it was a proud airline that could boast it had registered nurses ready to administer to riders on every flight. The idea of nurse-staffed airplanes didn't exactly reassure the more nervous passengers, and the registered nurse soon gave way to the more traditional hostess. Theirs was not an easy lot, as one writer stated:

> Their duties were to bolt the seats to the floor before each flight, offer cotton for passengers' ears to muffle noise, make sure the passengers chose the door to the toilet instead of the nearby emergency exit, warn against throwing lighted cigar butts out the window and "carry a railroad timetable in case the plane is grounded somewhere."[1]

In FLYING HOSTESS, Judith Barrett starred and her character had the opportunity to bail out of a plane at 5,000 feet and land a transport plane after the pilot had been knocked out. The picture was a good advertisement for TWA, which had its name prominently displayed on the planes.

Interestingly, FLYING HOSTESS was previewed to New York critics in the air. Twelve of them were taken to the airport at Newark, New Jersey, put on a TWA plane, and taken aloft for a showing on the film while flying over New York. (This was not the first in-flight sound film, however. That happened on January 3, 1935 when the first public showing of the film BABOONS occurred on board a plane which took off from Newark and also flew over New York. This plane had Eddie Rickenbacker as the co-pilot.)

Bruce Cabot starred in LOVE TAKES FLIGHT (1937),

the story of a commercial pilot who leaves his stewardess girl friend (Beatrice Roberts) to become a film star. Angry, she attempts a solo flight to Manila (she's also a stunt pilot) but he stows on board and eventually saves her, parachuting out of the plane so that she gets credit for the flight. The poorly-done film was made in cooperation with American Airlines, which is very obvious.

In TAIL SPIN (1939), a Twentieth Century-Fox film written by Frank Wead and directed by Roy Del Ruth, women speed fliers took center stage. The picture dealt with three women pilots, played by Alice Faye, Constance Bennett, and Nancy Kelly. The picture centered around the efforts of these women to win the Women's Air Derby (the "Powder Puff" derby) from Los Angeles to Cleveland at the 1939 Cleveland Air Races. The picture contained good aerial sequences, including several crack-ups, and Paul Mantz was one of the technical directors. TAIL SPIN was advertised by its own traveling air circus. A group of women fliers and studio beauties made a tour of twenty-five key cities plugging the picture.

Not to be outdone, Warners set WOMEN IN THE WIND (1939) against the background of the "Powder Puff" derby and starred Kay Francis, in her last contract picture for Warners, as a woman pilot out to get money for her brother, an injured flier. The picture also included the breaking of the round-the-world flying record and the breaking of a transatlantic record from Dublin when the pilot was really headed for Moscow. This was obviously inspired by the exploits of "Wrong Way" Corrigan, who would soon get his own picture.

AIR MAIL (VOZDUSJNAJA POTJATA, 1939) was a Russian film about a female aviator. She faces difficulties when she flies medicines to a remote Far East children's hospital.

FLIGHT ANGELS (1940) was a Warner Brothers picture dealing with stewardesses. American Airlines was plugged in the film, which told of a crack pilot (Dennis Morgan) who has plenty of girls but who likes the airline's top stewardess (Virginia Bruce); she, however, doesn't like him. To complicate matters, Morgan's eyesight fails as he and his co-pilot (Wayne Morris) are perfecting a high-flying plane. Jane Wyman was also featured as a stewardess who pursues Morris.

THEY FLEW ALONE (1942, released in the U.S. as WINGS AND THE WOMAN) was an RKO release dealing with the life of flier Amy Johnson (Anna Neagle), a woman whose rebellious nature led her to fight prejudice against woman fliers and become a national hero. She flew a DeHavilland DH60 Gypsy Moth from England to Australia in May 1930 and earned the name "Lady Lindbergh." She broke speed records from London to Tokyo and from London to Cape Town, and was the first woman to fly the Atlantic. She married Jim Mollison, the "Flying Scot" and they became known as the "Flying Mollisons." Among their joint efforts was a flight to America in 1933. They were divorced and when the war came they joined Air Transport Auxiliary and both ferried bombers. In January 1941 the plane Amy was ferrying broke up and she parachuted into the Thames estuary. A young British Navy Commander dove off his vessel to save her, but she drowned and he died of exposure. The film details her early interest in flying, her solo flight to Australia, her marriage to Jim Mollison, their flight to America, their divorce, Johnson's job as a ferry pilot, and her fatal crash. The blue Gypsy Moth (named "Jason") used in the film was Johnson's original plane and the one she used in her Australian flight. Critics praised the picture as a frank biography and Mollison, then flying British bombers to Africa, approved it in spite of the uncomplimentary things it included about him. The print was cut from 104 to 96 minutes for U.S. distribution.

PARACHUTE NURSE (1942) was a minor Columbia release about the training of nurses who parachute onto the battlefield. Much of the action was concerned with parachute packing.

The next aviation film was RKO's FLIGHT FOR FREEDOM (1943), originally called STAND BY TO DIE). The uneven picture starred Rosalind Russell as a pilot patterned after Amelia Earhart. She makes her first solo flight in 1932 and meets expert flier Fred MacMurray. They have a brief romance, but MacMurray doesn't think women should be pilots. Russell sets out to prove him wrong by breaking his records. She flies in the Bendix cross-country race and breaks the Los Angeles to New York record. When she decides on an around-the-world flight, the Navy asks her to lose herself in the Pacific so that the Navy can use a search for her as an excuse to photograph the Japanese

Mandated Islands. She finds her navigator is to be MacMurray, although she is now engaged to plane designer Herbert Marshall. She discovers the Japanese have learned of the plan and intend to rescue her quickly, so she crashes suicidally in the ocean to give a reason for the search. The film ends with MacMurray dive-bombing Japanese fortifications pinpointed as a result of Russell's sacrifice. The film begins with a preface that American naval actions in the Pacific were possible because of "one pretty girl." A few over-water shots were filmed at San Pedro, but the coastal defense prohibition of civilian flying forced the filmmakers to shoot most of the aerial sequences over land (in Phoenix, Arizona).

RKO did not confirm or deny that FLIGHT FOR FREEDOM had any connection with Amelia Earhart. But her husband, George **Putnam**, was given $7,500 when the story was bought, even though he didn't give RKO permission to use Earhart's name in the film or in its advertising. Obviously the film was based on Earhart's life, for the plane in which Russell dies is a twin-engined Lockheed Electra, like the plane used by Earhart.

THE LADY TAKES A FLIER (1958) had two pilots, Maggie (Lana Turner) and Mike (Jeff Chandler), operating a thriving international ferry service. They marry, but quarrel over the domestic chores. Their squabbles form the basis for this sometimes funny comedy. Written and directed by Jack Arnold, the film has some witty moments, particularly when Chandler has an argument about his little daughter with an ex-WAC babysitter. The flying shots are highlighted by a transatlantic hop by Chandler and a tense situation when Turner has to land in a London fog.

COME FLY WITH ME (1962) was an aviation comedy dealing with three stewardesses on a transatlantic run. On the route, the girls set out to get men from the assorted passengers. Donna Stewart (Dolores Hart) looks for a potential rich husband and finds a baron who uses her to smuggle diamonds. Hilda Birgstrom (Lois Nettleton) goes after a Texas multi-millionaire (Karl Malden). And Carol Brewster (Pamela Tiffin), the novice stewardess, aims for the affections of the first flight officer (Hugh **O'Brian**). The picture was filmed largely in Paris and Vienna, and the interior plane shots were done in a studio mock-up of a passenger jet. The film has a few good moments, as when a crew member solemnly explains to Tiffin the dangers of "cavitation," which can only be corrected by flushing the front and rear toilets of the aircraft every five minutes.

BOEING BOEING (1965) was a kind of sequel to COME FLY WITH ME, for it was the story of three more stewardesses. These three are kept on a string by a Paris-based newspaper man (Tony Curtis). The girls' flight schedules allow only one of them to be in Paris at any one time, so each thinks she's the only girl in Curtis's life. This arrangement is spoiled, however, when Boeing introduces a new jetliner which results in the girls' flight schedules being changed. The girls are pretty, Thelma Ritter is good as Curtis's housekeeper, and the film is an entertaining comedy.

WINGS (KRYLJA, 1966) was a film by female Russian director Larisa Sjepitkos which tells of a female aviator, ex-flying ace Nadiezda Pietruchina, who is told she can no longer fly, for health reasons. She is, however, able to overcome her problem and fly again.

WINGS OF FIRE (1967) was a below-average made-for-TV movie starring Suzanne Pleshette as a flier determined to win an air race to save her father's freight service.

The STEWARDESSES (1970) was a 3D, X-rated pornographic look at stewardesses' adventures. The picture was later released in a flat R-rated version. COFFEE TEA OR ME? (1973) was a made-for-TV movie starring Karen Valentine as a stewardess with a unique problem: a husband at each end of her New York-to-Los Angeles run. FLYING HIGH (1975), a made-for-TV movie about three stewardesses, spawned a short-lived (1978-1979) television series. In an effort to make the series more believable, the three stars of the show talked with real flight attendants to get a feel for the problems of stewardesses.

AMELIA EARHART (1976) was a two-and-one-half-hour made-for-television movie dealing with the aviatrix. Susan Clark played Earhart and John Forsythe played her husband, the publisher George Putnam. The film blended Earhart's public and private lives with some degree of success, but overall it was not a great film. Stephen Macht played Paul Mantz.

SKYWARD (1980) starred Bette Davis in an NBC television film about a former woman stunt pilot who takes a paraplegic (played by Suzy Gilstrap, a real life paraplegic) under her wing and teaches her to fly. Charlie Hillard served as chief stunt pilot for the film, which featured his Christen Eagle II. The film debuted at the Kennedy Center in Washington, D.C. as part of the ceremonies surrounding President Carter's proclamation of 1981 as the "Year of the Handicapped." The film was popular enough to warrant a sequel, and SKYWARD CHRISTMAS (1981) reunited the same cast and flight team.

SWING SHIFT (1984) starred Goldie Hawn as Kay, a woman whose world changes radically when her husband Jack

Goldie Hawn (center) goes to work in a Dauntless factory in SWING SHIFT (1984).

(Ed Harris) goes to war on December 8, 1941. Along with many other women, she gets a job riveting in an aircraft factory, at a California company that manufactures 7,500 SBD Dauntless dive bombers by the end of World War II. The women experience great resentment from the men who have been working at the plant, but they eventually overcome it. Kay also has a relationship with her supervisor (Kurt Russell), a trumpet-playing 4-F type who convinces Kay she should have the affair with him and not worry about her husband. When Jack returns on leave in 1944 and learns what's going on, he's understandably upset. The war ends, all the women workers are fired, and Kay and Jack are reconciled.

SWING SHIFT is a dreadful movie that captures neither the spirit of the 1940s nor the problems of factory workers. The film tries to cover too much time and too many themes. The movie juggles Kay's feelings about going to work, her relationship with her husband, her affair with her boyfriend, and her attitude toward one of her female co-workers to such an extent that none is dealt with satisfactorily. There are lots of shots of women riveting SBD fuselages, but the flying shots are done with AT-6s. The screenplay credits underwent several changes before the film was released, with Robert Towne among the several writers who asked that their names be removed from the film.

Women aviators have secured a unique place for themselves in aviation history, but they have received relatively little attention from filmmakers. Few films have effectively dealt with the multitude of problems these pilots faced.

CHAPTER 7

BANDITS, TWELVE O'CLOCK HIGH

"The battle for France is over. The battle of Britain
is about to begin." With these words Winston Churchill un-
derscored England's coming struggle. The first German attacks of World War II made such words as "blitzkrieg" and
"Stuka" part of the common language. The Battle of Britain
showed that the Luftwaffe could be beaten. And the strategic bombing of Germany added a whole new dimension to
aerial warfare. These events provided aviation filmmakers
with the material for some of the most exciting and dramatic
airplane films.

The first film dealing with the World War II air war
was a propaganda one, THE LION HAS WINGS (1939), a
British film that was also England's first propaganda picture
of the war. The picture was produced by Alexander Korda
during twelve days and nights, and starred Ralph Richardson and Merle Oberon. THE LION HAS WINGS, made with
the cooperation of the Royal Air Force, used a March of
Time-style technique (and Lowell Thomas' narration) to depict RAF operations, particularly during the raid on a pocket
battleship in the Kiel Canal (using some actual newsreel footage of planes taking off for the raid and returning) and the
repulsing of a fictional German air attack on London. Despite
the film's obvious propaganda, it impressed the critics favorably, and Time called it "... excellently made...."[1] Made in
the fall of 1939, the film had considerable material on balloon
barrages and munition factory interiors cut out by British
censors. The Kiel raid was made to look easy, causing Nazi
radio to call it "'A celluloid fairy tale.'"[2]

BOMBER WING LUTZOW (KAMPFGESCHWÄDER, 1940),
a Tobias production, was a sequel to the film D III 88. The
principal actors from that earlier film also starred in this

151

movie. As in D III 88, Hermann Braun and Heinz Welzel played two close friends who join a bomber squadron in August 1939 that attacks Poland. The film was backed by the German Ministry of Defense and featured actual combat footage. The two fliers ultimately see action against England. Both men love the same girl. Welzel is wounded in a raid, but gets his plane and crew safely to base before he dies.

The Russians produced a number of films dealing with the war. THE 5TH SQUADRON (ESKADRILJA NR. 5) was released in 1941. AN AIR TAXI (KRYLATYJ TZVOSTJIK, 1943) mixed comedy and romance in telling of a pilot battling the Germans. THE SKY FLIGHT (NEBESNYJ TICHOCHOD, 1945) dealt with a light reconnaissance squadron. THE WAY TO THE STARS (DOROGA KZVIODAM, 1942), WAIT FOR ME (ZDIMENJA, 1943), and THE MOSCOW SKY (or MOSCOW SKIES; NEBO MOSKUY, 1944) also depicted the war. This last film was the only one of the group to be shown in the West. The documentary (with English subtitles) detailed the defense of Moscow by air in the fall of 1941. The film mixed a tepid plot about a daring Army pilot who has an affair with an Army nurse with newsreel footage of aerial combat.

By the summer of 1941 more British documentary films were released in the U.S. Among a group of fifteen shown at the Museum of Modern Art under the title "The Art of Britain at War" was AIR COMMUNIQUE. This showed how aerial combat "kills" were tabulated. The film featured some good aerial combat scenes and Squadron 992 detailing the organization and training of a balloon barrage crew assigned to protect the Firth of Forth Bridge in Scotland.

DANGEROUS MOONLIGHT (1941, also called SUICIDE SQUADRON) was an RKO British production about a Polish flier (Anton Walbrook) who is also a musician. The film is told in a flashback, after the flier recovers his memory. When the Nazis invade Poland, the flier's friends convince him he should escape because his music is more important to the cause than his flying. Before leaving, he meets an American newswoman (Sally Gray). On a fund-raising concert tour of America, Walbrook meets Gray again and they are married. But Walbrook feels he must fly, and he goes to England and joins the Polish Squadron of the Royal Air Force. Eventually he rams a Nazi bomber, after his ammuni-

tion is exhausted, and loses his memory. Gray helps him to
recover it. The story and script were written by Terrence
Young, who, at the time of production, was a sergeant major
in the army. The director, Brian Desmond Hurst, felt that
escapism in a war-time environment was difficult and that
DANGEROUS MOONLIGHT's music would give people a chance
to relax. Walbrook played the piano in the film.

INTERNATIONAL SQUADRON (1941) starred Ronald
Reagan as an ex-air circus daredevil who ferries a bomber
to England and decides to stay to fly in the foreign squadron of the Royal Air Force. His individualistic manners at
first get him into trouble, but he eventually learns responsibility and team work. He goes to his death when he sets
out to blow up a munitions dump on the French coast. The
film, suggested by a play by Frank Wead, featured Mantz's
stunt flying. The picture opens with a test power dive and
features good aerial action.

The next major aviation film was Twentieth Century-
Fox's A YANK IN THE R.A.F. (1941), based on a story by
producer Darryl F. Zanuck (under the name of Melville Crossman) and directed by Henry King. The story dealt with a
former airline pilot, Tyrone Power, who ferries a bomber to
England for the money. While there, he meets a former girl
friend, Betty Grable, who is performing in a nightclub and
driving an ambulance. To be near her, he enlists in the
R.A.F. He is first assigned to a leaflet-dropping mission over
Berlin, but later sees combat during the raids and during air
cover for the retreating Dunkirk forces. The romance becomes a triangle with the involvement of a wing commander,
played by John Sutton. The original ending in which Power
is killed was unacceptable to a preview audience and it was
changed. The romantic triangle was never resolved.

The picture was filmed in both the United States and
England with the approval of Lord Beaverbrook, the British
Air Ministry, the R.A.F., and the American and Canadian
governments. It proved to be the first Hollywood film to use
dramatically the Battle of Britain and the Fall of France.
Production of A YANK IN THE R.A.F. involved recording
actual combat footage. Originally, Twentieth Century-Fox
planned to use British war department footage in the picture. But this was 16mm and the producers felt that when
this was blown up to 35mm the contrast with the rest of the

Publicity tie-in for A YANK IN THE R.A.F. (1941), showing
Tyrone Power and Betty Grable, his "dream" girl.

film's scenes would be too great. So two Fox cameramen went aloft with a defending squadron. Their plane was shot down in a dogfight and both were killed. They weren't the only filmmakers to go into battle. Joe Delfino, Fox's sound expert, explained: "This war has made valueless at least $100,000 in sound effects in our studio alone.... Even the roar of airplane motors of three years ago is archaic. The new types of bombs, shells and other explosives have to be recorded at great expense for future war pictures."[3] So a crew in England recorded these sound effects under fire.

Mantz flew for the film and the airfield footage was shot in California at night at the Lockheed airport, with a hundred Hudson bombers doubling for the planes at the R.A.F. base south of London. Lockheed employees served as extras, and fifty policemen, "... the largest number of guards ever posted around a movie set," kept order.[4] The Dunkirk sequence was shot in the studio tank, with the use of compressed air running through pipes under water to simulate bomb explosions. These "blasts" soaked and unnerved the extras to the point where they demanded stunt wages ($25 a day, compared to their usual $5.50). A compromise netted them $16.50.

The picture premiered in New York at the beginning of October 1941 at the Roxy Theatre, promoted by a carnival and a ball benefiting the British-American Ambulance Corps. Ironically, the film opened at a time when a Senate subcommittee was in its third week of investigation of alleged war-mongering in Hollywood (see Chapter 10). The film was generally well received by the critics.

Following A YANK IN THE R.A.F. was TARGET FOR TONIGHT (1941), a British film released in the U.S. by Warner Bros. The 48-minute picture, directed by Harry Watt, details one complete bombing mission of a plane labeled "F for Freddie." It covers from the reception of the reconnaisance photos which show that a new oil dump has been set up in Freihausen, Germany, through the pre-flight preparations and briefings, and the night attack of the Wellingtons on the dump, to the anxious waiting until all the planes from the mission have landed at their bases. The picture was made with the cooperation of the R.A.F. and released with the approval of the Ministry of Aviation. Each man played himself, and no professional actors were used. The bomber crew included Squadron Leader Dickson, former head of the Czech squadron; Flying Officer Willett, who made 40 trips over Germany before going to a training camp as an instructor; Flight Sergeant MacPherson, the navigator; and Flight Sergeant Lee, the radio operator and a footman at 10 Downing Street before the war. Also playing himself was Air Marshall Richard Peirse, Commander in Chief of the R.A.F. Bomber Command.

STUKAS (1941) was a German picture that was "... a kind of Nazi counterpart to Warners' 'Air Force.'"[5] The picture, directed by Karl Ritter, dealt with a Ju-87 Stuka squadron about the time of the fall of France and showed action against Liège, Dunkirk, the Marne, and combat with French tank formations. The film stressed the morale of the fliers, but without the kind of feeling of films such as AIR FORCE. If American producers sometimes thought they had distribution problems, they were nothing compared to trying to get STUKAS shown in the western hemisphere. The Nazis tried without success to smuggle it into Buenos Aires on a Portuguese vessel in 1942. Every Latin American country except Argentina had banned the showing of Axis pictures, and only some string-pulling got the film shown in Buenos Aires in 1943.

The year 1942 began with the British picture, SHIPS WITH WINGS, which dealt with German attempts to sink the aircraft carrier H.M.S. Ark Royal in the Mediterranean. The picture, made with the cooperation of the British Admiralty, took almost 18 months to produce, and cost about $600,000. The story tells of a pilot in the Fleet Air Arm, played by John Clements, who takes up a plane without permission. A crash takes the life of his passenger and Clements is court-martialed. He ends up running a one-man airline in the Mediterranean. He discovers a German ploy to sink the Ark Royal and warns the British. A great deal of aerial action ensues (much of it done with models), with the hero finally locking his plane with a German one and crashing both into a dam, which wipes out the Germans. The 140-minute film was cut to 91 minutes for U.S. release.

THE WIFE TAKES A FLIER (1942), a comedy, starred Franchot Tone as a downed pilot in Holland hidden by a Dutch household. A Nazi mayor moves into the household and Tone is passed off as the mentally defective husband of

Joan Bennett. Tone and Bennett fall in love and Tone flies them to England in a stolen German plane.

Next came a Warner Bros. picture, CAPTAINS OF THE CLOUDS (1942), directed by Michael Curtiz and shot in Technicolor. James Cagney played one of a group of bush pilots (the others played by Dennis Morgan, Alan Hale, Reginald Gardiner, and George Tobias) flying in northern Canada. Inspired by Churchill's "We Shall Never Surrender" speech, they enlist in the Royal Canadian Air Force. They are too old, however, to be sent into combat so they are assigned to train pilots. Cagney's individualism makes him a rebel and he is court-martialed and dismissed from the service when one of his pupils is killed. He redeems himself when, as a civilian, he is ferrying a bomber to England. The unarmed flight is attacked by a Messerschmitt and Cagney rams into it, killing himself but saving the flight.

Most of the picture was made in Canada in the summer of 1940 with the cooperation of the Canadian Government and the Royal Canadian Air Force. Appearing as himself in the film, giving wings to 1000 cadets, was Canada's Air Marshal William Avery "Billy" Bishop, the World War I ace. (Bishop's film biography was produced in 1983.) Elmer Dyer did the aerial photography and Mantz flew for the filmmakers. The film contains good aerial footage of the bush pilots flying over Ontario's North Bay country, as well as shots of the cadets training. The film premiered in February 1942, and 200 RCAF fliers, as well as several Canadian diplomats and war officials, came to New York for the occasion. There were simultaneous premieres in London, Cairo, Ottawa, Toronto, and Vancouver. The critics thought the film propaganda, but generally praised it.

THE DAY WILL DAWN (1942) was a British effort starring Ralph Richardson and Deborah Kerr. It told of an English journalist sent to Norway at the war's start. He returns to England when the Germans invade Norway and is asked by the War Office to guide the Royal Air Force to a secret U-boat base in a fiord. He parachutes in, signals the location of the base to the fliers, and is rescued by commandos.

EAGLE SQUADRON (1942) starred Robert Stack in a C. S. Forester story about American pilots who flew in the

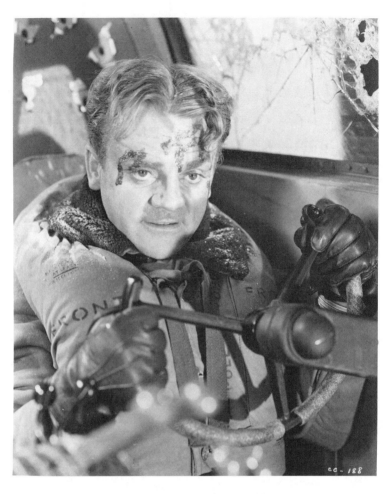

James Cagney gets set to ram a Messerschmitt with his Lockheed Hudson, in CAPTAINS OF THE CLOUDS (1942).

Eddie Albert (second from right) and fellow airmen in EAGLE SQUADRON (1942).

R.A.F. before America entered the war. The picture opened with a foreword, spoken by Quentin Reynolds, telling of these Americans while showing shots of some of them. Stack played a pilot who has trouble accepting the reserved British attitude. The picture includes aerial footage taken from 13,000 feet of combat footage shot by producer Walter Wanger's crew with the approval of the British Ministry of Information. The film contains dogfights, bombing raids across the Channel, air-sea rescue, and a climactic commando raid in which Stack steals a new secret German plane. While the aerial material was exciting, the film suffered from a below-average plot and indecision by its makers as to whether or not it should be a documentary. Originally, six real members of the Eagle Squadron were to have played the leads, one of these an ex-Hollywood

make-up artist by the name of Gus Daymond, holder of the
D.F.C.

ATLANTIC CONVOY (1942) was a Columbia release
starring Bruce Bennett and John Beal. It dealt with U.S.
air patrols off the coast of Iceland and a group of spies
providing shipping information to German U-boats. Beal,
a weatherman operator, is suspected of aiding the Nazis,
and in the end he vindicates himself by aiding U.S. planes
in the sinking of a fishing boat that is the contact with the
sub, even though he is on board the boat at the time.

FLYING FORTRESS (1942) was a minor Warners film
about an American playboy (Richard Greene) who becomes a
ferry pilot for the fun of it but then joins the Air Force
when he sees how desperately the English are fighting. The
major heroics occur when the hero climbs out of his plane to
patch a hole in its side; this was based on an actual incident.
The film was made in cooperation with the British authorities.

Raoul Walsh directed Warners' adventure film DESPER-
ATE JOURNEY (1942), which starred Errol Flynn, Ronald
Reagan, and Raymond Massey. It told of the crew of the
bomber "D for Danny" which is shot down on a raid into
Germany. The five surviving crew members, including
Flynn and Reagan, wreak considerable havoc in this comic
strip-type film before stealing a British bomber the Germans
had captured and flying it back to England.

The British-made ONE OF OUR AIRCRAFT IS MISSING
(1942) combined the documentary approach of TARGET FOR
TONIGHT (in showing the bombing mission) with the theme
of DESERPATE JOURNEY and came up with the story of six
members of a bomber crew whose Wellington ("B for Bertie")
is severely damaged in a raid on Stuttgart. They bail out
over Holland and are aided by Dutch citizens who help them
escape. Made in cooperation with the Netherlands government in exile, the picture was announced under the titles
ONE OF OUR AIRCRAFT HAS FAILED TO RETURN, ONE OF
OUR AIRCRAFT FAILED, and ONE OF OUR AIRCRAFT.

THE FIRST OF THE FEW was another British picture,
released in September 1942 but not shown in the U.S. until
the middle of 1943 (under the title SPITFIRE). Produced
and directed by Leslie Howard, it told the story of R. J.

Mitchell (played by Howard), who designed the Spitfire fighter. The film begins on September 15, 1940 when R.A.F. pilots have just downed 185 German planes during a single day in the Battle of Britain. The pilots are talking about their planes and discover that they know nothing about the man who designed the Spitfire. The station commander relates Mitchell's story and the film flashes back to 1922 when Mitchell gets the idea for an advanced fighter. He builds racing planes which capture victory in the Schneider Cup Races of 1927-29 and 1931. A visit to Germany in 1935 brings the realization that the Germans are building a powerful air force. Eventually, Mitchell convinces the British government of the need for Spitfires, but completing the work so injures his health that he dies in 1937 at the age of 42.

The film included action footage of the Battle of Britain and a re-creation of the 1927 Schneider Cup Race. A section of the Venice waterfront was re-created on a sound stage, complete with the winning plane, a blue and silver Supermarine S. 6.

Samuel Goldwyn acquired U.S. rights to the picture and released it through RKO. The film was cut from 118 minutes to 90 minutes for U.S. release. Ironically, it opened in the States only days after Howard died, killed when the plane he was flying in from Lisbon to London on government business was shot down.

By late 1942 another kind of aviation film had become established: documentary, training, and/or educational films dealing with aviation. Filmed in various lengths, they were produced by the U.S. government, the Armed Forces, or individual companies or organizations, and were available in silent, sound, and/or color versions in various film sizes. For example, BOMBER (1941) was made as a "defense report on film" by the Office for Emergency Management's film unit. It was made at the Glenn L. Martin Company's Baltimore plant and was a ten-minute documentary on the construction and flight of the B-26 bomber; it featured a commentary by Carl Sandburg. The Bell Aircraft Corporation offered to lend to any recognized organization its 25-minute, 16mm film CANNONS ON WINGS (1942), with a sound track and in color, detailing the construction and flight characteristics of the Bell P-39 Airacobra. Official Films provided WINGS FOR VICTORY, a feature-length film for home use (available in

8mm and 16mm silent and 16mm sound) about the Arctic air lanes and the development of the region for wartime use.

Of all the units producing this type of film, the most important was the Army **Air Force's** First Motion Picture Unit (FMPU) headed by Paul Mantz. Mantz, then a Major in the Air Force (later a Lieutenant Colonel), had been given the job of helping put together "... a Hollywood Air Force **capable of turning out millions of** feet of combat training film, and organize global teams of professional combat photography units to record [the operations of the AAF]."[6] So Mantz left United Air Service in charge of his wife and chief test pilot and went to FMPU, which was activated on July 1, 1942. On September 22 he became commanding officer, replacing Colonel Jack Warner who had left the Army and gone back to his studio. FMPU moved from Vitagraph into the Hal Roach Studios in Culver City in October; the studio became known as Fort Roach and its inhabitants the Culver City Commandos. Among the people Mantz assembled were Frank Clarke and Elmer Dyer, whom he needed to help train combat photographers. Hollywood writers, stars, directors, cinematographers and others were recruited and became members of the six active film units.

During its lifetime the FMPU produced more than 300 films and Combat Camera Units photographed 3,000,000 feet of overseas combat footage. Among these films were LEARN TO LIVE, the first Fort Roach training film, a flying safety film in which Mantz stunted his Boeing P-12 through barns and under bridges. PILOTS' HEAVEN showed how not to commit twelve fatal flying errors. BRIEFING FOR THE NORTH ATLANTIC gave pilots instruction on how to fly the North Atlantic ferry route. TARGET FOR TODAY, the American equivalent of TARGET FOR TONIGHT (because of course, the British bombed at night while the Americans practiced daylight strategic bombing), showed the Eighth Air Force bombers and fighters on raids against Europe. COMBAT AMERICA was a color film about flexible gunners on bombers, in part produced by Clark Gable who served in this capacity on five combat missions. (This film was not released because it duplicated the material of another film, THE MEMPHIS BELLE.) DITCH AND LIVE showed how to survive in the ocean, while LAND AND LIVE showed how to survive if downed on land. THE EARTHQUAKERS told about the 321st Bombardment Group's action with B-25's in North Africa. TARGET TOKYO gave detailed instruction on the flight path B-29s were to take on fire-bombing missions to Ota, Japan. Other films included MISSION OF A BOMB, FIGHTER GROUP, RESISTING ENEMY INTERROGATION, B-29 FLIGHT ENGINEER, and, one of the best of the FMPU films, THE MEMPHIS BELLE (discussed later).

Back in the commercial Hollywood world, SQUADRON LEADER X (1943) told of a German squadron leader (Eric Portman) who dresses in an RAF uniform and parachutes into a Belgian town as a spy.

BOMBER'S MOON (1943) starred George Montgomery in a Twentieth Century-Fox film as an American flier who goes down over enemy territory. He's captured by the Germans, but escapes with a woman Soviet medical corps lieutenant (Annabella) and a German spy (Kent Taylor). Montgomery and Annabella make it to Holland, where she takes a fishing boat to England while Montgomery steals an enemy bomber and flies it home. The film contained a few flying sequences.

THE PURPLE V (1943) was another low-budget film about a German schoolmaster who helps an American flier return to the Allied lines with secret information on the North African campaign.

Karl Ritter (director of STUKAS) made THE DORA CREW (BESÄTZUNG DORA, 1943). Banned by German censors and never shown in Germany during the war, the film told of a pilot (Hanner Stelzer) who flies Ju-88's on the Eastern Front and dreams of settling with his girl in occupied Russia after the war. By 1943 nobody, Hitler included, believed this would ever happen, so the film was banned.

The next documentary was Lieutenant Colonel Frank Capra's BATTLE OF BRITAIN (1943), the fourth in the WHY WE FIGHT series. The film was designed to be shown in U.S. Army basic training centers, and it consisted of previously-released newsreel clips (Army-released for the first time) and captured Nazi footage. The British liked it so much that American correspondents thought it should be shown commercially in the U.S.

The next film was one of the best aviation documentaries to come out of World War II: MEMPHIS BELLE (1944).

The 41-minute picture, made by Hollywood director Lieutenant Colonel William Wyler, noted cameraman Major William C. Clothier, and Lieutenant Harold Tannenbaum, told the story of the B-17 Memphis Belle's 25th mission, the last before it was sent home, from the pre-flight briefings to the attack on the heavily defended Wilhelmshaven, Germany, to the return home where the crew was decorated for its efforts. Paramount began distributing 500 prints of the four-reel film to almost 9,000 theatres in April 1944 on a non-profit basis, a gesture which prompted Army Air Force General H. H. Arnold to write a letter of thanks to the President of Paramount.

Production of MEMPHIS BELLE began when Lieutenant General Ira C. Eaker, chief of the Eighth Air Force, assigned Wyler to do the film. The crew set out for England in early summer of 1942, but their 35mm cameras and sound equipment was lost when the transporting ship didn't reach England. Most of the film, therefore, was shot with hand-held 16mm cameras using Kodachrome stock, which was processed in Technicolor and blown up to 35mm for theatrical release. Filming problems included enclosing the cameras in electrically heated pads to keep them from freezing in the 40° below zero temperatures in which the bombers operated at five miles up. Wyler and the crew made a total of thirteen flights over such targets as Brest, St. Nazaire, and Lorient, in France, and Bremen, Kiel, Vegesak, and Wilhelmshaven in Germany to get the footage they needed. Wyler and Clothier each flew five missions and Wyler was on board the Memphis Belle on its 25th mission. Unfortunately, Tannenbaum was killed on his fourth mission when his B-17 went down over Brest. (The Memphis Belle went on to fly another 25 missions and was never seriously damaged in combat.)

Wyler returned to the States in November 1943 with 16,000 feet of film. After about 20 different tries, he'd edited this down to a 4,000-foot film. The editing work was done at the FMPU's Fort Roach. One side effect was the stopping of general release of Clark Gable's COMBAT AMERICA; the Office of War Information felt it duplicated MEMPHIS BELLE. The OWI did release that seven-reel film in a 16mm version, but only for non-theatrical showings.

Critics praised MEMPHIS BELLE. Time called it "... one of the few genuinely exciting U.S. documentaries," and

The New York Times said, "It might literally be termed the duty of every American to see this film and learn from it why the debt to our young fliers is one we'll forever owe."[7]

COASTAL COMMAND (1944) was a sort of English equivalent to MEMPHIS BELLE, for this one-hour documentary dealt with one week in the life of a "T for Tommie" Sunderland flying boat, and its missions patrolling the waterways. Produced for the Ministry of Information and with the cooperation of the Royal Air Force and Royal Navy, the film depicted an attack on a German U-boat, patrolling on convoy duty, and an attack on a German cruiser. Continuing with the sea duty theme was a fictional story, FOR THOSE IN PERIL (1944), a British production about the operations of the English Air Sea Rescue service which, in the film at least, serves as a dumping ground for men who can't be fliers in the R.A.F. because they don't meet the physical requirements.

'TIL WE MEET AGAIN (1944) told the story of a French nun (Barbara Britton) helping a downed American aviator (Ray Milland) who must get to England with vital French underground information. RED DEVIL PARATROOPS (1944) was a Paramount News effort showing the airborne invasion of Arnhem. Although the film rightly stated that "the heroes of Arnhem" were British soldiers, the troops shown were American. The New York Times called this "... a reckless distortion of fact."[8]

A MATTER OF LIFE AND DEATH (1945, released in the United States as STAIRWAY TO HEAVEN) was an offbeat British film about a bomber pilot (David Niven) who jumps from a burning plane after his crew has been killed. He doesn't have a parachute, but he doesn't want to be burned to death. He doesn't die, however, because of a mix-up in heaven's bookkeeping. When heaven's emissary comes for him, Niven defends his right to live and wins his case.

JOURNEY TOGETHER (1945) was a British film starring Richard Attenborough and Edward G. Robinson. The semi-documentary was directed by John Boulting and featured members of the Royal Air Force, the Royal Canadian Air Force, and the U.S. Army Air Force. It told of two fliers training to be fighter pilots in the R.A.F. One of the pilots (Attenborough) washes out and has to settle for a navigator's position on a bomber.

THUNDERBOLT (1945) was a 43-minute Technicolor film about the 57th Fighter Group based in Corsica. Directed by William Wyler, the film told of air power's role in the bombing of enemy supply lines behind the Gustav line during the American and British advance in Italy. The footage came from automatic cameras installed in the Thunderbolts. The film was not completed until the war's end, and it did not go into general release.

The end of World War II brought with it an end to the war motion picture, and nowhere in the film industry was this more deeply felt than in the aviation film genre. The Second World War provided the aviation filmmaker with some of his best material. But by 1946 this material had become box office poison and it would not be until late in 1948 that major war films of any type were again made.

FALSELY EQUIPPED (BESPKOJNOJE CHOZJAJSTVO, 1946) was a Russian film about a group of men who build a phony air base to decoy the Germans. OUR HEART (NASJE SERDTSE, 1946) had a Russian airplane designer in the war determined to improve the efficiency of Soviet airplanes. The film takes liberties with Soviet jet development history. The picture ends with a round-the-world non-stop flight.

The year 1946 closed out with perhaps the best picture ever made about returning servicemen after a war, THE BEST YEARS OF OUR LIVES. Directed by William Wyler and written by Robert Sherwood (from the novel, Glory for Me), the film tells of three World War II returning servicemen: a middle-aged infantry sergeant (Fredric March) who comes home to a wife, two children, and a steady job at a bank; an Air Force bombardier captain (Dana Andrews) who is skilled only in dropping bombs on target and has to get a job in the place where he worked as a soda jerk before the war; and a double-amputee young sailor (Harold Russell, a real amputee) who must adjust, along with his family and girl friend, to the fact he has lost both his hands.

The film contains only one aviation sequence, showing the three men flying home in a B-17, hedgehopping across America. This was shot through the plexiglass nose of Mantz's B-25 camera ship. But the scene at the movie's end, when Dana Andrews wanders through a graveyard of stripped Fortresses (filmed at Ontario, California) beautifully

Dana Andrews re-lives his wartime experiences in a scrapped B-17 in THE BEST YEARS OF OUR LIVES (1946).

sums up the alienation that many veterans felt. They were
no longer at home in the service, but they didn't fit into
civilian life, either. Andrews relives his wartime B-17 experiences, and in doing so recalls the past and purges himself. He ends up getting a job with a junk dealer who is
stripping down B-17s for houses.

THEY ARE NO ANGELS (1948, BATAILLON DU CIEL),
a French film released in the United States with subtitles,
dealt with four hundred French paratroopers training in
England before D-Day and then in battle after the invasion.
The film is best in its first half, where brawls between the
men and comedy scenes are interspersed with the training of
paratroopers. The movie is given over to melodrama in the
second half as the men drop into occupied France to battle
the Germans in commando fashion. The best moments in the
film, and the main aviation shots, come during the mass formation parachute drop.

THE STORY OF A REAL MAN (POVEST O NASTOJASJ-
TJEM TJELOVEKE, 1948), a Russian version of REACH FOR
THE SKY, is about a legless pilot who learns to fly again.

By the end of 1948 Warner Brothers felt the public was
ready for a major war picture, and they released FIGHTER
SQUADRON. Not only was it the first major combat film to
appear after World War II; it was the first of a new series of
war films, aviation or otherwise. The film maintained the
blood-and-guts tradition of the war pictures of the early
forties and seemed a little out of place in the post-war environment.

FIGHTER SQUADRON details the actions of a group of
pilots stationed at the Third Fighter Group Base in England
and the evolution of fighter tactics immediately preceding D-
Day. The movie was a departure from previous European
war aviation films in that it told of pursuit planes and their
pilots. Most of the successful aviation pictures of World
War II were not primarily concerned with operations of this
type. To stress the offensive power of the U.S. there was
a concerted effort during the war to publicize bomber personnel and operations. Fighter pilots had been dealt with
in pre-war films.

The plot of FIGHTER SQUADRON concerns the fliers

who shoot down the enemy, strafe his ground troops, drink, kid each other, and constantly volunteer for an extra tour of duty. Their biggest battle is with the top brass, to persuade them to introduce new tactics into aerial fighting. These include dropping belly tanks before engaging the enemy and going to low altitude if necessary. Quite obviously, these aren't going to win the war overnight, nor are they particularly original. The film's characters embody the virtues one expects of movie fighter pilots. The tough squadron commander (Edmond O'Brien) chews out his best friend for the good of the outfit. The captain (Robert Stack) goes home to be married, but hurries back to rescue his major, even landing behind enemy lines to save him. (This was reportedly based on a real-life incident.) The film contains just about all of the air war picture clichés, but the director, Raoul Walsh, manages to make them bearable by manipulating the audience's emotions through a combination of light comedy and tense drama.

That the film belongs more with the group of propaganda pictures made during the war than with the post-war film trends is evidenced by the great pleasure the pilots take in killing the enemy. German planes are shot down to the accompaniment of dialogue like "Burn, yuh crumb, burn!"

The planes in FIGHTER SQUADRON are P-47 Thunderbolts supplied by National Guard units in Nashville and Savannah, which also supplied the pilots. The film was made under the supervision of Air Force technical advisors and shot at the Oscoda Air Base in Oscoda, Michigan. This base was chosen because filming there allowed the Eastern National Guard units to take their active duty training with the film company. Also, the base's terrain was similar to that of the English airfield represented in the film. Filming the aviation sequences presented the same problem that occurred with WINGS and HELL'S ANGELS: no clouds. It wasn't until the second week of shooting that some clouds finally appeared. As good as the studio-filmeed air shots are, they are surpassed by the actual combat footage supplied by the Army Air Force. This footage is well matched to the fictional scenes.

Aviation films turned from fighters to bombers with MGM's release of COMMAND DECISION at the very end of 1948. The movie deals very little with the men who actually fly the B-17s; it is rather the story of the men who decide what missions are to be flown. The events in the film are

Clark Gable and staff synchronize watches in the "Operation Stitch" command center in COMMAND DECISION (1948).

similar to those surrounding the October 14, 1943 raid on the ball-bearing factories at Schweinfurt, Germany. On that day, "Black Thursday," sixty Flying Forts and over 600 men were lost. The loss figures, the size of the raid, and the attempt to totally destroy a specific objective were carried through to the plot line of COMMAND DECISION.

Adapted from a play by William Wiston Hanes, the film deals with one man, Brigadier General K. C. Dennis (Clark Gable), who spends as much time fighting the brass as he does planning missions against the Germans. Given favorable weather, and the absence of his immediate superior, Dennis launches "Operation Stitch" ("a stitch in time"). This is a plan to bomb three Me-262 factories with a maximum effort, one factory at a time. The three days of raids will wipe out Messerchmitt jet fighter production and shorten the war. But Dennis is faced with the problem of continuing the raids under political pressure from Washington. His superior, Major General Roland Kane (Walter Pidgeon), and visiting Congressmen eventually become appalled by the loss figures. The first mission results in 48 B-17s being shot down, but total destruction of the target is achieved. The second mission ends with 52 planes lost, including the lead one flown by Dennis' friend. On top of that, the strike force hits the wrong target. This means that a fourth maximum effort will have to be launched. At this point a Congressional committee arrives at the air base. Kane is more concerned with his efforts to sell daylight precision bombing to the Congressmen than he is to make "Stitch" an immediate success, which puts him at odds with Dennis. The story reduces to the decisions Dennis must make and their consequences.

COMMAND DECISION is characterized by excellent acting. Gable gives a strong performance, which is never better than when he tries to talk down a damaged B-17 being flown by a navigator (the pilot is dead and the co-pilot wounded). He almost has the plane safely landed when it skids and bursts into flames, killing all on board. This piece brings home the agonies Gable suffers when he sends men out on a mission. Walter Pidgeon is excellent as the general who knows Gable is right but compromises himself to satisfy the politicians. The film doesn't portray all American leaders in a favorable light and sometimes makes the politicians look rather foolish. Because of this, the story was investigated by the House Un-American Activities Committee in November 1947. But Metro left the story intact, and its message is, once war is declared, military decisions are best left to military men.

The film was a success in the U.S. but, like OBJECTIVE BURMA, it drew heavy criticism in England. The British felt that it insulted them because it gave credit for the aerial destruction of Germany solely to the U.S. The film, however, depicts daylight operations which the British had abandoned as being too costly.

The aviation scenes are a model of restraint, consisting mostly of bombers taking off and landing. Most of the action takes place in several rooms at bomber command headquarters, in keeping with the play. COMMAND DECISION stands out as the first top-notch aviation film made after WWII.

Two scenes from TWELVE O'CLOCK HIGH (1949). At top, Gregory Peck embarks on a mission. Below, he briefs the aircrews before another mission.

TWELVE O'CLOCK HIGH (1949), like COMMAND DECI-
SION, told of the loneliness of commanding a B-17 group;
and like the previous film explored the late-forties philosophy that perhaps war was neither glamorous nor desirable,
no matter how just the cause. The film bears the personal
stamp of Darryl F. Zanuck, who bought the novel by Lieutenant Colonel Sy Bartlett and Colonel Bernie Lay, Jr.,
members of the 918th Bomb Group and friends of Mantz, in
1948. It deals with the U.S. Army's Eighth Air Force in
the fall of 1942. It opens with a flashback showing Dean
Jagger returning to the now-deserted field. Stationed at
Chelveston, England, the 918th Bombardment Group has become known as a "hard luck" outfit. Under pressure to
mount several "maximum efforts," the group begins to dis-
integrate. The other groups can always muster their full
complement of 21 aircraft, but the 918th is usually three or
four planes short. The group's loss of morale threatens not
only to discredit daylight precision bombing but also to
weaken the morale in other groups. The high command feels
that the present commander, Colonel Keith Davenport (Gary
Merrill), is too involved with his men and sends Davenport's
friend, General Savage (Gregory Peck), to replace him. (The
character of Savage was inspired by the life of Major General
Frank A. Armstrong, Jr., who led the first Flying Fortress daylight raid against Occupied Europe.) All the pilots put in immediately for transfers, but Savage delays these in order to
gain time to prove he's right. The group abandons missions
and begins training flying all over again. Savage puts all
the misfits into one aircraft, The Leper Colony, to shame
them into shaping up. By the time the group goes back into
combat, its morale is up and its losses decrease. All this
tells on Savage, however, because he too begins to care about
the men and cracks up. Pack gives an excellent performance
and he received an Oscar nomination for it.

TWELVE O'CLOCK HIGH surpassed COMMAND DECI-
SION in its shots of the B-17s, and the introduction says
that actual combat footage was used in the film. Director
Henry King went on an 11,000-mile trip to find the right
location. Saving the best for last, King has one major flying sequence at the film's end. Twentieth Century-Fox
bought bombers and fighters from the War Assets Administration and sent them to Elgin Field, Florida, for shooting.
Hundreds of aircraft seem to be in the air during the spectacular 12-minute bombing raid. Studio shots were skillfully
blended with the combat footage, some of it taken from the

Germans, and only minor technical lapses can be found, such as shots of "German" fighter machine guns firing when the guns are really mounted in P-47s.

The most spectacular aviation scene was staged for the picture. In this scene Mantz was to crash land a B-17 in front of the cameras, allow the plane to slide with its gear up into a group of tents, and then jump out of the plane. Inside one of the tents was a large iron post which was supposed to catch one wing so the plane would spin around. It was an extraordinarily difficult stunt, for Mantz would be flying the bomber without the help of a co-pilot. Mantz took the B-17 aloft, jettisoned the ball turret, and made his approach. He came in down wind and found the rudder ineffective when he cut the power because of a tail wind. But the B-17 began to roll on its wheels, even though they were still retracted, and Mantz controlled the plane with brakes. He avoided other B-17s parked on the runway and slid 1,000 feet into the tents, right on target. One of the iron poles in the tents flew up in the air, barely missing the cockpit. For this stunt Mantz received $6,000. (The stunt also appeared in the pilot episode of the television series.)

TWELVE O'CLOCK HIGH turned out to be the top-grossing aviation film of the late 1940s, making $3,225,000 in its first year of release. It and TASK FORCE made the European Command Motion Pictures Services' list of the top ten films shown in Army cinemas.

The situations and themes in TWELVE O'CLOCK HIGH were so universal that a television series was made based on the film. It ran from 1964 to 1967 on ABC. Quinn Martin, a bomber pilot with the Eighth Air Force in the war, produced the series. Filming took place at the Chino Airport in California. The producers worked with 3,000,000 feet of actual combat film and film shot for the original motion picture. Fifteen thousand feet of the combat film was edited into each series episode.

Bernie Lay, who wrote the novel on which the film was based, also wrote the TV pilot. Lay had commanded the 487th Bomb Group of the Eighth Air Force. He was shot down over France in 1944 while leading a raid involving 72 B-24s. He escaped the Germans with the help of the French underground. Robert Lansing, who took flying lessons while the series was being filmed, starred as General Savage, but his character was killed on a mission at the start of the second season. Paul Burke, playing Colonel Joe Gallagher, took over the lead role.

SECRET FLIGHT (1951), a British film, was a rather poor tribute to the people who developed radar. Written and directed by Peter Ustinov, the film has some good moments of comedy but the best parts are the documentary shots of British bombing missions over Europe. Once radar has been developed, it is used to locate a German night fighter and as a guidance aid for the pinpoint bombing of Cologne.

The British produced the first post-war film to deal with the Battle of Britain pilots, ANGELS ONE FIVE (1952). It was not shown in the US until two years later. The film is difficult to follow and most of the air action is depicted by means of messages to and from the operations room, with only the briefest glimpse of Spitfires and Hurricanes taking off. All the rest is ground action.

The plot follows three members of the RAF. One, a young officer, pushes to be transferred out of the operations center so he can fly a Hurricane. Another, an older officer, is not trying his hardest to help the war effort. And the third, a new replacement, isn't really accepted by the rest of the pilots. The base is presided over by "Septic" Baird (John Gregson) and "Tiger" Small (Jack Hawkins), both of whom play their roles with a reasonable degree of expertise.

THEY WHO DARE (1953) was a British film directed by Lewis Milestone. Dirk Bogard and Akim Tamiroff starred in this story of a commando raid on German-controlled Aegean air fields.

APPOINTMENT IN LONDON (1953) dealt with the bombing offensive against Germany. The action happens at the bomber base, except for one battle scene over Germany. The plot has Wing Commander Tim Mason (Dirk Bogard) flying missions in 1943. His great ambition is to fly 90 missions before he takes a desk job. When his mission total stands at 89, he is grounded by Bomber Command. He takes the place of an injured pilot, however, and manages to fly one more mission. The aerial sequence at the end is fairly realistic.

LANDFALL (1953), based on a Nevil Shute novel, tells of a young RAF pilot, Flight Lieutenant Rick Chambers (Michael Denison), assigned to the Coastal Command, who sinks what he believes to be a British submarine. A court of inquiry charges him with negligence, but his girl friend comes up with evidence to prove that it was really a German sub he destroyed. Not only is the pilot cleared, but he also proves his courage by testing an electrically controlled guided missile.

MALTA STORY (1953) had **Alec Guinness playing** a reconnaissance pilot on his way to Egypt in 1942. He stops off at Malta where his plane is destroyed, stranding him. Persuaded to help defend Malta, he loses his life taking vital pictures of a German convoy. The film deals mainly with the aerial bombing of the island and the gallant efforts of the people to hold out. Supplies that reach the island are destroyed almost as soon as they arrive, and the Spitfire pilots have a hard time beating back the German air force. Newsreel footage was used in the film, some of it captured from the Germans and never before shown.

PARATROOPER (1953, released in England as THE RED BERET) dealt with a paratroop regiment during World War II, following a group of men from their initial training through two combat assignments. Alan Ladd plays Canada (he's really an American), who is haunted by the death of his best friend who he ordered to jump at training school. So Ladd volunteers to join this new regiment, where he can simply take orders and not give them. The paratroopers drop into France and capture a device from a German radar station. Their British planes are replaced by USAAF transports and the men, now wearing the red berets they earned after their first combat mission, drop into North Africa to capture an airfield prior to the invasion. The Germans trap them, but Ladd's heroics save the day. The best aviation shots in this average film are the color shots of the mass parachute drop with white, yellow, red, and brown parachutes contrasting with the blue sky.

SKY COMMANDO (1953) begins in the Korean War with a jet pilot returning from a mission. The pilot blames the commanding officer (Dan Duryea) for his brother's death, and the picture flashes back to World War II. Duryea is the much-disliked leader of a reconnaissance squadron flying in southern Europe. He has all the cliché traits that mark a tough aviation leader and it takes a battle to prove to the men the value of their commander. A mission to the Ploesti oil fields in Romania proves to the pilots that Duryea is really a good squadron leader.

FIGHTER ATTACK (1953), released by Allied Artists, told of an air unit based in Corsica in 1944. The squadron, led by Steve (Sterling Hayden), has been chosen to locate and destroy a German supply dump so that the offensive in Italy can begin. Searching for the dump, Steve is shot down and is taken by Nina (Joy Page) to the headquarters of the underground. With their help he locates the dump and calls in the squadron to bomb it.

The next British effort was a top-notch war film, THE DAM BUSTERS (1954), based on the book Enemy Coast Ahead, by Guy Gibson. The film details the efforts of a scientist, Dr. Barnes Wallis (Michael Redgrave), to develop a bomb capable of destroying the Ruhr dams in Germany and to convince the high officials of the merits of his bomb. A unique device, it skips across the water until it hits the dam. Then it sinks to a predetermined depth and explodes. The bomb must be delivered with absolute precision, for it will not work unless it is dropped 600 yards from the dam while the plane is traveling at 240 miles per hour 60 feet above the water. The film deals with Wallis's efforts to perfect the bomb and with Wing Commander Guy Gibson (Richard Todd) and his training of the special bomber crews who will drop the bombs. The recreation of the bombing of the Moehne and Eder Dams in May 1943 provides the exciting conclusion to the movie.

The film's aviation scenes are especially exciting, which is quite remarkable considering that most of them, including virtually all of the dam bombing sequences, were staged with models. This is one of the few aviation pictures that made superb use of models, thanks to the special effects talents of Gilbert Taylor. A model dam about 20 feet across was built in a 100-feet-square studio set of the lake and surrounding countryside. Originally, the dam was to have been blown up by model planes, but it proved impossible to create a convincing water spout in this manner. A full-scale explosion was superimposed on the dam after the model scenes had been filmed.

Richard Todd (center) and the men who will destroy the German dams in THE DAM BUSTERS (1954).

The film created a stir that reached all the way to the House of Parliament. Word reached England that the movie had been doctored by the American distributor, Warner Brothers, to show B-17s attacking the dams instead of Lancasters! A member of Parliament protested, saying that the film "'jeopardizes good Anglo-American relations.'"[9] The charge is totally ridiculous, for except for one two-second scene of a B-17 crashing in a forest (apparently put in by a misguided American cutter to liven up the action), there is no question that all the planes are Avro Lancasters.

THE SEA SHALL NOT HAVE THEM (1954), another British release, dealt with the exploits of the British air-sea rescue service in 1944. Their mission is to rescue the crew of a Hudson aircraft shot down over the North Sea. An air commodore (Michael Redgrave) is on board with a brief-case that contains vital enemy secrets. After two days and nights of a search fraught with problems, the air-sea rescue team saves the men who are now drifting off the Belgian coast under heavy enemy gunfire.

THE DEVIL'S GENERAL (DER TEUFELS GENERAL, 1955) was based on a Carl Zuckmayer story about an anti-Nazi pilot general (similar to Ernst Udet) and a squadron of Junkers Ju-86 bombers. The Ju-86s used in the film came from Sweden, the only place where the planes were still in service when the film was made.

REACH FOR THE SKY (1956), a British production about the famous legless fighter pilot, Douglas Bader, is a solid affair telling of the flier's pain and courage. Bader himself served as technical advisor. Bader (Kenneth More) joins the air service in 1928. A bit of a reckless flier, he becomes a little too daring and loses both legs in a crash in 1931. The middle of the film deals with his efforts to over-come this seemingly insurmountable handicap. He masters everything he tries and applies for permission to fly again in the RAF. At first his petition is denied, but when WWII comes he is passed by a generous flight medic and ends up as a Wing Commander, leading a fighter wing in the Battle of Britain. He becomes one of England's first war heroes and a fighter ace. Eventually he is shot down and captured by the Germans. After he has made three attempts to es-cape the Germans place him in Colditz Castle, where he re-mains until the Americans rescue him. Although actual com-bat footage is used, the aviation scenes aren't that outstand-ing. It marked the start of U.S. distributing by J. Arthur Rank, a major figure in the British film industry.

THE STAR OF AFRICA (DER STERN VON AFRIKA, 1957) was a German biography of the World War II ace Hans Joachim, who shot down 152 enemy planes before his death on a mission in Africa. Because the film glorified a Nazi pi-lot, the picture was banned in Germany. The Spanish Air Force supplied the Me-109s, Heinkel 111s, and Ju-52s, as it would for THE BATTLE OF BRITAIN 12 years later.

THE STORY OF A FIGHTER PLANE (HISTORIA JED-NEGO MYSLIWCA, 1958), a Polish film, is based on the memoirs of Stanislav Skalski about Polish fliers in the RAF

UNSEEN HEROES (1958) tells of Michael Rennie and David Knight, who play two Polish underground agents who are sent in 1942 to investigate the German missile program. They locate a new secret missile base at Pennemunde and call in the RAF, who carry out a mass bombing raid which destroys the installation. They then capture a flying bomb and smuggle it back to England. Some actual newsreel footage is used in the bombing run.

PARATROOP COMMAND (1959) starred Richard Bakalyan as a paratrooper who becomes an outcast when he accidentally kills one of the other members of his unit. Throughout the film, he takes this problem with him to several combat assignments in North Africa, Sicily, and Italy. He exonerates himself by sacrificing himself for the good of the unit.

THE NIGHT WE DROPPED A CLANGER (1959) was an inept film involving an Air Force officer on a secret mission to France. To fool the Nazis, the British send his double to Cairo. Of course the two characters get on the wrong planes, so the double is now handling the secret mission. This British film is terrible.

NORMANDIA-NEIMAN (1960) was a joint Soviet-French production about a French fighter squadron flying with the Russians in the war. The squadron flew Yak 3 and Yak 9 planes. The Russian BALTIC SKY (BALLTIJSKOJE NEBO, 1961) also dealt with World War II.

AIRBORNE (1962) was a paratroop picture following the adventures of a naive country boy at Fort Bragg, home of the Fighting 82nd. The film is interesting only for its shots of paratroop training procedures. (Much better material concerning the 82nd Airborne is found in the 1962 non-aviation film, THE LONGEST DAY.)

Half of SMASHING OF THE REICH (1962), a documentary, is devoted to the aerial bombardment of Germany, with emphasis on the daylight bombing of the German oil industry. Most of the footage had been used before, and the film offers nothing new in the way of aerial shots.

THE WAR LOVER (1962), based on the book by John Hersey, starred Steve McQueen as an unruly but brilliant pilot of a B-17 and Robert Wagner as his co-pilot on missions over Germany in 1943. Conflicts arise from the fact both are in love with the same girl and because McQueen seems to enjoy war. He breaks the rules and gets away with it because he can fly his B-17 as no other pilot in the outfit can. He bombs an enemy base through a hole in the clouds after the planes have been ordered to turn back. He buzzes the field at extremely low level for the fun of it. (This stunt was performed by British stunt pilot John Crewdson.) In an ordinary situation he would be grounded, but his superiors realize that sometimes war has to be fought by psychopaths, and they allow him to keep flying. But McQueen's encounter with Wagner's girl friend shakes his blind faith in his flying ability. On one mission, the B-17 is badly damaged and everyone but McQueen bails out. He over-estimates his flying skill and tries to get the plane back to the base. He crashes into cliffs on the English coast line.

THE WAR LOVER contains usual combat footage, but it also has interesting shots of the B-17s taken from cameras mounted on various parts of the plane: the landing gear, the top of the fuselage, etc. Author Martin Caiden and several friends rebuilt three B-17s from scrounged spare parts and flew them to England for the picture, as detailed in Caiden's book, Everything But the Flak (Duell, Sloan, & Pearce, 1964). Flying these patched together aircraft across the Atlantic proved to be almost as dangerous as flying in combat, and Caiden had several close calls. Once the planes were in England, Les Hillman and his ground crew inflicted considerable damage on the planes so they would look like battle-damaged aircraft in the film. As Caiden stated "'On several occasions Hillman and his ground crews so mangled the bombers for flight scenes, John [Crewdson] refused to allow anyone to enter the plane with him and like Greg [Board], repeatedly took to the air as the sole occupant of the four-engined bomber.'"[10] Although no one was hurt during this dangerous stunt flying, British parachutist Mike Reilly died after parachuting from a B-17 into the English Channel for the film. His equipment weighted him down and he drowned before he could be picked up.

CAPTAIN NEWMAN, M.D. (1963) starred Gregory Peck as an Air Force psychiatrist charged with patching up the mental casualties of war. The setting is Colfax Army Air Base stateside in 1944. Peck has six weeks to cure his patients and return them to combat, or send them to a more

permanent mental hospital. Peck is unorthodox in his methods. He angers superiors, shanghais an orderly from another ward, and keeps a herd of sheep for use in laboratory
experiments. His three principal patients are a mad colonel
(Eddie Albert), finally driven to suicide because of all the
men he lost in combat; a nearly catatonic flier (Robert Duvall) who spent 13 months hiding in a cellar in a German-
occupied French town; and a guilt-ridden waist gunner (Bobby Darin) who escaped from his burning bomber, but did not
try to pull his buddy from the wreck. The film alternates
between drama and comedy to produce a weakly effective
combination.

INTERRUPTED FLIGHT (POZERWANG LOT, 1964) was
a Polish movie telling about a Russian pilot's difficulties in
German-occupied Poland.

633 SQUADRON (1964) was the first World War II aviation film made in Panavision and color. For this reason newsreel footage couldn't be used, and all the aerial sequences
had to be photographed especially for the picture. The Germans have built a special heavy water manufacturing plant at
the end of a Norwegian fiord. It is vital that the factory be
destroyed and, **since** it cannot be hurt by high-level bombing, a "Dam Busters" type of attack is called for. Wing
Commander Roy Grant (Cliff Robertson) must lead his Mosquito bombers up the fiord, which is heavily defended by
anti-aircraft batteries, and hit the plant in a head-on attack. The Norwegian underground fails in its efforts to destroy the anti-aircraft guns and, as a result, the planes
take a terrible beating as they make their bomb run. Enough
planes get through, however, to destroy the factory.

The planes are everything in this picture, for the plot
and acting are only mediocre. The Mirish production team
conducted an extensive search for the film's aircraft. **With
the help of London's Air Ministry in Whitehall they managed to**
locate the ten required Mosquitos at RAF bases at Exeter in
South Devon, Shawbury, Henlow, and the Central Flying
School at Little Rissington. Had the filmmakers waited two
more weeks, these "Mossies" would have been sent to Muse-
ums or scrapped. Several Bf-108s doubled for Me-109s; and
Martin Caiden ferried a B-25 across the Atlantic to be used
in the film.

633 SQUADRON was filmed in Scotland. The director, Walter Grauman, flew 56 missions as a B-25 bomber pilot in Europe in WWII. The Mosquitos of the M.A.F. (Mirish Air Force) were flown by British stunt pilots, some of whom flew in the Battle of Britain. The star, Cliff Robertson, held a private pilot's license but wasn't allowed to fly because of studio insurance regulations. Excellent special effects of exploding aircraft were coupled with flying shots to make the movie an exciting one.

Mosquito aircraft also figured in THE PATHFINDERS, a British television series of the 1960s about the pilots who flew ahead of the bomber formations, dropping incendiaries to mark the target. Scottish actor Robert Urquhart played the lead.

CALM PLACES (MESTA TUT TICHIJE, 1967) was a Russian film telling of battles against German U-boats in the Barents Sea. THE STORY OF A DIVE BOMBER (CHRONIKA PIKURUJUSTJEGO BOMBARDIROVSJTJIKA, 1967) dealt with three pilots in a dive-bomber squadron.

THE THOUSAND PLANE RAID (1969), directed by Boris Sagal, was a poor film. Christopher George plays the mastermind of a plan to send 1,000 B-17s against Germany's principal airplane manufacturing center. (The British launched the first 1,000-plane raid against Cologne, Germany on May 30, 1942.) His tough attitude endears him to no one and forms the basis for several minor character conflicts in the film. Other characters are a young, scared pilot, George's girl friend, and a cocky RAF ace sent to advise the Americans. What aerial footage there is consists mainly of stock film. The B-17 that served as Gregory Peck's plane in TWELVE O'CLOCK HIGH turned up as the Bucking Bronco in THE THOUSAND PLANE RAID and another B-17, a former drone, was resurrected from the Davis Monthan AFB storage depot. The aerial footage was shot at Santa Maria Airport in California.

THE BATTLE OF BRITAIN (1969) proved to be one of the most elaborate aviation movies of all time. Shot on a multi-million-dollar budget and using dozens of authentic aircraft, the film is one of the most detailed aviation movies ever made. Unfortunately, neither the plot nor any aspect

of the dramatic structure comes anywhere near to matching
the technical quality. (For an excellent account of the personal, financial, and logistical problems involved in making a
large-budget aviation film, see "Battle of Britain": The Making of a Film by Leonard Mosley, Ballantine Books, 1969.)

The movie chronicles the events between August 10,
1940 and September 15, 1940, the period which has been
called the Battle of Britain. There is some controversy over
this labeling. The Germans deny there was any such battle:
they say they merely conducted a series of air raids during
that period and stopped them when the results were not what
they hoped. Some of the British also feel this way. Wing
Commander H. R. Allen, of the RAF, wrote an article claiming that the battle title was invented by Churchill for propaganda purposes. He said the kill claims were exaggerated
and if the British had really won the battle, the Luftwaffe
never would have been able to launch its night raids on London.

A German bomber squadron in Northern France being re-
viewed in THE BATTLE OF BRITAIN (1969).

On July 10, 1940, the British had 49 operational squadrons, for a total of about 650 fighter aircraft. Most of these were Hurricanes, with about one-third being the faster and better Spitfires Mark I and Mark II, along with about 30 Boulton-Paul Defiants. Opposing the British in France were about 1,100 fighters (Me-109Es and Me-110s), 900 bombers (Heinkel 111s, Junkers Ju-88s, and Dornier Do17s) and 300 Junker Ju-87 Stuka dive bombers. Scandinavia had an additional 123 bombers and 34 long-range twin engined Me-110 fighters. The total came to more than 2,300 aircraft. The Spitfires were better than the Me-109s below 20,000 feet, but the German fighters were better at higher altitude. The Messerschmitts were faster than the Hurricane 1s, but the British **planes were sturdier than the German ones.** The Me-110s, one-fourth of the German fighters, were the poorest planes of the lot.

The Germans, determined to invade England, first had to knock the British out of the sky, and August 10, 1940 was set as Eagle Day: the beginning of the destruction of the RAF. Bad weather postponed the first attack until August 13. Outnumbered four to one, the British faced complete destruction. Heading the Fighter Command was Air Chief Marshall Sir Hugh Dowding. Dowding had a thorough knowledge of aerial combat techniques, but his conservative manner (he was an introvert, a vegetarian, and he didn't drink) earned him the nickname of "Stuffy." He had little facility for making political friends and a habit of making unpopular, though accurate, recommendations; such as not sending more planes to France when it was obvious that the country was doomed.

Dowding had four operational groups under his command: 13 **Group** in northern England and Scotland, 10 Group in west England, 12 Group in southeast England, and 11 Group assigned to London and the southeast coast of England. The last two were the most important, for they defended the area in which the Germans concentrated their attacks. Eleven Group, which bore the brunt of the fighting, was commanded by Air Vice Marshall Keith Park. Air Vice Marshall Trafford Leigh-Mallory headed 12 Group. Unfortunately, these two commanders had different ideas on how to beat the Germans, and they didn't work well together. Of the men most responsible for winning the battle, Dowding, Leigh-Mallory, and Park, only Leigh-Mallory would receive official recognition for his services during and after the war.

The German strategy centered on shooting down as many of the British fighters as possible, while bombing the airfields so that the survivors would have no place to land. The British had the advantages of radar and of being able to fight over their own territory. (The Germans also had radar, but they used it to track ships in the English Channel.) The German fighters also had fuel for only 30 minutes of flying over the south of England, and ten minutes over London, but they had superior numbers.

As the battle progressed, it became obvious that the Germans were winning. In two weeks, more than 450 Spitfires and Hurricanes were destroyed or badly damaged. Although the aircraft could be replaced, the pilots who flew them could not. Losses on both sides were high, with the Germans losing two or three times as many planes as the British. But the ratio dropped as the battle progressed, and the Germans could afford the losses.

Parks' airfields were coming under heavy attack, and Manston and Biggin Hill were hit so hard they were almost useless. Park depended on Leigh-Mallory's 12 Group to defend his airfields, but often when he called for help, Leigh-Mallory's planes didn't come. Mallory had developed the "big wind" concept, in which 40 or 50 aircraft were assembled to attack the Germans. But getting these planes together in the air took time, and during that time Park's airfields had already been bombed.

By the end of August, the British were all but defeated. German losses were now four to three, and the British couldn't afford to trade plane for plane. But on August 24, German planes that had strayed off course jettisoned their bombs over London. Hitler had specifically forbidden attacks on London; he and Churchill both knew that bombs falling on the city would rouse world-wide sympathy for England. The accidental London raid prompted a British one on Berlin on August 25, and although it did little damage, it put Goering, who vowed bombs would never fall on Berlin, into disgrace. The bombing so infuriated Hitler that he vowed to obliterate London, and on September 7 the Luftwaffe switched from attacking airfields and support facilities to all-out raids on London. This gave the RAF a rest at the very time it was going down to defeat and changed the course of the battle. Park's airfields were no longer under attack and

Two scenes from THE BATTLE OF BRITAIN (1969): top,
British pilots scramble to repel the Germans; below, a Spitfire burns.

now masses of planes were sent against the Germans as they
went to and from London. On September 15, 1940 the British scored their greatest victory to that point against the
German bomber streams, and claimed 185 planes shot down.
The real figure is closer to 60, but many more crashed flying back to base. Even the Germans couldn't afford such
losses. Goering switched to night bombings, Hitler canceled
plans for invading Britain, and the Battle of Britain was
over. Raids would continue for months, of course, but the
Luftwaffe never again threatened to destroy the RAF.

By the mid-sixties, over 150 books had been written
about the Battle of Britain, but no one had ever done a film
about the whole battle. Producer S. Benjamin Fisz had just
completed THE HEROES OF TELEMARK in September 1965
when he got the idea for a LONGEST DAY-type detailed account of the battle. He called his friend Freddy Thomas at
the Rank Organization and broached the idea. Thomas was
so interested that Fisz talked with playwright Terence Rattigan, who agreed to do the first draft of a script for $8,000.
Rank owned the rights to a Battle of Britain book called The
Thin Blue Line, so there would be no problem of rights to
the material.

By mid-October Fisz had firm plans for the project and
had lined up help from the British Air Ministry. The release date was set for September 15, 1967, the Battle of
Britain anniversary. But Rattigan couldn't finish the script
in time and upped his price to $280,000. Thomas and Fisz
quarreled over who would control the production. Fisz
hired James Kennaway to replace Rattigan and engaged Group
Captain Hamish Mahaddie to track down World War II aircraft
in different countries. In May 1966 Harry Saltzman called
Fisz about working on the film.

Saltzman was the innovative British producer who co-
produced the James Bond films. Saltzman was becoming
bored with the Bond pictures and wanted to do something
different. Fisz had to give up exclusive rights to the picture, but he gained a powerful ally. Rank agreed to put out
$3,500,000 in exchange for twenty per cent of the world-wide
profits and Eastern Hemisphere distribution, and Saltzman
promised he'd raise the rest of the $8-10 million cost of the
film. Rank also offered to put up $140,000 in preproduction
money, but only after Rank approved the script.

But at this point there wasn't any script. Kennaway hadn't finished it and it was taking time for him to do the research. Meanwhile, Saltzman brought director Guy Hamilton (GOLDFINGER) into the project, and Hamilton, too, started researching the battle. Kennaway couldn't go on with the script, so Paul Dehn was brought in. Dehn did a first draft and Kennaway went back to work.

On August 31, 1966 Thomas met with Saltzman and Fisz to finalize Rank's agreement on the film. But Thomas wanted better distribution terms. Saltzman refused, so Thomas withdrew Rank from the project. Paramount was approached and the film company, which had just been absorbed by Gulf & Western, agreed to make the picture. It would be Paramount's biggest investment since the $13-million TEN COMMANDMENTS in 1955. Paramount talked with Cinerama about making the film in that wide-screen process. But Paramount had differences with Saltzman and Fisz and decided to pull out of the whole deal. Saltzman postponed the film.

Hamilton agreed to go on working despite the money uncertainties, and he and Kennaway continued revising the script. Mahaddie continued to search for planes and the Ministry of Defense (Air) promised continued cooperation.

By 1967 a production staff had been gathered and had started working, using Saltzman's money. Work stopped when Saltzman announced that the film would not go into production the next year, but Saltzman then made a deal with United Artists and the company gave the go-ahead to make the film. There were still script problems, however, and Hamilton was having trouble reconciling the documentary aspects of the film with the necessity for a dramatic story. It was obvious that the German side of the battle would have to be portrayed. Hamilton agreed that the German sequences should be shot in German using English subtitles and German actors, but he worried about the Germans checking the accuracy of the film.

Fisz chose Adolf Galland, the great German ace and Battle of Britain flier, as the German technical consultant. (The German aerial commander in the film was based on Galland.) It took Galland a while to adjust to an objective viewpoint. Kennaway and Hamilton did not get along with

Galland at first, but Fisz warned Kennaway that if Galland complained of something that was untrue, the script would be changed. True incidents, whether Galland liked them or not, would stay in. In August 1967 a copy of the script was sent to Galland, who complained it was unfair and inaccurate. Kennaway and Hamilton took Galland's comments under advisement and went to work revising the script.

Meanwhile, searches for planes continued. Hamish Mahaddie had made buying planes for films a living and he knew where many could be found. He was able to locate 109 Spitfires around the world, but the German planes were more of a problem. Galland suggested Mahaddie try Spain for the Heinkel bombers and Messerschmitts. Mahaddie found that these planes were, indeed, available and on March 29, 1966 he went to a Spanish air base outside Seville. Some fighters were in good condition and some were on the scrap heap, but Saltzman told Mahaddie to buy all of them; out of the lot Mahaddie figured he could salvage 30 Messerschmitts, which he bought at auction.

The British ambassador in Madrid helped Mahaddie deal with the Spanish so that the filmmakers could film the Spanish air force's fifty Heinkels in flight. The Spanish generously granted their permission, and even refused payment for fuel, flight crew time, etc. The filmmakers concluded that the Spanish offer saved them $420,000.

By the end of 1967 Mahaddie had collected 50 Heinkels (on loan from Spain), 28 Messerschmitts (seven of which had only 200 hours), a Ju-52 transport, two squadrons of Spitfires and an equal number of "runners" for ground scenes, and four Hurricanes (there were only six left in the world), one of which was rebuilt from a Canadian scrap heap and flown by its restorer, an ex-RCAF pilot, across the Atlantic to appear in the film. The only differences between these planes and those used in the Battle of Britain was that the Messerschmitts had four-bladed props and Rolls Royce engines, unlike the Me-109s. The film now had the world's third largest air force.

In addition to the full-sized aircraft, some radio controlled models were built. Half-size 20-foot Stukas were built, powered with Percival Proctor engines, and used in the radar station bombing sequences. British modelers Jack

Morton, Chris Olsen, Mick Charles, and Dave Platt were
hired to build several 7- to 10-foot-wingspan replicas of the
various planes, including a Hurricane, a Stuka, and an Me-
110.

Saltzman had talked with United Artists and the budget
was announced at $8,500,000. But the film was already cost-
ing $56,000 a week and when shooting started that figure
might rise to $56,000 a day, not counting stars' salaries.
The start of production was set for March 11, 1968 and the
first construction crews went to Seville and San Sebastian in
Spain on January 29, 1968 to begin their work. Their task
was to make Huelva Beach look like Dunkirk, convert Spanish airfields to resemble German ones, put German markings
on the planes, make a small harbor in San Sebastian look
like a French port for the invasion of England scenes, and
convert some of San Sebastian's streets into those of Berlin.

Hamilton still worked on the script in February 1968
while crews scouted British locations. In the meantime, Fisz
was going after stars. By March 10, 1968 the script had
been finished and Alec Guinness was offered the role of Sir
Hugh Dowding. The postponement of production made it impossible for him to take the part and it went to Sir Laurence
Olivier.

Filming began on March 13, 1968, and on March 18 a
brightly painted B-25 camera plane called the Psychedelic
Monster flew in, piloted by John Hawke, a 30-year old RAF
pilot and member of the RAF's Red Devils acrobatic team.
John Blake, a member of the Royal Aeronautical Club, was in
charge of the flying sequences. Skeets Kelly and Johnny
Jordan were the B-25 camera men. Jordan had lost part of
one leg below the knee while filming a helicopter sequence on
YOU ONLY LIVE TWICE, but he still continued as an aerial
photographer.

Hawke's B-25 had flown in the Pacific. The nose had
been replaced by clear plexiglass to allow a 65mm camera to
be mounted in the front. Cameras could shoot through the
side windows, a camera was placed in the tail, and another
could be lowered through the bomb bay to shoot over a 360°
field of view, controlled by the cameraman above it. The air
unit director watched the action from a large plexiglass dome
in the center of the fuselage and ahead of him rode the air

traffic controller. Everyone in the plane was in intercom
contact: the air controller could talk to the other planes in
the air and Hawkes would talk to the ground. Television
cameras had been installed in the film camera positions so
that the air unit director could see what was being filmed
on a TV monitor and play the action back on a video tape
machine.

Galland flew into Seville on March 23, 1968 to observe
the filming. His friend Wing Commander **Stanford-Tuck** was
technical advisor for the RAF scenes. Another friend, Com-
mandante Pedro Santa Cruz, a Spanish Civil War pilot and
flier with the Germans against the Russians, was selected to
fly with and command the Messerschmitt pilots in the film.
Besides the Spanish air force pilots, four Texans from the
Confederate Air Force, Lloyd Nolan, **Martin** Gardner, Gerald
Martin, and Wilson Edwards, brought some Spitfires and Messerschmitts from America, and these four flew the German
planes as Luftwaffe Colonels. The filmmakers were trying to
film during weather that was similar to that during the Battle, but the Spanish weather didn't cooperate and there were
delays.

On March 29, 1968 an incident happened that threatened to disrupt the whole film. When Hamilton was filming
the farewell scene in which Goering berates General Oster-
kamp and Kesselring as his train pulls out, Hamilton thought
the two men merely saluting Goering lacked dramatic bite.
Luftwaffe men did not give the Nazi salute, but since Kesselring was also a Nazi, Hamilton reasoned that the scene
would have more power if Kesselring raised his arm in salute to Goering. Galland watched the scene as it was being
filmed and became enraged. He stalked off the set and
threatened never to return. The filmmakers were worried
about adverse German reaction because of Galland's stand.
It wasn't until about three weeks later, when Galland saw
the filmed scene, that he grudgingly admitted its dramatic
value and decided to remain with the film.

United Artists had started to worry about the budget.
The bad weather was resulting in a $50,000-a-day expendi-
ture for nothing. UA had now spent $7,000,000 of the
$8,000,000 budget and the film was only one-quarter done.
Pilots and technicians threatened a walkout.

By May 1968 the cast of the film had been selected. Besides Olivier for Dowding, Robert Shaw (whose character was based on a real ace), Christopher Plummer, Michael Caine, Susannah York, and Trevor Howard were hired. Caine's role had to be changed because of filming delays. Rex Harrison had originally been selected for Howard's role (Keith Park), partly because Harrison had been in 11 Group in the war, but Harrison couldn't adjust his schedule to fit the filming delays, and he was replaced. This caused an angry reaction from Park, who was living in New Zealand. Park thought the replacement of Harrison, who would play Park sympathetically, was a plot against him and he issued an angry statement charging the filmmakers with trying to cover up "a dirty little wartime intrigue" which led to Dowding's sacking and Park's being assigned to a training squadron. The filmmakers couldn't afford this kind of publicity, and enlisted Dowding's help in reassuring Park that his role was being played fairly.

Several participants in the actual battle visited the set at one time or another. The 86-year-old Dowding came in a wheelchair and was very moved by the scenes. Pilots Ginger Lacey, Lord Snowdon, Peter Townsend, and Douglas Bader also came.

The last big scene to be filmed was the bombing of Duxford airfield. The earlier scenes of burning buildings along the waterfront during the London Blitz, in which the Greater London Council had turned over part of Bermondsey to the filmmakers to demolish, had gone off without much of a problem. But there were problems at Duxford. The filmmakers had not gotten permission from the British Ministry of Defense to destroy one of the hangars, an important element in the scene. Saltzman and Hamilton went ahead anyway. The first attempt to blow the hangar failed, but the second succeeded.

A rough cut of the film was shown to the heads of United Artists, David and Arnold Picker, on September 23, 1968. They liked it well enough to advance enough money to finish the rest of the flying scenes, bringing the total budget to $13,000,000. The weather still posed a problem, but all the filming was completed by the end of September.

The BATTLE OF BRITAIN was released in London on

September 15, 1969, one year later than the original target
date. Coinciding with the film's release was an attempt to
win an official promotion to full Marshal of the Royal Air
Force for the 87-year-old Lord Dowding, by his assistant
in the last stages of the Battle, Robert Wright. A book,
Dowding and The Battle of Britain, was also released at this
time. The film met with indifferent audience and critical reaction. Vincent Canby best evaluated the film; he praised
the air sequences but went on to call it "... one of those
all-star nonmovies, of a somewhat lower order than 'The
Longest Day,' that attempt to recapitulate history, but add
nothing to one's understanding. The mixture of minor-key
fiction and restaged fact is ... never particularly satisfying,
since it is denied the prerogatives and possibilities of both
the documentary and the fiction film."[11] Hamilton never successfully resolved his dilemma over how to handle the documentary and fictional elements. The attempt to integrate
fictional elements into the film, particularly the conflict between Christopher Plummer and his WAAF wife, Susannah
York, fails and the viewer is left with no feeling for the
characters.

Unfortunately, the same thing holds true for the real
incidents. Tension is generated during the German attacks,
but the whole fails to hold the viewer. One of the most important aspects of the Battle, the feud between Park and
Leigh-Mallory, is only mentioned twice and Mallory appears
in just one brief scene. The airplane sequences are spectacular; among the best ever filmed. But even these grow
monotonous, and it isn't until the final lengthy airplane sequence, with no dialogue, that the filmmakers really capture
the spirit of the Battle.

The next major WWII aviation film dealing with the
European theater was completely different in tone and style
from THE BATTLE OF BRITAIN. CATCH-22 (1970), for
those who see the film without reading Joseph Heller's book,
is often confusing. The story concerns the oddest squadron of B-25s that ever existed, based on the Mediterranean
island of Pianosa. Yossarian (Alan Arkin), a bombardier,
has been very disturbed by the death of a novice tail gunner. He is now determined to escape war and save himself
by any means possible. He is thwarted in his efforts by
most of the other men on the base. Colonel Cathcart (Martin Balsam) wants to be featured in The Saturday Evening

Post and will do anything to get his wish. His planes only bomb civilian targets because the bomb patterns on the re- connaissance photos look neater; and he continually raises the number of missions a man must fly before he can be transferred. Captain Orr (Robert Balaban) ditches so many planes in the ocean that no one will fly with him (he is real- ly practicing for the time when he can safely ditch and es- cape to Sweden). Milo Minderbinder (Jon Voight), the squad- ron's mess officer, runs a gigantic commercial enterprise. He sells the men's parachutes and places shares in his company in their empty parachute packs. He even makes a deal with the Germans to have his own men attack his air base if the Germans will take some surplus supplies off his hands. It is no wonder that Yossarian wants to escape, and the end of the film finds him optimistically paddling out to sea in a one- man life raft, headed for Sweden.

A great deal of money was spent on the aerial shots, but only a small amount of this B-25 footage was used. (About one and one-half hours of spectacular flying se- quences never made it into the film.) The planes are main- ly photographed on the runway, their engines stirring up clouds of sand and their shapes distorted by heated air ris- ing from the tarmac; the film opens with eighteen 20-ton B-25s thundering down the airstrip 100 yards apart. There are some good take-off and landing scenes, such as one where a plane skids on landing and bursts into flames, and a comic scene where General Dreddle (Orson Welles) visits the base in his white-sidewall-tired plane.

Frank Tallman collected 18 B-25s from all over North America and stripped them down and rebuilt them so they would pass FAA tests. For five months he and the other pilots flew them from the Catch-22 airfield in Guaymas, Mex- ico. There was only one way in and out of the field and the cross winds made flying difficult. Thirty-six mechanics, 36 pilots and co-pilots, 20 flight engineers, and six camera plane pilots worked on the picture. The script required that a dummy on a raft be cut in two by an L-5 Army spot- ter plane, but when the scene was filmed the plastic "hand" became lodged in the elevator of Tallman's plane, almost causing a crash. Besides cutting the dummy, Tallman had to fly through flak and skim very low over the **Mexican** beaches. Filming was done with three Cessnas, the L-5, and a helicopter. Tragically, Johnny Jordan died when he fell out of the tail turret of a B-25 camera plane piloted by Frank Pine. Planes also transported the newly shot film daily from Mexico to Los Angeles.

The movie was based on Heller's own experience during WWII. He served as a B-25 bombardier and on his 37th mission his plane ran into trouble over Avignon. His gunner was wounded and bled a great deal into his flight suit. The experience so unnerved Heller that he sailed home after the war and did not ride in another plane until fifteen years later. Heller said he wrote his novel during the Korean War and designed it for the one after that. But translating Heller's complex novel to the screen proved **exceptionally** difficult, and much of the book had to be eliminated. As a result, the film never captures the novel's essential elements. Many of the characters are not well drawn and much of the film is confusing. CATCH-22 was an interesting experiment, but it is a failure.

MOSQUITO SQUADRON (1970) was a British film directed by Boris Sagal. The trite film had David McCallum as an RAF bomb crew leader ordered to destroy German rocket installations. The sites can only be eliminated by a special skip-bomb. Complicating the mission is the fact that the Germans have imprisoned captured RAF fliers at the sites, and one of the pilots is the husband of the woman McCallum loves. The only good aerial shots come during the bombing and rescue mission at the end of the film, although the explosions are well done with models, and stock aerial footage is blended with all too obvious process shots.

MURPHY'S WAR (1970) had Peter O'Toole as Murphy. Near the end of WWII, a German submarine sinks a merchantman at the mouth of a Venezuelan river. The Germans machine-gun the survivors and only one, Murphy, escapes. Vowing to destroy the submarine, he is taken to a Quaker missionary (Sian Phillips, Mrs. Peter O'Toole) by Brezen (Philippe **Noiret**), a French oil engineer who merely wants to sit out the rest of the war in peace. The missionary patches Murphy up. A wounded airman is brought to the mission and before the Germans kill him he begs Murphy to keep his plane out of German hands. Murphy decides to patch up the plane and use it to bomb the German sub. The only trouble is, he doesn't know how to fly. He rigs gasoline bombs to his wings, manages to get the plane in the air,

and drops the bombs on the sub. It's not destroyed, however. The war ends but Murphy's private war goes on and
he takes the barge on which Brezen lives and goes after
the sub. He blows up the sub with one of its own torpedoes
but he is drowned when the barge sinks.

The scenes of Murphy learning to fly the Grumman
J2F-6 Duck are very exciting. The hair-raising flying was
done by Frank Tallman. The film was shot on location on
Venezuela's Orinoco River and Tallman's plane was flown
there for the shots. No models or trick techniques were
used. Tallman did rip large panels of fabric off the wing
on three occasions and clipped several trees. Once he damaged the lower wing when he struck a hidden object in the
water, but he managed to land safely.

THE BIRDMEN (1971, retitled ESCAPE OF THE BIRD-
MEN) was a made-for-TV movie starring Doug McClure and
Chuck Connors about Allied POWs in a German castle who
build a glider so that they can fly to Switzerland, ten miles
away.

The most recent aviation sequences about the European
war occurred in A BRIDGE TOO FAR (1977). The picture
dealt with the Allied invasion of Holland, which proved to be
the greatest airborne assault in history. Most of the film
deals with the planning and combat of the invasion, but the
sequences of the air assault by two American divisions and a
British one are exciting.

The West German documentary, BOMBS OVER BERLIN
(BOMBEN AUF BERLIN, 1983), depicted the strategic bombing of Berlin from the viewpoint of German civilians. During
the last 18 months of the war, Berliners spent half of their
time in air raid shelters. A February 3, 1945 raid on the
center of Berlin by the British resulted in more than 2,000
dead and left over 100,000 homeless. By contrast, the German bombing of London throughout all of 1940 killed slightly
over 200 and made 9,000 homeless. BOMBS OVER BERLIN
traces the history of the city during the war, and includes
much rare footage.

The European war has provided aviation filmmakers
with some of their greatest images. From the fighters of
THE BATTLE OF BRITAIN to the B-17s of TWELVE O'CLOCK

HIGH, the aerial battles in the war have received thorough and expert attention. This is the single largest group of aviation films, and it provides some of the most exciting flying to be found on the screen.

CHAPTER 8

FLYING TIGERS

The Japanese strike on Pearl Harbor, December 7, 1941, dramatically demonstrated the important role aviation would play in the war in the Pacific. In action ranging from the epic carrier battles to the fire bombing of Japan, thousands of aviators fought and died in the blue Pacific skies. Their exploits provided the material for some exciting aviation films, films that matched the best ones to come out of the European Theater.

NIPPON'S WILD EAGLE (1941, also called NIPPON'S YOUNG EAGLES) was one of the rare Axis aviation films to be discussed in the Allied press. The film, shown in Berlin to an audience that included Goebbels, dealt with the training of pilots and Japan's attacks on Pearl Harbor, Malaya, the Philippines, and Borneo.

A few other Japanese aviation films were made during the war. THE BURNING SKY (1940), directed by Yutaka Abe, an aviation enthusiast, contained documentary footage of Japan's pre-World War II military actions. THE WAR AT SEA FROM HAWAII TO MALAYA (1942) dealt with Japanese Navy fliers and won a prize for the best film of the year in Japan. THE SOARING PASSION (1941) dealt with sailplanes and was directed by Eiichi Koishi, who also made GENERAL KATO'S FALCON FIGHTERS (1944). Flying cadets were the subject of TOWARDS THE DECISIVE BATTLE IN THE SKY (1943); and NAVY (1943) dealt with the pilots who bombed Pearl Harbor. THE DIVINE SOLDIERS OF THE SKY (1942) was a documentary about Japanese paratroopers.

REMEMBER PEARL HARBOR (1942) was a minor Republic effort starring Republic's western star Donald Barry as a soldier in the Philippines who unknowingly becomes

involved with Axis fifth columnists, turns on them, and suicidally crashes a plane into a Japanese troop transport.

WINGS FOR THE EAGLE (1942) dealt with the workings
of the California Lockheed plant (helpfully near the Warners'
Burbank lot) and the extra efforts necessary to get the
2,000th plane through production. Dennis Morgan played a
factory worker who makes himself so important in the production of Hudson bombers and P-38s that he escapes the draft.
But Pearl Harbor changes that and he goes into Army aviation. George Tobias played a Lockheed boss, fired from his
job because he doesn't have his citizenship papers but reinstated after he takes the oath of allegiance. He makes the
planes and his son flies them, until the son is killed in the
Philippines. Ann Sheridan provided the feminine touch while
Billy Curtis, a midget, showed one way of solving a fuselage
construction problem.

WAKE ISLAND (1942) was the first major Pacific aviation film. The Paramount picture starred Brian Donlevy,
Robert Preston, and Macdonald Carey in a story of the defense of the island by some 385 Marines against the Japanese.
Directed by John Farrow, the film was written by W. R. Bur-
nett and Frank Butler and based on an "original story by the
United States Marines," according to the credits as cited
from the Marine Corps records of the battle. The terse,
unfrilled account of the battle during the two weeks following
Pearl Harbor captured the imagination of the American public
and led to high praise from many critics. Newsweek called
it "... Hollywood's first intelligent, honest, and completely
successful attempt to dramatize the deeds of an American
force on a fighting front."[1] The New York Times stated:
"Here is a film which should surely bring a surge of pride
to every patriot's breast."[2] In this story of concentrated
air (with F4Fs), ground, and naval action, Americans had a
new group of heroes. Although the characters in the film
were fictional, their defiance of the enemy in the face of
overwhelming odds (and replies like "Send us more Japs,"
when they were asked if they wanted anything) meant that
Americans no longer had to identify with fighting men by
proxy through British or other Allied soldiers.

WAKE ISLAND began with four months' work on the
script. The script was returned to the studio by the Navy
for some minor technical revision and the filmmakers had

Brian Donlevy (center) and fellow Marines under attack in
WAKE ISLAND (1942).

Marine Corps cooperation and approval of the effort. The
Salton Sea in the Southern California desert, about 200
miles from Los Angeles, was used as a location because of
coastal defense restrictions placed on the filmmakers. The
crew was housed in a camp built to simulate the civilian
labor camp on Wake Island, and a set was built in ten days.
This included a mile-long runway, built by the man who had
built the runway on Wake, a garrison, a town, gun emplace-
ments, radio towers, and docks. Set designers worked from
photographs and newsreels.

The major problem in shooting arose from the gales
that blew through the area and created sandstorms. Farrow tried to use wind machines to counteract the sand, but
these didn't do the job. The sand clogged guns and ruined
battle sequences. It also irritated people's eyes and everyone would have to retreat inside tents until the storm passed.

WAKE ISLAND received enthusiastic support, as could well be expected. At the Quantico Marine base 2,000 Marines "... cheered it with thunderous applause."[3] And in Detroit on September 17, the audience paid for their admission by buying $1,300,000 worth of war bonds. After the picture, 350 young men from Detroit and other parts of Michigan were sworn into the Marine Corps.

The Asian war generated one of the greatest aviation documentary films to come out of World War II, THE BATTLE OF MIDWAY (1942). The 18-minute Technicolor film was made by one of Hollywood's top directors, Commander John Ford, U.S.N.R., who headed a Navy film unit. It was the first release of the Motion Picture Industry's War Activities Committee. Filmed in silent 16mm (a soundtrack was added) and blown up for theatre distribution, much of it, dealing with one of the most significant naval battles in history, was personally filmed by Ford, who was on Midway Island and was wounded and knocked unconscious during the battle. Two of the three cameras photographing the island fighting were destroyed. The film was the first battle photographed in Technicolor and "... the first official shots of U.S. troops in actual combat...."[4] Five hundred prints were distributed by Twentieth Century-Fox as part of the Activities Committee War Bond Drive. The exciting jerkiness of the battle had a great impact on audiences, especially given the overwhelming victory scored against the Japanese. The film served as the nucleus for MIDWAY (1975), a dramatization of the battle.

John Wayne starred in the average Republic adventure, FLYING TIGERS (1942). Limited by its routine aerial action, the story of a hot-shot pilot (John Carroll) who has to learn the meaning of the war from his squadron leader (Wayne) was weak. The film began with a foreword by Generalissimo Chiang Kai-Shek and Republic had intended to include a scene in which the Chinese leader brings Carroll back to the American base in his own car. The Hays Office vetoed the idea, saying it would not be proper to show Chiang without permission; so the scene was rewritten and Carroll died instead.

The final scene of FLYING TIGERS featured a flying Capelis transport. This model work was done by the Lydecker brothers, who worked at Republic Studios in the

1930s and 1940s. Rather than film models on a sound stage with artificial light, they photographed outdoors in the clear air of Arizona against real backgrounds. They won a 1943 Oscar nomination for Best Special Effects for their efforts. (This technique was revived for THE RIGHT STUFF.)

The year 1942 closed out with NIGHT PLANE FROM CHUNGKING, a poor plane-crash film about a group of people, including Robert Preston as an American pilot serving with the Chinese army, on board a transport plane shot down by the Japanese while traveling from Chungking to the Indian border. They are betrayed to the Japanese by a Nazi agent, but Preston sees to their rescue.

LADY FROM CHUNGKING started off 1943. It was a Producers Releasing Corp. picture about a Chinese guerrilla leader who helps two Flying Tigers.

Next came one of the best films to come out of World War II, Howard Hawks' AIR FORCE (1943). The Warner Bros. production was written by Dudley Nichols, who worked from Army Air Force records. It told the story of the B-17 "Mary Ann" and her crew, from the bombing of Pearl Harbor through the Battle of the Coral Sea. The film begins when the Mary Ann and eight other B-17s take off from Mather Field in San Francisco for Hawaii on Dec. 6, 1941. The bombers arrive at Pearl Harbor in the middle of the attack and the Mary Ann is detoured to Maui. Fifth columnists attack the plane, and the bomber returns to Hickam Field. The plane is ordered to Wake Island, which is under attack by the Japanese, and then on to Clark Field in the Philippines. The Mary Ann attacks a battleship and is badly damaged. Most of the crew bails out, but a gunner stays with the plane and brings it in for a crash landing. Amid attacks by the Japanese the plane is repaired and takes part in the Battle of the Coral Sea. It limps away after the battle, finally ending up on an Australian beach.

The Mary Ann's crew was made up of actors who were not big box-office draws. This reinforced the idea of dealing with the bomber and crew as a unit, rather than having the film be a vehicle for a particular actor. John Ridgely played the pilot, Capt. Quincannon, a man who loves his airplane. Arthur Kennedy portrayed the bombardier, Lieutenant McMartin, whose sister was wounded at Hickam Field.

John Garfield grabs the controls of the crippled Mary Ann in AIR FORCE (1943).

Gig Young played the role of the co-pilot, Lieut. Williams, who is in love with Kennedy's sister. The crew chief, Sgt. White, portrayed by Harry Carey, is a man who fought in World War I and whose son has just been killed in World War II. Comic relief was provided by the assistant crew chief, Corp. Weinberg, played by George Tobias. John Garfield played Sgt. Winocki, the gunner filled with bitterness because he failed to become a pilot. Rounding out the group was Charles Drake as Lieut. Hauser, the navigator, Ward Wood as Corp. Peterson, the radio operator, and James Brown as a pursuit pilot picked up as a passenger to Manila.

The film was made with the cooperation of the War Department and included actual historical incidents, some accurate and some not. For example, there was a flight of B-17s coming into Pearl Harbor during the attack. In the film, John Garfield cuts a hole in the rear of the plane and mounts a gun there to cover this blind spot. (The Mary Ann is a B-17C, which was not equipped with a tail gun.) This was based on an actual incident. An attack against a Japanese battleship, the Haruna, depicted in the film was based on reports of such an attack by Colin Kelly, who had taken his B-17 off from Clark Field on December 9, 1941 in search of targets. He attacked what he believed to be a battleship and his crew believed it had been bombed to a burning hulk. People wanted to believe serious damage had been done to the Japanese and Kelly became a hero. Martin Caidin wrote: "So chaotic were conditions at air force headquarters that the official communiques of the events involving Kelly's bomber (false to begin with) were distorted and swiftly expanded into a major victory for the United States."[5]

AIR FORCE was made at the suggestion of Lt. Gen. H. H. (Hap) Arnold, chief of the Army Air Forces, who insisted on complete authenticity. As a result, the film's budget ran to around $2,500,000. Interior sets of a B-17 were built at a cost of $40,000. These were fully detailed, except for secret military devices. (The B-17 used in the flying scenes was eventually lost in action in the South Pacific.) Much of the picture was shot in six weeks at Drew Field, Tampa, Florida, where Hickam Field was recreated by a technical crew of about 150 men. Models were used in the scene in which the Japanese fleet is attacked. Ten cameras, under the direction of cinematographer James Wong Howe, photographed the ground action, while Elmer Dyer did the aerial

photography with three camera planes brought from Hollywood. Paul Mantz served as chief pilot. To shoot the South
Pacific island footage, the crew moved to a jungle area ten
miles outside of Tampa. To make it suitable for filming (because of the soft ground), the jungle had to be moved intact
across a highway and two hundred extras worked in the 100°
Florida heat. Aerial pictures were shot from the wings of
diving planes and, when planes dove almost into the cameras,
from the ground. One **Major** diving a P-43 was 20 feet from
the ground when an explosion simulating a bomb blast buffeted his plane. He threatened to quit if exposed to more
of the same. Advising the filmmakers were Majors Sam Trif-
fy, Jack Coulter, and Capt. Hewitt T. Wheless, whom President Roosevelt had cited in a Fireside Chat for bringing his
crippled B-17 home after bombing six Japanese transports.
The film opened with a quotation from the **Gettysburg** Ad-
dress and included a broadcast of Roosevelt's declaration-
of-war speech to Congress.

AIR FORCE premiered on February 3, 1943 at the Hollywood Theatre in New York to enthusiastic critical reception.
Time called it "... easily the best aviation film to date,"[6]
while Variety labeled it "... one of the sock war pictures of
this or any other war."[7] The New York Times called it "...
truly an epic, in the very best sense of the word...."[8] Besides being popular on the home front, AIR FORCE scored
with the GIs; in a survey done by the Army Motion Picture
Service for Variety, AIR FORCE ranked second in Army theatre box office receipts (after CRASH DIVE) in the 1942-43
period. Contemporary critics have also praised the film, and
Robin Wood in his book, Howard Hawks, calls it "... one of
[Hawks'] greatest works."[9]

AERIAL GUNNER (1943), made with Army cooperation,
was a low-budget Paramount film about two enemies in civilian
life, Chester Morris and Richard Arlen, thrown together at
the Harlingen aerial gunnery school. The film detailed pre-
combat training and **climaxed** with a furious air battle against
the Japanese. Morris and Arlen's plane force-lands on a
Japanese occupied island and Morris sacrifices his life so that
Arlen can take off and get away.

PILOT NO. 5 (1943) was an MGM film about a pilot in
the Philippines, played by Franchot Tone, once involved in
machine politics, who goes on a suicide mission against a

Japanese carrier. After he has taken off, his four pilot companions tell in flashbacks what they know about his past. The film featured the Republic Seversky EP-1, a fighter which was already obsolete when the war broke out.

A GUY NAMED JOE (1943) was reportedly the first fiction film to show the Lockheed P-38 and it remains one of the very few movies in which this fighter has appeared. Spencer Tracy played a squadron commander who is killed at the beginning of the film but returns as a reluctant guardian angel to another flier (Van Johnson), although this flier can neither see nor hear him. Since this pilot falls in love with Tracy's former girl friend (Irene Dunne), Tracy is not interested in helping him. But Tracy's commander in heaven says Tracy owes a debt to other fliers that must be paid. To save Johnson, Dunne (who is a ferry pilot) flies the hazardous mission and destroys a Japanese supply dump. In 1983 MGM/UA was considering a remake of the film, titled ALWAYS and directed by Steven Spielberg.

BOMBARDIER (1943) was another service picture, this time dealing with the U.S. Army's theories of high-level precision bombing and the training of bombardier cadets. Pat O'Brien played a dedicated believer of high-level bombing in this RKO film, while Randolph Scott served as his foil in the role of a pilot who doesn't share O'Brien's beliefs. Scott eventually dies when he sets himself and his downed plane afire to guide the other planes to the target in a raid against Japan. Ann Shirley provided the love interest. The film was made in cooperation with the Air Force and some of it was shot at Kirkland Field, Albuquerque, and at Blythe, California. The film features a B-17E and a B-18.

WINGS OVER THE PACIFIC (1943) was a poor Monogram production about a WWI veteran whose island paradise is disturbed when a German pilot and a U.S. Navy flier land after a dogfight.

Walt Disney produced VICTORY THROUGH AIR POWER (1943), a 65-minute animated look at the history of air power from 1903 to 1939. The Technicolor film, dedicated to General Billy Mitchell, was based on Major Alexander P. de Seversky's book of the same title. Seversky, a Russian designer and WWI flier, had strong theories about air power and appeared in the film; he was asked questions about his theories and the answers were provided in animated sequences. Two chief themes were the necessity for the United States to have an air force separate from any other branch of the service, and that the defeat of Japan could be accomplished by building fleets of giant long-range bombers that would fly from bases in Alaska and bomb Japan into submission.

Critics praised the film for its straightforward way of presenting history and concepts of aviation so that they were easily understandable by children and adults alike. The New York Times called it "... an extraordinary accomplishment ... a new milestone in the screen's recently accelerated march toward maturity."[10] The picture was Disney's first feature-length war film, and he planned to follow it with THE GREMLINS, a collection of Royal Air Force legends dealing with the beings who were said to help or hinder pilots in battle.

The U.S. Army Signal Corps' REPORT FROM THE ALEUTIANS (1943) dealt with the Aleutian campaign from six months following the landing on Adak Island. Shot in 16mm Kodachrome and blown up to 35mm Technicolor, the picture was made by Hollywood director Captain John Huston and Captain Ray Scott. The principal aerial action consisted of a raid with Liberators and a B-17 against Kiska. Scott flew to the targets nine times in six days and received the Air Medal for his efforts. Huston was nearly killed twice, during a crash landing and when a 20mm shell from a Zero killed the waist gunner sitting three feet away from him. The raid shown in the film was really a composite of fifteen separate trips made by various members of the six-man film unit. Release of the picture was delayed two months because of haggling over its length. The Office of War Information felt the 47-minute length was "awkward" and the film should be reduced to two reels. The Army felt that the film should not be cut, and although they had their way, the delay meant the film was not shown during the May-June attack on Attu, when public interest in the Aleutians was at its height. Huston's father, Walter, provided some of the narration.

THE PURPLE HEART (1944) was the first aviation film to deal with the April 1942 Doolittle raid on Tokyo. The film, written by Darryl Zanuck under the name of Melville Crossman (because exhibitors objected to Zanuck's name on scripting credits for so many films--in one year he wrote 19) was a fictional effort based on the Japanese announcement that

Dana Andrews (l.), Sam Levene (r.) and a companion face
capture in THE PURPLE HEART (1944).

eight American fliers captured on the raid had been executed after "investigation and confession." Most of the film took place in a Japanese courtroom and centered on two themes: the efforts of the Japanese to learn, through torture, the take-off point of the bombers, and the internal wrangling between the Japanese Army, which claimed the bombers had taken off from an aircraft carrier (which they had) and the Navy, which said that wasn't possible. The Americans were charged with murder for deliberately bombing non-military targets and killing children, and were tried in a civil court, although they were legally prisoners of war. Lewis Milestone directed and Dana Andrews and Richard Conte starred.

Critics praised the film for its effective portrayal of the brutal Japanese. Variety commented: "The Jap military caste, their matter-of-fact innate, senseless cruelty, their insanely nationalistic fanaticism, have been drawn in cold, stark, deliberate, devastating strokes. It is, so far, the strongest indictment of the savagery and sadism of the Japs to be projected."[11]

ATTACK! THE BATTLE FOR NEW BRITAIN (1944), a six-reel documentary dealing with the assault on the island of New Britain, included shots of B-25s softening up the shore. The film, distributed by RKO, proved to be one of the company's most sought-after releases and was booked in about 15,000 locations.

WING AND A PRAYER (1944) was a 95-minute carrier picture that told part of the story of the American Navy after Pearl Harbor. An unnamed aircraft carrier, Carrier X (a footnote on the credits said for military reasons the carrier and other ships in the film could not be named), is given the job of making the Japanese think the American Navy is scattered and disorganized. To do this, the ship runs away from an encounter with the enemy, lulling the Japanese into a false sense of security until the American Navy fights back at Midway. Members of Squadron Number Five on board the carrier, which contains the usual cross section of "average" Americans engaged in war, included Dana Andrews and Don Ameche.

WING AND A PRAYER was directed by Henry Hathaway, who, with a camera crew, spent seven weeks on board a carrier in order to shoot 50,000 feet of factual footage.

The Navy then provided the filmmakers with combat footage and soundtracks from the Battle of Midway. Much of the film was shot on board the Yorktown II during her shake-down cruise, during which time the first Curtiss SB2C Hell-divers were attempting to qualify for carrier operation. Some of the Grumman TBF Avenger crash footage was ac-complished by placing pieces of aircraft in tanks of water on the Twentieth Century-Fox back lot. The picture was per-haps inspired by Stanley Johnson's book, <u>Queen of the Flat Tops</u>, for Fox had offered to buy the book for $20,000 but backed out when the author and publisher refused to sign a contract which said that Fox, which was supposedly buying only the title, could not be sued if some material from the book was inadvertently used. Johnson and the publisher, E. P. Dutton, won a settlement against Fox when they sued in 1946.

The next aviation film was THIRTY SECONDS OVER TOKYO (1944), the story of the Doolittle raid in April 1942. The screenplay was written by Dalton Trumbo and based on the book by Captain Ted W. Lawson and Robert Considine. The picture, therefore, concentrated on Lawson, played by Van Johnson, and although Spencer Tracy as Lieutenant Colonel Doolittle got top billing he had only a small role. The film followed Lawson and his men from their B-25 car-rier training early in 1942 through the raid, and detailed the subsequent experiences of the men after they crashed on the China coast, where Lawson's leg was amputated. The romance between Lawson and his wife was added.

Directed by Mervyn LeRoy, the 138-minute picture is best when dealing with the flying experiences of Lawson's B-25, The Ruptured Duck. The filmmakers recreated the flight deck of the aircraft carrier Hornet and mixed process shots with real footage of the raid to achieve the desired effect. Of particular interest is the take-off from the Hor-net in a storm, the low-level bombing of Japan, and a B-25 flying under the Golden Gate Bridge.

Critics praised the aviation footage but found parts of the picture overly sentimental, as in the farewell party at the beginning.

The next aviation film was WINGED VICTORY (1944), directed by George Cukor (William Wyler was a possible first

Van Johnson (c.) and crew members from The Ruptured Duck struggle ashore after crashing off the Chinese coast, in THIRTY SECONDS OVER TOKYO (1944).

choice) and written by Moss Hart, based on his own play. It was a documentation of the training of six American young men from diverse parts of America who have become members of the Army Air Force. The film follows them through basic training, aptitude tests, solo flights, graduation, and finally combat in New Guinea. The cast consisted largely of the Broadway troupe who were brought to Hollywood for the production. All the male roles were filled by actual members of the Army Air Force, including Sergeant Edmond O'Brien, Corporal Lee J. Cobb, and Corporal Red Buttons. The wives of the men were given ten-week contracts by Fox and served as extras.

Moss Hart completed his script in March 1944 and the film began shooting on June 15 and finished on September 25. The Christmas party scene occupied a mile and a quarter of

Part of the cast of Army Air Force personnel from WINGED VICTORY (1944)

beach front, necessitating the use of walkie talkies, reportedly the first time these were used in the production of a picture. Locations at twenty or more military camps in California were used. The proceeds from the film were donated to Army charities and the 130-minute film was well received by the critics, although it wasn't substantially different in tone from the recruiting films of the 1930s.

The year 1944 closed out with THE FIGHTING LADY, a 61-minute U.S. Navy documentary detailing the operations of an Essex class carrier in the Pacific. The picture dealt with a typical carrier from the time its complement of planes arrived on board in 1943 through her combat experiences in raids on Marcus Island, Kwajalein, Truk, Guam, Saipan, Tinian, and the Marianas in the battle of the Philippine Sea in June 1944 during which the "Great Marianas Turkey Shoot" took place and the Japanese lost 346 planes and two carriers.

The idea for a picture giving the home front a complete view of life on board a carrier was conceived by Captain H. B. Miller, USNR, Bureau of Aeronautics, in 1943.
The picture was shot over a period of fifteen months by six
enlisted men under the direction of Lieutenant Commander
Dwight Long and supervised by noted photographer Captain
Edward Steichen. Much of the film's impact came from the
combat footage gleaned from the gun cameras of Hellcat fighters, Avenger torpedo bombers, and Helldiver dive bombers.
By one report, more than 500,000 feet of film was used.
This 16mm **Kodachrome** stock was processed into Technicolor
and blown up to 35mm for the final version of the film.

The Navy worked out an arrangement with Twentieth
Century-Fox by which Fox produced the film for commercial
release. This was the first time a commercial studio had
undertaken the releasing of a feature-length documentary
made by the armed forces under normal trade conditions.
(Fox had distributed the British DESERT VICTORY, but
American battle films such as MEMPHIS BELLE had been given
free to theatres by the Office of War Information and the motion picture industry's War Activities Committee.) Fox intended THE FIGHTING LADY as the first in a series of
"journalistic features" dealing with war-related subjects and
produced by Louis de Rochemont. After the footage shot
had been studied by Navy Intelligence, 60,000 feet of it
went to Rochemont (producer of THE MARCH OF TIME) and
he edited it down to a final version 7,500 feet long. A narration for the film was written by John Steward Martin and
spoken by Lieutenant Robert Taylor, USN.

The film was completed at the end of 1944 and premiered on January 17, 1945 in New York. The profits of
the film went to the Navy Relief Society. The critics were
enthusiastic about the film, particularly enjoying the gun
camera footage and the scene where a Japanese plane almost
crashed into the carrier. Time said: "For violent air action and pure visual magnificence, THE FIGHTING LADY is
not likely ever to be beaten."[12] On the negative side, com-
plaints were raised that the film had been edited too sharply
and that scenes of American planes being shot down were almost completely eliminated. Upon seeing the picture, Admiral
Chester Nimitz called the film "'A real picture of real men
and real fighting.'"[13] Nimitz went on to suggest one of the
most unusual methods of distribution ever proposed for a film.

He felt the film was so effective in presenting the United States that it should be dropped over Tokyo for the Japanese to view. Long quoted Nimitz as saying, "... the Japanese should see this picture some day with our bombs and our compliments."[14]

OBJECTIVE BURMA (1945) was a top-notch actioner starring Errol Flynn. It told the story of a group of paratroopers dropped into the Burmese jungle to wipe out a Japanese radar station. The aerial action consisted of paratroop drops at the beginning and end of the film, supply drops, and a glider evacuation of Flynn and his men at the close of the picture. The film proved very popular, but created a furor among the British. The film, they said, implied that the Americans beat the Japanese in Burma single-handed and completely ignored the large role played by the British Fourteenth Army. England's Lord Chancellor banned the film and Warners suspended the picture's general release in England.

GOD IS MY CO-PILOT (1945) was, like THIRTY SECONDS OVER TOKYO, an aviation film based on a best-selling book. The Warners film starred Dennis Morgan as Colonel Robert Lee Scott, Jr. and told of his experiences with the Flying Tigers. The film followed Scott from his boyhood interest in aviation (jumping off a barn with an umbrella, building model planes, flying the mail) to the time of Pearl Harbor when Scott was rejected for combat because of his age (34). Scott persisted, however, and managed to get an assignment on a B-17, which took him to India. When a planned raid on Tokyo was shelved, Scott hauled freight in an unarmed Fortress to Claire Channault's (Raymond Massey) Flying Tigers in China. Scott began flying a P-40 against the Japanese and when the USAAF took over the group in 1942, Scott stayed on as commander of the 23rd Flying Group. The real Scott served as a special advisor on the film and the aerial footage was shot at Luke AFB, Arizona with P-40Fs.

GOD IS MY CO-PILOT is an uneven film that mixes some good combat sequences with worn-out aviation film clichés, particularly the presence of a Japanese ace, Tokyo Joe, who taunts the Americans over the radio. The film's weakest moments are those in which a priest, Big Mike (Alan Hale), discusses with Scott the appropriateness of the film's title, because Scott has faith only in himself.

The year 1945 closed out with two documentaries.
THE FLEET THAT CAME TO STAY was a 20-minute picture
about the Kamikaze attacks on Okinawa. The film was shot
during the three months of the Okinawan operation by 103
Marines, Coast Guard and Navy cameramen, one of whom was
killed. The picture was edited by the Navy Photographic
Services and showed striking scenes of the attacks on the
American ships. The Navy claimed its pilots and gunners
destroyed "4,232 Japanese planes" during the action.

In JUNGLE PATROL (1948) eight pilots are based at a
temporary airfield near Port Moresby, New Guinea. They
are to hold off the Japanese planes until a permanent airstrip can be built. They manage to blow up 100 enemy
planes without losing a single pilot, but the men know they
could be killed on their next mission. No aerial action is
shown; the air battles are all heard on Operations Radio.

Warner Brothers produced the next aviation film, TASK
FORCE (1949). The movie, dealing with the history of naval
carrier aviation from the USS Langley to the USS Franklin D.
Roosevelt, was conceived in 1945. The producers planned to
use Navy, Marine, and Coast Guard color footage shot off
Iwo Jima, Okinawa, and elsewhere. Delmer Daves got the
directing chores and the technical advisors were to be Captain Morton T. Seligman, executive officer of the carrier
Lexington, sunk in 1942, and Lieutenant Oliver Jensen, author
of Carrier War. But the abrupt end of World War II caused
Warners to abandon the project in August 1945, because the
film wouldn't be released until 1946 and Warners realized that
this would be a bad time to launch a war film. (Warners also
scuttled another aviation film, TARGET JAPAN, in 1945. It
was to be about the activities of bomber crews based on Saipan.) But inspired by the upswing in World War II films
toward the end of the 1940s, Warners reactivated the project.

Before the actual start of production in October 1948,
producer Jerry Wald and director Delmer Daves examined
4,000,000 feet of color film shot by the Navy at naval bases
and on board vessels during the war. From this they ex-
tracted 2,200 feet of superb color combat film which formed
the film's core. Ample footage existed for the period after
1940, but depicting the origins of naval aviation presented a
problem. Wald and Daves uncovered footage of the Langley,
a collier converted into the Navy's first carrier, and the

Saratoga, but the film was in black and white and had been
shot at silent speed. The filmmakers first planned to have
Mantz fly a 1923 plane and mix shots of this with miniatures
of the early carriers, but finally decided to make the first
part of the film in black and white, switching to color when
the Enterprise was shown at Pearl Harbor.

The release date of the film was advanced because of
a controversy between the Navy and the Air Force over carrier aviation versus the B-36 bomber, and to take advantage
of aircraft exhibitions put on by the Navy to promote the
film. TASK FORCE had a two-ocean premiere, being shown
on September 20, 1949 aboard the carriers Midway in the Atlantic and the Valley Forge in the Pacific, where 300 repre-
sentatives of the press, broadcasting, and motion pictures
watched the premiere. Warner Brothers received the Navy
Distinguished Public Service Award for producing the film.

Unfortunately, TASK FORCE's dramatic action leaves
something to be desired. Gary Cooper is good as the naval
commander who fights for the aircraft carrier, but the romantic scenes between him and Jane Wyatt detract from the
overall effect of the film. All the characters are completely
overshadowed by the aerial footage, and the planes run the
gamut from the Navy's earliest to the latest jets. This
makes TASK FORCE an excellent chronicle of the rise of
naval air power.

The Army and the Navy had received wide treatment
in aviation films after World War II but the Marines had been
neglected until FLYING LEATHERNECKS (1951), a John Wayne
adventure. The director, Nicholas Ray, combined spectacular
aviation footage with a meager plot to produce a film that is
only good in the air.

The story concerns a small squadron of Marines based
in the Pacific, first near Guadalcanal and then near Okinawa.
The commander, Dan (Wayne), pressures headquarters for
closer air support for the ground troops on Guadalcanal.
Since this air support comes from his squadron, this results
in the loss of some of his pilots. All this disturbs Dan's
executive officer, Griff (Robert Ryan), who feels that Dan
is too ruthless with the men's lives. He learns from Dan,
however, and in the end Dan is content to have Griff command the squadron.

The Technicolor film is best when the camera is in the air. Studio shots and actual combat pictures of Guadalcanal, **kamikaze** strikes, and other similar combat scenes are skillfully blended to produce exciting air action. Over Guadalcanal, Leyte, Tarawa, Iwo Jima, and Okinawa the fliers deal with Japanese troop ships, Zeros, and kamikazes. Most of the movie was shot at Camp Pendleton and at the El Toro Marine Base, with the cooperation of the U.S. Marine Corps and Marine Aviation.

The story of flying Marines in the Pacific was also told in the television series BLACK SHEEP SQUADRON, which ran between 1976 and 1978 on NBC TV. The series was based on the exploits of Gregory "Pappy" Boyington (played by Robert Conrad), who flew for the Flying Tigers before being given command of VMF 214 in the South Pacific. Boyington was the top-scoring Marine ace of the war with 28 victories (six of them as a Flying Tiger). He was shot down in combat, captured by the Japanese, and spent the rest of the war as a POW. He wrote an exciting account of his experiences, <u>Baa Baa Black Sheep</u>. Boyington served as technical advisor to the series.

Robert Conrad, an avid aviation enthusiast, fought hard to have the series made and them had to fight to keep it on the air. The first-season title of BAA BAA BLACK SHEEP was changed because the network felt some viewers thought it was a children's program. NBC canceled the series at the end of the 1976-1977 season, but Conrad's efforts got it back on the air.

For the series, the filmmakers collected F4U-1, -4, -5, -7, and FG-1 versions of the plane. The Zeros were modified T-6 trainers. The Corsair pilots often had to do tricky flying to make it seem as though the T-6s were flying faster than the Corsairs. Some of the aerial photography was done with the Tallmantz B-25, but many shots were filmed with a T-28, painted blue in case it ever accidently appeared in any of the shots. Jim Greenwood explained the camera set-up in the T-28:

> The T-28's rear cockpit was stripped to provide working space for a cinematographer and his hand-held 35 (millimeter) Arriflex camera. Small remote TV scopes were installed in both cockpits so that

[Jim] Gavin and the cinematographer could monitor two fixed cameras slung in pods under the wings (including a remote-controlled zoom lens on one camera). For every stunt they could expose three sets of film--two from the fixed cameras and one shot over Gavin's shoulder with the Arriflex.[15]

Stunt fliers for BLACK SHEEP included Frank Tallman, Jim Gavin, Steve Hinton, Tom Friedkin, and Ted Janczarek. Two other pilots, Glenn Riley and Tom Mooney, had actually flown with VMF 214 at the end of World War II. The pilots flew out of Indian Dunes, near Los Angeles. Because the narrow runway simulating the squadron's airbase was only wide enough for one airplane, formation take-offs were accomplished by having an airborne plane with its gear down fly low past a taxiing Corsair, giving the impression that several planes were taking off at once.

Unquestionably, BLACK SHEEP SQUADRON contains some of the best flying footage ever to appear in a television show. Unfortunately, equivalent attention wasn't lavished on the scripts. The series tended to concentrate more on fist fights between the fliers than on the real war. The show suffered from lack of character identification, and only Conrad stood out. The other "regular" characters weren't developed to the point where the viewer wanted to identify with them from week to week. For aviation buffs, the flying was enough, but it's easy to see why the show didn't last.

The end of 1951 was marked by one of the only two films ever devoted solely to the B-29 Superfortress: THE WILD BLUE YONDER (the other was ABOVE AND BEYOND). As long as the movie shows actual combat footage and studio shots of the B-29s, it's somewhat interesting, but the love triangle is dull. Captain Harold Calvert (Wendell Corey) and Major Tom West (Forrest Tucker) are both in love with an Army nurse (Vera Ralston). West is a neurotic and afraid to face a raid after 24 successful missions. Calvert gets wounded on a mission, but recovers. West, determined to prove himself, is killed while trying to save a crew member from the wreckage of a bomber. In THE WILD BLUE YONDER the director, Allan Dawn, is much more at home with the planes than the characters.

ABOVE AND BEYOND (1952) was a good, though uneven film about the flight crew assigned to drop the first
atomic bomb. In 1943 Colonel Paul Tibbets (Robert Taylor)
complains to a general about a bomb run carried out at six
thousand feet. He feels it would be safer to bomb at 20,000.
His complaint attracts the attention of the Air Force brass
and he is chosen to test the new B-29. He does so well that
he is selected to command the atomic bomb fliers' training
school at Wendover Field, Utah under the code name of Operation Silverplate. The result of his efforts is a graphic
bomb run over the target in the Enola Gay and, of course,
the detonation of the bomb.

The film has much in common with THE WILD BLUE
YONDER. As long as it sticks to the documentary-type
story of testing the B-29s, training the flight crews, and
dropping the bomb, it's a good aviation film. It falls apart
when it takes up the marital problems of Tibbetts. His wife
(Eleanor Parker) continually quarrels with him because his
top secret work takes up so much of his time. She raises
such a fuss that she becomes a security risk and is expelled
from the base; and this segment detracts from a genuinely
fine film.

ABOVE AND BEYOND has some good flying scenes and
some fine moments, particularly shots of the Enola Gay crew
attending evening prayers a few hours before take-off. Later,
when asked how it feels to have just killed all those people,
Taylor replies, "How do they feel about it?" Although the
film is based on real events, the filmmakers ironically include
the warning that "Any similarity to actual persons living or
dead ... is purely coincidental." The Tibbets story was
filmed again as the television movie ENOLA GAY: THE MEN,
THE MISSION, THE ATOMIC BOMB (1980), and it featured
the Confederate Air Force's B-29, the only flyable B-29 left.

FLAT TOP (1952) offered nothing new. A new carrier
group, led by Joe Rodgers (Richard Carlson), boards the
carrier USS Princeton in 1944 to find it run by a tough commanding officer (Sterling Hayden). The men all think Hayden is a slave driver until they realize that his methods offer the best chance for survival. Actual combat footage of
carrier action adds excitement to the film. Earlier films had
made good use of World War II combat footage, but it was
now ten years old and had lost its novelty. Also, it didn't

Two scenes from ABOVE AND BEYOND (1952): above, Robert Taylor and Eleanor Parker look intense over coffee; below, Taylor and scientists at work.

now match studio film. Like TASK FORCE, FLAT TOP had its premiere on a carrier, this time on the hangar deck of another USS Princeton.

THE PURPLE PLAIN (1954) was a British film. Squadron Leader Forrester (Gregory Peck) of the RAF, along with his navigator (Lyndon Brook) and another officer (Maurice Denham), crashes his Mosquito fighter in the Japanese-held Burmese jungle. The navigator suffers burns and cannot walk. The other officer suffers fits of depression. It is left up to Peck to get them all to safety and the trek to their own lines takes up most of the movie. After days in the jungle Denham shoots himself but Peck manages to get the navigator to safety. The main attraction of the picture is the romance provided by a Burmese actress, Win Min Than, who toured the US with 32 colorful saris to promote the picture. It was lensed in Sri Lanka with the cooperation of the Royal Air Force.

BATTLE STATIONS (1956), a poor film, told the story of an Essex class carrier from the time it leaves the Alameda Naval Air Station, after repairs of war damage, to the time when it returns to Brooklyn after an engagement with the Japanese. The film is basically a chronicle of life aboard an aircraft carrier, and not much time is devoted to the battle action. The film used a lot of stock footage.

WEEP, PEOPLE OF JAPAN--THE LAST PURSUIT PLANE (1956) was a Japanese war film directed by Hiroshi Noguschi. ZERO FIGHTER (1961) was a Japanese film about the A6M5 Zero fighter directed by Toshio Masuda.

A STORM FROM THE SEA (retitled I BOMBED PEARL HARBOR, 1961) was a Japanese movie telling of a young flight lieutenant (Yosuke Nataki) who first feels the exultation of victory after the attack on Pearl Harbor and then the bitterness of defeat at Midway. Noted actor Toshiro Mifune appeared in the film. Most of the aerial action was staged with models. The picture was directed by Shue Matsubagashi, who also did WINGS OF THE SEA (1962), a story of kamikaze pilots.

KAMIKAZE (1962) was a documentary that followed the aerial war in the Pacific from the Japanese preparations to bomb Pearl Harbor to the atomic bombing. The film is geared for a western audience, for the scenes of the Japanese home front match the stereotyped conception of the average Japanese citizen. The aerial footage is merely interesting.

NONE BUT THE BRAVE (1965) told of a group of Americans who crash on a remote island and make peace with a Japanese patrol. McHALE'S NAVY JOINS THE AIR FORCE (1965) has bumbling Ensign Parker (Tim Conway) accidently assuming the role of an Air Force officer. This impersonation eventually leads to the sinking of the Japanese fleet and an audience with President Roosevelt. MISSION BATANGAS (1969) had Dennis Weaver as an American pilot determined to save Philippine government gold from the Japanese during the 1942 fall of Corregidor. A poor film, shot in the Philippines.

In the fall of 1970 the most expensive aviation film ever made, TORA! TORA! TORA!, was released. The picture provided World War II flying scenes the like of which will never be seen again.

The exact reasons why Darryl F. Zanuck and Twentieth Century-Fox wanted to bankroll this $25,000,000 epic are somewhat unclear. (The movie cost more than it cost the Japanese to stage the original attack.) The picture, based on the books Tora, Tora, Tora by Gordon W. Prange and The Broken Seal by Ladislas Farago, deals with the Japanese attack on Pearl Harbor on December 7, 1941. Zanuck had produced THE LONGEST DAY in the early 1960s. That epic about the invasion of Normandy was both a critical and a popular success and it help restore Zanuck to power at Fox. But it had portrayed an American victory. Why would people be interested in a film about the worst disaster in American military history?

Zanuck presented his case this way: "'Audiences may not think they are waiting for TORA! but audiences never know what they want until it's put in front of them. TORA! TORA! will say something about today.'"[16] When a controversy later broke out over the film, Zanuck, at a cost of $15,000, placed full-page ads in the New York Times and the Washington Post to explain his position. The ad read, in part:

TORA 3 is an American-Japanese historical film

officially approved by the American Department of
Defense as well as the Japanese Department of Defense. The basic reason for producing this film ...
was to arouse the American public to the necessity
for preparedness in this **acute** missile age where a
sneak attack could occur at any moment.... This is
not merely a movie but an accurate and dramatic
slice of history that should never have occurred but
did occur, and the **purpose** of producing this film is
to remind the public of the tragedy that happened to
us and to ensure that it will never happen again.[17]

Another view, expressed by Elmo Williams, the film's producer, was that no matter how historically conscientious
filmmakers are, they are generally in the business to make
money.

Whatever the motive, preliminary work began on the
film in 1966 and full pre-production began in early 1967.
American filming began on December 7, 1968. The film was
divided into two parts: the American sequences and the
Japanese scenes. Richard Fleischer was hired to direct the
American section and Akira Kurosawa, the world-renowned
Japanese director, was signed to do the Japanese scenes.
Kurosawa bowed out because of ill health and he was replaced by the **lesser-known** Japanese directors, Toshio Masuda and Kinji Fukasaku. The Japanese sequences were
shot at Osaka and Ashiya Air Force **Base** on Kyushu, with
the filmmakers' headquarters located in Kyoto. At Ashiya,
three-quarters of the aircraft carrier Akagi, the Pearl Harbor attack force flagship, was reconstructed (for aircraft
take-offs) and a full-sized replica of the battleship Nagato,
Admiral **Yamamoto's flagship, was built next** to it for static
carrier footage. Built from the original plans, the Nagato
was 660 feet long and ten stories high, making it the largest
film set ever built in Japan. Japanese technical advisors
included Minoru Genda, the principal architect of the Pearl
Harbor strike; the aircraft advisor was Kanoe Sonokawa, the
Zero pilot who led the air strike that sank the HMS Prince
of Wales and **HMS Repulse off Malaya**; and the naval advisor,
Kuranosuke Isoda, a member of Yamamoto's staff.

The American sequences were more complex because of
the necessity of coming up with planes and locations. Several B-17s owned by Aviation Specialties of Mesa, Arizona

were flown in to double as the flight that landed at Pearl during the attack, while "flat" plywood B-17's were used on Hickam Field. Aviation Specialties was responsible for the aircraft and engines. Two flyable P-40 Warhawks were used, one an E model and the other an N model. Model Bs were based at Wheeler during the raid, but the mock-ups were copied from the P-40E so that all of the planes would match. Several PBYs were barged to Hawaii for the Ford Island scenes and one was flown in for the flying sequences. Jack Canary made plaster molds from the flyable P-40s and then fiberglass P-40 fuselage sides were placed around welded steel frames. C-45 Beechcraft outer panels served as the wings, T-6 main gears and Curtiss Electric props were used, and P-40 tail gears and wheels were found. Some of these planes were used as dummies on the airstrip while others were fitted with original Allison engines so that they could taxi.

Canary also designed the modifications to other planes to turn them into Kates, Vals, and Zeros, each rebuilt at a cost of $20,000. (Canary was later killed flying a BT-13 from the East Coast for rebuilding.) The original idea was to use authentic Japanese planes in the film. A research team scoured the Solomons, the Yap group, and other islands in the Pacific, some of which had been by-passed by American task forces in the drive across the Pacific. Original planes were found, but they had deteriorated too far to be used. The Fox survey team calculated it would take at least five authentic wrecks to make one complete Japanese plane, not counting the fact that the planes would require new engines and the great difficulty of getting them off the islands and back to the U.S. Thirty-one accurate scale-replicas were made for the Kates, Vals, and Zeros. The two main types used were the Vultee BT-13 and the AT-6, a North American advanced trainer.

Vals were created from BT-13s by the Stewart-Davis Company in Long Beach, California. The BT-13 fuselage was lengthened, the vertical fin shape was changed, new wing tips were added, wheel parts and gear fairings were redesigned, the canopy revamped, and a 600 h.p. Pratt and Whitney R-1340 AN-1 engine and three-bladed prop was installed. The T-6 cowl was re-worked. Reportedly the rebuilt Val flew better than the Japanese version. Gas-fired rear guns were installed for a realistic effect. Planes were equipped with electronic strobe machine guns.

The Cal-Volair Company, also from Long Beach, "manufactured" the Zekes from AT-6s. Twenty-five such aircraft were produced. New canopies and new wing tips were installed. Guns, gun wells, air scoops, and landing gear fairings were added. Tail hooks were installed for carrier landings. The BT-13 tail gear with its hard rubber wheels was installed for carrier operation. These "Zekes" were also equipped with the R-1340 engine. Cal-Volair also produced the Kates. The front half of a T-6 airframe and the back half of a BT-13 were mated, along with a new seven-foot center section to create a Kate.

Only a few of each aircraft were able to land on a carrier. These planes had to make at least 20 arrester-hook landings on land before they were allowed to land on board the USS Valley Forge, the Navy helicopter landing ship chosen to substitute for the Akagi.

The Kawasaki Aircraft Company in Japan also rebuilt 19 T-6s. Off duty Navy and Air National Guard pilots flew the raid on Pearl Harbor. The total cost of the air operations turned out to be $2,500,000.

A good deal of model making also went into the film. Twenty-six ships, with an average length of 30 feet, were built over a period of six months by 80 studio model builders under the direction of Gaile R. Brown. The American ships were built at a 3/4" to one-foot scale ratio; the Japanese ships were 1/2" to the foot. Most of the model ships weighed almost a ton. A major portion of Pearl Harbor was recreated in model form and the models were burnt and capsized.

The rear section of the Arizona was rebuilt. It stretched 309 feet long and the tower stood 144 feet high. Ford field served as Hickam because Hickam itself had been modernized.

In a project of this magnitude, Defense Department cooperation was essential, but criticism was leveled at Fox because of the high degree of the Navy's involvement. The fact that six off-duty servicemen were burned during filming on April 12 did not help Fox's case. Zanuck took out newspaper ads defending the film (discussed earlier) after Representative John M. Murphy, Democrat of New York, introduced a bill "to prohibit the use of armed forces personnel and equipment in the production of certain films made for profit."[18] Murphy drafted the bill as a response to a letter from one of the burned servicemen, among other things. The Pentagon, however, reaffirmed its policy of giving aid to filmmakers as long as the assistance was paid for. Not satisfied, Murphy urged the Justice Department to file suit against Fox for costs of the aid, claiming that "... the Navy had virtually subsidized the film."[19] Fox claimed it had paid for the help, and no action was taken against the studio. In May 1969, on a "60 Minutes" segment, Mike Wallace had questions about the Navy carrying 30 planes on USS Yorktown from San Diego to Hawaii.

The principal photography was completed on June 6, 1969. Fox billed the epic as "The Most Spectacular Film Ever Made!" but it opened in September 1970 to generally unfavorable critical reaction. Perhaps the most noted critical comment came from Vincent Canby, who labeled the film "Tora-ble, Tora-ble, Tora-ble." Canby said it was "... possessed by a lack of imagination so singular that it amounts to a death wish."[20] He and other critics faulted the film for its lack of drama and the poor nature of the special effects dealing with Pearl Harbor. The problem with the picture arose from trying to recreate the event without dealing with the people involved. The audience was equally unenthusiastic; and the film was not a big money-maker.

The film does have some strong points, however. The flying sequences are superb; among the best on film. And the picture effectively captures the small events on which history turns: the slowness of a typist in the Japanese embassy, for example, which delays the Japanese declaration of war until after the start of the attack.

MIDWAY (1976) turned out to be an exceptionally disappointing combination of TORA! TORA! TORA! footage and newsreel shots, with the opening of the picture taken from THIRTY SECONDS OVER TOKYO. Conceived by Walter Mirish as a tribute to America's bicentennial, it coupled badly mismatched aviation footage with a ridiculous subplot about the aviator son of an American Naval officer (played by Charlton Heston) who is in love with a Japanese girl interned as a security risk. The Department of Defense wanted to cooperate in the making of the film, but could provide only limited assistance because of the lack of old equipment.

The film, of course, chronicles the epic carrier battle in World War II. The Japanese had hoped to lure the American fleet into a vulnerable position and destroy it. The Americans husbanded their scanty resources and, aided by excellent code breaking, destroyed the backbone of Japanese carrier airpower. Big name stars were signed to play the historical roles, with the only major fictional character being that played by Charlton Heston.

Only two authentic F4Fs were used in the film. The filmmakers got limited access to the carrier USS Lexington for dockside and atmosphere shots. The Navy, however, refused to allow the F4Fs to fly off the Lexington, even though they were airworthy. As a result, director Jack Smight could use the planes only as props.

Extensive use was made of actual combat footage and a statement was included at the beginning of the film saying all the combat shots were real. The problem was, much of this footage was badly mismatched. At one point a two-place Avenger torpedo bomber turns into an F4F when it crashes into the sea. In another sequence, a crippled F4F crash lands on a carrier and turns into an Avenger in the process! The crash that kills Heston at the film's end didn't even come out of World War II: Heston's plane was of Korean War vintage. In addition, there were considerable problems in blowing up the 16mm combat film to fit a wide-screen format. Footage from TORA! TORA! TORA!, of course, didn't pose this problem, but it is painfully obvious where these scenes came from. In spite of the mismatched footage and its plot problems, MIDWAY did turn out to be a box office success.

Two films at the end of the 1970s took an unconventional look at Americans at the time of the Pearl Harbor attack. 1941 (1979) has turned out to be director Steven Spielberg's only unsuccessful major film. The madcap comedy of panic in California immediately following Pearl Harbor failed at the box office, but it did feature some exciting stunting with a P-40 (flown by John Belushi's character) and exquisite model work.

THE FINAL COUNTDOWN (1980) had a United States nuclear-powered aircraft carrier ("played" by the U.S.S. Nimitz) becoming trapped in a "time tunnel" storm and being whisked back to 1941. The officers and men of the carrier realize they have a unique opportunity: they can stop the Pearl Harbor attack. After some agonizing over whether or not history should be tampered with, the Captain (Kirk Douglas) launches his jets to intercept the Pearl Harbor strike force. The time tunnel conveniently reappears, however, and returns the planes to the present day. The film's interesting premise is spoiled by the ending: the characters have no choice about being returned to the present. An interesting story would have been generated if Douglas could have chosen whether to come back to 1980, or to stay and change the course of World War II.

ATTACK FORCE Z (1981) was an **Australian-Taiwanese** film about a group of criminals sent to rescue plane crash survivors on a Japanese-occupied island.

The war in the Pacific abruptly ended with the dropping of the atomic bomb. Filmmakers continued to be fascinated with the aviation aspect of the war. While more epics like TORA! will probably never be produced, excellent films can come from the more limited stories provided by the war.

CHAPTER 9

MIG ALLEY

Between the end of World War II and the Korean War, combat aircraft underwent considerable development. The piston-driven planes of the Second World War gave way to supersonic jets that eventually stalked each other with air-to-air missiles. In the thirty years since the end of the Korean War, increasingly sophisticated aircraft have duelled in several conflicts: Vietnam, the Arab-Israeli Wars, the Falklands. But none of these aerial wars have made it to the motion picture screen; and the jet combat aviation film is the most neglected of all airplane film categories.

The United States entered the Korean conflict expecting to fight a highly mobile war. For a while it was, but soon the soldiers found themselves entangled in trench warfare reminiscent of World War I. While the foot soldiers battled over meaningless terrain, the aviators fought in the clouds. But there was none of the World War I gallantry between enemy pilots. Shot-down American pilots could expect torture and brainwashing if they were not quickly rescued.

MISSION OVER KOREA (1953) was one of the first, but not one of the best, aviation films dealing with the Korean War. It is concerned with the American Air Force in the early stages of the conflict. John Hodiak and John Derek play pilots who spend most of the time fidgeting in their cockpits, which are photographed against an obvious studio background. Hodiak, a stern officer, and Derek, a neurotic youngster, clash over methods of discipline. Maureen O'Sullivan appears as Hodiak's wife and Rex Reason plays a down-to-earth major. It has some shots of the Korean countryside taken from actual combat footage.

FLIGHT NURSE (1953) was a poor story of the Air

Force nurse corps. Nurse **Joan** Leslie falls madly in love
with a helicopter pilot (Arthur Franz). They have their
romantic problems until Leslie forgets her love affair to de-
vote herself entirely to her work, in spite of a lady-killing
C-47 pilot (Forrest Tucker). Thrown into the film are documentary shots of Communist atrocities.

SABRE JET (1953) was a weak Korean War actioner
that dealt with a fighter unit flying from a base in Japan.
It **tried**, but failed, to deal realistically with the problems
of the wives who must wait while their husbands fly combat
over Korea. Colonel Gil Manton (Robert Stack), second in
command at the base, has his problems with his wife (Coleen
Gray) who is a war correspondent. She wants to write a
story about the wives who wait anxiously by a special gate
for their husbands to return to base. She feels that this is
not only good material but that it will also further her career
as a journalist. Stack is appalled by this, feeling his wife
shouldn't try to capitalize on the sufferings of others.

The women are weak characters who are driven to near
hysteria when their husbands are flying. Some shots of the
jets, with fliers shooting at MIGs and strafing the ground,

Robert Stack on a mission in SABRE JET (1953).

are moderately interesting. The film was made in cooperation with the Air Force and some actual combat footage is used. Cameras with wide-angle lenses were mounted on the planes' fins to provide realistic shots.

DRAGONFLY SQUADRON (1954) told of the training of the South Korean Air Force just before the war. An Air Force major (John Hodiak) is sent to Kongu in 1950 to train South Korean pilots so that they will be ready in the event of war. It pays off in the end when the South Koreans repel a wave of Communist tanks. (The problems of the fledgling Korean Air Force were much better dealt with in BATTLE HYMN.)

MEN OF THE FIGHTING LADY (1954) was based on two articles that appeared in The Saturday Evening Post, "The Forgotten Heroes of Korea," by James Michener, and "The Case of the Blind Pilot," by commander Harry A. Burns, U.S.N., which served as the climax of the movie. A jet fighter squadron is based aboard the USS Princeton, stationed off Korea. Their task is to fly bombing missions against North Korean installations. A tough squadron leader, Lieutenant Commander Paul Grayson (Frank Lovejoy), an advocate of low-level flying, takes the outfit too low while attacking a target at Wosan. He indirectly causes the loss of one of his men and earns a rebuke from his commander. The climax comes when Lieutenant Howard Thayer (Van Johnson) uses the radio to guide a pilot blinded by antiaircraft fire to a safe landing on the carrier's deck. (This was based on a World War II incident in which a blinded Hellcat pilot was guided to a crash landing on a Pacific beach.)

The film is best when it shows Grumman F9F Panther jets. An air of excitement is created when planes are raised to the flight deck and made ready to go. Actual combat footage, some of it shot below 300 feet, is skillfully blended with studio shots to provide a realistic account of the bombing of a North Korean railway junction. This footage also shows the rescue of a flier downed in the ocean and a spectacular crash when a pilot (Keenan Wynn) slams into the flight deck. The acting is credible, with Walter Pidgeon, as the flight surgeon, and Louis Calhern, as Michener, providing an occasional profound thought about war.

William Holden and Mickey Rooney head for cover in Communist-held territory in THE BRIDGES AT TOKO-RI (1954).

Korean war films became bigger and better with THE BRIDGES AT TOKO-RI (1954). The picture, based on a Pulitzer Prize-winning James Michener novel, tells of the USS Oriskany and the USS Kearsarge operating in the China Sea and the Sea of Japan. Lieutenant Harry Brubaker (William Holden) served with distinction in World War II and is angry at being called up to fight in the forgotten war in Korea. He leaves his wife and children to serve aboard a carrier where he is taken under the wing of Rear Admiral George Tarrant (Fredric March). The admiral likes Brubaker because he reminds him of his son, who was killed in the war. Brubaker's wife (Grace Kelly) and his two daughters

come to Tokyo to be near him and this makes him even more
reluctant to risk his life. From the start, his missions are
ill-fated and he begins to think more about death. Returning from one sortie he has to crash his damaged plane in the
ocean, and almost dies before he is rescued by a jaunty helicopter pilot (Mickey Rooney) whose trademark is a green silk
hat and scarf. Another time he has to make an emergency
landing on the carrier's flight deck. And finally the admiral
has to send his unit on a very hazardous mission: destroy
five vital bridges at Toko-Ri in Korea's interior. Brubaker
is shot down, but makes it out of the crashed Panther jet.
Rooney and his helicopter come to the rescue but are shot
down, and Rooney is killed. Waves of Chinese soldiers make
their way toward Brubaker as American jets stream overhead,
strafing them. For every Chinese killed, however, ten take
their place. The result is inevitable: Brubaker is killed.

The film is exciting both in the air and on the ground.
The planes, fliers, and carriers were supplied by the Navy,
which also helped stage some of the action. The shots of the
jets taking off and landing, of daring helicopter operations,
of fighter missions, of high-altitude scenes, and of spectacular crashes make this one of the best naval aviation movies.
The picture has excellent special effects. They were so good,
in fact, that Pentagon officials at a special screening were
aghast to see planes crashing and burning on the flight deck.
Several admirals demanded to know if planes had been deliberately crashed to accommodate the Hollywood film crew!
They were assured that the shots were all done with models.
The film won an Oscar in 1954 for best technical effects.

William Holden turns in an excellent performance as a
man who can't understand why he has to serve his country
twice. He's told it's because he's there and other people are
somewhere else. He fights because he happens to be in the
right place at the right time, not from noble sentiments.
This, one of the best Korean war films, like many World
War I films (such as THE DAWN PATROL), stresses the futility of war.

In BATTLE TAXI (1955), it was the US Air Service's
actions in Korea that captured the filmmaker's imagination.
Made in cooperation with the Defense Department, the film
is a poor account of helicopter pilots. Sterling Hayden plays
the head of an air rescue squadron whose job it is to con-

vince the eager pilots that it is more important for them to
save lives than to try to kill the enemy.

THE McCONNELL STORY (1955), which opens with a
dedication to the USAF as a guardian of the peace, is the
biography of America's first triple jet ace, Joseph McConnell,
who shot down 16 MIGs in nine months of flying in Korea.
Alan Ladd plays McConnell. During World War II he quits
the Medical Corps to become a navigator on a B-17, and he
flies 25 missions. He really wants to be a pilot, however,
and takes flying lessons on the side. He is rescued from a
post-war desk job and becomes a pilot. He's assigned to a
P-47 base after the war, is shunted from base to base, and
ends up flying F-86s in Korea and battling the Communist
MIG-15s (really F-84F Thunderstreaks). On August 25,
1954, McConnell tests an F-86H over the Rodgers Dry Lake
Desert in California. The Sabre jet goes out of control and
he's killed. The next day another pilot takes his place as
test pilot, because of the extreme importance the H model
will play in the war.

The picture had its premiere in New York. A parade,
at which the Air Force Wives Association was honored, preceded the opening of the film. Officers from all four branches
of the service attended the premiere and among the guests
were Captain Peter Fernandez, USAF, who was technical advisor on the film, and Mrs. James Doolittle, who presented a
citation to the AFWA members honoring the wives of American fliers.

HELL'S HORIZON (1955) was a poor picture in which
John Ireland and Bill Williams play the pilot and co-pilot of
a bomber sent out on a special mission in the Korean war.
A one-plane raid is planned for them and they are to fly
from their base in Okinawa and bomb a strategic bridge over
the Yalu River. The mission is to take place in bad weather
to give them cover from enemy fighters. On the way the
weather clears and the Red fighters attack. The Americans
survive, however, making it back to base and crash-landing
with an empty tank.

BATTLE HYMN (1956) is the story of Colonel Dean
"Killer" Hess, an ordained minister of the Disciples of Christ
who flew 62 missions as a fighter pilot in World War II. When
the Korean war started he reentered the Air Force and volun-

Two scenes from BATTLE HYMN (1956): above, Rock Hudson leads his P-51s into battle; below, airlifting the orphans.

teered for hazardous duty in Korea. He managed to muster
a few airplanes and began to train South Korean pilots to
fly P-51 Mustangs. They flew from the worst possible fields,
usually situated as close as possible to the fighting. Flying
his Mustang with South Korean markings and the inscription
"By Faith I Fly" painted in Chinese characters on the front
of the aircraft, Hess made a phenomenal 250 missions. Hard-
ly, if ever, showing the usual signs of fatigue and nervous-
ness that constant combat bring on, Hess became the pride
of the Fifth Air Force. He had a constant fear of killing
civilians (he had accidently bombed an orphanage in WW II)
and became touched by the plight of the many Korean orphans.
Organizing "Operation Kitty Car," he airlifted over 800 of
them to Cheju Island where he set up an orphanage.

The film stars Rock Hudson as Hess and was directed
by Douglas Sirk. Hess sold his story to Hollywood for
$60,000 to raise money for his orphanage and he served as
technical advisor on the film, a fact which distressed Sirk.
Every time Sirk would try to add a fictional scene to make
a better film, Hess would say that wasn't the way it happened and Sirk would have to leave the scene out. Twenty-
five children from the Cheju Orphanage were brought by
Universal to the US to be used in the film. The film contains some realistic dogfights and strafing shots filmed near
Nogales, Arizona.

JET ATTACK (1958) used stock war footage and studio
shots. Tom Arnett (John Agar) and two of his buddies are
shot down behind North Korean lines. A Russian nurse (Aud-
rey Totter) offers them help but Arnett's buddies don't trust
her. He does, however, and she helps them rescue a captured US scientist whom Arnett flies to safety in a stolen
MIG.

THE HUNTERS (1958) had a weak plot but exciting
aerial action. Major Cleve Saville (Robert Mitchum) is a
World War II ace assigned to a fighter group made up of
younger men and based near the Yalu River in Korea in
January 1952. A professional soldier, he is known as the
"Iceman" because of his complete lack of fear. Saville begins to fall in love with the wife (May Britt) of his wing-
man, Lieutenant Abbott (Lee Philips), a young pilot who
drinks and neglects his wife because of his overpowering
fear of combat. Over enemy territory, Abbott gets shot

down and Saville, instead of leaving him so that he can have Abbott's wife, belly-lands his jet to rescue Abbott. Another pilot (Robert Wagner) bails out to help Saville and they spend the last third of the movie getting Abbott back to their lines.

There are some exciting aviation scenes when Saville is chased by a MIG (an F-84F, predecessor of the F-86) flown by the enemy's top ace, "Casey Jones." Saville's F-86 Sabre jet twists and turns until he gets the advantage and shoots Casey down in a ball of fire. Radio-controlled model planes were used to stage the aerial explosions and a five-foot-span static model was used for some of the other shots. The real flying was done by ten crack fighter squadrons at Luke Field, Arizona.

OPERATION AIR RAID: RED MUFFLER was made in 1964 but not shown outside of Korea until 1966. The Korean production is the story of a Republic of Korea air force group in 1951 that is about to fly its 100th mission against an important North Korean bridge. The picture is adequately made and the aerial battles and the destruction of the bridge are reasonably well done.

By the time of the production of OPERATION AIR RAID, the Vietnam conflict was well under way. The Vietnam War proved so unpopular that only a handful of films have been made on the subject. Of these, only APOCALYPSE NOW (1979) has major aerial action. But while the helicopter attack on the Vietcong village is one of the most exciting flying sequences of the 1970s, the film is not an aviation one. The major aerial campaigns, such as the B-52 bombing of the Ho Chi Min trail and Rolling Thunder, the coordinated attack on strategic targets in North Vietnam, have not been dealt with in fictional films.

The Arab-Israeli wars fought since the 1950s have had numerous examples of jet combat, particularly the 1982 conflict in Lebanon in which the Israelis achieved an **astonishing** 80-to-1 kill ratio against Syria. But these aerial battles, like Vietnam, have not made it to the commercial movie screen. The cost of recreating these battles is a factor, but mainly it is because recent wars have been so unpopular that filmmakers have not been encouraged to tackle them.

CHAPTER 10

PEACE IS OUR PROFESSION

Peacetime military aviation presents something of a paradox. On the one hand the military tries to spur recruitment, fund projects, and stress the need for a strong military; at the same time it tries to avoid the appearance of warmongering. Aviation filmmakers face something of the same challenge: how to make peacetime military aviation films exciting. As we shall see, they have gone about it in a variety of ways.

FLYING WITH THE MARINES (1918) was the first in a long list of aviation pictures dealing with American peacetime military flying. A documentary about Marine aviation, the film contained some excellent footage. Although these sequences might seem routine to a modern audience, to the 1918 filmgoer they brought new thrills and a sensation of actually flying. As The New York Times stated: "Never before, perhaps, have the camera and the airplane been brought together with such thrilling results as in these pictures."[1]

The film opens with shots of the Marine aviation base at Miami, Florida. Squadrons of planes fly in standard battle formations. Individual aircraft loop, dive, and spin. At the picture's end, there are shots, taken from the ground, of an airplane stunting. The film then cuts to footage from a camera mounted on the plane to give a pilot's perspective of the acrobatics.

Quartermaster Sergeants John M. LaMond and Freeman H. Owen photographed the film's three reels, with LaMond cranking the camera while his plane was piloted through stunts. This is one of the first times that moving picture

footage was shot with a plane-mounted camera for the express purpose of producing a mass audience film. It also
illustrates the influence the American military has had on
aviation films from the start, for FLYING WITH THE MA-
RINES was certainly intended to "sell" Marine aviation. (The
production of peacetime military aviation films, made in cooperation with the armed services to stimulate enlistments,
reached its height near the end of the 1930s.) A favorable
reception greeted FLYING WITH THE MARINES, and it was
the most successful early aviation film. At the Rivoli Theatre in New York the film outdrew most previous audiences,
and even beat out a Douglas Fairbanks feature for audience
size.

WASHINGTON'S SKY PATROL (1918) had scenes similar to those in FLYING WITH THE MARINES, only this time
the viewer was treated to aerial stunting over Washington
and the Capitol.

THE NON-STOP FLIGHT (1926) didn't have much aviation action, but it did tell of the U.S. Navy's efforts to make
a non-stop flight from San Francisco to Hawaii. The plane,
the PN9, runs out of fuel, lands in the ocean, and drifts to
an uncharted island where adventures befall the plane's crew.

More closely related to fact was the documentary WINGS
OF THE FLEET (1928), a 22-minute film. Produced by the
Navy with the intent of showing the advancement of naval
aviation, it offered nothing unusual and consisted mainly of
newsreel footage.

THE FLYING FLEET (1929), with sound, was made in
cooperation with the U.S. Navy. Lieutenant Commander Frank
"Spig" Wead, USN and Byron Morgan produced the story of
six buddies who decide to join the Navy Air Corps. Eventually their group is reduced to two (Ramon Novarro and
Ralph Graves). Frank Wead would go on to become the dean
of aviation film writers, taking over that position from John
Monk Saunders. Wead had to abandon his career in Naval
aviation when a fall down a flight of stairs crippled him.
With nothing to do but lie in bed, he started to write stories. After a while they began to sell and he went into film
writing. (Wead's story was detailed in THE WINGS OF EA-
GLES, discussed later.)

The flying shots in THE FLYING FLEET offered some excitement, especially during the climax in which Graves crashes in the sea and Novarro goes to his rescue. This sequence included some of the first aircraft carrier shots to be used in a fictional film.

FLIGHT (1929), an all-dialogue Columbia picture made with the cooperation of the U.S. Marine corps, was directed by Frank Capra and photographed by Elmer Dyer and Joe Novak. Ralph Graves, one of the film's stars, wrote the story, which dealt with flying Marines hunting bandits in Nicaragua. The film had good aerial footage. When it opened in New York, the theatre's female ushers dressed in blue French fliers' uniforms and several Marines were present in the theatre. Perhaps the most notable part of the film is when one flier places his dead buddy's body on the wings of a cracked-up plane and sets fire to it.

LO STORMO ATLANTICO (ATLANTIC FLIGHT, 1931) was an Italian documentary about General Italo Balbo's 12-man flight, at the end of 1930 and the beginning of 1931, from Italy to Brazil. The silent picture was released in the United States with Italian titles and was a routine, uninspired documentary.

HELL DIVERS (1931), based on a story by Frank Wead, took a look at naval aviation and had Wallace Beery and Clark Gable play two rival naval aviators (Windy Riker and Steve Nelson). Beery is a champion airplane gunner, a position threatened by the arrival of Gable, who defeats Beery in a gun camera contest. The rivalry intensifies when Beery plays a trick on Gable and his girl friend, and continues when the two are shipped to Panama. On a flight, Gable and a companion get into trouble. Gable breaks his leg parachuting and his companion is badly injured. Beery comes to the rescue and takes a desperate chance by trying to fly the two injured men back to their aircraft carrier, the Saratoga. Beery tries to land on the carrier but the plane crashes and burns. Gable and the other man are saved, but Beery dies.

HELL DIVERS was made with the assistance of the U.S. Navy, which provided authentic planes as well as the use of the Saratoga. Shots of the aircraft landing, taking off, and other operations aboard the carrier provided some of the first glimpses of scenes that would become standard in carrier aviation films. In addition, the Saratoga is shown going through the Panama Canal. The aerial photography was done under the supervision of Charles A. Marshall.

Next came an Italian Picture, ITALY SPEAKS (L'ITALIA PARLA, 1934, also known as THE WINGED ARMADA--L'AR-MATA AZZURRA), a documentary best summed by by the New York Times as "... a motion picture record of Italy's 1932 naval and airplane manoeuvres, followed by a series of Sicilian folk songs and dances...."[2]

DEVIL DOGS OF THE AIR (1935), released as a sequel to HERE COMES THE NAVY, was based on a story by John Monk Saunders. The Warner Bros. film, shot in eight weeks on a budget of $350,000, glorified Marine aviation and starred James Cagney as a hot-shot pilot who shows what can be done with a plane, including hopping over an ambulance a couple of times, but who learns discipline. Pat O'Brien co-starred. The aviation footage is exciting and well done. The Government cooperated with Warners by providing the San Diego naval training station as a filming site, and, of course, generated considerable propaganda for itself in the process. The film was, incidentally, the first Cosmopolitan production for Warners and as such received considerable publicity in the Hearst Press.

WEST POINT OF THE AIR (1935) dealt with Army aviation. The story for the MGM film was written by John Monk Saunders and was adapted by Frank Wead, who would shortly replace Saunders as the major aviation film writer. Part of the camera work was done by Elmer Dyer and Mantz did the stunt flying. Mantz built a replica of a 1910 Curtiss pusher for Wallace Beery to fly because he couldn't find an original. The film told of an Army sergeant, Wallace Beery, and his efforts to make an ace flier out of his son, Robert Young. The story was a confusing one, with numerous subplots. The flying sequences were well done, but by now this was becoming routine in aviation films. The New York Times summed up the film by saying it included "... a prefatory note of tribute 'to the fliers of the United States Army,' half a mile of sound track devoted to speeches on obedience and loyalty, and a panoramic air scene in which the fledgling war birds form a great U.S.A. and roar down the sky toward the attentive M.-G.-M. cameras."[3]

R.A.F. (1935) was a British film not released in the U.S. Made with the cooperation of the British Air Ministry and the Admiralty, the plotless film showed the training of recruits for the Royal Air Force. The men are taught mechanics, and then move on to blind flying, bombing, landing on an aircraft carrier, desert air tactics, and aerobatics.

AIR CITY (AEROGRAD, 1935), a Russian film dealing with the establishment of an aviation city outpost in Siberia as a defense measure against Japan, set out to show that the Soviet air force would play a major role in the defense against any invasion. Written and directed by the noted Russian director Alexander Dovzhenko, the film was designed to help raise the level of art in the industry, as well as serve as propaganda. THE AVIATORS (LIOTTJIKI, 1935) and THE FLYING PAINTER (KRYLATYJ MALJAR, 1935) dealt with training Soviet Air Force pilots.

YOUTH OF TODAY (UNGDOM AV IDAG, 1936) was a Swedish film about training pilots for the Swedish Air Force.

DEVIL'S SQUADRON (1936), a Columbia picture, starred Richard Dix in a story about test pilots flying new planes for the Army. The film presents the theory that these test pilots are merely human guinea pigs for designers' sometimes unsafe modifications. The test pilot theme would be done much better in TEST PILOT. BORDER FLIGHT (1936) detailed the aerial activities of the U.S. Coast Guard fighting a gang of smugglers. The climax comes when one pilot crashes the smugglers' plane into a boat which is trying to prevent a rescue.

WINGS OVER HONOLULU (1937), a Universal **picture** made in cooperation with the U.S. Navy, told of a flier, Ray Milland, who marries Wendy Barrie but is then sent immediately to Pearl Harbor. Barrie follows but has problems being a Navy wife. Milland shows up at a party given by Barrie's former boy friend and cracks up a new plane. For this he is to be court-martialed, but Barrie intervenes and saves him. There are some nice aerial shots, including one of a bombing squadron of flying boats silhouetted against a moonlit sky.

CLIPPED WINGS (1938) was a cheaply-made film dealing with Army aviation, G-men, and oil thieves. Elmer Dyer did the photography, but the aerial scenes were uninspired.

AIR DEVILS (1938) was another cheaply-made film dealing with military aviation.

L'ESCADRILLE DE LA CHANCE (1938) was a French film about a French north African air squadron which "... possesses considerable propaganda for the French air force and colonial army, which is too obvious to be anything but distasteful."[4]

LUCIANO SERRA, PILOT (1938) was an Italian picture glorifying Italian military aviation. After World War I, Luciano Serra, a pilot in the Italian Air Service, drifts around in search of flying adventures to satisfy his restless spirit. Serra disappears on a transatlantic flight but his son, Aldo, becomes a flier. In the Ethiopian campaign Aldo is wounded and his plane is shot down. He is helped by Italian soldiers, one of whom is his father. Serra dies saving Aldo's life.

POUR LE MERITE (1938) was a German film by Karl Ritter about World War I fliers. (Ritter himself had been a fighter pilot during the war.) The war's end does not mean surrender for one squadron leader (Paul Hartman). He takes his planes and pilots back to Germany, only to find the country being ravaged by Communism. The pilots weather the dark years, however, until the rise of National Socialism. The film ends with Hartman being given a new command by Goering. Goering reviews the new squadron, which is equipped with Me-109s.

The Germans sent the United States D III 88 (also known as D III 88, THE NEW GERMAN AIR FORCE ATTACKS --D III 88, DIE NEUE DEUTSCHE LUFTWAFFE GREIFT AN). (D III 88 is the identification number of the Fokker Dr I triplane that appeared in the film, the last original, flyable example of this plane.) The film depicted the daily life of a fighter pilot. Two young fliers (Heinz Welzel and **Hermann Braun**), who are friends, quarrel. They make an unauthorized flight into bad weather and crash. They are grounded but are given a chance at an important mission and succeed. The picture was quite well done, and the New York Times remarked, "Technically, this Tobis production cannot be praised too highly. Such brilliant photography and attention to detail in the air and on land and sea are rarely seen on the screen."[5]

WINGS OF THE NAVY (1939), Warners' next aviation picture, starred George Brent, Olivia de Havilland, and John Payne and told about the training of Navy fliers at the Pensacola and San Diego Naval Air Stations. Elmer Dyer did the aerial photography and the Navy provided full cooperation for the use of its planes and equipment, worth about $40,000,000, particularly PBY's. Variety summed up the aerial action:

> Picture is studded with numerous eye-filling sequences of flying against beautiful cloud formations.... Routine of instruction covers seaplanes, landplanes, blind flying, formation bombing, bomber warding off attack of pursuit planes, and general insight into operations and equipment of the various aircraft in the service. [6]

The Navy would not allow its fliers to do dangerous stunts, so Mantz and Clarke did the flying for the film.

An ironic note to the film, in view of the fierce rivalry between the Army and the Navy, was the depiction of five Army bombers in a drawing advertising the picture. The Army had made some bomber flights out to sea and the Navy practically ordered them back, resulting in a temporary suspension of such flights.

WINGS OF THE NAVY did, of course, have considerable propaganda value for the Navy, as Variety pointed out: "[The film] is a convincer to mold public opinion and support in favor of current Government plans for wide expansion of American air defense forces." [7]

COAST GUARD (1939) was a Columbia picture in the military service genre with Randolph Scott doing some Arctic flying. The New York Times pointed out, "... looks as if the boys are patrolling a pretty ambitious coast--from something that looks like Southern California to ... the Arctic." [8]

FLIGHT COMMAND (1940) was MGM's first feature film to deal with the beefing up of the air defense effort. Harvey S. Haislip, USN retired, served as technical advisor and co-authored the story and screenplay about a new Navy flying recruit from Pensacola (Robert Taylor) who is assigned to the crack "Hell Cats" squadron at the San Diego Naval

Base but who is not accepted by his flying mates until he proves himself, partly by developing a radio-beam fog landing device. Critics were divided about the film's plot but not about the picture's flying scenes, which were excellent and included shots of formation flying and carrier footage. Mantz participated in the filmmaking and some of this footage was shot during war games off Hawaii. The film was made in cooperation with the Navy, which, in return for the concession, required MGM to make a one-reel film dealing with naval flying and the life of recruits. CLOUD HOPPERS was the result.

I WANTED WINGS (1941) was a Paramount film starring Ray Milland, William Holden, Wayne Morris (who eventually became a U.S. Navy fighter pilot), Brian Donlevy, Constance Moore, and Veronica Lake in the story of three men from different backgrounds who enlist in the U.S. Army Air Corps. Milland plays a Long Island playboy socialite who makes it through the program and becomes a B-17 pilot. Holden, a garage mechanic and Milland's friend, washes out by taking the blame for a crash, and Morris is a football star with natural flying ability who dies in a crash. Their story was framed against the over-all training program for Army pilots at Randolph and March Fields. Moore and Lake provided the love interests that hindered, more than helped, the plot. The film was based on a story by Eleanor Griffin and Frank Wead, taken from a book by Lieutenant Bernie Lay, Jr., Air Corps Reserve, who also co-wrote the screenplay.

The film was designed as an Air corps recruitment vehicle and to this end the U.S. Army provided lavish help. One hundred and thirty members of the Hollywood community traveled to Randolph and Kelly Fields in Texas and arrived almost simultaneously with a new group of cadets. Filming began near the end of August 1940 and lasted until Thanksgiving. The Army provided about 1,160 planes, worth $25,000,000, and for extras, 1,050 cadets, 450 officers and instructors, and 2,543 enlisted men. They grounded 700 planes on one day because their engine noise was interfering with the sound recording, and they allowed Randolph Field's grass to be painted green because the sun had burned it brown. The only restriction placed on filmmakers was "... that every photograph taken on the premises be passed by the Army censor...."[9]

Back projection makes this crash safe for the actors in
I WANTED WINGS (1941).

To photograph the aerial sequences, director Leisen
and Army radio engineers developed a plane-to-plane-to-
ground system of communication and The New York Times
called the film "... a new departure in the history of aerial
photography."[10] A three-way radio was installed between
Lieutenant Fred Gray's plane (he was head of the flight formation squadron), Mantz's camera plane, and the look-out
tower of assistant director Harold Rosson. In this way, Rosson and Elmer Dyer, riding in Mantz's plane, could ask for
and get the exact aerial action they wanted. It worked so
well that they even had a plane flying in time to music. No
shots were faked. Close-ups of the pilots were shot with a
special automatic camera strapped to a strut. No models
were used in the film's three crashes. In addition, the film
had a scene shot inside a Flying Fortress in flight, the first
time the American public had been able to see the insides of
the aircraft. The aviation sequences make the film, and while
these were praised, the critics sometimes had less than enthusiastic reactions to the plot.

PARACHUTE BATTALION (1941) was a lackluster RKO film about the training of parachute cadets at Fort Benning, Georgia. The original screenplay was written by John Twist and Major Hugh Fite, U.S. Air Corps, who supplied the 501st Parachute Battalion. It dealt with three cadets (Robert Preston, a football hero; **Edmond O'Brien**, the commander's son; and hillbilly Buddy Ebsen) in a story similar to I WANTED WINGS. It was made in cooperation with the U.S. Army, but the weak plot detracted from the genuinely interesting shots of parachute training. As Variety pointed out: "What it naturally needs to give it excitement are some hair-raising incidents--or accidents. That wouldn't serve to get recruits for the parachute corps, however, and so the writers have detoured to the detriment of their story."[11]

The next major aviation film was Warner Bros.' DIVE BOMBER (1941), filmed in Technicolor. The picture, written

Fliers administer to a stricken comrade in DIVE BOMBER (1941).

by Frank Wead and Robert Buckner and based on a story written by Wead, marked a departure in "service" aviation films. Instead of dealing directly with Navy aviators, its main topic was aviation medicine. Made in cooperation with the U.S. Navy, the film starred Errol Flynn as a Navy doctor interacting with three aviators, played by Fred MacMurray, Regis Toomey, and Louis Jean Heydt. Heydt dies under Flynn's care in Hawaii and then Flynn again treats the other two at the Naval Air Station in San Diego. Flynn's specialty is studying the effects of power dive blackouts on fliers. Toomey is grounded because of pilot fatigue; he joins the R.A.F. but crashes ferrying a plane. MacMurray dies in a crash while testing a high altitude suit. The film featured Vindicator dive bombers and a Lockheed Hudson with a pressurized cabin supposedly going way above its rated altitude.

As with many aviation films, the critics praised the flying sequences but not the plot. The New York Times said: "never before has an aviation film been so vivid in its images, conveyed such a sense of tangible solidity when it is showing us solid things or been so full of sunlight and clean air when the cameras are aloft. Except for a few badly matched shots, the job is well nigh perfect. And the story? Well, again we face a necessary evil."[12]

Production of DIVE BOMBER involved special problems. Filming the aerial sequences for MEN WITH WINGS involved using a stripped down 250-pound Technicolor camera, but for DIVE BOMBER it became necessary to take a 600-pound camera aloft, along with the 250-pound model. Mantz had charge of the aerial photography, along with three cameramen, one of whom was Dyer. Since the film concerned power dives, mounting the 600-pound camera in a plane that would dive alongside the target ship involved special difficulties. Two planes were used. The 250-pound camera was bolted to the floor of a Ryan so that it couldn't move. If the camera had to be turned, the plane had to be turned with it. The 600-pound camera was positioned in a twin-engined Stinson. The filmmakers cut another door in the fuselage opposite a standard one. Between these three-foot-wide times five-feet-high doorways a track was laid so the camera could be dollied from one side of the plane to the other. Byron Haskin, head of Warner Bros.' special effects department, helped design the camera mounts. Shooting included three days at sea with the carrier Enterprise.

By the middle of 1941, there had been so many military films produced that isolationist **senators** in Congress called in September a hearing of the subcommittee of the Committee on Interstate Commerce to investigate Hollywood's "warmongering." Harry Warner, Darryl Zanuck, and other movie men said they were not making propaganda films. As Suid reported:

> Warner acknowledged that his company during the past eight years made feature films about the armed forces. But he stressed the studio "needed no urging from the government and we would be ashamed if the government would have had to make such a request of us. We have produced these pictures voluntarily and proudly."[13]

The antagonistic senators remained unconvinced, however, and the hearings were temporarily adjourned. Before they could be reconvened, the **Pearl Harbor attack ended any** questions about whether filmmakers were trying to lead America into war.

FLYING CADETS (1941) told of a flier (William Gargan) who wants to establish a flying school for future Army fliers as well as win a government contract for his new fast plane. The film contained a wooden mock-up of the Curtiss SB2C Helldiver, which was in an experimental stage when the film was released. Mantz flew for the film.

The Swedish Air Force assisted the production of THE FIRST **SQUADRON (FORSTA DIVISIONEN**, 1941), which told the story of a dive-bomber squadron. A flier is slowly going blind. He has to quit flying, but gets a chance to fly a mission as a signaler. The pilot of the plane tries to land in the fog and the pilot and signaler are killed.

THUNDER BIRDS (1942) was a Technicolor film based on a story by Darryl Zanuck (writing under the name of Melville Crossman) and directed by William Wellman. The film was shot at the Thunder Bird Army Air Force field in Arizona and starred Preston Foster as an instructor, John Sutton as a British cadet with a conditioned reflex that makes him sick when he flies, and Gene Tierney as the woman who can't make up her mind between the two men. This average picture had a prologue and epilogue by John Gunther and featured shots of flying lessons, Foster bailing out in a sand-storm, and Sutton making a dead-stick landing.

THE WAY TO THE STARS (1945) was a British film re-leased in the U.S. as JOHNNY OF THE CLOUDS. It told the story of the takeover by the Americans of an RAF airdrome and of a girl who lived near the field, in the best tradition of Jeannine in LILAC TIME. The girl, played by Rosamund John, bears a son to an RAF pilot (Michael Redgrave) but he is killed. She has a romance with an American flier who comes to the base with the Eight Air Force. He too is even-tually killed.

The film was made with cooperation of officers of the RAF and USAAF, but the camera never took to the air, so the aviation footage was limited to what could be seen from the ground. The film starts in the present, with the air-field deserted and gone to grass, and then goes into a flash-back, a technique that would be better used in TWELVE O'CLOCK HIGH, five years later. The American title came from a poem in the film.

The Swedish film, THREE SONS JOINED THE AIR FORCE (TRE SONER GICK TILL FLYGET, 1945) told of a test pilot working for a SAAB aircraft factory. The film featured two Swedish-built airplanes, the B-17 and the B-18A. WE HEAD FOR RIO (VI FLYGER PA RIO, 1949) was a Swedish-Norwegian film about the difficulties of Swedish and Norwegian pilots flying DC-4s on newly opened routes to South America.

SLATTERY'S HURRICANE (1949) starred Richard Wid-mark as a Navy weather pilot flying out of an east Florida coast base. In trying to atone for a wrong done to a friend, Widmark takes the friend's plane on a flight into a hurricane. With one engine dead and the plane being tossed about, Wid-mark thinks back over his life as a heel. A wartime Navy pilot who single-handedly sank a Japanese cruiser, Widmark becomes a candy manufacturer's chauffeur after the war. He becomes involved with dope smuggling and generally messes up the lives of two women, Linda Darnell and Veronica Lake. Of course, he redeems himself at the end.

Warner Brothers released CHAIN LIGHTNING in Febru-ary 1950. It was the first film devoted solely to jets. Be-fore this, jet planes had appeared only in short segments of

Humphrey Bogart as a wartime aviator who later becomes a jet test pilot in CHAIN LIGHTNING (1950).

films, as in TASK FORCE. Warners made use of the fact this was a new type of film. Their ads proclaimed the movie as a "Tremendous Warner First, [the] Screen's First Story of Jet Planes."

The picture opens with B-17 bombing raids during WWII. The squadron shown is led by a heroic pilot, Matt Brennan (Humphrey Bogart), who fearlessly flies his bomber through the worst opposition the Germans can mount. Down on his luck after the war, he takes a job as a test pilot for Leland Willis (Raymond Massey). Willis is trying to convince the Air Force that his jet, the JA-3, which has a speed of 1,400 miles per hour, flies at 90,000 feet, and can stay aloft for four hours, is just what they need. The truth is, the plane is almost obsolete. A better version is in the works and it has a pod for pilot ejection at high altitude. To prove the worth of the JA-3 Brennan takes it on a flight from Alaska

to Washington by way of the North Pole. He runs out of
fuel near the finish and has to glide the rest of the way.
The Air Force is sold on the plane, but Brennan learns that
the pod's designer has been killed testing the pod in the
newer version of the plane. Against orders he takes the
newer model up, successfully tests the pod, and insures
that the Air Force gets the best possible aircraft.

The film excels in its shots of the jets, which were
staged using models and a plane that could only taxi on the
ground. Warners paid Mantz $15,000 to build a futuristic
jet for the taxi scenes. He and Vince Johnson took a Bell
Airacobra, added some jet-age plumbing to it, and produced
a plane so realistic that many people thought it was a new
Air Force jet that actually flew. The plot, however, is rather
poor.

The screenwriter of CHAIN LIGHTNING, J. Redmond
Prior, was really Lester Cole, one of the Hollywood Ten who
refused to cooperate with the House Un-American Activities
Committee. Since these ten were blacklisted from Hollywood,
Warners claimed that while it knew J. Redmond Prior was a
pseudonym when they purchased the story in 1948, they did
not know Cole had written it. By the time this was discovered the film had been released, and no one criticized it for
being "un-American."

The next major aviation film was THE BIG LIFT (1950).
This story of the Berlin airlift has its good and its bad spots.
Woven into the flights of the C-47s and C-54s is a romantic
story of two Americans and two German girls. Danny Mac-
Cullough (Montgomery Clift), a sergeant, is a young, inno-
cent Midwesterner who is taken in by a German girl (Cornell
Norchers). She merely wants to use him as a way of getting
to the U.S., where her husband is living. MacCullough's
companion, Hank (Paul Douglas), who talks down the planes
flying the supplies, hates the "Krauts" because he was in
a prisoner of war camp. He preaches democracy to his Berlin girl friend (Bruni Lobel) but finds out that she is more
democratic than he is.

THE BIG LIFT was in preparation in Germany for nine
months, three of which were used for location shooting in
Berlin. George Seaton, the director, submitted the completed script to the four-power authorities for approval

before shooting began. The Russians at first refused to allow the crew to film in the Russian sections of the city. They later relented, but continued to harass the filmmakers. At one point, members of the **Young** Communist League shouted every time the signal was given to commence filming, stopping as soon as the "cut" order came. The crew reversed signals and went ahead with the filming.

Released at the same time as THE BIG LIFT was the independently produced OPERATION HAYLIFT (1950), in which the U.S. Air Force is given the task of feeding cattle and sheep. The film deals with the efforts of the Air Force to save the animals during the blizzards of January 1949 in Nevada. Interwoven into this exploit is the story of two brothers struggling to preserve their way of life. The movie's most interesting moments come during sequences of the Flying Boxcars, lent by the Air Force for the film. The picture was made entirely at Ely, Nevada, the center of the actual operation.

ZUKOVSKI (1950) was a Russian biography of the Soviet aviation designer.

STARLIFT (1951, Warner Bros.) was a musical dealing with top stars' entertainment of men at California's Travis Air Force Base.

The next major aviation film, AIR CADET (1951), followed the adventures of three **pilots through preliminary** flight training at Randolph Field, Texas and on to their assignments at Williams Field, Arizona, where they fly F-80 Shooting Stars. The pilots are: Joe (Alex Nicol), an ex-sergeant who wants to fly jets; Russ (Richard Long), who is trying to surpass his dead brother's war exploits; and Walt (Robert Arthur), a rich boy who wants to make it on his own. They are led by Major Jack Page (Stephen McNally), a hard-driving man who is still troubled over the men he lost in World War II. The aerial shots are the only bright spots in the whole film, and the best of these are the aerobatic sequences in which the men fly a four-ship diamond formation with wing tips eighteen inches apart.

JUMPING JACKS (1952) was a comedy with Dean Martin and Jerry Lewis as a pair of bunglers at a paratroop camp.

The 1954 Swedish film, THE YELLOW SQUADRON (GUBA DIVISIONEN), featured the SAAB J-29, the "Flying Barrel," and had a flier stunting under a Stockholm bridge.

Don Siegel directed AN ANNAPOLIS STORY (1955). The film starred John Derek in a story about the training of jet pilots.

STRATEGIC AIR COMMAND (1955) had Lieutenant Colonel Robert Holland (Jimmy Stewart) retire from the air force, after commanding a B-24 wing in World War II, to become a third baseman for the St. Louis Cardinals. He is called back for a 21-month tour of active duty with the Strategic Air Command, which he bitterly resents. Having served his country once, he doesn't see why he has to do so again. This also disturbs his wife (June Allyson) but both are finally convinced of the necessity of Holland's work.

Holland serves at a base that's phasing out the propeller-driven B-36s and converting to B-47 jet bombers. The picture was shot in a process developed by Paramount called VistaVision, which allowed the movie to be shown on a huge screen. The premiere was held at the Paramount Theatre in New York under the sponsorship of the Air Force Association. The film was made with generous help from the Air Force, which provided the planes, men, airfields and facilities. The picture was shown on the world's largest seamless screen, 70 by 40 feet. It was given a great deal of publicity as 3,500 guests attended the premiere and interviews held in the theatre lobby were telecast on the Arthur Godfrey show. The guests were impressed with the full-sized shots of the big aircraft. Expert special effects were employed in a dramatic sequence when Stewart crash-lands a flaming B-36 on the Greenland icecap.

The film grew out of Stewart's interest in SAC. (Stewart had flown 25 bombing missions into Germany in a B-24 in World War II.) He spent a day talking with General Curtiss LeMay, chief of SAC, and was so convinced of SAC's importance that he talked Paramount into making the movie. Stewart had received the **Distinguished Flying** Cross for leading a raid on the German aircraft factories at Brunswick, and finished the war as a colonel. He placed great faith in the Air Force and believed that SAC was "'the biggest single factor in the security of the world.'"[14] He was right in his belief that SAC would make a good subject for a film.

TOP OF THE WORLD (1955) dealt with the establishment of an Air Force weather station on an ice island in the Arctic. Dale Robertson starred as a bitter pilot divorced from his wife after their World War II marriage ended on a **tragic** note. Too old to be allowed to fly jets, Robertson is sent to Alaska to aid Frank Lovejoy in the weather observation unit. He learns that Lovejoy is in love with his ex-wife. The picture has some exciting moments during survival and rescue scenes. William Clothier did the aerial photography.

At the end of 1955 Warner Brothers released a public service documentary designed to explain to Americans the working of the USAF's Air Defense Command. The theme of 24-HOUR ALERT, a 31-minute short, is that it is better to be disturbed at night by friendly jets overhead than never wake up because of an enemy attack. In the early 1950s many people complained to the USAF about the jet noise, and this picture was made to help quell some of the local opposition to having an Air Force base a few hundred yards down the road. It stars Jack Webb, who narrates it, and tells how a local jet unit is able to overcome opposition to its operation. It was shown in New York along with Warner Brothers' THE COURT-MARTIAL OF BILLY MITCHELL.

THE COURT-MARTIAL OF BILLY MITCHELL (1955) tackled justice, the faults of the military, and the need for a strong air arm. On July 21, 1921, Brigadier General William Mitchell of the Army Air Force sent nine biplanes off the Virginia coast to bomb the "unsinkable" German battleship, Ostfriesland, thus **providing the airplane to be a formid**able weapon. Unfortunately, not many top US officials realized this fact and Mitchell was broken to colonel and assigned a desk job in Texas. The accidental destruction of the Navy airship Shenandoah prompted him to say that such crashes "are the result of the incompetency, the criminal negligence and almost treasonable administration of our national defense by the Navy and War Departments." For this statement, he was court-martialed in 1925. He used the trial to expound his theories of air power, predicting the Pearl Harbor attack, extensive wartime use of paratroops, and supersonic aircraft. In 1947 he was posthumously restored to his former rank.

The film had a difficult time getting to the screen. In January 1942 RKO announced that it had purchased the screen

Gary Cooper (at far right) helps a pilot walk away from a crash in THE COURT-MARTIAL OF BILLY MITCHELL (1955).

treatment of Mitchell's life, entitled "General Billy Mitchell" and written by William Rankin with the approval of the general's family. The studio said that Howard Hawks, brother of producer William Hawks, would direct the film. But by June 1942 William Hawks announced that the film would no longer be made, feeling that "it is unwise to revive the Mitchell controversy during the war."[15] Warner Brothers felt that the climate in the mid-fifties had become more conducive and went ahead with production, with Otto Premminger directing and Gary Cooper playing a convincing Mitchell.

ON THE THRESHOLD OF SPACE (1956) explored the methods and equipment used in high-altitude flight. Although the film deals mainly with rocket sleds and high-altitude balloons, there are some interesting shots of high-altitude bail-outs from speeding jets. Guy Madison and John Hodiak star as fictional Air Force men testing new methods and equipment. It was made under the supervision of Air Force technical experts and shot at Elgin Air Force Base in Florida and at Holliman Air Force Base in New Mexico.

TOWARD THE UNKNOWN (1956) also dealt with experimental jets. This time the setting was Edwards Air Force Base and the aircraft the Bell X-2 experimental rocket plane. Major Lincoln Bond (William Holden, in his first independent production) was captured in Korea, broke under brainwashing, and signed a germ-warfare confession. Back in the U.S. he seeks and is given a chance to recover both his self-respect and his girl (Virginia Leith). He is given the job of test flying the X-2 rocket plane (the actual aircraft set a speed record in July 1956 of 1,900 miles per hour, and in September of that year set an altitude record of 126,000 feet.) He successfully completes his mission and recovers his girl and his pride.

The plot is weak, but the aerial sequences are good. The director, Mervyn LeRoy, wanted to get a shot of two F-94s flying with the wing-tip tank of one plane tangled in the drag chute, which had accidently opened, of the other. No matter how much he tried, the shots looked fake, so Paul Mantz and Colonel Pete Everest (the man who flew the X-2 on its 1,900-mile per hour flight) piloted the F-94s, with the wings tied together by rope, through a series of perfect maneuvers. The film ends with shots of the USAF Thunderbirds' aerobatics. TOWARD THE UNKNOWN was the forerunner of that great rocket plane movie, X-15.

HEROES OF THE AIR (HEROES DEL AIR, 1957) was a Spanish film. Two Spanish Civil War fliers (Alfredo Mayo and Julio Nunez) meet in the 1950s when Mayo is commander of an Air Rescue Service. The men remember their adventures as Nationalist fliers. In a plot device from WINGS, Nunez shoots down Mayo, who has stolen a Republican plane, but, in a departure from the WINGS scenario, Mayo survives. Back in the present, Nunez foils a plan to blackmail his sister (who is Mayo's wife) but loses his life in a crash.

THE WINGS OF EAGLES (1957) cost $2,600,000, was directed by John Ford, and tells the sometimes not too factual account of Commander Frank "Spig" Wead (John Wayne). Both Wayne and Ford were friends of Wead and for this reason Ford was reluctant to do the film. Fearing that another director might not do justice to Wead, however, Ford decided to go ahead with the picture.

The early days of naval aviation were fraught with

danger, mostly from Wead's flying. He flew through hangars, landed in a swimming pool, and in general did considerable damage. At 30 he fell down a flight of stairs and broke his neck. Grounded by the accident, Wead learned to write aviation stories and eventually went to Hollywood where he became the dean of the aviation film writers of the thirties, producing scripts for such films as DIRIGIBLE, HELL DIVERS, TEST PILOT, CEILING ZERO, and DIVE BOMBER. He finally re-entered the Navy and won the Legion of Merit for his ideas on the support "jeep" carrier, a vessel designed to resupply other aircraft carriers with planes to replace those lost in battle. THE WINGS OF EAGLES leaves something to be desired. Most of the aerial shots, which feature a J-1 Trainer, occur in the first part of the movie.

BAILOUT AT 43,000 (1957) was a remake of the CBS television program "Climax." The picture deals with Major Paul Peterson (John Payne), who is assigned to the Air Research and Development Command branch of the Air Force. This department has been given the job of developing and testing, under actual flying conditions, a downward ejection seat for the B-47 jet bomber. Colonel Hughes (Paul Kelly), head of the project, senses that Peterson is nervous about the test and assigns two other officers to carry out the test before Peterson. This, of course, makes Peterson even more unsure of himself and he begins to wonder if he'll chicken out when his turn comes. The first man to test the ejection seat lands with a broken neck. The next officer is suddenly hospitalized for an emergency appendectomy. This puts Hughes in the ejection seat, and he successfully carries out the test and reaffirms his faith in himself.

HIGH FLIGHT (1957), a British film, deals with a three-year training course for new RAF pilots. Wing Commander Rudge (Ray Milland), who presides over Cranwell Flying College, is having problems with a new cadet (Kenneth Haigh). Haigh is a natural pilot but an undisciplined hothead. Rudge has trouble disciplining the new pilot because Rudge's own recklessness had caused the death of Haigh's father during the war. Haigh creates tough situations for Rudge. At the end of the picture, however, Rudge saves Haigh's life on an operational flight and the two become friends. The film featured the Percival Provost and Hawker Hunter planes, and some of the aerial footage was shot at the Farnborough Air Display.

JET PILOT (1957) was made by Howard Hughes, who began shooting it in 1949. It was considered completed in 1951 but was not released until 1957 because Hughes wanted time to "improve" it. For six years he dabbled with it and the film got worse. In the early 1950s, he sold his interest in RKO, the studio that made the film, but retained the rights to the picture. He finally persuaded Universal to release it. It was not, as he had hoped, another HELL'S ANGELS. Instead, movie critic Hollis Alpert called it "one of the most idiotic movies ever made."[16]

The picture stars Janet Leigh as a Soviet Air Force pilot who flies a MIG to an Alaskan air base commanded by Colonel John Wayne. She says she has escaped from the Russians. Wayne is given the job of getting information out of her. He takes her around the country and shows her most of our latest air secrets. They end up in Palm Springs, fall in love, and get married. Then it turns out that Leigh is a spy. The U.S. Government arranges for her to "escape" with Wayne, who becomes a U.S. spy in Russia. In Siberia and later in Moscow Leigh has a change of heart. Wayne steals an experimental rocket plane ("played" by the Bell X-1) and they escape to the United States.

Because of the time lag between production and release, much aviation footage had to be cut out because it was obsolete. Hughes, who spent $180,000 photographing the bad air shots, turned to Mantz to bail out the picture. Mantz's appraisal of the film was, "it stinks." Mantz agreed to shoot some more footage and got Colonel Chuck Yeager, the first supersonic pilot, to fly acrobatics in an F-86 Sabre jet over Kelly Field, Texas. On the downward leg of a loop he lost his dive brakes and then lost the entire tail section in the steep dive that followed. He managed to land the ship using only ailerons and emerged unharmed. The talents of Mantz and Yeager couldn't save matters, however; the multimillion dollar film is terrible.

The next film was the second in the SAC trilogy. BOMBERS B-52 (1957) deals with a SAC unit whose obsolete B-47s are being replaced with B-52s, the new Stratofortress jet bomber. Karl Malden plays a line crew chief, Sergeant Chuck Brennan, who is both proud and happy to work on the eight-engined bombers. His wife (Marsha Hunt) and especially his daughter (Natalie Wood) don't like living on

Line-crew chief Karl Malden checks over an aircraft in
BOMBERS B-52 (1957).

the base and think he would be better off if he took a high-
paying job with a civilian aircraft company. Colonel Jim
Herlihy (Efrem Zimbalist, Jr.) comes to take over command
of the air base, and Brennan has something else to be upset about. Brennan dislikes Herlihy because of a Korean
war incident, so he is not too happy when Herlihy begins
dating his daughter. Just as Brennan gives in to his family and sends in his retirement papers, the new B-52s arrive. Since he's the best crew chief in the Air Force, pressure is put on him to delay his retirement until he can train
crews to properly maintain the new bomber. He agrees, but
the price for staying is that Herlihy stops seeing his daughter. A new computer panel has been developed for the B-52
and Herlihy and Brennan are told to test it out under actual
combat conditions. (Why a non-stop flight to Africa and
back simulates actual combat conditions is never explained.)
The plane is almost home when the panel short-circuits and

starts a fire. The rest of the crew bails out and Herlihy safely lands the plane. Rescue teams pick up all the crew except Brennan, who is missing and possibly injured. Herlihy goes looking for him, finds him, and stays with him until help arrives. Brennan realizes he's misjudged Herlihy, decides to stay in the Air Force, and allows Herlihy to date his daughter again.

The $1,400,000 picture, which is dedicated to the Air Force crew chiefs and ground personnel, contains good aerial footage. The $9,000,000, four hundred thousand-pound B-52s are photographed from every conceivable angle: from looking toward the tail as the drag chute unfolds to shots taken from the landing gear wheel wells. Tense moments are provided when the plane is on fire and when the forward gear sticks on a training flight (it's the master control relay in the forward wheel well). The planes fly at 650 miles per hour. Every so often one of the characters breaks into a speech about how important it is to have these bombers in readiness as a war deterrent. It is the best film about B-52s.

THUNDERING JETS (1958) had Rex Reason as a jet ace who heads an Air Force test pilot training school. Instead of being desk bound, however, he wishes to fly again. His frustration is taken out on his students and his girl. He is almost ready to quit the service when one of the new pilots freezes at the dual controls of an aircraft and is saved by Reason's quick thinking. This earns Reason a surprise party and he realizes how important his desk job really is. One subplot deals with the leading girl-chaser at the school, who makes a pass at Reason's girl. The other subplot concerns two students, one of whom had his brother killed over Germany in World War II, and one who flew for the German air force during the war. The picture is poor and has only routine aerial shots.

NO TIME FOR SERGEANTS (1958) told the story of Airman Will Stockdale, a country bumpkin who turned the Air Force upside down. The comedy was based on the novel by Mac Hyman, which was made into a play in 1955 and then filmed in 1958, both versions starring Andy Griffith. The story was also made into a TV series, NO TIME FOR SERGEANTS, which starred Sammy Jackson and ran from 1964 to 1965.

In November 1961, X-15 was released. X-15 is a semi-documentary about the successor to the Bell X-2. Narrated by Jimmy Stewart, the film follows Matt Powell (David Mc-Lean), Lieutenant Colonel Lee Brandon (Charles Bronson), Major Ernie Wilde (Ralph **Taeger**), and their sweethearts as the characters become involved in the X-15 testing program. The men are led by Tom Deparma (James Gregory), who directs them as they take turns flying the X-15 and its two chase planes. Of course the men have romantic problems: Powell has a flighty fiancée, Brandon's wife wants a baby, and Wilde's wife opposes, but eventually succeeds in tolerating, her husband's dangerous work.

The film chronicles the technical experiments and the conditioning of the men that precede the X-15 flights. Some fictional material is included in the picture, but it wasn't necessary. The plane is the star of this film, which has some exciting aerial footage. The test flights are a combination of vapor trails, seen reflected in the plane's canopy, beautiful high-altitude photography, and kaleidoscopic views of the X-15 mirrored in the escorts' cockpits. Even on the ground the footage is good, as when a jet skims at tree-top level guiding in a damaged ship for a landing, with fire trucks racing to the plane.

X-15 was chosen to lead the list of nine American film entries in the International **Aeronautical** Film Festival held in June 1965 in Vichy, France.

A GATHERING OF EAGLES (1962) was the last film in the SAC trilogy which included STRATEGIC AIR COMMAND and BOMBERS B-52. A GATHERING OF EAGLES, however, lacks the impact of the previous two films and is the poorest of the three.

Jim Caldwell (Rock Hudson) is assigned as the new commander of the 904th Strategic Air Command Wing, based at Carmody Air Force Base in California, because the Wing has failed to pass its Operational Readiness Inspection. There is a surprise visit by a SAC inspector-general who notes how the base responds to unexpected wartime exercises. Caldwell cold-heartedly proceeds to whip the base into shape by firing base personnel, including his best friend, Hollis Farr (Rod Taylor), and the base commander,

SAC wing commander Rock Hudson (r.) and his B-52 crew
run into trouble in A GATHERING OF EAGLES (1962).

Colonel Fowler (Barry Sullivan), who drinks too much. This
disgrace is too much for Fowler, and he shoots himself. All
this upsets Caldwell's wife (Mary Peach) and she threatens
to leave him and return to England. When it comes time to
test Caldwell's efficiency, he has to pull a few tricks (like
ordering a plane aloft with only eighty percent power in one
engine), but the base passes the Operational Readiness Inspection. This, of course, causes Caldwell's wife to realize
how important he is and she comes back to him.

The biggest disappointment in the film is the flying
shots. There are a few good airplane scenes, as when the
giant B-52s scream down the runway at 15-second intervals,
and when Caldwell's bomber is being refueled in flight and
the fuel line breaks, forcing him to make a risky flaps-up
landing to avoid an explosion, but the aerial footage fails to
meet the standards set by BOMBERS B-52. Along with the
scenes of the B-52s there is some footage of a KC135 tanker,
adapted from Boeing's civilian 707, and a T-33 jet. The picture was filmed at the Beagle Air Force Base in California

and much of the shooting took place during an actual SAC exercise. Sy Bartlett, the producer and a reserve colonel in SAC, is reputed to be the first American to drop a bomb on Berlin during World War II. Delbert Mann, the director, flew 35 missions in bomber in World War II. Mann had always wanted to make a bomber picture and this film gave him his chance.

The best aspect of A GATHERING OF EAGLES is the effective view it gives the audience of the kind of life SAC men lead. They are always on constant alert, waiting for the red phone to ring and inform them war has been declared. Every time they scramble there is always the nagging doubt whether this time the alert is merely another training exercise or not. The picture also provides a view of the complex operations of SAC and the safeguards against accidental nuclear war. By the end of the film the viewer realizes that SAC is much more than, as Rock Hudson first thought, "'Jimmy Stewart and a big airplane.'"[17]

In 1964, the last two aviation films dealing with SAC were released. But unlike the previous trilogy, which stressed the benefits and necessity of SAC, DR. STRANGE-LOVE and FAIL-SAFE explored the potential of SAC for igniting a nuclear war.

DR. STRANGELOVE: OR HOW I LEARNED TO STOP WORRYING AND LOVE THE BOMB (Columbia, 1964) satirized the military and political establishment with all the brilliance and insight its director, Stanley Kubrick, could muster. Before starting the film, **Kubrick** read every book available on nuclear warfare, and his careful research shows.

The film opens with a disclaimer that the incidents portrayed could never happen. A right-wing SAC commander, General Jack D. Ripper (Sterling Hayden), under the provisions of a directive called Wing Attack Plan R, seals off his base and sends his planes past their fail-safe points to bomb Russia. He believes the Communists are responsible for everything from the Cold War to fluoridation of water, which attacks the "vital bodily fluids." The film cuts back and forth between the hilarious efforts of Major King Kong (Slim Pickens) to get his B-52 to the target and the struggles of U.S. President Muffley (Peter Sellers, who also plays Group Captain Mandrake and Dr. Strangelove), and General Buck

Major King Kong (Slim Pickens, at right) is determined to
get his B-52 to the target in DR. STRANGELOVE (1964).

Turgidson (George C. Scott) to recall the bombers or shoot
them down before they reach their targets. The Army attacks Ripper's base and fights its way in past the billboards
proclaiming SAC's motto: "Peace Is Our Profession." The
President almost succeeds in stopping the bombers, but Kong
gets through, thereby setting off the Russian doomsday device that will destroy all life on earth.

The exterior aviation shots are done almost entirely
with models. Kubrick, of course, got no help from the Air
Force concerning the interior construction of B-52s, but
from one interior photograph published in an aviation magazine and Kubrick's own knowledge of civilian aircraft, he
constructed an extremely realistic mock-up of a B-52. The
film is characterized by outstanding performances by all the
principals, and Kubrick's guiding hand makes it one of the
best aviation films ever made.

FAIL-SAFE (1964), a Columbia film, repeated the material in STRANGELOVE, but in a serious manner. Columbia
sued the authors of the book Fail-Safe, claiming it was pla-

giarized from the book on which DR. STRANGELOVE was
based. The issue was resolved when Columbia took over
financing and distribution of the movie FAIL-SAFE. In the
Omaha headquarters of SAC a piece of equipment fouls up
and transmits the attack order to a flight of bombers over
Alaska. The picture details the efforts of the U.S. President (Henry Fonda) to get the bombers to turn back. When
this fails, the Russians are warned of the danger and told to
shoot down the bombers, as in DR. STRANGELOVE. One
B-52 gets through, however, and destroys Moscow. Fonda
then must bomb New York to prove to the Russians that it
really was an accident, and thereby prevents a war. The
film contains a minimum of aviation footage and, while it's
interesting, it's not as good as DR. STRANGELOVE.

FLIGHT FROM ASHIYA (1964) depicted the efforts of
the American Air Rescue Service in the China Sea. Richard
Widmark played the no-nonsense pilot of a Grumman SA-16
Albatross. The climax comes with a rescue mission staged
by Widmark, George Chakiris, and Yul Brynner in an intense storm.

THE GREAT SANTINI (1979, also called THE GIFT OF
FURY) had Robert Duvall as Marine Colonel Bull Meechum.
The picture is set in 1962, and Duvall is a combat pilot with
no missions to fly. The movie centers on the conflicts between Duvall and his family, particularly his 18-year-old son.
The **conflicts reach a critical stage before Meechum realizes**
that he must soften his attitude. The reconciliation comes too
late, however, because Meechum is soon killed on a routine
flight. THE GREAT SANTINI featured F-4s, and it was
filmed at the Beaufort, S.C. Marine Air Station with Clay
Lacy directing the aerial scenes. The film started out as a
venture for cable TV, but became popular enough to be
shown in the theatres.

RED FLAG: THE ULTIMATE GAME (1981) was a made-
for-TV movie dealing with fighter training at Nellis Air Force
Base, Nevada, and was filmed on location. The film starred
Barry Bostwick and William Devane. Clay Lacy supervised
the aviation sequences in this story of war games that become too realistic. The film used some stock Air Force and
Northrop Aviation footage. For the flying sequences, newly
photographed for the picture, the Air Force charged the
filmmakers $3,200 an hour for use of each F-4 and $1,100

for the F-5Es which took the part of Russian MIG-21s. A far cry from the free assistance offered in earlier days!

THE RIGHT STUFF (1983), based on the best-selling book by Tom Wolfe, proved to be a good, but flawed, film. The picture deals with the manned space program, from Chuck Yeager's breaking of the sound barrier in 1947 to the last Mercury 7 flight in 1963. The episodic movie first focuses on Yeager (Sam Shepard), a unique pilot with the combination of courage and daring that qualifies as "the right stuff." A few broken ribs don't prevent him from piloting the Bell X-1 through the sound barrier on October 14, 1947, making him "the fastest man alive." Because of him and other pilots, Edwards Air Force Base becomes the place to go if a man wants to "push the envelope." It is here that government officials come looking for the first astronauts. But Yeager didn't go to college, and he's passed over as a Mercury 7 candidate. The astronauts who are chosen find life difficult. They're subjected to exhaustive testing and have to fight to be thought of as test pilots and not guinea pigs. But they persevere, and Alan Shepard (Scott Glenn) becomes the first American into space. John Glenn (Ed Harris) emerges as the spokesman for the group, and his orbital flight makes him an instant hero. Gordon Cooper (Dennis Quaid) is the last of the original seven to go into space; he flies twenty-two orbits in 1963 and becomes, for a time, "the fastest man alive."

The film version of THE RIGHT STUFF began in 1980. William Goldman (THE GREAT WALDO PEPPER) wrote a script that dealt primarily with the Mercury 7 astronaut training. Phil Kaufman, the director, didn't like the script and he spent a year rewriting it, inserting the Chuck Yeager material. He sent the script to Yeager, who liked it so much that he agreed to be the film's technical advisor. (Yeager also appeared in the film as Fred, the bartender.) As in AIR FORCE, Kaufman wanted to portray the astronauts as a group and he therefore did not hire big-name actors. The biggest problem, of course, was recreating the flying sequences.

About eighty aircraft either appeared in the film or were used in making it. Three T-33s were provided by the California Air National Guard's 144th FIS based at Fresno. Flight Systems International supplied the F-86F that appears

as the Edwards' chase plane. The last F-104 Starfighters
had long been retired from the U.S. Air Force, so two German planes were flown to Edwards in May 1982 for the NF-
104 sequence. In July 1982 the film crew went on board
the carrier Coral Sea for a three-day cruise. No planes
were on board the ship, but two A-4s and two A-7s were
flown to the vessel.

Of all the aircraft, the rocket planes were the most
difficult to recreate. The filmmakers talked with the Air
Force Museum about using the real X-1 and X-15 for ground
shots, but it proved too expensive to truck them to California. The possibility of constructing a flyable X-1 and dropping it from the Confederate Air Force's B-29 was raised,
but Yeager refused to fly any such mock-up; it would thus
have been dropped just once, and was far too expensive a
venture to contemplate. As it was, the FAA wouldn't pass
the B-29 with the wooden X-1 mock-up for flight, so it
could only taxi. If duplicating the X-1 proved difficult, recreating the X-15 became impossible. The movie makers acquired an X-15 mock-up from the Pima County Air Museum in
Arizona and refinished it. But filming any X-15 sequences
proved too costly, and since the X-15 didn't involve Yeager
directly this material was dropped from the film. The filmmakers wanted to use the D-558-2 Douglas Skyrocket from the
Planes of Fame Air Museum at Chino Airport, California. The
expense of transporting this aircraft to the shooting site prevented its use. Kaufman used Al Letcher's British Hawker
Hunter jet as a substitute for the Skyrocket. The Confederate Air Force's B-29 flew in the film, while the interior B-29
scenes were done in Pima County Museum's B-29 fuselage,
which appeared in THE LAST FLIGHT OF NOAH'S ARK. Lt.
Col. Duncan Wilmore (Ret.) served as a technical advisor and
planner for the aerial sequences.

Much of THE RIGHT STUFF was shot at Edwards. The
abandoned South Base, site of the X-1 and D-558-2 scenes,
was where the actual events had occurred 35 years earlier.
The NF-104 sequences were done at Edwards' Main Base.
The abandoned Hamilton Air Force Base in San Francisco was
used for filming after its hangars had been turned into sound
stages. Locations around San Francisco served as settings
for the non-flying scenes, which the Cow Palace doubling for
the Houston Astrodome. Pancho Barnes' Happy Bottom Riding
Club, destroyed by fire in the mid-1950s, was rebuilt near
South Base at Edwards.

THE RIGHT STUFF made extensive use of models. A radio-controlled B-29 dropped an Estes rocket-powered X-1 model for one shot. Gary Gutierrez's USFX studios constructed the other miniatures. Rather than use computer-directed replicas on a sound stage, Gutierrez believed he could achieve a better look if the models were photographed outdoors. Three X-1 replicas were built. A 4"-long one was constructed from styrene, while the 6" and 2' versions were cast in polyurethane and skinned with a metal-like finish. The filmmakers powered these with Estes rockets and shot them horizontally down a 200'-long wire. A PT boat camouflage fogger provided the clouds.

Besides the specially-created models, stock plastic F-104 models were also used. The special effects team bought fifty or so Hasegawa 1/32 and Monogram 1/48 kits. Some were carried aloft on a helium balloon on a fifty-foot wire. Others were fired from a large crossbow to get the illusion of the real plane against the sky. Men holding a cargo parachute tried to catch these F-104s. The ones they missed were quickly repaired so that they could be used again.

THE RIGHT STUFF, a 22-million-dollar film, opened in 100 70mm-equipped theatres in 85 cities on October 21, 1983, and in mid-December in the rest of the country. The film gained publicity because John Glenn was running for the Presidency, and there was much speculation about whether the film would help his campaign. The movie garnered universally enthusiastic reviews. Critics praised the story, acting, and special effects. The film presented American heroes in a believable light, with both their strengths and weaknesses very much in evidence. Strangely, the movie quickly earned the reputation that it wasn't a money-maker and people weren't going to see it, in spite of all the favorable press.

THE RIGHT STUFF has much to recommend it. It's very well made. The flying shots, even those done with models, are among the best ever photographed. They capture magnificently the sensation of speed associated with challenging the sound barrier. The acting is excellent, with all the principals turning in believable performances. But the film is also seriously flawed, and these defects keep it from being a great picture. Director Kaufman would probably have been better off had he stuck to Goldman's original script dealing only with the astronauts. THE RIGHT STUFF tries to cover too much ground. The winged space program and the capsule space program each need three hours of screen time. They don't compress well into a single story. The omission of X-15 material is a serious flaw; the X-1 experiments foreshadowed the spectacular Mach 4 flights of the X-15. The astronauts and test pilots are portrayed as heroes, but the scientists, administrators, and politicians are all presented as fools and idiots, men who throw temper tantrums and want human cannonballs as astronaut candidates.

Several television shows have also dealt with military aviation. AIR POWER, a documentary series narrated by Walter Cronkite and made in cooperation with the U.S. Air Force, ran from 1956 to 1958. The series traced the rise of aviation and its impact on world social and military history. STEVE CANYON (1958-1959) was based on the comic strip by Milton Caniff. Dean Fredericks played Canyon, a pilot and troubleshooter for the Air Force. Filming was done on Air Force bases with the blessing of the government, which saw the series as a possible recruitment aid. THE BLUE ANGELS was a syndicated show, 39 episodes long, released in the fall of 1960. As a history of television stated:

> Since the real Blue Angels spent most of their
> time simply flying ... considerable ingenuity was
> needed to lend this series variety. The producers
> managed to concoct all sorts of unlikely plots, such
> as having the pilots, on the spur of the moment,
> chase smugglers, romance pretty bystanders, fly
> life-saving supplies to a dying woman, scare a ju-
> venile delinquent into going straight by giving him
> a wild airplane ride, and even stop a holdup--much
> of this off duty. The U.S. Navy, which cooperated
> in the production of the series, protested some of
> this, but producer Sam Gally barked back, "How the
> hell does the Pentagon know what happens to a Blue
> when he's off duty?" [18]

EMERALD POINT N.A.S. debuted in the fall of 1983. The series had much more to do with bedroom escapades than Navy aviation, however; it was a nighttime soap in the tradition of DYNASTY. Dennis Weaver and Robert Vaughn played the heads of two prominent families, while Sela Ward and Jill St. John portrayed the evil women popular in this type of drama.

Peacetime military aviation films have been the most controversial of any group of flying films. The public concern over "hawkishness" has clashed with the Pentagon's desire to spur recruitment. Some of the most interesting aviation films have come out of this struggle.

CHAPTER 11

MAYDAY! MAYDAY!

"Trouble in the air" films fall into two categories: stories that deal with a plane crash and the problems faced by the survivors; and films in which an airplane experiences an emergency which must be overcome by the passengers and crew. Filmmakers have often alarmed airline executives with these stories, for films dealing with the perils of flying certainly do not reassure the faint-hearted airline passenger. These pictures are most often soap opera melodramas, but a few excellent movies have been made on the hazards of aviation.

THE GREEN GODDESS (1923, re-made in 1930), which dealt with a doctor crash-landing in a mythical kingdom, was the first "air crash" picture. Airplane crash films often have little in the way of aviation shots; after the initial crash most of the action takes place on the ground. The air-crash device generally serves to place an individual or group of suitably diverse people in some out-of-the-way place (deserts, jungles, etc.). THE BROKEN WING (1923) combined aviation comedy with the air-crash device in telling of a flier who crashes in Mexico and is nursed by Inez (Miriam Cooper). Held prisoner by bandits, the flier repairs his aircraft and escapes with Inez.

SINNERS IN HEAVEN (1924), an air-crash picture, was also the first aerial "sex" film. A young girl (Bebe Daniels) and her chaperon accompany an English aviator (Richard Dix) on a world's flight to lay out an air mail route for the British government. The plane crashes in the ocean with only the girl and the aviator surviving. Sex comes in a semi-nude bathing scene featuring Daniels, although the actress did wear a white bathing suit. But this was still exciting stuff for 1924, prompting Variety to remark that "... some small town boys will get a real thrill out of this."[1]

CONQUEST (1929) involved two airplane crashes on expeditions to the South Pole.

THE BROKEN WING (1932), based on a play, had an American aviator (Melvyn Douglas) crashing in Mexican bandit country, losing his memory, and becoming the object of the bandit chief's girl's (Lupe Velez) affections. The most notable aspect of the picture is that in July it was banned by the Mexican Federal District Government because it "... slurred Mexico."[2] In addition, Señorita Velez was censured for being in the picture. This political influence extended outside Mexico, for when the film was shown in Panama City it was stopped halfway through at the request of the Mexican Minister, although the picture had been previously passed by the Panama Board of Censors.

By the 1930s, airline passenger travel had increased dramatically, and Hollywood produced the first film dealing with a commercial airport. CENTRAL AIRPORT (1934), directed by William Wellman, starred Richard Barthelmess in a routine story about a crash-prone flier (Barthelmess) who has lost his job as a passenger pilot because of a crash. He teams up with a barnstorming parachute jumper, Sally Eilers, who wants to marry him. Believing that fliers should not be married, he refuses, and she marries his kid brother out of spite. Barthelmess has to rescue his brother and some passengers whose plane has gone down in the Gulf of Mexico. For this sequence the filmmakers dredged out a 600 feet by 400 feet pond on the First National lot in North Hollywood, to a depth of 30 feet, so that a Ford Trimotor could fit in it. Waves were made in the pond and water dumped into the scene and blown about by several large airplanes stationed on the shore with their propellers turning at full speed. After the rescue, however, Barthelmess can't find the field because of a thick fog. The airport boss stations many cars on a hill and they use their light to guide the pilot. He runs out of fuel and dead-sticks in.

CENTRAL AIRPORT proved to be one of Paul Mantz's most dangerous films. Wellman needed some night shots of a Trimotor, and Mantz called Howard Batt, asking to rent the plane. Batt insisted on coming and flew the plane to United Airport. He quickly checked out Mantz, who had never flown this type of plane, and they took off into the night. Batt circled at 1000 feet and then started the camera run. Mantz thought something was wrong and then realized that one of the red lights on a high-tension pole at the east end of the airport, in line with Runway 25, had burned out. He pointed it out to Batt but Batt paid little attention. He came in nose-high to land short as Wellman wanted, and Mantz realized that they were under-shooting. Dwiggins explained what happened:

> Mantz, disregarding all the rules of airman's eti-
> quette, grabbed the control wheel, shoving the throt-
> tles wide open just as the ship's underbelly smashed
> into the darkened pole. The sky blazed as more
> than 150,000 volts spun off the middle propeller in
> a rain of orange and blue sparks. [3]

Mantz landed on the runway as power went out all over the city. Batt, who had thought he knew what he was doing, refused to speak to Mantz for months. The film cost Mantz the only broken bone he ever received while flying for films. The stunt called for Mantz, in a runaway plane, to crash through a hot dog stand and then into a plane piloted by Barthelmess. Mantz was supposed to jump out as he hit, but the tail caught him and he broke his collar bone. He was back in action in a week, but a doctor advised an operation to completely repair the damage. Mantz felt he couldn't afford the time out from his flying business, and the shoulder bothered him for the rest of his life.

FORCED LANDING (1935) featured criminals on board a transcontinental airliner. Included were numerous details about how the plane's crew operates and the plane being forced down by a storm.

CEILING ZERO (1936), directed by Howard Hawks, was written by Frank Wead, based on his stage play of the same name. The Warner Brothers film teamed James Cagney and Pat O'Brien in a story about the Federal Air Lines, based at Hadley Field in Newark. Reviewers were enthusiastic about the picture. The New York Times called it "... a constantly absorbing chronicle of life in and around a commercial air-port." [4]

The story involved two fliers, Dizzy Davis (Cagney) and Texas Clarke (Stuart Erwin), both in love with the same girl. Davis fakes sickness so he can have a date with the girl and Clarke flies in his place. Clarke's plane becomes lost in a fog, his radio fails, and he dies in a spectacular crash into some high-tension wires as he tries to land (which almost happened to Mantz in CENTRAL AIRPORT). (Hawks would repeat and refine this type of tragic death over a woman in ONLY ANGELS HAVE WINGS, three years later.) In the end, Davis takes off in bad weather and dies when his plane's wings ice up and he crashes. The picture began with a tribute to the pioneers of commercial aviation.

This story of dangerous happenings around an airport did not sit well with airline executives, as Jim Greenwood explained:

> But before the movie's release, commercial airline officials nervously remembering that many potential air travelers were scared out of their wits during the play's run on Broadway, sent emissaries to plead with the studio. They wanted the production company to withdraw the film.
> It was an exercise in futility: the film couldn't be scrapped, there was ... money at stake. However, studio chiefs did allow the airlines to inscribe a foreword.... "This picture depicts pioneer days in air travel," the caption read. "As a result of these heroic events, we have arrived at today's safety." ... Needless to say, the airline disclaimer didn't help much. [5]

An incident during the filming of CEILING ZERO indicates the value of having the air action directed not only by a good stunt pilot but also by a person very astute about every aspect of filmmaking, as Paul Mantz was. Mantz was hired to fly the camera ship for the picture. When he arrived at the shooting location, he told Hawks that the numbers on the tail of the plane Cagney was supposed to fly should be changed. Since the numbers were 1313, Hawks asked if Mantz was superstitious. Mantz replied "no," but if Hawks wanted to flip shots to show the plane flying in the opposite direction, the numbers should read the same backward and forward. Hawks had them changed to 8118.

13 HOURS BY AIR (1936) had pilot Fred MacMurray and various other characters in an airliner being forced down in a snowstorm and menaced by crooks. Ironically, the Paramount filmmakers thanked United Airlines for its cooperation

in making the picture, which showed air travel as anything but safe. FUGITIVE IN THE SKY (1937), a Warners' remake of 13 HOURS BY AIR, told the story of a criminal taking control of an air liner which is forced down in a dust storm.

LOST HORIZON (1937, remade in 1973) told of Hollywood's most famous group of crash survivors, the passengers of a downed airplane in the Himalayas who reach Shangri-La.

FIVE CAME BACK (1939), a low-budget RKO picture written by Jerry Cady, Dalton Trumbo, and Nathanael West, told of the crash of the airliner "Silver Queen" in the South American jungle. Of the twelve passengers on board, including Lucille Ball and Chester Morris, five come back. The picture was remade in 1956 as BACK FROM ETERNITY with John Farrow as the director and was little changed from the earlier version. A plane piloted by Bill (Robert Ryan) and Joe (Keith Andes) runs into a storm and crashes in the South American jungle. On board are a murderer (Rod Steiger) who is being sent home to be executed, a bullying coward (Gene Barry), his fiancée (Phyllis Kirk), a hooker (Anita Ekberg), and six other people. Ryan manages to repair the plane, but it can take only half of them to safety out of head-hunter country. The passengers reveal their real character as they decide who will have to stay.

One aviation film planned in 1939 that was not made was THIRTEEN GO FLYING. After informal objections from the U.S. Government, Samuel Goldwyn canceled plans to make a picture based on the crash of the flying boat Cavalier on a flight to Bermuda. Goldwyn said: " 'I certainly do not want to place any hindrance in the path of American aviation's fine progress.' "[6]

In SEVEN WERE SAVED (1947), a plane crashes in the Pacific and the passengers float on a life raft awaiting rescue. The film is part raft survival instructions, part details of the air search, and part conflicts between the characters on the raft. The film ends with a power boat being dropped by plane to take them to safety.

Jimmy Stewart starred in NO HIGHWAY IN THE SKY (1951, also known as NO HIGHWAY), produced by Twentieth

James Stewart and Marlene Dietrich on board the Reindeer that will soon crash unless they take action, in NO HIGHWAY IN THE SKY (1951).

Century-Fox. In it he played an eccentric scientist, Theodore Honey, who works as a research engineer in the Royal Aircraft Establishment laboratories while raising his daughter Elspeth (Janette Scott). He has discovered that a new transatlantic plane, the Reindeer, suffers from metal fatigue, which causes the tail section to break off without warning after 1,400 flying hours. He works diligently to prove his theory while the planes continue in service, piling up flying hours. Dragged out of the laboratory, he is sent by his boss (Jack Hawkins) to Labrador to investigate the crash of one of the planes. And, of course, he travels on a Reindeer. En route he informs a stewardess (Glynis Johns) and a movie star (Marlene Dietrich) that he has just concluded that the plane

they are on has already flown 1,420 hours. They make it to
Gander Airport, Newfoundland, where Honey retracts the
landing gear while the plane sits on the runway, in ord *r* to
wreck it and keep it from flying. So impressed with honey
are Dietrich and Johns that they accompany him back to England to help clear him from a lunacy charge and to prove the
planes are unsafe. He becomes the hero of British aviation.
The film was based on a Nevil Shute novel and the action
takes place in the lab or on board the plane.

BROKEN JOURNEY (1948) was a well acted vehicle
about a plane crash in the Alps. Inspired by the Alpine
crash of an American Army Dakota in November 1946, the
English film showed characters who found new strengths or
weaknesses when faced with survival on the glacier's slope.
MIRACULOUS JOURNEY (1948) had characters downed in a
jungle when their plane crashes. The passengers, are, of
course, a **cross-section** of society and there is even a blind
girl on her way to an operation to restore her sight. The
intrepid band is rescued when pilot Rory Calhoun walks out
of the jungle and returns via helicopter to rescue them.
DAUGHTER OF THE JUNGLE (1949) had a female Tarzan
leading the victims of an airplane crash to safety. THE
GREAT PLANE ROBBERY (1950) dealt with a daring robbery
and two murders on a transcontinental airliner.

DESPERATE SEARCH (1952) told of Canadian Western
Airlines Flight Number 7 from Vancouver to San Francisco
crashing in the wilderness after the port engine catches fire.
The only survivors are two small children. Their remarried
father (Howard Keel), a bush pilot, begins a desperate search
to find them before they die in the rugged country. As if
he didn't have enough troubles, Keel develops an inferiority
complex brought on by the self-assurance of his ex-wife, a
famed aviatrix. He gets hold of himself in time to save the
children, however. The film has an extremely poor model
plane crash, which is offset by good shots of the bush pilots' airplanes as they search for the children in the wilderness terrain.

The Czechoslovakian film HIJACKING (UNOS, 1952)
dealt with the hijacking of a plane to West Germany. The
film severely criticized America, but the director, Jan Kadar,
has lived in exile in the U.S. since 1968.

ISLAND IN THE SKY (1953) was directed by William Wellman. John Wayne played the pilot of an Air Transport DC-3 Command plane that crashes in Labrador. Wayne and his four crewmen must struggle to stay alive in the **unchartered Arctic waste until** they are rescued. For five days Wayne fights to hold the crew together, and on the sixth day they are saved. Wellman expertly shifts from the tense drama at the crash site to the planning and execution of the search. Snow-covered Donner Lake near Truckie, California doubled for the Labrador location. The good ground photography at this site, the well-done aerial shots of William Clothier, and the expert acting make ISLAND IN THE SKY one of the best of the plane-crash films.

THE HIGH AND THE MIGHTY (1954) was also directed by William Wellman. Produced by Warner Brothers, the film was the first to show the tribulations of the passengers and crew of a "doomed" airliner. This idea has formed the basis for several popular films which are discussed later. It is interesting to note that in these films, no matter what caused the aerial emergency, the plane always lands safely, with no additional people being injured. THE HIGH AND THE MIGHTY starred John Wayne as the co-pilot and Robert Stack as the pilot of a plane bound from Honolulu to San Francisco. Among the 22 people on board are a maniac who is out to kill one of the other passengers, a couple on their way home to get a divorce, a disillusioned atomic scientist, and a crippled rich boy. Stack is obsessed with the idea that something's going to go wrong on the flight, while Wayne is full of remorse because his wife and child died when a plane he was piloting crashed. The four-engined plane loses a propeller, which ruptures a wing tank. This leaves a nearly empty fuel tank and the bad engine hanging from the nacelle. The navigator panics and computes a course in statute miles instead of nautical miles. As the fuel situation becomes critical, the passengers receive ditching instructions and a stewardess sobs in the rear cabin. The navigator finally plots a correct course and figures that they can make the coast if they can pick up eleven extra flying minutes. Stack becomes hysterical and urges that they ditch immediately. Wayne slaps Stack around and takes command, cutting power to save fuel. Stack finally regains control of himself and feels that they now have a chance to land safely. He manages to land in San Francisco with 30 gallons of fuel to spare. There is some good aviation photography by William **Clothier**.

Understandably, the airlines were rather upset by the film. Many people who had flown previously without giving it a second thought now took another look at airline safety. One film critic said, "'You may decide never to step into an airplane again after seeing THE HIGH AND THE MIGHTY.'"[7] Dimitri Tiomkin received an Oscar for his haunting score for the movie.

THE NIGHT MY NUMBER CAME UP (1955) was a British film based on an actual incident that happened to Air Marshall Sir Victor Goddard (of the Royal New Zealand Air Force) in 1946. In Shanghai, on his way to Tokyo, Goddard (Michael Redgrave) is told by a naval commander about a dream. The commander dreamt about a Dakota (DC-3) with eight passengers on board which crashes, killing a high official, a civil servant, and a young woman. Since Goddard is to fly to Tokyo the next day in a Liberator carrying only four people, he's not worried. By flight time, however, a Dakota has been substituted for the original plane and four more passengers have been added, including a VIP and a woman secretary. The plane runs into an electrical storm, loses the use of the radio, and becomes lost at high altitude, with the passengers gasping for breath. The plane crashes but the characters survive, breaking the truth of the dream. Skillfully acted and ably directed, it is a fine picture.

JULIE (1956) was a minor aviation film starring Doris Day as a woman fleeing from her insane, murdering husband. At the end of the picture, the husband kills the pilots of an airliner and Day has to land the plane. TARZAN AND THE LOST SAFARI (1957) has an airplane crashing in the jungle and it's up to Tarzan (Gordon Scott) to get the passengers out of dangerous country.

The British DECISION AGAINST TIME (1957) devoted thirty minutes of its length to an English test pilot (Jack Hawkins) who is circling his damaged air-cargo plane over an airport. His boss (Walter Fitzgerald), the owner of a small plane factory, has all his capital tied up in the crippled plane but nevertheless urges Hawkins to bail out. Hawkins refuses, makes a desperate landing, and saves the airplane and the company.

In ZERO HOUR (1957) two pilots of a passenger plane flying between Winnipeg and Vancouver are stricken with food poisoning, along with some of the passengers. One of the passengers (Dana Andrews) is a former flight leader of an RAF Spitfire squadron active during World War II and it falls to him to land the plane safely. Not only has he not flown for 12 years, but the reason he stopped flying was because he lost his flying nerve after accidentally leading his squadron to destruction. A hostess presses him into service and the airline's chief test pilot (Sterling Hayden) is called to the tower to talk him down. Hayden, however, knows of Andrews' wartime experiences and has little confidence in him. Andrews saves the plane and the doctor on board is able to save the passengers. Before it was made into a film, the story was shown on TV (in 1955) under the title of "Flight into Danger." The story returned to TV again in 1971 when it appeared as a television movie starring Doug McClure as a helicopter pilot just home from Vietnam who has to fly the plane. And ZERO HOUR served as the basis for the satire on disaster pictures, AIRPLANE.

CRASH LANDING (1958) tells the story of a plane in trouble over the Atlantic. The plane has to ditch in the ocean and everyone is safely rescued by a U.S. Navy destroyer. The pilot of this plane is Steve Williams (Gary Merrill), a tyrant who pushes his music-loving son to be a boy of action. The notables on board are a retired businessman, a school teacher, a rugged tycoon, and a Portuguese grandmother on her first flight to America to see her grandchildren. The film is amateurish, with Los Angeles Airport doubling for the one in Lisbon, and the rim of a studio tank in plain view during the rescue scenes.

THE ISLAND OF LOST WOMEN (1959) had an American radio commentator (Jeff Richards) and his pilot (John Smith) make a forced landing on a tiny uncharted Pacific island. The only inhabitants are a brilliant atomic scientist (Alan Napier), who is convinced that the rest of the world is mad, and his three daughters, who have never seen another man before. To prevent Richards from returning to civilization and reporting his whereabouts, Napier destroys the plane. An explosion set off by Napier, however, is detected by the Australians, and they send investigators to the island and expose Napier's hiding place. This is one of the worst of the plane crash movies and the plot is ridiculous.

S.O.S. PACIFIC (1959), a British film, was not much

better. A group of diverse characters is on board a sea-plane. The pilot likes to drink and the co-pilot likes only himself. The passengers include a tough sea captain being brought back to face a smuggling charge, a middle-aged spinster, and a shy young German scientist. The plane runs into a hurricane and catches fire. The pilot is injured, the co-pilot killed, and the plane crashes in the Pacific. The survivors end up on a remote island which is soon to be the site of an atomic test. They have five hours to neutralize the bomb. One of the characters manages to disarm the bomb and survives the ordeal (in the American version he is killed). Shot in the Canary Islands, the film has a few interesting aviation shots.

JET STORM (1959) was a British film telling of an airliner flying from London to New York. One of the passengers (Richard Attenborough) accuses another passenger of being the hit-and-run driver who killed his child. Obviously mentally disturbed, he says he will kill the passenger and he denounces the human race. He has smuggled a bomb on board and the captain of the plane (Stanley Baker) and some of the stronger-willed passengers decide that he must be overpowered. The picture is marred by melodramatics, poor acting, and a contrived ending.

The German-made FAREWELL TO THE CLOUDS (ABS-CHIED VON DEN WOLKEN, 1959) told of an airliner flying over Bermuda. Among the passengers are a general running away with his country's treasury, an old Nazi, and a Dutch adventurer. The captain of the airliner (Peter van Eyck) and the Dutchman overcome the Nazi and the general when they cause trouble, and the plane makes a belly landing.

JET OVER THE ATLANTIC (1960) was a poor film featuring an assortment of characters, including George Raft, Virginia Mayo, and Guy Madison, flying on an airliner that develops engine trouble over the ocean. THE CROWDED SKY (1960) had characters who did not know they were in danger: only the audience knows that a Navy jet and an airliner are heading toward a mid-air collision. As the Navy plane piloted by Dale Heath (Efrem Zimbalist, Jr.) speeds toward the airliner flown by Dick Barnett (Dana Andrews), the personal quirks of the pilots and passengers are revealed. The airliner survives the collision, but the Navy jet and its crew are destroyed.

THE FLIGHT THAT DISAPPEARED (1961) tells of an airliner en route from Los Angeles to Washington. On board are a famous nuclear physicist, his assistant, and a rocket propulsion expert. They have been summoned to the Pentagon to discuss a new superbomb that has been developed. The plane suddenly begins climbing out of control and rises to an extreme altitude. All the passengers but these three lose consciousness and the plane lands on a cloud-shrouded plateau far above the earth's atmosphere. They are taken by a mysterious figure to be tried by unborn future generations for developing a bomb that can destroy all life. Twenty-four hours later the plane lands in Washington, the scientists having been sobered by the experience. The incredible plot makes the film all but unwatchable.

WINGS OF CHANCE (1961) was a poor film concerning the attempts to rescue a group of people downed in the northern woods. The only notable feature of the film is that it is one of Jim Brown's first pictures.

FATE IS THE HUNTER (1964) tells of a civilian jet crash that kills 53 people, and of the investigation that follows. As the Civil Aeronautics Board and the FBI investigate the incident they find that the pilot (Rod Taylor) had been drinking prior to the flight. This, then, is assumed to be the cause of the crash. But the airline vice president (Glenn Ford), an old friend of Taylor's who flew with him in World War II, doesn't believe it and sets out to clear him. He interviews the only survivor of the crash, a stewardess (Suzanne Pleshette), makes a test flight simulation of the take off of the plane, and finds the cause of the crash. A cup of coffee had spilled over an instrument box and short-circuited vital wiring.

The film has a variety of aircraft. The flying scenes were staged using a six-foot-span model. A full-sized airplane was built so that it would not resemble any existing airliner. The airlines were reluctant to have one of their planes crash in the film, so Twentieth Century-Fox purchased a DC-6B and converted it by sweeping back the wings, removing the engines, redesigning the tail, and adding jet pods to the horizontal stabilizer. The aircraft was then broken up to form the nucleus of the plane crash set on the Fox Culver City back lot. The set looked so realistic that the co-pilot of a northbound Electra flying overhead reported over the radio that an airliner had crashed in Culver City. Besides the jet shots, prop planes are featured in a World War II flashback. A C-54 and a Fairchild rescue plane were among the aircraft used in the simulation of an airfield in Burma (the scene was shot at Whiteman Park in the San Fernando Valley).

SANDS OF THE KALAHARI (1965) proved to be one of the best crash films. This time the crash leaves a group of assorted characters stranded in the Kalahari Desert. The group finds a series of caves to take shelter in and, while some of them go for help, O'Brien (Stewart Whitman) wages a one-man war against the baboons that live in the area, shooting them when he gets the chance. A helicopter comes to the rescue but O'Brien refuses to return to civilization to be tried for a murder he has committed. As the helicopter leaves, O'Brien runs out of bullets, fights the king of the baboons with his bare hands, and wins, becoming leader of the tribe. Visually exciting, the film makes the most of the desert country.

MISSING AIRCRAFT (FLYGPLAN SAKNAS, 1965) was a Swedish film about an S-32 Lansen reconnaissance plane. The pilot and the navigator are forced to ditch into the water and they float on their rafts awaiting rescue. The film follows the search from the time they're reported missing until they are found, by which time the pilot has died.

The beginning of 1966 saw the release of the best crash movie ever made, THE FLIGHT OF THE PHOENIX, based on a novel by Elleston Trevor, a World War II Spitfire pilot. Robert Aldrich directed the $5,000,000 picture, which stars Jimmy Stewart as Frank Towns, a "seat-of-the-pants" pilot who distrusts the new breed of airplanes and is therefore reduced to flying an obscure cargo run for a Middle East oil company, Arabco Oil. On a flight to Benghazi his C-82 Skytruck runs into a sand storm and crashes in the Sahara. Of the 14 passengers on board, two are killed and the rest of the mixed group is left with oil-rig tools, dried dates, and little else. Towns' hard-drinking navigator (Richard Attenborough) failed to check out the radio before they left and now Towns finds it will not work. Captain Harris (Peter Finch), a British officer, tries to walk for help but later returns to the crashed plane nearly dead from thirst. A group of Arabs camp nearby, but out of

sight of the plane, and when Harris tries to enlist their aid
he is brutally killed. At this point the German in the group
(Hardy Kruger) reveals that he is an aircraft designer and
suggests they build a plane out of one boom of the C-82.
Towns distrusts him, but agrees to the scheme as a way of
keeping up the men's morale. As the "Phoenix" nears completion, Towns' respect for the German grows and he wants
to know what planes the German has designed. Towns finds
out, to his horror, that the German is a model aircraft designer. He's upset that a "toy" designer has been ordering
him about. The German explains that a model plane must be
extremely stable because it has to fly itself. The "Phoenix"
proves to be a flyable aircraft and, with the survivors strapped
to the wing, Towns flies it to an oil drilling station.

THE FLIGHT OF THE PHOENIX, based on a true World
War II incident, is basically the story of the conflict between
those who work with their hands (Towns) and those who work
with their heads (the German). It is also a confrontation between the old and the new. Towns represents the old way
of thinking and although he doesn't like the German, he needs
him to design the plane. The German needs Towns to pilot
the airplane. The end result is a mutual admiration between
the two men.

The C-82 flying sequences were done with a six-foot
wing-span model. The flying shots of the Phoenix, however,
were done for real and resulted in the tragic death of Paul
Mantz. Otto Timm, an old friend of Mantz, helped build the
Phoenix out of parts salvaged from a twin-engined Beech C-
45 and a North American T-6 trainer. Two versions of the
movie plane were actually built, and flight experiments were
made with both. The final version used in the movie looked
like a disaster, but the plane passed all homebuilt aircraft
regulations set by the FAA.

The Phoenix was shipped to Buttercup Valley, 20 miles
west of Yuma, Arizona, in June. Frank Tallman had been
signed as the pilot, but he had fallen while pushing his son's
go-cart and smashed his left kneecap. (The leg would later
have to be amputated above the knee.) **Twentieth Century-
Fox executives** were reluctant to have Mantz fly the plane
because the stunt pilot was nearly sixty-two years old.
Mantz, however, felt he was quite equal to the task.

Upon flying the plane, Mantz found it noseheavy but manageable. Technical problems, such as the engine over-heating and the landing gear failing, dogged the production. The script called for the Jimmy Stewart character to fly the plane, with the other survivors of the crash lying on the wings. Dummies were tried, but it was found that they blanked the controls, just as Bobby Rose's body had on THE GALLOPING GHOST, Mantz's first film-flying assign-ment many years earlier. Plywood cutouts were then used to simulate the passengers. Bobby Rose rode in the cock-pit behind Mantz.

Mantz was supposed to take off from the floor of the valley, struggle to remain airborne, and just clear the sand dunes. But a take-off from the sand seemed impossible, so the eventual plan was to take off from Blythe airport, dip down into the valley until the wheels touched, and climb again. The flying shots were scheduled for the early morn-ing because the temperature often climbed to 140° in the af-ternoon. Mantz took off at 6:10 a.m. on July 8, 1965, with Bobby Rose in the rear seat. Mantz flew to the filming lo-cation and made an excellent pass in front of the cameras, lightly touching down and barely clearing the sand dunes. But the filmmakers wanted one more pass as an insurance shot, so Mantz headed in again. He touched down and his right gear hit a small mound, perhaps made by a prairie dog. The fuselage split in two as the plane flipped on its back and crumpled into the ground. Mantz was killed, crushed by the engine. Bobby Rose jumped clear and, although badly in-jured, lived. Three cameras recorded the action, but the movie ends as originally intended, with the characters fly-ing to safety. Like Locklear before him, Mantz died doing a stunt already "in the can." Mantz's death cost the studio $200,000 for lost time, insurance, and a new plane. (The original plane cost $90,000.) But that was insignificant com-pared to the loss of one of aviation's greatest pilots.

Mantz had come out of semi-retirement to do the film, as a favor to the studio. But he had been disturbed by the aerodynamics of the Phoenix and had spent sleepless nights worrying about the plane. He was also troubled by a feel-ing he couldn't identify. Perhaps this is why, when the Civil Aeronautics Board released its report on the crash in January 1967, they stated that Mantz was "under the influ-

ence of alcohol" when he died. They cited the probable
cause of the accident as "impaired efficiency and judgment
of the pilot caused by the consumption of alcohol and 'over-
load failure of the fuselage structure.'"[8] Whatever the con-
tributing factors, Hollywood lost its greatest stunt pilot.

THE DOOMSDAY FLIGHT (1966) was a made-for-TV
film scripted by Rod Serling and starring Jack Lord and
Edmond O'Brien. O'Brien blackmails an airline by planting
an altitude-activated bomb on a passenger plane. His plan
is thwarted, however, when the plane lands in Denver,
whose elevation is above the altitude that will trigger the
bomb. The film inspired such a rash of telephone bomb
hoaxes to the airlines that Serling regretted having written
the script. In May 1971, when the film was being shown in
syndication, Qantas Airlines paid $560,000 to two extortion-
ists who were later apprehended. On August 3, 1971, a
week after the film was shown in Canada, a B.O.A.C. 747
from Montreal to London had to be diverted to Denver because a caller said a bomb would explode if the plane
dropped below 5,000 feet. The plane landed safely and no
bomb was found. In August 1971, the Federal Aviation Administration asked 500 TV stations not to show the film because of the threats.

VALLEY OF MYSTERY (1967), a television pilot expanded for theatrical release, had a Boeing 707, on a routine passenger run, encountering a hurricane and crashing
in the South American jungle. The notables on board include
a murderer (Fernando Lamas), a novelist (Peter Graves) who
is looking **for his sister who's** married a missionary, a liquor
saleswoman (Lois Nettleton), and a neurotic school teacher
(Julia Adams). The whole film is rather boring, and in fact
is interesting only for its errors in logic. During the storm
the 707 loses its starboard outboard engine and wing tip but
manages to glide to a safe landing in a valley surrounded by
high mountain peaks. Of the 130 people on board, only one
is injured and that's because his seat belt was deliberately
unfastened. And only 15 or 20 people are ever shown. What
happened to the others?

SULLIVAN'S EMPIRE (1967) was also a TV pilot. An
American businessman, John Sullivan (Arch Johnson), crashes
in the Brazilian jungle and his three sons set out to look for
him. The poor film was shot entirely on a Hollywood sound

stage. TERROR IN THE JUNGLE (1968) was a terrible story of a boy who survives a plane crash in Peru's Amazon jungle. He is found by some Incas who think he's a blond god. LAST FLIGHT (1969) was a television film about a group of survivors of a commercial jet that crash-lands on a Pacific island.

THE SKY PIRATE (1970) was the first American film to deal with hijacking. Filmmakers lagged behind the times in treating this new aerial subject and this movie was an underground one shot in 16mm. The story is told in flashbacks when Charlie (Claudia Leacock) hears over the radio that her uncle Joe (Michael McClanathan) has hijacked a Boeing 707 to Cuba. Most of the rest of the film deals with Joe's relations with the few people that know him. There's a lot of talking but the film is still interesting.

In January 1970 Carlo Ponti planned the production of THEY ROBBED ME OF $200 AND I TOOK IT BACK, the story of real-life hijacker Raffaele Minichello, then in jail awaiting trial. Ponti wanted to create the events as accurately as possible, including the use of the hijacked plane's crew. For this and other items he needed the assistance of TWA, which flatly refused to have anything to do with the project. Although Ponti was determined to go ahead without their cooperation, he found the lack of assistance too great an obstacle and the film was never made.

AIRPORT (1970) proved to be the top money-making aviation film of all time, earning $44,500,000 in the film rentals by the end of 1971. It's the only "blockbusting" aviation film. The workings of the Lincoln International Airport (location shots were done at the Minneapolis-St. Paul International Airport) form the basis for the film. It is a day when everything happens at once. The worst blizzard of the year strikes, closing most of the area's airports and most of Lincoln's runways. A mad bomber (Van Heflin) has boarded Trans-Global Airlines' flight to Rome and plans to destroy the plane over the ocean so that his wife (Maureen Stapleton) can collect his flight insurance. A little old lady (Helen Hayes) is found to be a professional stowaway, is held in the terminal, and escapes on to the flight to Rome. Outside the terminal a group of angry citizens pickets for jet plane noise reduction. On the field, a jet has skidded and is now blocking the only usable runway. These problems that the airport

This jet blocks a crucial runway in AIRPORT (1970).

manager (Burt Lancaster) faces are beyond the comprehension of his social-climbing wife (Dana Wynter) and she wants a divorce. He therefore turns to the head of his guest relations department (Jean Seberg) for comfort. The bomb on the plane goes off and the pilot (Dean Martin), who is married to Lancaster's sister (Barbara Hale) but is having an affair with a now-pregnant stewardess (Jacqueline Bisset), tries to keep the plane in the air long enough to return to the airport. On the ground the ace crew chief (George Kennedy) works frantically to clear the runway of the plane that skidded. He succeeds, Martin lands the plane, and Lancaster goes home with Seberg to sample her scrambled eggs.

AIRPORT spawned three sequels, all featuring George Kennedy as the crew chief. (Roy Davis, head of TWA's Chicago maintenance section, was the basis for Kennedy's character. He convinced Kennedy to learn to fly and Kennedy got his pilot's license.) AIRPORT 1975 (1974) starred

Pilot Dean Martin has more than his share of problems in
AIRPORT (1970).

Charlton Heston in the story of a Boeing 747 which collides with a twin-engine Beechcraft Baron. The crew of the 747 is disabled or killed and a large hole is smashed in the nose. A stewardess (Karen Black) puts the plane's controls on automatic while ground controllers decide how to save the plane. They decide they must lower a pilot by helicopter so that he can climb into the 747 through the hole and land the plane. The first man to attempt this is killed, but Heston succeeds.

Jim Gavin served as second unit director for AIRPORT 1975. Stuntman Joe Canuck was lowered to within 18 feet of the 747's nose, giving the illusion that he made the transfer. This difficult scene was shot near Salt Lake city, Utah.

Gavin also worked on AIRPORT '77 (1977). A luxury jet belonging to the character portrayed by Jimmy Stewart and loaded with art treasures crashes and sinks in the ocean. The plane remains watertight, however, and the passengers

Passengers panic as their 747 collides with a private plane in AIRPORT 1975.

are rescued when the plane is raised from the bottom. Surprisingly, this plot is better than it sounds. Extra footage was added when the film was shown on television.

THE CONCORDE--AIRPORT '79 (1979) was by far the worst of the AIRPORT series. It had not one, but three stories of people out to stop the Concorde's flight. Gavin had charge of the aerial sequences, which he pegged at $50,000 per flying hour. Jean T. Franchie, Aerospatiale's (the company that built the Concorde) chief pilot, flew the plane for the flying scenes, filmed with Clay Lacy's Learjet photoplane and a Bell Ranger helicopter. Gavin considered this film the most difficult of his career, because of the high costs involved. At the present time a further sequel, AIRPORT 2000, is planned.

WILD IN THE SKY (1972, retitled BLACK JACK) told of three prisoners who hijack a plane. FAMILY FLIGHT (1972), a made-for-television film starring Rod Taylor, was about a troubled family that crashes while on a flying vacation and finds they must work together to survive.

SKYJACKED (1972) was directed by John Guillermin (THE BLUE MAX) and based on the novel Hijacked by David Harper. The film stars Charlton Heston as the pilot of a 707 hijacked by a deranged passenger (James Brolin) who orders the plane flown to Anchorage and then to Moscow. On board are the usual assortment of passengers including the stewardess ex-love of Heston (Yvette Mimieux) and a US Senator (Walter Pidgeon). Aerial sequences in the $1,700,000 film were shot by Don Morgan and directed by James W. Gavin. Four F-4s represented Russian fighters that intercept the 707 when it enters Russian air space. Heston actually flew a 707 at 30,000 feet over New Mexico and no models were used in the film.

SKYJACKED, made at a time when hijacking had reached alarming proportions, was the first major aviation film to deal with this theme. Because it didn't make hijacking seem glamorous, the film received the sanction of the FAA, but that didn't stop it from alarming some people. Partly as a result of an Air Transport Association campaign to downplay information about hijackings, television ads for the film were not shown on some stations. The film was banned in Australia for about six months, in the interests of passenger safety.

The latter half of the 1970s saw a rash of made-for-television "Mayday" films. MAYDAY AT 40,000 FEET (1976) starred David Janssen as the pilot of a 747 plagued by troubles, including a ruthless killer on board. FLIGHT TO HOLOCAUST (1977) depicted a group of trouble-shooters trying to rescue passengers from a private plane that has crashed into a skyscraper and become stuck there. SST--DEATH FLIGHT (1977, also called SST--DISASTER IN THE SKY) told of sabotage against the maiden flight of America's first supersonic transport. CRASH (1978) recounted the story of the 1972 crash of a plane in the Florida Everglades. THE GHOST OF FLIGHT 401 (1978) also dealt with this crash. Ernest Borgnine played the ghost of the pilot of the downed airliner who haunts subsequent flights. The film was based on the book by John C. Fuller. AND I ALONE SURVIVED (1979) was based on Lauren Elder's ordeal after she crashed in the Sierra Nevada mountains in the spring of 1976. CRISIS IN MID-AIR (1979) dealt with an over-age air traffic controller charged with the responsibility for a mid-air collision.

In the Russian-made THE CREW (EKIPAZY, 1979) an Aeroflot passenger plane, a Tupolev Tu-154, lands to rescue people who are menaced by a volcano. The overloaded plane takes off, but loses an engine. The crew manages to get out on the engine nacelle at the rear of the plane and repair the engine. The plane lands safely at Moscow.

THE LAST FLIGHT OF NOAH'S ARK (1981) was an unusual film by Walt Disney, set after the end of World War II. It was based on a story by Ernest K. Gann and filmed at Waikiki Beach. Elliott Gould played a charter pilot who takes a job flying Genevieve Bujold and some animals and children to the South Pacific in his surplus B-29. The plane crahses on an island where two Japanese soldiers think the war is still going on. A truce is arranged, and the plane wreck is converted into a boat so that the group can sail to safety.

The plane crash was done with models. The Confederate Air Force provided its B-29 for the flying scenes and the Navy gave the filmmakers three B-29 wrecks from their China Lake Testing Range.

AIRPLANE! (1980; also known as FLYING HIGH in Britain) was the hilarious retelling of ZERO HOUR. The $3,000,000 film was written and directed by Jim Abrahams

Julie Hagerty and Robert Hays try to fly the plane in the hilarious spoof of trouble-in-the-air films, AIRPLANE! (1980).

and David and Jerry Zucker. It is a marvelous satire of trouble-in-the-air films. The passengers and crew of an airliner are stricken with food poisoning and it's up to a washed-up pilot (Robert Hayes) to land the pland. The film fires sight and verbal gags at a mile-a-minute; and the entire cast plays the material with a straight face, to great effect.

Unfortunately, the same cannot be said for AIRPLANE's sequel, AIRPLANE II (1982). This absolutely dreadful film tells of trouble on a passenger space shuttle mission to the moon. Many of the scenes and jokes from the first film were reused and overused. The only scrap of this picture that bears watching is William Shatner's hamming it up as the moon-base commander.

The Japanese AFARIKA MONOGATARI (1981) starred Jimmy Stewart as the overseer of an African game preserve into which a pilot crashes. The film was also known as A TALE OF AFRICA and THE GREEN HORIZON.

The made-for-television movie FLIGHT #90: DISASTER

ON THE POTOMAC (1984) told in uninspired detail the story
of the January 13, 1982 crash of Air Florida Flight 90, which
slammed into Washington, D.C.'s 14th Street Bridge and sank
into the Potomac River after taking off from National Airport.
Seventy-four people on the plane and four on the bridge were
killed. The first part of the picture is a standard trouble-
in-the-air film, with various characters making serious statements which foreshadow the crash. The latter part of FLIGHT
#90 focuses on the rescue efforts, but one of the two heroes
of the crash is not depicted. Roger Olian and Lenny Skutnik
dived into the icy water to save the passengers, but only
Olian (Richard Masur) is shown. The filmmakers claimed
Skutnik wanted too much money for his cooperation, while
Skutnik said he didn't like the movie's producer. The film
stresses the necessity for following the correct take-off procedures in a snowstorm, and the cockpit transcript of the ill-
fated plane was used as a basis for some of the film's dialogue.

Trouble-in-the-air films are among the easiest aviation
films to produce. Often only the interior of a plane or a
plane wreck is all that's needed in the way of aviation shots.
They often play on people's fears of flying, which provides
a ready-made point of terror. This, coupled with their great
soap opera potential, has made them very popular, particularly on television.

CHAPTER 12

LIGHTER THAN AIR

Ever since the first manned balloon ascension in France
in 1783, men have been fascinated by lighter-than-air flight.
For 120 years balloons remained the only way to stay aloft
for any length of time. And during the early, primitive
years of heavier-than-air aviation, zeppelins offered luxury
air travel. German zeppelins bombed London in World War I,
and after the war dirigibles crisscrossed the Atlantic. The
Hindenberg disaster in 1937 put an end to lighter-than-air
passenger service, but ballooning has continued to be a popular sport.

Late in 1917, Thomas Ince produced THE ZEPPELIN'S
LAST RAID, the first lighter-than-air film. The war scenes
particularly, borrowed much from Ince's epic CIVILIZATION,
gave credence to the belief that both films were made at the
same time. THE ZEPPELIN'S LAST RAID is set against the
workings of a huge dirigible. A young woman works in a
secret movement to overthrow a tyrannical government. She
persuades the captain of the zeppelin to join in the movement. He does so and, when ordered to bomb a city which
is in revolt, refuses. His crew attacks him. Mortally wounded, he throws a switch to destroy the airship.

A factual German zeppelin replaced Ince's fictional one
in THE LAST RAID OF ZEPPELIN L-2 (1918), a semi-documentary, two-reel accumulation of newsreel footage and studio
shots depicting the zeppelin raids on England. The film
showed British anti-aircraft guns shooting at the zeppelin,
a British seaplane crashing, the destruction caused by the
air ship, the zeppelin dropping bombs, searchlights locating
the dirigible, and English planes attacking it. The zeppelin
falls in flames when a flier drops a bomb on it and sets it
on fire.

AROUND THE WORLD VIA GRAF ZEPPELIN (1929) was a documentary, with inserted sound, of newsreel shots taken on board the Graf Zeppelin on a round-the-world trip. The airship is shown leaving Lakehurst, New Jersey, flying over Germany and Russia, Los Angeles, and Chicago, and stopping at Lakehurst. On-board shots included an electrical storm over the Pacific.

THE LOST ZEPPELIN (1930) was a modest picture that told of an airship expedition to the South Pole, quite probably an attempt to cash in on Admiral Byrd's South Pole expedition.

MADAM SATAN (1930), directed by Cecil B. DeMille, had for its high point an elaborate masked ball staged aboard a giant dirigible in typical C.B. fashion. The climax comes

The masked ball on board the dirigible in MADAM SATAN (1930).

when the airship, moored to a mast, is struck by lightning and the passengers parachute to safety.

Director Frank Capra's DIRIGIBLE (1931) was based on a story by Frank Wead. Lieutenant Commander Jack Brandon (Jack Holt) sees great potential in the use of dirigibles, while Lieutenant "Frisky" Pearce (Ralph Graves) favors heavier-than-air craft. Brandon proposes a trip to the South Pole in the giant dirigible Los Angeles, and Pearce agrees to go. But Pearce's wife fears for her husband's safety and convinces Brandon not to take Pearce. Pearce is given a false reason why he can't go along and becomes resentful of Brandon.

Louis Rondelle heads up the polar expedition. But the airship is damaged in a storm and the expedition has to return home. (The scene of the dirigible in the storm has been compared favorably to the zeppelin sequence in HELL'S ANGELS.) This gives Pearce the chance to show up Brandon's airship philosophy by taking a Ford Trimotor over the South

Parachuting onto the ice in DIRIGIBLE (1931).

Pole. Rondelle agrees to go along. The adventurers plan to fly over the Pole and drop a U.S. flag, à la Admiral Byrd, but once over their destination they can't resist the temptation to land. Their plane cracks up on landing and they are stranded. Naturally enough, Brandon rescues them when he pilots a dirigible to the Pole.

To film the picture, Capra enlisted the aid of the U.S. Navy, and the film is dedicated to that group. The Navy Bureau of Aeronautics allowed the movie crew the use of aircraft, equipment, and personnel and permitted the use of the Naval Air Station at Lakehurst, New Jersey, where the dirigible Los Angeles (used in the film) and other airships were moored. The 230-foot-high steel hangar housing these dirigibles was so large that water condensed inside the structure, causing rain.

Use of the Los Angeles was not without problems. Temperature was a critical factor for flying the airship for photographic purposes. The airship's helium expanded and contracted with the temperature, and it was only at a suitable density to permit filming in the early morning, not the best time to shoot. To overcome this, special emulsions and sensitized film were developed.

Another problem with the Los Angeles concerned the necessity to record in-flight sound for the film's soundtrack. The airship was photographed from the J-3, a smaller Navy dirigible. But the pitch of the Los Angeles' motors was different from that of the J-3; a microphone had to be placed in the outboard motor compartments of the larger airship, while the J-3's motors were idled down. In addition, sound equipment had to be adapted for temperature and altitude changes.

Elmer Dyer was the aerial photographer, heading up a group of cameramen, many of whom had never been up in any kind of aircraft before. The most interesting airplane sequences occurred when the cameras photographed aircraft hooking on to the Los Angeles and the Ford Trimotor overturned and burning. U.S. government planes from the airbase in Anacostia were fitted with special camera mounts and motor driven cameras to film the hooking up. In addition, cameramen were squeezed into the motor gondolas to place them in a better filming position. The crash of the Trimotor was accomplished by allowing a real aircraft, with its motor running, to roll along the ground before being tipped on its nose. Of the fourteen cameras used in this sequence, two, placed directly in front of the plane with remote motors, were totally destroyed.

One other aviation tidbit is notable: two world's parachute records were claimed by members of the crew. One was for the largest number of men ever to jump at a single time; the other was for coming closest to the designated landing spot (one Navy parachutist landed within four feet of his aiming point).

In filming, Capra faced the problem of creating Antarctic conditions in the 93-degree climate of the San Gabriel Valley. The three-acre Antarctic "ice-cap" had three inches of salt that could move in the wind like snow. Snowy mountains in the background cost $5,000 to paint. And a dozen wind machines and tons of cornflakes were ready to provide a studio blizzard. But Capra wasn't satisfied. There was still the dead giveaway that the actors' breath didn't show. He looked into the problem and a friend hit upon the idea of putting dry ice in wire cages and placing the cages in the actors' mouths. So Capra had a dentist build the cages. The scene to be shot was the planting of a flag at the South Pole, and Hobart Bosworth, Ralph Graves, Clarence Muse, and three others gamely tried to struggle through the scene with the cages in their mouths. Their breath showed but Bosworth, fumbling his lines, threw the cage away in disgust and placed the dry ice directly in his mouth. The result was the loss of three lower teeth, two upper ones, and part of his jawbone, along with some dead tissue. Returning to the set after taking Bosworth to the hospital, Capra found the sign, "'For sale--DRY ICE--Cheap,'" and a cup full of his cages. The experiment was not without success, however, because Clarence Muse's breath showed up well against his black face, causing one critic to ask, "'How come Clarence Muse got more close-ups in DIRIGIBLE than the stars?'"[1]

DIRIGIBLE, Columbia Studio's most expensive film to date, premiered in Los Angeles at Grauman's Chinese Theatre on April 18, 1931 and met with great success, especially sweet to Harry Cohn, head of Columbia. The picture was able to capitalize on Byrd's Polar flight while at the same time taking dramatic liberties that the public would accept because most had not seen Byrd's own WITH BYRD AT THE SOUTH POLE.

LOST IN THE STRATOSPHERE (1935) involved two junior Army officers in a stratospheric balloon flight. IT'S IN THE AIR (1935), an MGM comedy featuring Jack Benny, was partly set in a high-altitude balloon.

THE RED TENT (1969), an Italian-Russian production based on a true incident, dealt with the ill-fated attempt of General Umberto Nobile (Peter Finch) to land a dirigible at the North Pole in 1929. A storm forces him to turn back and the airship crashes. Rescue parties are sent out and a small group of survivors (who painted their tent red to attract search aircraft) is located. The plane that finds them, however, is only a two-seater and the pilot will only take General Nobile to safety. The rest of the men perish and Nobile is disgraced for abandoning his men. Forty years later the General is still haunted by their ghosts and still trying to justify his actions to himself.

The picture is a good adventure story, but it tries, and fails, to be a deep psychological drama. It is interesting for its aerial shots, as much footage is devoted to both the interior and the exterior of the dirigible. The interior sets of the airship are well done and the viewer is given a complete tour of the aircraft.

ZEPPELIN (1971) was set in World War I. The film starred Michael York playing a British officer with German ancestors. This makes him useful to British intelligence, who arrange his "escape" from England so that he can find out what the Germans are up to. The Germans plan to fly to Scotland in a zeppelin and steal the Magna Carta from its wartime hiding place in a castle. York is aghast at this, since he suffers from vertigo. He conceals his condition, goes on the mission, and aids in getting the Zeppelin shot down. It crashes in the English channel but York survives.

The design for the airship used in the film came from German plans for the airship L661, built in 1914-15. A 12-foot model and a 37-foot-long model were built, as well as a full-sized gondola. The dirigible hangars at Cardington, Bedfordshire, England were used to simulate German hangars.

The film was marked by tragedy. Burch Williams, head of the firm which supplied vintage aircraft to filmmakers and brother of film producer Elmo Williams, and veteran aerial cameraman Skeets Kelly were killed on August 18, 1970 when a French Alouette collided with a German biplane off the Irish coast while filming a dogfight. French helicopter pilot Gilbert Chomat and the Irish Air Force pilot flying the biplane were also killed.

HINDENBERG (1975) proved to be the most elaborate airship movie ever made. In 1972 the book The Hindenberg was published and Universal, which liked the drama of the book, decided it would make an excellent film. Veteran director Robert Wise was signed to direct the story of the ill-fated German airship, which told of the dirigible's last voyage, speculating the airship was destroyed by sabotage when it tried to land at Lakehurst, New Jersey on May 6, 1937. George C. Scott starred as a Luftwaffe intelligence officer assigned to protect the Hindenberg.

The filming began on August 12, 1974, with Munich doubling for pre-war Berlin. Sequences were also done at the El Toro Marine Air Base, which had two 1000-foot hangars for lighter-than-air ships. The passenger area, gondola, and superstructure of the dirigible were built on a Universal sound stage. The original interior furnishings and colors were matched as closely as possible. A 50-foot full-size nose cone was constructed. A twenty-five-foot exact replica of the Hindenberg "flew" on Universal Stage 27, with a 24-hour guard to protect the $35,000 model. The model took 80 men four months to construct, or a total of 70,000 man-hours work. It contained eight tons of aluminum, 11,000 yards of muslin, 24,000 feet of sash cord, and two million rivets. When the explosion sequence was filmed, a hole had to be cut in Stage 12's roof to allow the heat from the fire to escape. To add detail, Universal hired Confederate Air Force Col. Gerald Martin and his CASA HA.1112-MIL, N109ME, a Spanish-built version of Bf109 in markings of Condor Legion. These aircraft scenes were filmed at the semi-abandoned Oxnard AFB in southern California.

The original Hindenberg was the largest airship ever constructed, 803 feet long and capable of carrying 50 passengers in luxury ocean liner style. All blueprints for the Hindenberg were destroyed during WWII. The art director,

Ed Carfagno, talked with some engineers who worked on the original. Technical advisor George Lewis, a mechanical engineer, had been employed by Goodyear in the 1930s and spent one and a half years in Germany observing the construction of the real Hindenberg, and had crossed the Atlantic both ways on the Hindenberg and the Graf Zeppelin. Lewis was also at Lakehurst when the accident occurred.

Herb Morrison, a commentator from radio station WLS in Chicago, was in Lakehurst to cover the landing and he made the famous recording of the disaster. Of the 97 people on board, 35 died; 13 of them passengers and 22 crew. One member of the ground crew died. The explosion took only 34 seconds, but it forever ended the era of the luxury dirigibles.

BLACK SUNDAY (1977) was based on the best-selling novel by Thomas Harris. Bruce Dern played the pilot of a Goodyear blimp involved in the plot of a terrorist group to kill 80,000 spectators at the Miami superbowl, including the President.

THE FLIGHT OF THE EAGLE (INGENIOER ANDREES LUFTFAERD, 1982; originally titled THE AIR VOYAGE OF ENGINEER ANDREE) was a Swedish-West German-Norwegian co-production originally made in a television version about an ill-fated 1897 North Pole balloon flight. Max Von Sydow starred as Solomon Andree. Ignoring warnings that their balloon would never survive, Andree's group took off from Spitsbergen and went down three days later. They lasted three months on foot before succumbing to the elements. Although the film received an Oscar nomination for best foreign film, and although it was done by noted director Jan Troell, it is a tedious affair.

There have been relatively few movies dealing with balloons and zeppelins, but those that have been made provide an interesting look at this aspect of aviation.

CONCLUSION

When one looks back over aviation film history, several aspects stand out. Much like the western film genre, aviation movies have most often stressed individualism. A solitary aviator, fortified with guts and "seat-of-the-pants" flying ability, battling the elements and stretching his plane's capacity to the limit, is the most frequent theme in aviation films. This "technical cowboy" prevails not only in American films but in foreign movies as well. Even the airplane movies made in Fascist Germany and communist Russia stress individual courage and initiative. When filmmakers have tried to broaden the scope of aviation films beyond this individual level, the result has often been failure, as in TORA! TORA! TORA! and THE BATTLE OF BRITAIN.

For all their excitement and breath-taking aerial sequences, aviation movies have not been trend-setting films. WINGS did initiate a whole series of flying pictures, but two earlier films showed that World War I could be box-office. THOSE MAGNIFICENT MEN IN THEIR FLYING MACHINES, THE BLUE MAX, THE BATTLE OF BRITAIN, and TORA! TORA! TORA! were made in the 1960s in response to the trend toward big-budget spectaculars at that time, but they didn't start it. There's no GRADUATE of the aviation cinema; no ground-breaking movie that influenced the whole style of filmmaking. Perhaps this is why relatively little has been written about aviation films. Aviation movies are seldom singled out and studied for their uniqueness.

With the exception of films dealing with hijacking, few airplane movies have tackled controversial issues. The public-safety conscious climate that inspired THE CHINA SYNDROME and SILKWOOD didn't spawn an equivalent film dealing with the air traffic controllers' strike, certainly as great a menace to the public safety as nuclear pollution.

305

But whatever negative characteristics plague aviation in the cinema, its positive aspect cannot be denied. Besides providing exciting action sequences, these movies stand as invaluable historical records, far more alive than any museum-bound plane. Besides, these movies are fun, giving us all a chance to go on a dawn patrol or rocket through the sound barrier. The best such films work both as escapist entertainment and as examinations of the human experience, in a way that few other films can match.

REFERENCES

Chapter 1

1. Art Ronnie, Locklear: The Man Who Walked on Wings,* p. 93.
2. Ibid., p. 223.
3. Jim and Maxine Greenwood, Stunt Flying in the Movies, p. 36.
4. The New York Times Film Reviews, 1913-1968, p. 1380.
5. Bara, "Criminals of the Air," Variety, August 18, 1937, p. 9.
6. "Cinema," Time, June 26, 1939, p. 46.
7. Barn, "Flying G Men," Variety, March 22, 1939, p. 30.
8. The New York Times Film Reviews, 1913-1968, p. 1689.
9. Walt, "Power Dive," Variety, April 9, 1941, p. 16.
10. Art, "Emergency Landing," Variety, June 18, 1941, p. 18.
11. Marc Scott Zicree, The Twilight Zone Companion, p. 136.

Chapter 2

1. Greenwood, p. 82.
2. Ronnie, p. 13.
3. Don Dwiggins, Hollywood Pilot, p. 46.
4. Ibid., pp. 53, 54.
5. Greenwood, p. 107.

Chapter 3

1. Ronnie, p. 115.

---

*Full bibliographic citations are given in the Bibliography, which follows these References.

2. Ibid., p. 124.
3. Rush, "Air Mail," Variety, November 8, 1932, p. 17.
4. Dwiggins, pp. 46, 47.
5. The New York Times Film Reviews, 1913-1968, p. 1633.

Chapter 4

1. Sterling Seagrave, Soldiers of Fortune, p. 76.
2. Arch Whitehouse, Legion of the Lafayette, pp. 60, 61.
3. The New York Times Film Reviews, 1913-1968, p. 380.
4. The New York Times Film Reviews, 1913-1968, p. 461.
5. Shan, "The Last Flight," Variety, June 19, 1929, p. 30.
6. "Ask 'Hell's Angels' Ban," The New York Times, June 19, 1931, p. 21.
7. Ibid.
8. George P. Garrett, O. B. Hardison, Jr., and Jane R. Gelfman, eds., Suggestions for Instructions to Accompany Film Scripts One and Film Scripts Two, p. 26.
9. Ibid.
10. The New York Times Film Reviews, 1913-1968, p. 1560.
11. Greenwood, p. 186.
12. Philip Strick, "Ma Barker to von Richthofen: An Interview with Roger Corman," Sight and Sound, Autumn 1970, p. 183.

Chapter 5

1. "London Critics Differ on the Merits of the Byrd Expedition's Film Record," The New York Times, July 27, 1930, Section 3, p. 6.
2. Hobe, "Atlantic Flight," Variety, September 22, 1937, p. 18.
3. Thomas M. Pryor, "Merrill of the Movies," The New York Times, September 26, 1937, Section 11, p. 5.
4. Otis Ferguson, "Lenin and the Dead Pilots," The New Republic, May 11, 1938, p. 19.
5. Dwiggins, p. 62.
6. "Cinema," Time, November 7, 1938, p. 41.
7. The New York Times Film Reviews, 1913-1968, p. 1542.
8. "Army Demands Changes in Film as a Condition to Use of Its Planes," The New York Times, May 29, 1938, Section 2, p. 1.
9. Douglas W. Churchill, "Peace vs. Propaganda," The

New York Times, May 29, 1938, Section 9, p. 3.
10. Fred Stanley, "What's the News in Hollywood?" The New York Times, May 9, 1943, Section 2, p. 3.
11. Fred Stanley, "Hollywood Atom Race Ends," The New York Times, March 24, 1946, Section 2, p. 3.
12. A. H. Weiler, "Random Notes About Pictures and People," The New York Times, July 20, 1947, Section 2, p. 3.
13. Ibid.

Chapter 6

1. Oliver E. Allen, The Airline Builders, p. 136.

Chapter 7

1. Time, November 20, 1939, p. 80.
2. C. A. Lejeune, "London Comes Up for Air," The New York Times, November 19, 1939, Section 9, p. 4.
3. "Behind the Eight Ball," The New York Times, June 8, 1941, Section 9, p. 4.
4. Ibid.
5. Ray, "Stukas," Variety, August 25, 1943, p. 10.
6. Dwiggins, p. 130.
7. "Cinema," Time, April 17, 1944, p. 94; Bosley Crowther, "The Real Thing," The New York Times, April 16, 1944, Section 2, p. 3.
8. Bosley Crowther, "Thinking Out Loud," The New York Times, October 8, 1944, Section 2, p. 1.
9. Robert Hotz, "The Dam Busters," Aviation Week, December 5, 1955, p. 138.
10. Greenwood, p. 166.
11. The New York Times Film Reviews, 1969-1970, p. 90.

Chapter 8

1. "Movies," Newsweek, August 31, 1942, p. 60.
2. The New York Times Film Reviews, 1913-1968, p. 1887.
3. Ibid.
4. "Cinema," Time, September 28, 1942, p. 82.
5. Martin Caiden, The Ragged, Rugged Warriors, p. 189.
6. "Cinema," Time, February 8, 1943, p. 85.

7. Abel, "AIR FORCE," Variety, February 3, 1943, p. 14.
8. Bosley Crowther, "The New Tax on Credulity," The New York Times, February 7, 1943, Section 2, p. 3.
9. Robin Wood, Howard Hawks, p. 92.
10. The New York Times Film Reviews, 1913-1968, p. 1948.
11. Mori, "The Purple Heart," Variety, February 13, 1944, p. 10.
12. "Cinema," Time, January 22, 1945, p. 91.
13. Thomas M. Pryor, "'Lady' with a Punch," The New York Times, January 21, 1945, Section 2, p. 1.
14. "Films of 'Fighting Lady' Are Destined for Tokyo," The New York Times, February 10, 1945, p. 15.
15. Greenwood, p. 150.
16. Lawrence H. Suid, Guts and Glory, p. 275.
17. Darryl Zanuck, "Why 'Tora! Tora! Tora!'?" The New York Times, June 16, 1969, p. 10.
18. A. H. Weiler, "Fox Pays $15,000 to Defend Its Movie," The New York Times, June 17, 1969, p. 40.
19. "Suit Against Film Concern For Navy's Bill Demanded," The New York Times, October 6, 1969, p. 26.
20. Vincent Canby, "Tora-ble Tora-ble Tora-ble," The New York Times, October 4, 1970, Section 2, p. 1.

Chapter 10

1. The New York Times Film Reviews, 1913-1968, p. 38.
2. Ibid., p. 909.
3. Ibid., p. 1162.
4. Hago, "L'Escadrille de la Chance," Variety, July 20, 1938, p. 13.
5. The New York Times Film Reviews, 1913-1968, p. 1865.
6. "Wings of the Navy," Variety, January 18, 1939, p. 12.
7. Ibid.
8. The New York Times Film Reviews, 1913-1968, p. 1631.
9. "Shooting from the Wings," The New York Times, March 9, 1941, Section 9, p. 4.
10. Ibid.
11. Herb, "Parachute Battalion," Variety, July 16, 1941, p. 8.
12. The New York Times Film Reviews, 1913-1968, p. 1807.
13. Suid, p. 38.
14. "The Big Blue Yonder," Newsweek, May 9, 1955, p. 102.
15. Thomas F. Brady, "New Hollywood Curbs," The New York Times, June 7, 1942, Section 8, p. 3.

16. Hollis Alpert, "SR Goes to the Movies," Saturday Review, October 12, 1957, p. 31.
17. Paine Knickerbocker, "Jet-Propelled 'Eagles,'" The New York Times, August 26, 1962, Section 2, p. 7.
18. Tim Brooks and Earle Marsh, The Complete Directory to Prime Time Network TV Shows 1946-Present, pp. 93, 94.

Chapter 11

1. Fred, "Sinners in Heaven," Variety, September 10, 1924, p. 27.
2. The New York Times Film Reviews, 1913-1968, p. 812.
3. Dwiggins, p. 50.
4. The New York Times Film Reviews, 1913-1968, p. 1246.
5. Greenwood, p. 181.
6. "Cancels Air-Crash Movie," The New York Times, March 7, 1939, p. 19.
7. FS, "Scare Movie," Aviation Week, July 26, 1954, p. 67.
8. "Stunt Pilot's Crash Linked to Drinking," The New York Times, January 11, 1967, p. 14.

Chapter 12

1. Frank Capra, The Name Above the Title, p. 128.

BIBLIOGRAPHY

Film Reviews and Articles

"A Repulo Arany," Variety, December 27, 1932, p. 54.

Abel. "Air Force," Variety, February 3, 1943, p. 14.

_____. "Devil Dogs of the Air," Variety, February 12, 1935, p. 19.

_____. "The Lost Squadron," Variety, March 15, 1932, p. 14.

_____. "Night Flight," Variety, October 10, 1933, p. 23.

_____. "Only Angels Have Wings," Variety, May 17, 1939, p. 12.

_____. "The Sky's The Limit," Variety, September 8, 1943, p. 16.

_____. "The Story of Vernon and Irene Castle," Variety, April 5, 1939, p. 15.

_____. "Test Pilot," Variety, April 20, 1938, p. 15.

_____. "Victory Thru Air Power," Variety, July 7, 1943, p. 8.

"Aflame in the Skies," Variety, November 2, 1927, p. 24.

"Air Eagles," Variety, January 26, 1932, p. 23.

"Air Film Flood," Variety, August 17, 1927, p. 13.

"Air Hawks," Variety, June 12, 1935, p. 41.

312

"Air Patrol, The," Variety, January 18, 1928, p. 19.

"Air Power on the Screen," The New York Times, July 26, 1943, p. 18.

"Air Wives at Premiere," The New York Times, September 29, 1955, p. 39.

Albarino, Richard. "'Blue Max' into 561-Seat Suttom, Part of 'Winning the East Side'; Trade Scrutinizes 20th's Tactics," Variety, June 1, 1966, p. 7.

Alpert, Hollis. "Battle Hymn," Saturday Review, February 16, 1957, p. 28.

_____. "SR Goes to the Movies," Saturday Review, December 3, 1955, p. 39.

_____. "SR Goes to the Movies," Saturday Review, March 9, 1957, p. 27.

_____. "SR Goes to the Movies," Saturday Review, October 12, 1957, p. 31.

_____. "SR Goes to the Movies," Saturday Review, July 16, 1966, p. 43.

"Also Showing," Time, August 16, 1943, p. 94.

"An Angel to 'Angels'" The New York Times, May 11, 1930, Section 9, p. 6.

"Angels Could Do No More," The New York Times, February 17, 1929, Section 9, p. 7.

Archerd, Army. "'Flight of the Phoenix' $100,000 London Junket a Feedback for Oscar," Variety, January 19, 1966, p. 36.

"Army Demands Changes in Film as a Condition to Use of Its Planes," The New York Times, May 29, 1938, Section 2, p. 1.

"Arnold Praises Film," The New York Times, April 27, 1944, p. 18.

Art. "Emergency Landing," Variety, June 18, 1941, p. 16.

_____. "Flight Angels," Variety, May 15, 1940, p. 16.

"Ask 'Hell's Angels' Ban," The New York Times, June 19, 1931, p. 21.

"Attack!" Variety, June 14, 1944, p. 10.

"Audience Buys $11,300,000 Bonds," The New York Times, Sept. 19, 1942, p. 17.

"Author Talks on Flying," The New York Times, March 15, 1925, Section 8, p. 5.

"'The Aviator' Very Funny," The New York Times, January 11, 1930, p. 21.

"The Aviation Cycle," Newsweek, February 20, 1939, p. 29.

B., T. "The Screen," The New York Times, July 6, 1942, p. 18.

Bakshy, Alexander. "Films," The Nation, September 3, 1930, p. 254.

"Banana-Town Airline," Newsweek, May 22, 1939, p. 35.

Bang. "Around the World Via Graf Zeppelin," Variety, November 6, 1929, p. 31.

_____. "Dance Hall," Variety, December 18, 1929, p. 28.

Bara. "Criminals of the Air," Variety, August 18, 1937, p. 39.

Barn. "Danger Flight," Variety, December 6, 1939, p. 16.

_____. "Flight to Fame," Variety, December 14, 1938, p. 15.

_____. "Flying G-Men," Variety, March 22, 1939, p. 30.

_____. "Sky Patrol," Variety, November 29, 1939, p. 18.

_____. "Stunt Pilot," Variety, July 26, 1939, p. 15.

_____. "Yukon Flight," Variety, January 10, 1940, p. 16.

"Bars American Film," The New York Times, July 7, 1932, p. 20.

Bart, Peter. "Paul Mantz, Stunt Flier, Is Killed in Crash During Filming of Movie Scene in Arizona," The New York Times, July 9, 1965, p. 14.

"Behind the Eight Ball," The New York Times, June 8, 1941, Sec. 9, p. 4.

"Behind the Scenes: The Film That Waited," Newsweek, September 23, 1957, p. 94.

Behlmer, Rudy. "World War I Aviation Films," Films in Review, August-September 1967, pp. 413-433.

Bennett. "Aerograd," Variety, January 1, 1936, p. 58.

Berger, Meyer. "About New York," The New York Times, April 15, 1957, p. 49.

"Berlin Sees Tokyo Film," The New York Times, June 11, 1942, p. 4.

Bert. "Flight Into Nowhere," Variety, May 4, 1938, p. 15.

"Big Blue Yonder, The," Newsweek, May 9, 1955, p. 102.

Bige. "The Broken Wing," Variety, March 29, 1932, p. 24.

_____. "Captain Swagger," Variety, December 26, 1928, p. 27.

_____. "Ceiling Zero," Variety, January 22, 1936, p. 14.

_____. "Central Airport," Variety, May 9, 1953, p. 14.

_____. "China Clipper," Variety, August 19, 1936, p. 16.

_____. "The Cloud Dogger," Variety, November 28, 1928, p. 20.

_____. "Parachute Jumper," Variety, January 31, 1933, p. 12.

_____. "The Sacred Flame," Variety, November 27, 1929, pp. 21, 31.

_____. "13 Hours By Air," Variety, May 6, 1936, p. 18.

_____. "West Point of the Air," Variety, April 10, 1935, p. 17.

"Blaze of Noon," Time, March 24, 1947, p. 100.

"Blue Max, The," Air Classics, May 1965, pp. 4-8.

"Bombardier's Day, The," Newsweek, June 21, 1943, p. 102.

Bon. "Men On Wings," Variety, June 12, 1935, p. 41.

Brady, Thomas F. "Dry Cleaned by Hollywood," The New York Times, June 14, 1942, Section 8, p. 3.

_____. "From Out of the West," The New York Times, October 18, 1942, Section 8, p. 3.

_____. "Hollywood Takes Uncommon 'Pain,'" The New York Times, May 31, 1942, Section 8, p. 3.

_____. "Hollywood Turns to Facts of War," The New York Times, October 4, 1942, Section 8, p. 3.

_____. "Hollywood Wire," The New York Times, October 17, 1948, Section 2, p. 5.

_____. "New Hollywood Curbs," The New York Times, June 7, 1942, Section 8, p. 3.

_____. "Roundup of Hollywood Matters of Moment," The New York Times, September 27, 1942, Section 8, p. 3.

Bran. "Sky High," Variety, January 30, 1974, p. 6.

"Breaking Through the Sound Barrier," Newsweek, December 1, 1952, p. 87.

"Bridges at Toko-Ri, The," Time, January 24, 1955, p. 75.

"Brig. Gen. Gable," Newsweek, January 24, 1949, p. 73.

Brog. "Above and Beyond," Variety, November 19, 1952, p. 6.

_____. "Air Cadet," Variety, February 21, 1951, p. 6.

_____. "Arctic Fury," Variety, May 11, 1949, p. 18.

_____. "Battle Hymn," Variety, December 19, 1956, p. 7.

_____. "Battle Stations," Variety, February 1, 1956, pp. 6, 18.

_____. "Blaze of Noon," Variety, March 5, 1947, p. 8.

_____. "Chain Lightning," Variety, February 8, 1950, p. 11.

_____. "Command Decision," Variety, December 29, 1948, p. 6.

_____. "Desperate Search," Variety, November 26, 1952, p. 6.

_____. "Dragonfly Squadron," Variety, February 3, 1954, p. 6.

_____. "Fighter Attack," Variety, November 25, 1953, p. 24.

_____. "Fighter Squadron," Variety, November 24, 1948, p. 6.

_____. "Flat Top," Variety, November 19, 1952, p. 16.

_____. "Flight to Tangier," Variety, October 14, 1953, p. 6.

_____. "The 49th Man," Variety, May 13, 1953, p. 18.

_____. "God Is My Co-Pilot," Variety, February 21, 1945, p. 8.

_____. "High and the Mighty," Variety, May 26, 1954, p. 6.

_____. "High Barbaree," Variety, March 12, 1947, p. 12.

_____. "Island in the Sky," Variety, August 12, 1953, p. 6.

_____. "Jet Job," Variety, March 26, 1952, p. 16.

_____. "Jump Into Hell," Variety, March 30, 1955, p. 8.

_____. "Jungle Flight," Variety, February 26, 1947, p. 11.

_____. "Jungle Patrol," Variety, September 22, 1948, p. 8.

_____. "The McConnell Story," Variety, August 17, 1955, p. 6.

_____. "Men of the Fighting Lady," Variety, May 12, 1954, p. 6.

_____. "On the Threshold of Space," Variety, March 7, 1956, p. 6.

_____. "Sabre Jet," Variety, September 9, 1953, p. 6.

_____. "Seven Were Saved," Variety, February 19, 1947, p. 9.

_____. "Sky Liner," Variety, August 3, 1949, p. 16.

_____. "Starlift," Variety, November 7, 1951, p. 6.

_____. "Tarzan and the Lost Safari," Variety, March 27, 1957, p. 6.

_____. "The Thousand Plane Raid," Variety, July 23, 1969, p. 6.

_____. "Thunder in the East," Variety, October 29, 1952, p. 6.

_____. "Top of the World," Variety, May 4, 1955, p. 6.

_____. "Toward the Unknown," Variety, September 26, 1956, p. 6.

_____. "12 O'Clock High," Variety, December 21, 1949, p. 8.

_____. "The Wild Blue Yonder," Variety, December 15, 1951, p. 6.

_____. "The Wings of Eagles," Variety, January 30, 1957, p. 6.

"Broken Wing, The," Variety, October 11, 1923, p. 27.

Byro. "Sullivan's Empire," Variety, June 7, 1967, p. 6.

_____. "Terror in the Jungle," Variety, November 20, 1968, p. 36.

Canby, Vincent. "Paramount Plans Costly War Film," The New York Times, November 23, 1966, p. 34.

_____. "Tora-ble, Tora-ble, Tora-ble," The New York Times, October 4, 1970, Section 2, pp. 1, 7.

Cane. "Broken Journey," Variety, April 21, 1948, p. 13.

"Capra's 'Battle of Britain' Newsreels Vividly Tell of Nazis' British Blitz in '40," Variety, September 15, 1943, p. 10.

"Carrier Show Given for Civilian Guests," The New York Times, September 21, 1949, p. 5.

"Catholic Office Hangs 'B' on 'Max,'" Variety, June 22, 1966, p. 7.

"Ceiling Zero: What Happens When Love Gets Mixed Up with the Airmail," Newsweek, January 18, 1936, p. 41.

"Chain Lightning," Newsweek, March 6, 1950, pp. 84, 85.

"Chain Lightning," Variety, January 24, 1950, p. 21.

Char. "Bomber's Moon," Variety, July 14, 1943, p. 18.

_____. "Clipped Wings," Variety, May 4, 1938, p. 15.

_____. "Cock of the Air," Variety, January 26, 1932, p. 23.

_____. "Hell in the Heavens," Variety, December 18, 1934, p. 13.

_____. "Hell's Angels," Variety, January 17, 1940, pp. 14, 24.

_____. "Legion of Lost Fliers," Variety, November 1, 1939, p. 14.

_____. "Men With Wings," Variety, October 26, 1938, p. 13.

_____. "Pilot No. 5," Variety, April 7, 1943, p. 8.

_____. "Secret Service of the Air," Variety, March 8, 1939, p. 18.

_____. "Storm Over the Andes," Variety, October 2, 1935, p. 16.

_____. "Wing and a Prayer," Variety, July 19, 1944, p. 18.

Chic. "Eagle and the Hawk," Variety, May 16, 1933, p. 21.

_____. "It's in the Air," Variety, November 13, 1935, p. 16.

_____. "Skyway," Variety, October 24, 1933, p. 22.

"China Clipper," Time, August 24, 1936, p. 32.

Churchill, Douglas W. "The Academy Convenes," The New York Times, February 26, 1939, Section 9, p. 5.

_____. "Bette Davis and Warners Solve a Problem," The New York Times, January 5, 1941, Section 9, p. 5.

_____. "Dogfights Roar over Hollywood," The New York Times, July 20, 1941, Section 9, p. 3.

_____. "Hollywood Dries Up," The New York Times, March 13, 1938, Section 9, p. 5.

_____. "Out Again In Again Corrigan," The New York Times, November 13, 1938, Section 9, p. 5.

_____. "Peace vs. Propaganda," The New York Times, May 29, 1938, Section 9, p. 3.

_____. "Rely on Hollywood," The New York Times, August 28, 1938, Section 9, p. 3.

"Cinema," Time, November 7, 1938, p. 41.

"Cinema," Time, January 2, 1939, p. 17.

"Cinema," Time, June 26, 1939, pp. 45, 46.

"Cinema," Time, November 20, 1939, p. 80.

"Cinema," Time, September 15, 1941, pp. 78, 79.

"Cinema," Time, October 13, 1941, p. 94.

"Cinema," Time, March 2, 1942, pp. 74, 75.

"Cinema," Time, May 4, 1942, p. 86.

"Cinema," Time, July 13, 1942, pp. 86, 87.

"Cinema," Time, September 14, 1942, pp. 94, 95.

"Cinema," Time, September 28, 1942, p. 82.

"Cinema," Time, November 16, 1942, pp. 99, 100.

"Cinema," Time, February 8, 1943, pp. 85, 86.

"Cinema," Time, June 21, 1943, pp. 54, 55.

"Cinema," Time, June 28, 1943, pp. 54, 56.

"Cinema," Time, March 6, 1944, pp. 94, 96.

"Cinema," Time, April 17, 1944, pp. 94, 96.

"Cinema," Time, January 22, 1945, p. 91.

"Cinema," Time, April 2, 1945, pp. 90, 92.

"Cinema," Time, August 6, 1945, p. 98.

"Cinema," Time, January 24, 1949, p. 87.

"Cinema," Time, January 30, 1950, pp. 84, 86.

"Cinema," Time, March 6, 1950, p. 92.

"Cinema," Time, May 8, 1950, pp. 90, 92.

"Cinema," Time, November 10, 1952, pp. 120, 123, 124.

"Cinema," Time, January 5, 1953, p. 70.

"Cinema," Time, January 19, 1953, p. 98.

"Cinema," Time, May 25, 1953, pp. 101, 103, 104.

"Cinema," Time, January 11, 1954, p. 80.

"Cinema," Time, May 31, 1954, p. 72.

"Cinema," Time, March 14, 1955, p. 106.

"Cinema," Time, May 2, 1955, p. 98.

"Cinema," Time, August 22, 1955, pp. 82, 84.

"Cinema," Time, October 17, 1955, pp. 114-116.

"Cinema," Time, December 26, 1955, pp. 59-61.

"Cinema," Time, January 2, 1956, p. 56.

"Cinema," Time, October 8, 1956, p. 104.

"Cinema," Time, March 4, 1957, p. 98.

"Cinema," Time, March 11, 1957, p. 98.

"Cinema," Time, May 13, 1957, p. 106.

"Cinema," Time, December 9, 1957, pp. 108, 112.

"Cinema," Time, May 17, 1963, p. 117.

"Cinema," Time, July 26, 1963, p. 80.

"Cinema," Time, June 18, 1965, p. 100.

"Cinema," Time, February 4, 1966, p. 103.

"Cinema," Time, July 8, 1966, p. 84.

Cleaver, Thomas. "Interview: Portraying a Hero," Plane & Pilot, November 1983, pp. 30, 33.

_____. "Making Movies: The Right Stuff," Plane & Pilot, November 1983, pp. 28, 29, 31, 51.

Clem. "Malta Story," Variety, July 8, 1953, p. 16.

_____. "Reach for the Sky," Variety, July 18, 1956, p. 6.

_____. "The Red Beret," Variety, August 19, 1953, p. 6.

"Coastal Command," Variety, April 19, 1944, p. 12.

Cocks, Jay. "Nose Dive," Time, June 26, 1972, p. 68.

"'Command Decision' Assailed in London," The New York Times, August 22, 1949, p. 14.

Cowley, Malcolm. "Emperor Hughes," The New Republic, October 1, 1930, p. 180.

Crichten, Kyle. "The Flying Hawks," Colliers, January 16, 1943, pp. 36, 37, 53.

Crist, Judith. "The Week's Movies," TV Guide, March 31, 1984, p. A-5.

Crowther, Bosley. "Accentuating the Implausible," The New York Times, February 13, 1966, Section 2, p. 1.

_____. "Army Movie of Landings at Arawe and Cape Gloucester Showing Here," The New York Times, June 21, 1944, pp. 1, 22.

_____. "Castles in Pictures," The New York Times, April 12, 1939, Section 10, p. 5.

_____. "Command Decision," The New York Times, November 2, 1947, Section 2, p. 1.

_____. "Contrasting 'Attack! The Battle of New Britain' and the Invasion Newsreels," The New York Times, June 25, 1944, Section 2, p. 3.

_____. "Disability Pictures," The New York Times, May 5, 1957, Section 2, p. 1.

_____. "Happy Medium," The New York Times, November 26, 1944, Section 2, p. 1.

_____. "The Hero Breed," The New York Times, February 24, 1957, Section 2, p. 1.

_____. "Imagination and Skill," The New York Times, November 16, 1952, Section 2, p. 1.

_____. "Is It Man or Is It Myth?" The New York Times, Aug. 19, 1945, Sec. 2, p. 1.

_____. "Is This Cinema of the Absurd?" The New York Times, June 27, 1965, Section 2, p. 1.

_____. "It's An Old Story," The New York Times, January 23, 1955, Section 2, p. 1.

_____. "Men at War," The New York Times, January 23, 1949, Section 2, p. 1.

_____. "New Giant, Screen," The New York Times, April 24, 1955, Section 2, p. 1.

_____. "The New Tax on Credulity," The New York Times, Feb. 7, 1943, Sect. 2, p. 3.

_____. "'The Purple Heart,'" The New York Times, March 19, 1944, Section 2, p. 3.

_____. "The Real Thing," The New York Times, April 16, 1944, Section 2, p. 3.

_____. "Realistic Romance," The New York Times, April 30, 1950, Section 2, p. 1.

_____. "Screen: Airborne Drama," The New York Times, December 20, 1955, p. 39.

_____. "Screen: 'Goliath and the Barbarians,'" The New York Times, January 7, 1960, p. 24.

_____. "Screen, The," The New York Times, June 4, 1942, p. 22.

_____. "Screen, The," The New York Times, October 29, 1942, p. 19.

_____. "Some Reflections," The New York Times, November 18, 1945, Section 2, p. 1.

_____. "Strictly Big Business," The New York Times, May 16, 1954, Section 2, p. 1.

_____. "Thinking Out Loud," The New York Times, October 8, 1944, Section 2, p. 1.

_____. "The War in Retrospect," The New York Times, January 29, 1950, Section 2, p. 1.

_____. "What to Do About War," The New York Times, October 5, 1941, Section 9, p. 5.

"Current Feature Films," The Christian Century, March 22, 1950, p. 383.

"Current Feature Films," The Christian Century, May 16, 1951, p. 623.

"Current Feature Films," The Christian Century, September 26, 1951, p. 111.

"Current Feature Films," The Christian Century, June 18, 1952, p. 725.

Dain. "Dr. Strangelove: Or How I Learned to Stop Worrying and Love the Bomb," Variety, January 22, 1964, p. 6.

"Dangerous Moonlight," Variety, July 30, 1941, p. 20.

"Dark Angels of the World War," The New York Times, February 5, 1928, Section 8, p. 7.

"Daring Deeds," Variety, January 25, 1928, p. 13.

Davidson, Bill. "Man the Battle Stations: Only Murders, Trials and Love Triangles Will Keep This Navy Afloat," TV Guide, Feb. 25, 1984, pp. 18-21.

"Desert Song," Newsweek, July 12, 1965, p. 90.

"Desperate Journey," Variety, August 19, 1942, p. 8.

Dietrich, Noah. "My 32 Years with Howard Hughes," True, April 1972, pp. 28A-28H, 92A-92H.

"Difficulties in Making 'Wings,'" The New York Times, July 8, 1928, Section 8, p. 4.

"Dive Bomber," Time, September 8, 1941, p. 67.

"Documentaries," Time, June 23, 1941, pp. 88, 89.

"Dog of the Regiment," Variety, November 2, 1927, p. 24.

Doll, S/Sgt. Bill. "On Filming 'Winged Victory,'" The New York Times, December 17, 1944, Section 2, p. 5.

Doren, Mark Van. "Films," The Nation, May 7, 1938, pp. 540, 541.

Dorr, John H. "Von Richthofen and Brown," Take One, July-August 1970, p. 8.

"Down Movieland's Runway," Air Classics, August 1969, pp. 44-49.

"Eagles and The Hawks," The New York Times, Jan. 24, 1943, Sect. 2, p. 4.

Earl. "The Sky Spider," Variety, October 6, 1931, p. 29.

"Eddie off the Raft," Newsweek, August 13, 1945, pp. 86, 88.

Eddy. "Atlantic Convoy," Variety, July 8, 1942, p. 8.

Edga. "Flying Hostess," Variety, December 16, 1936, p. 14.

_____. "Sky Parade," Variety, April 22, 1936, pp. 14, 29.

"8 War Pix Among Top '50 Grossers," Variety, January 3, 1951, p. 59.

Elson, Kathy. "John Simone: R/C's Movie Magician," Flying Models, October 1983, pp. 24-27.

"End Old Crate Flying After Death, 2nd Crash on 'Von Richthofen' Pic," Variety, September 23, 1970, p. 2.

"Entertainment," Newsweek, April 25, 1938, p. 27.

"Entertainment," Newsweek, December 12, 1938, p. 25.

"Entertainment," Newsweek, February 23, 1942, p. 54.

"European GIs Favor War Pix," Variety, January 3, 1951, p. 58.

"Events in a Movie Zoo," The New York Times, May 21, 1939, Section 10, p. 4.

"F.A.A. Asks TV Outlets to Bar Bomb-Hoax Film," The New York Times, August 11, 1971, p. 75.

"Fact and Application," The New Republic, February 12, 1945, p. 227.

"Fair Warning," Newsweek, March 5, 1956, p. 91.

"Famous Fliers," The New York Times, August 7, 1927, Section 7, p. 5.

"Fantastic Promotion for Two Films," Literary Digest, November 28, 1936, p. 22.

Farber, Manny. "A British Movie Biography," The New Republic, August 24, 1942, p. 228.

_____. "The Heroes of The Mary Ann," The New Republic, Feb. 22, 1943, pp. 254, 255.

Farmer, James H. "Aces of the Silver Screen," Airpower, May 1973, pp. 52-63.

_____. "Aircraft of 'The Right Stuff,'" Air Classics, January 1984, pp. 34-41, 66-70, 72, 73.

_____ . "The Catch-22 Air Force," Air Classics, December 1972, pp. 18-25, 58, 59.

_____ . "Filming 'The Right Stuff,'" Air Classics, December 1983, pp. 46-51, 72, 75, 78-81.

_____ . "Movie Forts," Airpower, November 1972, pp. 50-57.

"Fate Is the Hunter," Air Classics, March-April 1965, pp. 22, 23.

"Fate Is the Hunter," Scale Modeler, May 1972, p. 11.

"Father Takes The Air," Variety, June 20, 1951, p. 22.

Ferguson, Otis. "Air, Land and Sea," The New Republic, November 3, 1941, p. 587.

_____ . "Lenin and the Dead Pilots," The New Republic, May 11, 1938, p. 19.

_____ . "Movies: When They Are Good," The New Republic, January 5, 1936, p. 369.

_____ . "Two-on-the-Same-Screen Department," The New Republic, March 3, 1941, p. 307.

"Few, The," Air Classics, April 1970, pp. 18-59.

"Fighter Squadron," Time, December 6, 1948, pp. 107, 108.

"Fighting Lady, The," Films in Review, March 1945, pp. 174, 179.

"Fighting Planes," Newsweek, December 6, 1948, pp. 94, 96.

"Film Writer Sues Hughes and R.K.O.," The New York Times, January 28, 1958, p. 31.

"Filming 'Fighting Lady,'" The New York Times, January 14, 1945, Section 2, p. 3.

"Films of 'Fighting Lady' Are Destined for Tokyo," The New York Times, February 10, 1945, p. 15.

Finch, Bob. "Movie World, USA," Air Classics, January 1972, pp. 39-43.

"'Flat Top' Ruling Costs 20th 20G; Sets Oral Pact," Variety, April 17, 1946, p. 3.

"Flight at Midnight," Variety, August 30, 1939, p. 14.

"Flight Commander, The," Variety, October 12, 1927, p. 16.

"Flight Commander," Variety, May 9, 1928, p. 17.

"Flight for Freedom," Time, April 5, 1943, p. 56.

"Flight Nurse," National Parent Teacher, January 1954, p. 39.

"Flight of the Eagle, The," Variety, April 6, 1983, p. 18.

"Flight of the Phoenix," Air Classics, July 1966, pp. 34, 35.

"Flight over Wilhelmshaven," The New York Times, April 15, 1944, p. 10.

Flin. "Flight from Glory," Variety, August 11, 1937, p. 19.

Flint, Ralph, "Here and There in Hollywood," The New York Times, June 8, 1930, Section 9, p. 6.

"Flying Deuces, The," Variety, October 11, 1939, p. 13.

"Flying Fool, The," Variety, August 28, 1929, p. 31.

"Flying Irishman, The," Time, March 27, 1939, p. 67, 68.

"Flying Leathernecks," Time, October 8, 1951, pp. 114, 116.

"'Flying Machines' for Hard Ducats," Variety, March 3, 1965, p. 4.

"Flying Pat," Variety, December 17, 1920, p. 40.

"For Those in Peril," Variety, May 10, 1944, p. 10.

"Forty-ninth Man, The," National Parent Teacher, May 1953, p. 38.

Fran. "Lady from Chun King," Variety, January 20, 1943, p. 20.

Fred. "The Air Mail," Variety, March 25, 1925, pp. 37, 38.

_____. "Sinners in Heaven," Variety, September 10, 1924, p. 27.

Freeman, Marilla Waite. "New Films from Books," Library Journal, July 1954, p. 1304.

"From Zeppelin to Blimp," 1001 New Model Airplane Ideas, 9172, pp. 10-21.

FS. "Scare Movie," Aviation Week, July 26, 1954, pp. 67, 68.

G., W. "The Current Cinema," The New Yorker, January 13, 1945, p. 55.

_____. "The Current Cinema," The New Yorker, March 24, 1945, p. 82.

_____. "The Current Cinema," The New Yorker, August 18, 1945, p. 49.

"Gable Film Restricted," The New York Times, November 19, 1944, p. 48.

"Gallant Journey," Time, October 7, 1946, p. 104.

"Gary Cooper's Mitchell," Newsweek, January 9, 1956, p. 7.

Gelmis, Joseph. "'The Great Waldo Pepper' Flyboys: Stunt-man Tallman, Boss George Hill," The Burlington Free Press, May 2, 1975, p. 25.

Gene. "Jet Pilot," Variety, September 25, 1957, p. 6.

_____. "The Spirit of St. Louis," Variety, February 20, 1957, p. 6.

_____. "Strategic Air Command," Variety, March 30, 1955, p. 8.

Gilb. "Daredevils of the Clouds," Variety, July 21, 1948, p. 10.

_____. "Daughter of the Jungle," Variety, March 16, 1949, p. 11.

_____. "Flight Nurse," Variety, November 4, 1953, p. 6.

_____. "Sky Commando," Variety, August 26, 1953, p. 6.

"Glamor, Gunplay, and Gable," Newsweek, October 6, 1941, pp. 60, 61.

"Glorifying Aviation," Literary Digest, August 22, 1936, p. 24.

"Great Mail Robbery, The," Variety, July 20, 1927, p. 18.

Greenspun, Roger. "Oh! What a Lovely Spy," The New York Times, August 9, 1970, Section 2, p. 1.

_____. "O'Toole Heads Cast in 'Murphy's War,'" The New York Times, July 2, 1971, p. 26.

_____. "'Von Richthofen and Brown' Opens," The New York Times, July 29, 1971, p. 49.

Hago, "L'Escadrille de la Chance," Variety, July 20, 1938, p. 13.

Hall, Mordaunt. "An Air Mail Drama," The New York Times, October 15, 1933, Section 9, p. 3.

_____. "An Amusing Imposter," The New York Times, March 13, 1932, Section 8, p. 4.

_____. "At The South Pole," The New York Times, June 29, 1930, Section 8, p. 3.

_____. "Byrd's Flight Told in Graphic Film," The New York Times, June 20, 1930, p. 6.

_____. "Degrees of Violence in Comedies," The New York Times, October 16, 1927, Section 9, p. 7.

_____. "Exciting Air Battles," The New York Times, August 24, 1930, Section 8, p. 5.

_____. "Laughter and Tears," The New York Times, March 22, 1931, Section 8, p. 5.

_____. "Luminous Reflections in a Mirror," The New York Times, May 21, 1933, Section 9, p. 3.

_____. "Messrs. Beery and Hatton," The New York Times, December 12, 1927, p. 31.

_____. "Mr. Jannings as a Jealous Burlgar," The New York Times, March 20, 1932, Section 8, p. 4.

_____. "Old George Ade Play Amusing," The New York Times, November 13, 1927, Section 9, p. 7.

_____. "Pictures of Past Week," The New York Times, March 30, 1930, Section 8, p. 5.

_____. "Pictures of Past Week," The New York Times, October 12, 1930, Section 8, p. 5.

_____. "The Screen," The New York Times, September 19, 1929, p. 17.

_____. "'Skippy' on the Screen," The New York Times, April 12, 1931, Section 9, p. 5.

_____. "Winged Warriors," The New York Times, August 21, 1927, Section 7, p. 3.

_____. "Youth in the Clouds," The New York Times, September 9, 1928, Section 9, p. 5.

Hartung, Philip T. "Ariz. and Pa. Do Their Best," The Commonweal, November 13, 1942, p. 97.

_____. "Bomber's Moon," The Commonweal, September 10, 1943, pp. 514, 515.

_____. "Eagles Soar; Lions Roar," The Commonweal, July 17, 1942, pp. 304, 305.

_____. "Flight Command, The Commonweal, January 24, 1941, p. 152.

_____. "Flying Leathernecks," The Commonweal, November 2, 1951, p. 94.

_____. "Following the Films," Senior Scholastic, April 12, 1961, p. 39.

_____. "Hollywood's Reply to Dec. 7," The Commonweal, December 22, 1944, pp. 254, 255.

_____. "Lest We Forget," The Commonweal, September 15, 1944, pp. 518, 519.

_____. "Lotsa People: Lotsa Excitement," The Commonweal, July 16, 1954, p. 365.

_____. "Of Men and Mice," The Commonweal, November 18, 1938, p. 105.

_____. "Pilot No. 5," The Commonweal, June 25, 1943, p. 252.

_____. "Put Out More Flags," The Commonweal, December 17, 1948, p. 259.

_____. "The Screen," The Commonweal, August 6, 1943, pp. 393, 394.

_____. "The Screen," The Commonweal, April 14, 1944, pp. 651-653.

_____. "The Screen," The Commonweal, January 28, 1949, p. 400.

_____. "The Screen," The Commonweal, February 3, 1950, p. 464.

_____. "The Screen," The Commonweal, November 30, 1951, pp. 200, 201.

_____. "The Screen," The Commonweal, November 14, 1952, p. 141.

_____. "The Screen," The Commonweal, February 20, 1953, p. 499.

_____. "Sequels," The Commonweal, June 30, 1939, p. 259.

_____. "The Stage & Screen," The Commonweal, December 30, 1938, p. 273.

_____. "The Stage & Screen," The Commonweal, December 22, 1939, p. 206.

_____. "War and War," The Commonweal, February 9, 1945, pp. 426-428.

_____. "Wings for the Eagle," The Commonweal, Aug. 21, 1942, p. 424.

Haskell, Molly. "Reach for Your Airsick Bag," Village Voice, July 27, 1972, p. 56.

Hatch, Robert. "Movies: Broadway in Hollywood," The New Republic, June 7, 1948, p. 29.

_____. "Movies: Men Are Such Babies," The New Republic, May 15, 1950, pp. 23, 24.

_____. "Movies: The War Goes On," The New Republic, January 30, 1950, p. 30.

_____. "No Highway in the Sky," The New Republic, October 22, 1951, p. 22.

Haze. "Battle Taxi," Variety, January 12, 1955, p. 6.

"Heinkel How-To," 1001 New Model Airplane Ideas, Winter 1970, pp. 80-87.

Heln. "Luciano Serra, Pilot," Variety, September 21, 1938, p. 25.

Herb. "Parachute Battalion," Variety, July 16, 1941, p. 8.

Herm. "They Are Not Angels," Variety, June 2, 1948, p. 14.

Hift. "Malta Story," Variety, July 14, 1954, p. 6.

"High and the Mighty, The," Time, July 12, 1954, p. 94.

"High Barbaree," Time, June 9, 1947, p. 100.

Hobe. "Air Devils," Variety, May 11, 1938, p. 16.

_____. "Atlantic Flight," Variety, September 22, 1937, p. 18.

_____. "Bombardier," Variety, May 12, 1943, p. 8.

_____. "Flying Wild," Variety, April 16, 1941, p. 16.

_____. "The Great Plane Robbery," Variety, November 20, 1940, p. 18.

_____. "High Flyers," Variety, November 10, 1937, p. 19.

_____. "Junior G-Men of the Air," Variety, May 27, 1942, p. 8.

_____. "It's in the Air," Variety, December 11, 1940, p. 16.

_____. "The Lion Has Wings," Variety, January 24, 1940, p. 14.

_____. "Riding on Air," Variety, June 30, 1937, p. 20.

Holl. "Das Luftschiff," Variety, May 23, 1983, p. 22.

_____. "The Hunters," Variety, August 6, 1958, p. 6.

_____. "Landfall," Variety, May 13, 1953, p. 22.

_____. "Letaloto," Variety, April 1, 1981, p. 18.

_____. "24-Hour Alert," Variety, December 7, 1955, p. 8.

Hotz, Robert. "The Dam Busters," Aviation Week, December 5, 1955, p. 138.

"Hunters, The," Time, August 25, 1958, p. 78.

Hurl. "Death in the Sky," Variety, February 17, 1937, p. 23.

_____. "Love Takes Flight," Variety, August 18, 1937, p. 39.

_____. "Mysterious Pilot," Variety, December 22, 1937, p. 24.

_____. "Sky Giant," Variety, July 20, 1938, p. 12.

"Inland Sun Beckons Pilots 'Fogged In' by Coast Rules," The New York Times, June 14, 1942, Section 9, p. 22.

"It's a Wild, Wild Blue," Newsweek, July 5, 1965, p. 83.

"Irish Army Will Aid 'Blue Max' Shooting," Variety, August 4, 1965, p. 14.

"Johnny Comes Flying Home," Variety, March 20, 1946, p. 8.

Jolo. "Britain's Far-Flung Battle Line," Variety, August 9, 1918, p. 33.

_____. "The Day Will Dawn," Variety, June 3, 1942, p. 9.

_____. "The First of the Few," Variety, September 2, 1942, p. 17.

_____. "Flying Fortress," Variety, July 15, 1942, p. 9.

_____. "The Great Air Robbery," Variety, February 20, 1920, p. 40.

_____. "Last Raid of Zeppelin L-21," Variety, May 10, 1918, p. 43.

_____. "Marriage by Aeroplane," Variety, January 14, 1914, p. 17.

_____. "One of Our Aircraft Is Missing," Variety, April 29, 1942, p. 8.

_____. "Q Planes," Variety, March 15, 1939, p. 18.

_____. "R.A.F.," Variety, July 3, 1935, p. 14.

_____. "A Romance of the Air," Variety, November 15, 1918, p. 46.

_____. "Ships with Wings," Variety, January 7, 1942, p. 45.

_____. "Spies of the Air," Variety, April 26, 1939, pp. 12, 37.

_____. "Squadron Leader X," Variety, January 27, 1943, p. 8.

_____. "They Flew Alone," Variety, May 13, 1942, p. 8.

_____. "The Zeppelin's Last Raid," Variety, November 9, 1917, p. 55.

Jones, Idway. "A Flier in Technicolor," The New York Times, October 23, 1938, Section 9, p. 4.

Jose. "Miraculous Journey," Variety, August 11, 1948, p. 8.

_____. "Thunderbolt," Variety, October 31, 1945, p. 17.

Kahn. "Adventures of the Flying Cadets," Variety, Sept. 23, 1943, p. 16.

_____. "Task Force," Variety, July 20, 1949, p. 6.

_____. "Winged Victory," Variety, November 22, 1944, p. 10.

Kali. "Im Pokerisetsa Nebo," Variety, July 31, 1963, p. 12.

Kauf. "Flying Devils," Variety, August 29, 1933, p. 14.

_____. "Happy Landing," Variety, August 28, 1934, p. 15.

_____. "Lo Stormo Atlantico," Variety, July 28, 1931, p. 24.

_____. "Wings in the Dark," Variety, February 5, 1935, p. 14.

Kell. "Ingenioer Andrees Luftfaerd," Variety, September 1, 1982, p. 22.

_____. "Mosquito Squadron," Variety, July 8, 1970, p. 14.

"Kids Not Interested in Aviation's Past?" Variety, June 2, 1965, p. 2.

Knickerbocker, Paine. "Jet Propelled 'Eagles,'" The New York Times, August 26, 1962, Section 2, p. 7.

Knight, Arthur. "SR Goes to the Movies," Saturday Review, November 22, 1952, pp. 38, 39.

_____. "SR Goes to the Movies," Saturday Review, January 24, 1953, pp. 27, 28.

_____. "SR Goes to the Movies," Saturday Review, March 12, 1955, p. 27.

_____. "SR Goes to the Movies," Saturday Review, January 14, 1956, p. 21.

_____. "SR Goes to the Movies," Saturday Review, February 9, 1957, p. 29.

_____. "SR Goes to the Movies," Saturday Review, January 25, 1958, p. 27.

_____. "SR Goes to the Movies," Saturday Review, July 6, 1983, p. 16.

_____. "SR Goes to the Movies," Saturday Review, June 26, 1965, p. 22.

Kolchek, Carl. "The Hindenberg," Air Classics, March 1975, pp. 48-57, 78, 79.

"Korean War Drama," The New York Times, August 27, 1958, p. 33.

Kove. "Destination 60,000," Variety, July 10, 1957, p. 6.

Land. "The Air Legion," Variety, November 14, 1928, p. 26.

_____. "Clouds Over Europe," Variety, June 21, 1939, p. 16.

_____. "Conquest," Variety, February 13, 1929, p. 24.

_____. "The Court-Martial of Billy Mitchell," Variety, December 14, 1955, p. 6.

_____. "Crimson Romance," Variety, October 16, 1934, p. 15.

_____. "The Flying Fleet," Variety, February 13, 1929, pp. 13, 24.

_____. "Green Goddess," Variety, February 19, 1930, p. 21.

_____. "Lost Zeppelin," Variety, February 5, 1930, p. 19.

_____. "Wings Over Ethiopia," Variety, October 16, 1935, p. 22.

_____. "Young Eagles," Variety, March 26, 1930, p. 39.

Lardner, David. "The Current Cinema," The New Yorker, February 6, 1943, pp. 52, 53.

_____. "The Current Cinema," The New Yorker, July 3, 1943, p. 38.

Lardner, John. "The Current Cinema," The New Yorker, December 2, 1944, p. 85.

"Last Flight," Variety, June 19, 1929, p. 30.

Lejeune, C. A. "Libyan Battle on Film," The New York Times, February 7, 1943, Section 2, p. 3.

_____. "London Comes up for Air," The New York Times, November 19, 1939, Section 9, p. 4.

_____. "New Faces in London," The New York Times, November 9, 1941, Section 9, p. 4.

_____. "Polish Influence in London," The New York Times, January 26, 1941, Section 9, p. 4.

"Leo Nomis, Famous Film Stunt Flier, Killed When Spin in War Picture Turns into Crash," The New York Times, February 6, 1932, p. 2.

Lichter. "Black 13," Air Classics, December 1965, pp. 16-21, 65.

"Lilac Time," Variety, August 8, 1928, p. 12.

Lockhart, Jane. "Looking at Movies," The Rotarian, February 1949, p. 35.

_____. "Looking at Movies," The Rotarian, May 1949, p. 34.

_____. "Looking at Movies," The Rotarian, May 1950, p. 40.

_____. "Looking at Movies," The Rotarian, August 1950, p. 43.

Loit. "Going Up," Variety, October 11, 1923, p. 27.

"London Critics Differ on the Merits of the Byrd Expedition's Film Record," The New York Times, July 27, 1930, Section 3, p. 6.

"Lost Squadron," Variety, March 15, 1932, pp. 12, 13.

Loyn. "Swing Shift," Variety, April 18, 1984, p. 10.

McCarten, John. "The Current Cinema," The New Yorker, May 29, 1948, p. 66.

_____. "The Current Cinema," The New Yorker, January 29, 1949, p. 53.

_____. "The Current Cinema," The New Yorker, February 4, 1950, p. 78.

_____. "The Current Cinema," The New Yorker, April 29, 1950, pp. 96, 97.

_____. "The Current Cinema," The New Yorker, November 22, 1952, p. 107.

_____. "The Current Cinema," The New Yorker, May 15, 1954, p. 74.

_____. "The Current Cinema," The New Yorker, July 10, 1954, p. 59.

_____. "The Current Cinema," The New Yorker, July 24, 1954, pp. 40, 41.

_____. "The Current Cinema," The New Yorker, January 29, 1955, p. 79.

_____. "The Current Cinema," The New Yorker, April 30, 1955, pp. 116, 117.

_____. "The Current Cinema," The New Yorker, December 31, 1955, p. 36.

_____. "The Current Cinema," The New Yorker, February 9, 1957, p. 108.

_____. "The Current Cinema," The New Yorker, February 23, 1957, pp. 75, 76.

_____. "The Current Cinema," The New Yorker, March 1957, p. 88.

MacDonough, Scott. "Michael York: A Quiet Actor Dedicated to Doing 'Good Thing,'" Show, June 1972, pp. 24-27.

McGilligan, Pat. "Hollywood Toys with Disaster," The Boston Globe, September 8, 1974, Section A1, p. 8.

MacKenzie, Robert. "Review," TV Guide, March 31, 1984, p. 40.

McLove. "Fliers," Variety, May 29, 1935, p. 34.

Magnus. "Fliegende Schatten," Variety, May 10, 1932, p. 62.

"Making Aviation Films," The New York Times, July 20, 1930, Section 8, p. 4.

"March of Time's 'FBI Front,' 'Midway' Point up Stronger Crop of Shorts," Variety, September 16, 1942, p. 20.

Mark. "An Aerial Revenge," Variety, May 14, 1915, p. 24.

_____. "The Sky Ranger," Variety, November 14, 1928, pp. 26, 30.

_____. "Warfare in the Skies," Variety, August 7, 1914, p. 18.

_____. "Young Whirlwind," Variety, October 17, 1928, pp. 16, 24.

Marshall, Ernest. "London Film Notes," The New York Times, February 23, 1930, Section 8, p. 6.

Martin, Harold H. "The Pious Killer of Korea," The Saturday Evening Post, July 21, 1951, pp. 26, 27, 87-90.

Maxi. "L'Aviateur," Variety, February 18, 1931, p. 35.

_____. "Ombres Fuyantes," Variety, July 12, 1932.

Medjuck, Joe. "An Interview with Roger Corman," Take One, July-August 1970, pp. 6-9.

Meisler, Andy. "Coptermania!" TV Guide, November 26, 1983, pp. 57-62.

"Metro's 'Skyjacked' Producer Riled by Teleblurb Blackout," Variety, May 31, 1972, pp. 2, 61.

Mezo. "SOS Gleiseherpilot," Variety, March 25, 1959, p. 23.

"Midway Refought," Newsweek, September 11, 1944, p. 111.

Miha. "Pacific Banana," Variety, June 3, 1981, p. 23.

_____. "The Survivor," Variety, September 23, 1981, p. 22.

"Mild Blaze," Newsweek, March 17, 1947, p. 103.

Milne, W. S. "Pageant, Propaganda and Parturition," Canadian Film, January 1940, p. 327.

"Model-Plane Boom Simulates Hazardous Flights for Movies," Popular Science Monthly, December 1942, pp. 52, 53.

"Model World," American Modeler, October 1967, p. 8.

Moore, Kevin. "The Tallmantz Story and The Carpetbaggers," Air Classics, Summer 1964, pp. 14-17.

"More Hollywood Notes," The New York Times, August 26, 1945, Section 2, pp. 1, 3.

Mori. "Canal Zone," Variety, April 1, 1942, p. 8.

_____. "Code of the Air," Variety, December 19, 1928, p. 23.

_____. "Flying Luck," Variety, March 21, 1928, p. 26.

_____. "Flying Romeos," Variety, April 4, 1928, p. 28.

_____. "Flying Tigers," Variety, September 23, 1942, p. 8.

_____. "Fury in the Pacific," Variety, March 21, 1945, p. 10.

_____. "A Hero for a Night," Variety, December 28, 1927, p. 16.

_____. "Night Plane from Chunking," Variety, December 30, 1942, p. 16.

_____. "The Purple Heart," Variety, February 13, 1944, p. 10.

_____. "The Purple V," Variety, March 24, 1943, p. 20.

_____. "Wings of Victory," Variety, November 19, 1941, p. 20.

"Moscow Screen Looks to Language," The New York Times, July 8, 1934, Section 9, p. 2.

Mosher, John. "The Current Cinema," The New Yorker, May 30, 1942, p. 49.

Mosk. "Aerograd," Variety, August 7, 1968, p. 6.

_____. "High Flight," Variety, March 19, 1958, p. 6.

_____. "The Sea Shall Not Have Them," Variety, December 15, 1954, p. 28.

_____. "Wings of Danger," Variety, March 26, 1952, p. 16.

"Movie Is Rushed to Free British Actors for War," The New York Times, September 11, 1938, p. 35.

"Movie Shown in Plane," The New York Times, January 4, 1935, p. 26.

"Movies," Newsweek, March 31, 1941, pp. 66, 67.

"Movies," Newsweek, September 1, 1941, pp. 48, 49.

"Movies," Newsweek, July 6, 1942, p. 59.

"Movies," Newsweek, August 31, 1942, p. 60.

"Movies," Newsweek, September 21, 1942, p. 80.

"Movies," Newsweek, November 11, 1942, pp. 76, 77.

"Movies," Newsweek, February 8, 1943, pp. 83, 84.

"Movies," Newsweek, April 19, 1943, p. 74.

"Movies," Newsweek, November 13, 1943, p. 104.

"Movies," Newsweek, November 20, 1944, p. 98.

"Movies," Newsweek, January 22, 1945, pp. 86, 87.

"Movies," Newsweek, April 2, 1945, p. 78.

"Movies," Newsweek, October 21, 1946, pp. 102, 104.

"Movies," Newsweek, May 1, 1950, p. 75.

"Movies," Newsweek, March 26, 1951, p. 94.

"Movies," Newsweek, July 14, 1952, p. 90.

"Movies," Newsweek, February 2, 1953, p. 77.

"Movies," Newsweek, November 16, 1953, p. 104.

"Movies," Newsweek, January 18, 1954, p. 90.

"Movies," Newsweek, June 7, 1954, p. 56.

"Movies," Newsweek, March 14, 1955, p. 103.

"Movies," Newsweek, October 10, 1955, pp. 116, 117.

"Movies," Newsweek, April 16, 1956, p. 116.

"Movies," Newsweek, February 11, 1957, p. 89.

"Movies," Newsweek, February 25, 1957, pp. 118, 119.

"Movies," Newsweek, December 4, 1961, p. 88.

"Movies: Wide Blue Yonder," The New Republic, February 7, 1949, p. 30.

Murf. "Ace Eli and Roger of the Skies," Variety, April 25, 1973, p. 18.

_____. "Airport 1975," Variety, October 16, 1974, p. 14.

_____. "The Blue Max," Variety, June 22, 1966, pp. 6, 20.

_____. "Boeing, Boeing," Variety, December 1, 1965, p. 6.

_____. "Catch 22," Variety, June 10, 1970, pp. 18, 26.

_____. "The Great Waldo Pepper," Variety, March 5, 1975, pp. 20, 21.

_____. "Lost Command," Variety, May 25, 1966, p. 6.

_____. "Mission Batangas," Variety, November 13, 1968, p. 6.

_____. "Skyjacked," Variety, May 10, 1972, p. 20.

_____. "This Is a Hijack," Variety, June 13, 1973, p. 22.

_____. "Von Richthofen and Brown," Variety, May 26, 1971, p. 20.

"Murphy's War," Air Classics, December 1971, pp. 22-25.

Myro. "Angels One Five," Variety, April 2, 1952, p. 22.

_____. "Appointment in London," Variety, February 25, 1953, p. 18.

_____. "The Dam Busters," Variety, June 1, 1955, p. 6.

_____. "The Men in the Sky," Variety, January 25, 1957, p. 6.

_____. "The Night My Number Came Up," Variety, March 30, 1955, p. 9.

_____. "Out of the Clouds," Variety, February 23, 1955, p. 8.

_____. "The Purple Plain," Variety, September 22, 1954, p. 6.

_____. "Sound Barrier," Variety, July 30, 1952, p. 18.

"Mystery Plane," Variety, March 29, 1939, p. 14.

Naka. "Remember Pearl Harbor," Variety, May 13, 1942, p. 8.

Nald. "Operation Air Raid: Red Muffler," Variety, April 13, 1966, p. 20.

"Navy-Aided Film Will Be Speeded," The New York Times September 4, 1949, p. 32.

"Navy Movie, Army Planes Cause Air Corps Laughs," The New York Times, February 12, 1939, p. 31.

"Navy's Wings: A Light, Intelligent Comedy Drama of Flying

Adventure in Hawaii," Literary Digest, May 22, 1937, pp. 28, 29.

Neal. "Arctic Flight," Variety, July 30, 1952, p. 6.

_____. "Bailout at 43,000," Variety, May 15, 1957, p. 22.

"New Films," Newsweek, January 23, 1950, p. 79.

"New Films," Newsweek, January 14, 1952, p. 82.

"New films, The," Theatre Arts, April 1949, pp. 86, 87.

"New Pictures, The," Time, October 13, 1935, p. 59.

"New Pictures, The," Time, August 3, 1936, p. 29.

"No Highway in the Sky," Newsweek, October 8, 1951, pp. 100, 102.

"No Highway in the Sky," Time, October 8, 1951, pp. 112, 114.

"No Reich Protest on Film," The New York Times, November 21, 1930, p. 9.

"Notes for the Amateur Photographer," The New York Times, Sept. 27, 1942, Sect. 2, p. 10.

Nugent, Frank S. "By Way of Contrast," The New York Times, April 24, 1938, Section 9, p. 3.

_____. "Film Men of the Air Force," The New York Times Magazine, April 30, 1944, pp. 14, 30.

_____. "Good Old Standbys," The New York Times, May 14, 1939, Section 11, p. 3.

_____. "History, Histrionics and Humor," The New York Times, June 18, 1939, Section 9, p. 3.

_____. "Postscript on the Zanuck Touch," The New York Times, May 30, 1937, Section 9, p. 3.

_____. "Present from the Warners," The New York Times, Jan. 26, 1936, Sec. 9, p. 5.

_____. "The Screen," The New York Times, June 26, 1937, p. 20.

_____. "The Screen," The New York Times, January 22, 1938, p. 19.

_____. "Yes, No Revolution," The New York Times, October 30, 1938, Section 9, p. 5.

Odec. "Death Flies East," Variety, March 6, 1935, p. 21.

_____. "Mercy Plane," Variety, October 30, 1940, p. 15.

_____. "Murder in the Clouds," Variety, January 1, 1935, p. 18.

_____. "Speed Wings," Variety, April 3, 1934, p. 27.

O'Hara, Bob. "Big Screen Banzai," Air Classics, February 1969, pp. 14-20, 62, 66.

_____. "The 'Reel' Planes," Air Classics, July 1976, pp. 12-15, 63.

_____. "Tora Tora Tora," Air Classics, October 1969, pp. 18-35, 66, 67.

"One for the Navy," Newsweek, January 17, 1955, p. 86.

"Only Angels Have Wings," Time, May 22, 1939, p. 57.

"Our Department of Belles Lettres," The New York Times, June 5, 1938, Section 9, p. 4.

"Pacific Adventure," Variety, December 3, 1947, p. 11.

"Pacifist End to War Movie Is Out; Film Capital Sees Army's Hand," The New York Times, May 28, 1938, p. 17.

"Panama Bans Velez Film," The New York Times, July 17, 1932, p. 11.

"Par Gets Hall's Summer Spot for Its 'Darling Lili,'" Variety, January 21, 1970, p. 3.

"Parachuting into France," Newsweek, June 7, 1947, p. 82.

"Past Week's Offerings," The New York Times, August 12, 1928, Section 7, p. 3.

"Picturing a Tropical Storm," The New York Times, April 2, 1933, Section 9, p. 3.

"Picturing Air Scenes," The New York Times, April 19, 1931, Section 8, p. 6.

"Pilot #5," Time, July 12, 1943, p. 96.

"Pirates of the Skies," Variety, April 12, 1939, p. 18.

"Pirates of the Sky," Variety, May 11, 1927, p. 21.

Pit. "Aces High," Variety, May 26, 1976, p. 18.

_____. "Kamikaze," Variety, October 3, 1962, p. 7.

_____. "Smashing of the Reich," Variety, October 3, 1962, p. 6.

"Plane Crash for Camera," The New York Times, April 1, 1928, Section 9, p. 6.

"Plane Crash Movie Ignores the Big Hero," The Burlington Free Press, March 23, 1984, p. 50.

Pockett, Roy. "Curse You, Red Baron!" Air Classics, November 1971, pp. 16-21.

"Poet Puts Rythm [sic] into Film Epic," The New York Times, November 29, 1927, p. 6.

Pow. "Crash Landing," Variety, February 5, 1958, p. 20.

_____. "Lafayette Escadrille," Variety, February 5, 1958, p. 6.

Powe. "Here Come the Jets," Variety, June 3, 1959, p. 6.

_____. "Jet Attack," Variety, March 26, 1958, p. 6.

_____. "Paratroop Command," Variety, January 28, 1959, p. 6.

Prat. "The Lift," Variety, October 20, 1965, p. 26.

"Protests American Film," The New York Times, September 6, 1931, p. 19.

Pryor, Thomas M. "By Way of Report," The New York Times, September 24, 1944, Section 2, p. 3.

_____. "Disney, The Teacher," The New York Times, July 25, 1943, Sec. 2, p. 3.

_____. "Filming Our Bombers Over Germany," The New York Times, March 26, 1944, Section 2, p. 3.

_____. "Hollywood Canvas," The New York Times, July 17, 1955, Section 2, p. 5.

_____. "'Lady' with a Punch," The New York Times, January 21, 1945, Section 2, p. 1.

_____. "Merrill of the Movies," The New York Times, September 26, 1937, Section 11, p. 5.

_____. "Pot Shots at the News," The New York Times, June 2, 1940, Section 9, p. 3.

_____. "Random Notes on the Film Scene," The New York Times, August 6, 1944, Section 2, p. 3.

"Publicity Madness," Variety, October 19, 1927, p. 29.

Ray. "Stukas," Variety, August 25, 1943, p. 10.

"Remake Salvage from WB, 'Patrol' May Roll for UA," Variety, June 21, 1961, p. 5.

"Report from the Aleutians," Variety, July 14, 1943, p. 22.

"Reported Missing," Variety, September 1, 1937, p. 29.

Rhode, Bill. "The History of Hollywood in Aviation," AAHS Journal, October-December 1957, pp. 260-263.

Rich. "High Flight," Variety, September 25, 1957, p. 6.

_____. "Jet Storm," Variety, September 2, 1959, p. 6.

_____. "Murphy's War," Variety, January 27, 1971, p. 17.

_____. "The Night We Dropped a Clanger," Variety, September 23, 1959, p. 18.

_____. "S.O.S. Pacific," Variety, October 28, 1959, p. 6.

_____. "Unseen Heroes," Variety, May 21, 1958, p. 6.

_____. "Zeppelin," Variety, April 14, 1971, p. 16.

"Richthofen," Variety, September 11, 1929, p. 18.

Rick, "Airport," Variety, February 18, 1970, p. 17.

_____. "The Flying Doctor," Variety, October 21, 1936, p. 23.

_____. "The Sky Pirate," Variety, February 11, 1970, p. 16.

"RKO Will Screen the Life of 'General Billy Mitchell,'" The New York Times, January 16, 1942, p. 9.

Robe. "Sands of the Kalahari," Variety, October 27, 1965, p. 26.

_____. "Valley of Mystery," Variety, August 26, 1967, p. 6.

Robinson, Douglas. "From Cheju Island to California," The New York Times, May 5, 1956, Section 2, p. 5.

Rogow, Lee. "SR Goes to the Movies," The Saturday Review, July 3, 1954, p. 33.

_____. "SR Goes to the Movies," The Saturday Review, January 22, 1955, pp. 43, 44.

_____. "SR Goes to the Movies," The Saturday Reivew, May 14, 1955, pp. 26, 27.

Ron. "Thundering Jets," Variety, April 16, 1958, p. 6.

Ronnie, Art. "Box Office Ace," Air Classics, February 1969, pp. 6-11, 21, 53, 63.

_____. "Stand-in Stuntman," Air Classics, November 1966, pp. 32-37, 50, 54, 55, 64.

Rowl. "Wings Over Honolulu," Variety, June 2, 1937, p. 15.

"Runaway Balloon Found," The New York Times, December 27, 1944, p. 32.

Rush. "Air Mail," Variety, November 8, 1932, p. 17.

_____. "Air Mail Pilot," Variety, May 2, 1928, p. 26.

_____. "Flying High," Variety, February 23, 1927, pp. 17, 19.

_____. "Going Wild," Variety, January 28, 1932, pp. 15, 40.

_____. "Now We're in the Air," Variety, December 14, 1927, pp. 18, 19.

_____. "Shield of Honor," Variety, December 14, 1927, p. 23.

_____. "The Sky Spider," Variety, February 20, 1929, p. 17.

_____. "With Byrd at the South Pole," Variety, June 25, 1930, p. 109.

Rye, P. H. "Films," The Nation, March 14, 1942, p. 320.

"SAC-cessful," Newsweek, July 22, 1963, p. 86.

Saditiak. "De Vliegende Hollander," Variety, July 24, 1957, p. 27.

Saunders, John Monk. "The War-in-the-Air," The New York Times, July 31, 1927, Section 8, p. 3.

Schickel, Richard. "Genevieve with Wings," Life, June 25, 1965, p. 15.

_____. "High Flying," Time, March 24, 1975, pp. K3, K5.

_____. "Sad Saga of a Flying Bumpkin," Life, July 8, 1966, p. 8.

Schnepf, Ed. "Tora Tora Tora!" Scale Modeler, August 1971, pp. 36-43.

Scho. "Border Flight," Variety, June 24, 1936, p. 29.

Schwartz, Delmore. "Films," The New Republic, March 14, 1955, pp. 28, 29.

Seaton, George. "Film-Maker Reviews Soviet 'Cooperation' While Shooting 'Big lift' in Berlin," The New York Times, April 16, 1950, Section 2, p. 5.

Sege. "Nothing by Chance," Variety, January 29, 1975, p. 17.

"17 War Films Among the Top 60 Show in 1942-45 to GIs," Variety, December 25, 1946, p. 2.

Shan. "Air Hostess," Variety, January 24, 1933, pp. 21, 48.

_____. "Last Flight," Variety, August 25, 1931, pp. 14, 20.

_____. "Lost in the Stratosphere," Variety, March 6, 1935, p. 21.

_____. "The Sky Raiders," Variety, June 2, 1931, p. 31.

"Shooting from the Wings," The New York Times, March 9, 1941, Section 9, p. 4.

Shuster, Alvin. "Promotion Is Sought for Air Hero, 87," The New York Times, September 16, 1969, p. 55.

Sid. "Body and Soul," Variety, March 18, 1931, pp. 14, 24.

_____. "The Flying Fool," Variety, October 20, 1931, p. 27.

_____. "The Flying Mail," Variety, June 29, 1927, p. 26.

_____. "Hard Boiled Haggerty," Variety, August 24, 1927, pp. 23, 26.

_____. "Hell's Angels," Variety, June 4, 1930, p. 25.

_____. "Legion of the Condemned," Variety, March 21, 1928, p. 19.

_____. "The Lone Eagle," Variety, December 21, 1927, p. 24.

_____. "Pajamas," Variety, November 9, 1927, pp. 24, 25.

_____. "Sky Devils," Variety, March 8, 1932, p. 14.

_____. "Sky Hawk," Variety, December 18, 1929, p. 22.

_____. "Wings," Variety, August 17, 1927, p. 21.

Sime. "The Dawn Patrol," Variety, July 16, 1930, p. 15.

_____. "Dirigible," Variety, April 8, 1931, p. 18.

_____. "Dizzy Heights," Variety, December 31, 1915, p. 24.

_____. "Flight," Variety, September 18, 1929, p. 15.

_____. "Maid of the West," Variety, August 5, 1921, p. 27.

"633 Squadron," Air Classics, Summer 1964, pp. 43-45, 50.

Skig. "The Green Goddess," Variety, August 16, 1923, p. 27.

"Sky Bride," Variety, April 26, 1932, p. 25.

"'Sky Raider' Jumps Rail to $5,000," Variety, April 8, 1925, p. 31.

"Skyhigh Saunders," Variety, December 14, 1923, p. 26.

"Some Difficulties of a Producer," The New York Times, July 10, 1927, Section 8, p. 3.

"Spaatz Sees Film Debut," The New York Times, January 27, 1950, p. 29.

"Spies, War and Romance in New Film," Literary Digest, July 25, 1936, p. 18.

"Spotlight on Fighter Pilots," The New York Times, November 14, 1948, Section 2, p. 4.

Spinrad, Leonard. "Business as Usual," The New York Times, June 20, 1948, Section 2, p. 4.

Stal. "The Big Lift," Variety, April 12, 1950, p. 6.

Stanley, Fred. "A Belated Tribute to G.I. Joe," The New York Times, March 12, 1944, Section 2, p. 3.

_____. "Bulletins from Hollywood," The New York Times, June 4, 1944, Section 2, p. 3.

_____. "Hollywood Atom Race Ends," The New York Times, May 9, 1943, Sec. 2, p. 3.

_____. "Hollywood Faces Facts," The New York Times, June 18, 1944, Section 2, p. 3.

_____. "The Hollywood Slant," The New York Times, August 6, 1944, Section 2, pp. 1, 3.

_____. "What's the News in Hollywood?" The New York Times, May 9, 1943, Section 2, p. 3.

Sten. "Cowboy in the Clouds," Variety, January 26, 1944, p. 12.

_____. "Memphis Belle," Variety, March 22, 1944, p. 18.

"Storm Over the Andes," Time, September 23, 1935, p. 46.

"Stranger Than Fiction," Variety, December 16, 1921, p. 37.

Strat. "The Aerodrome," Variety, November 30, 1983, p. 22.

Strick, Philip. "Ma Barker to von Richthofen: An Interview with Roger Corman," Sight and Sound, Autumn 1970, pp. 179-183.

Strauss, Theodore. "Delayed Report," The New York Times, Aug. 8, 1943, Sec. 2, p. 3.

_____. "New Primer for the Armed Forces," The New York Times, June 8, 1941, Secion 9, p. 4.

Strnad [sic], Frank. "Additional Aviation Movies," AAHS Journal, July-September 1958, pp. 152-157.

_____. "Bibliography of Hollywood Aviation Motion Picture Material," AAHS Journal, July-September 1958, pp. 158-160.

_____. "Bibliography of WWI Motion Picture Material," AAHS Journal, October-December 1957, p. 264.

"Studio Sparks," The New York Times, February 19, 1928, Section 8, p. 3.

"Stunt Pilot's Crash Linked to Drinking," The New York Times, January 11, 1967, p. 14.

"Suit Against Film Concern for Navy's Bill Demanded," The New York Times, October 6, 1969, p. 26.

T., H. H. "Screen: 2 From Britain," The New York Times, August 1, 1957, p. 20.

"Tail Spin," Variety, February 1, 1939, p. 13.

Talb. "The Way to the Stars," Variety, June 20, 1945, p. 11.

"Talkers Invade Skies," The New York Times, April 12, 1931, Section 9, p. 6.

"'Task Force' to Get 2-Ocean Premiere," The New York Times, September 18, 1949, Section 2, p. 5.

"'Task' Forces 'White Heat,' Beacoup in the Blackout of the B-way Strand," Variety, September 28, 1949, p. 7.

"Technicolor Goes Aloft," The New York Times, June 1, 1941, Section 9, p. 4.

"'Test Pilot' Suit Ordered to Trial; Other Film Litigations East, West," Variety, August 9, 1939, p. 6.

"Those Magnificent Men in Their Flying Machines," Air Classics, May-June 1965, pp. 4-8.

"Three Miles Up," Variety, September 28, 1927, p. 25.

"Thrills of the Fleet Air Arm," Newsweek, January 6, 1941, p. 52.

"Top-Grossers of 1949," Variety, January 4, 1950, p. 59.

"Tora Tora Tora! Postscript," Air Classics, May 1972, pp. 20-25, 63.

Torme, Mel. "When the War Birds Invaded Hollywood," Cavalier, November 1961, pp. 27-31, 68-75.

"Transport," Time, November 18, 1935, p. 56.

"Trapped in the Sky," Variety, May 3, 1939, p. 16.

Travers, Peter. "Swing Shift," People, April 30, 1984, p. 12.

Tube. "Airborne," Variety, June 13, 1962, p. 7.

_____. "Come Fly with Me," Variety, April 3, 1963, p. 6.

_____. "The Crowded Sky," Variety, August 24, 1960, p. 6.

_____. "Flight from Ashiya," Variety, April 1, 1964, p. 23.

_____. "A Gathering of Eagles," Variety, June 6, 1963, pp. 6, 20.

_____. "I Bombed Pearl Harbor," Variety, November 29, 1961, p. 6.

_____. "The War Lover," Variety, October 24, 1962, p. 6.

_____. "X-15," Variety, November 15, 1961, p. 6.

"Twelve O'Clock High," The Christian Century, March 22, 1950, p. 383.

"2 Australians Plead Guilty In $560,000 Airliner Hoax," The New York Times, December 17, 1971, p. 4.

"2 Die As Plane, Copter Collide During Lensing of 'Zeppelin' Air Scenes," Variety, August 26, 1970, p. 2.

"UA's 'X-15' Going to Aero Film Festival," Variety, June 16, 1965, p. 5.

"United Artists to Sponsor 'The Battle of Britain' Film," The New York Times, June 21, 1967, p. 32.

"Up in the Air," The New York Times, September 1, 1946, Section 2, p. 3.

"U.S. War Film Banned in Dublin," The New York Times, September 24, 1943, p. 8.

"Van on an Island," Newsweek, June 23, 1947, p. 84.

"Veteran Calls Battle of Britain Myth Created Partly by Churchill," The Burlington Free Press, September 16, 1978, p. 5A.

"Vintage Flying Crates on Hard Ducats Sans Presold Property and Names," Variety, June 9, 1965, pp. 5, 56.

"Vintage Vans," Newsweek, June 27, 1966, p. 94.

Von Hausen, Kirk. "Zeppelin," Air Classics, September 1971, pp. 46-51.

W., A. "The Screen in Review," The New York Times, May 11, 1953, p. 25.

"Wake Island," Variety, August 12, 1942, p. 8.

" 'Wake Island,' Colorado," The New York Times, August 2, 1942, Section 8, p. 4.

Walt. "Aerial Gunner," Variety, March 24, 1943, p. 20.

_____. "Captains of the Clouds," Variety, January 21, 1942, p. 8.

_____. "Charter Pilot," Variety, November 27, 1940, p. 16.

_____. "Dive Bomber," Variety, August 13, 1941, p. 8.

_____. "Eagle Squadron," Variety, June 17, 1942, p. 8.

_____. "The Fighting Lady," Variety, December 20, 1944, p. 17.

_____. "Flight Command," Variety, December 18, 1940, p. 16.

_____. "Flight for Freedom," Variety, February 3, 1943, p. 14.

_____. "Flying Blind," Variety, August 20, 1941, p. 9.

_____. "Forced Landing," Variety, July 9, 1941, p. 14.

_____. "Give Us Wings," Variety, November 13, 1940, p. 16.

_____. "I Wanted Wings," Variety, March 26, 1941, p. 16.

_____. "International Squadron," Variety, August 13, 1941, p. 8.

_____. "Keep 'Em Flying," Variety, November 26, 1941, p. 9.

_____. "Men Against the Sky," Variety, August 28, 1940, pp. 16, 20.

_____. "Murder Over New York," Variety, December 4, 1940, p. 12.

_____. "Northern Pursuit," Variety, October 20, 1943, p. 12.

_____. "Power Dive," Variety, April 9, 1941, p. 16.

_____. "Sky Murder," Variety, September 25, 1940, p. 15.

_____. "Thunder Birds," Variety, October 21, 1942, p. 8.

_____. "The Wife Takes a Flier," Variety, April 22, 1942, p. 8.

Waly. "Ace of Aces," Variety, November 14, 1933, p. 30.

_____. "The Aviator," Variety, January 15, 1930, p. 22.

_____. "The Big Hop," Variety, January 9, 1929, p. 45.

_____. "The Flying Marine," Variety, August 8, 1929, p. 208.

_____. "Forgotten Men," Variety, May 16, 1933, p. 21.

_____. "Man and Moment," Variety, August 7, 1929, p. 201.

_____. "The Sky Rider," Variety, July 24, 1929, p. 39.

"War Film Cut in Turkey," The New York Times, February 12, 1932, p. 24.

"War Films Are Hell," Newsweek, September 15, 1958, p. 106.

"War Is Not All Bad," Newsweek, February 27, 1957, p. 119.

"Warner's in $100,000 Campaign," The New York Times, November 18, 1938, p. 40.

"Warners Suspend 'Burma' in Britain," The New York Times, September 26, 1945, p. 27.

"War's End Halts 'Task Force' Film," The New York Times, August 22, 1945, p. 17.

Watts, Stephen. "'Those Magnificent Men in Their Flying Machines' Take Off," The New York Times, August 23, 1964, Section 2, p. 7.

_____. "Viewing the Screen Scene Along the Thames," The New York Times, August 24, 1952, Section 2, p. 5.

Wear. "Best Combat Pix Yet," Variety, May 23, 1945, p. 19.

_____. "Bombay Clipper," Variety, January 14, 1942, p. 8.

_____. "Captain Eddie," Variety, June 20, 1945, p. 11.

_____. "Crack-Up," Variety, January 13, 1937, p. 13.

_____. "Dawn Patrol," Variety, December 14, 1938, p. 14.

_____. "Devil's Squadron," Variety, May 13, 1936, p. 14.

_____. "Flight Lieutenant," Variety, August 5, 1942, p. 27.

_____. "Flying Cadets," Variety, October 15, 1941, p. 8.

_____. "Forced Landing," Variety, January 1, 1936, p. 58.

_____. "Great Plane Robbery," Variety, March 8, 1950, p. 6.

_____. "L'Equipage," Variety, October 26, 1938, p. 15.

_____. "Marines Fly High," Variety, March 6, 1940, p. 18.

_____. "Moscow Skies," Variety, January 24, 1945, p. 10.

_____. "Murder in the Air," Variety, July 10, 1940, p. 12.

_____. "Parachute Nurse," Variety, June 3, 1942, p. 9.

_____. "Stirring British War Documentaries Good Model for U.S. Pic Propaganda," Variety, June 11, 1941, p. 14.

_____. "Target for Tonight," Variety, October 15, 1941, p. 8.

_____. "Wings for the Eagle," Variety, June 3, 1942, p. 9.

_____. "Wings Over Africa," Variety, August 2, 1939, p. 25.

_____. "Wings Over the Pacific," Variety, June 30, 1943, p. 20.

_____. "Women in the Wind," Variety, April 19, 1939, p. 22.

Weiler, A. H. "By Way of Report," The New York Times, July 1, 1945, Section 2, p. 3.

_____. "By Way of Report," The New York Times, July 15, 1945, Section 2, p. 3.

_____. "Fox Pays $15,000 to Defend Its Movie," The New York Times, June 17, 1969, p. 40.

_____. "Mild Blue Yonder," The New York Times, July 18, 1954, Section 2, p. 1.

_____. "Random Notes About Pictures and People," The New York Times, July 20, 1947, Sec. 2, p. 3.

_____. "'Wings' of 1927 to Be Re-Issued as Silent Movie," The New York Times, May 20, 1969, p. 41.

_____. "'Zeppelin' Carries Flimsy Tale," The New York Times, October 7, 1971, p. 58.

"What's in a Name?" The New York Times, May 6, 1951, Section 2, p. 4.

Whit. "Back from Eternity," Variety, August 29, 1956, p. 6.

_____. "Bombers B-52," Variety, October 30, 1957, p. 6.

_____. "The Bridges at Toko-Ri," Variety, December 29, 1954, p. 6.

_____. "Charley Varrick," Variety, October 10, 1973, p. 12.

_____. "Clipped Wings," Variety, November 25, 1953, pp. 6, 24.

_____. "Darling Lili," Variety, June 24, 1970, p. 17.

_____. "Decision Against Time," Variety, July 10, 1957, p. 6.

_____. "Fail Safe," Variety, September 16, 1964, p. 6.

_____. "Fate Is the Hunter," Variety, September 16, 1964, pp. 6, 19.

_____. "The Flight of the Phoenix," Variety, December 15, 1965, p. 6.

_____. "The Flight that Disappeared," Variety, September 20, 1961, p. 6.

_____. "The Gypsy Moths," Variety, August 27, 1969, p. 18.

_____. "Hell's Horizon," Variety, November 23, 1955, p. 6.

_____. "Island of Lost Women," Variety, April 8, 1959, p. 6.

_____. "McHale's Navy Joins the Air Force," Variety, June 9, 1965, p. 6.

_____. "Operation Haylift," Variety, April 19, 1950, p. 8.

_____. "Secret Flight," Variety, October 3, 1951, p. 22.

_____. "Sky High," Variety, April 16, 1952, p. 16.

_____. "The Tarnished Angels," Variety, November 20, 1957, p. 6.

_____. "Those Magnificent Men in Their Flying Machines," Variety, June 2, 1965, p. 6.

_____. "Zero Hour," Variety, October 23, 1957, p. 6.

Wideatt, Mary Fabyan. "The Stage and Screen," The Commonweal, April 29, 1938, p. 21.

"Winged Victory." Time, December 25, 1944, pp. 48, 50.

"'Wings' A Hit in Berlin," The New York Times, January 11, 1929, p. 20.

"Wings and the Woman," Variety, August 5, 1942, p. 8.

"Wings of Adventure," Variety, August 13, 1930, p. 31.

"Wings of Eagles, The," Time, March 11, 1957, pp. 100, 102.

"Wings of the Fleet," Variety, April 11, 1938, p. 13.

"Wings of the Navy," Variety, January 18, 1939, p. 12.

"Wings Over Africa," The New York Times, July 15, 1934, Section 9, p. 2.

"Wings Over Honolulu," Time, May 31, 1937, p. 30.

Wise, Naomi. "The Hawksian Woman," Take One, January-February 1971, pp. 17-19.

"Wolves of the Air," Variety, May 4, 1927, p. 23.

"Women in the Wind," Variety, February 1, 1939, p. 13.

"Won in the Clouds," Variety, May 2, 1928, p. 36.

Wood. "Charter Pilot," Variety, December 25, 1940, p. 16.

"Yank in the R.A.F., The," Variety, September 10, 1941, p. 8.

Zanuck, Darryl. "Why 'Tora! Tora! Tora!'?" The New York Times, June 16, 1969, p. 10.

"Zanuck's '12 O'Clock' Bid for Oscar, Ditto 'Pinky,'" Variety, October 19, 1949, p. 9.

Pressbooks and Promotional Material

"Blue Max, The." Twentieth Century-Fox Film Corp.: 1966.

"Gallant Journey." Columbia Pictures Corp.: 1946.

"Gathering of Eagles, The." Rank Film Distributors: 1963.

"High Road to China." Warner Brothers, 1983.

"Okinawa." Columbia Pictures Corp.: 1952.

"Right Stuff, The." Ladd Company: 1983.

"Those Magnificent Men in Their Flying Machines." Twentieth Century-Fox Film Corp.: 1965.

"Tora! Tora! Tora!" Twentieth Century-Fox Film Corp.: 1970.

Books

Allen, Oliver E. The Airline Builders. Alexandria: Time Life Books, 1981.

Angelucci, Enzo. The Rand McNally Encyclopedia of Military Aircraft, 1914-1980. New York: The Military Press, 1983.

Ball, Eustace Hale. Legion of the Condemned. New York: Grosset & Dunlap, 1928.

Barbour, Alan G. Days of Thrills and Adventure. London: Collier-MacMillan, 1970.

Baxter, John. Hollywood in the Sixties. New York: A. S. Barnes and Co., 1972.

_____. Hollywood in the Thirties. New York: A. S. Barnes and Co., 1968.

Bogdanovich, Peter. John Ford. Berkeley: University of California Press, 1968.

Bowen, Ezra. Knights of the Air. Alexandria: Time-Life Books, 1980.

Boyington, Gregory. Baa Baa Black Sheep. New York: Bantam Books, 1977.

Brooks, Tim and Earle Marsh. The Complete Directory to Prime Time Network TV Shows, 1946-Present. New York: Ballantine Books, 1979, 1981.

Brownlow, Kevin. The Parade's Gone By. New York: Ballantine Books, 1968.

Caiden, Martin. The Ragged, Rugged Warriors. New York: Ballantine Books, 1966.

Capra, Frank. The Name Above the Title. New York: The Macmillan Company, 1971.

Denby, David, Editor. Film 70/71. New York: Simon and Schuster, 1971.

Dwiggins, Don. Hollywood Pilot. New York: Modern Literary Editions Publishing Co., 1967.

_____. Howard Hughes: The True Story. Santa Monica: Werner Book Corp., 1972.

Fowler, Guy. Lilac Time. New York: Grosset & Dunlap, 1928.

Garrett, George P., O. B. Hardison, Jr., and Jane R. Gelfman, Editors. Suggestions for Instructions to Accompany Film Scripts One and Film Scripts Two. New York: Meredith Corp., 1971.

Goldman, William, and George Roy Hill. The Great Waldo Pepper. New York: Dell Publishing Co., 1975.

Gow, Gordon. Hollywood in the Fifties. New York: A. S. Barnes and Co., 1971.

Greenwood, Jim and Maxine. Stunt Flying in the Movies. Blue Ridge Summit: Tab Books, Inc., 1982.

Gussow, Mel. Don't Say Yes Until I Finish Talking. New York: Pocket Books, 1972.

Halliday, Jon. Sirk on Sirk. New York: The Viking Press, 1972.

Halliwell, Leslie. The Filmgoer's Companion. New York: Hill and Wang, 1965, 1967.

Higham, Charles and Joel Greenberg. Hollywood in the Forties. New York: Paperback Library, 1970.

Kael, Pauline. Going Steady. New York: Bantam Books, 1971.

Kagan, Norman. The War Film. New York: Pyramid Publications, 1974.

Krafsur, Richard P., Executive Editor. The American Film Institute Catalogue of Motion Pictures: Feature Films, 1961-1970. New York and London: R. R. Bowker Co., 1976.

Lahue, Kalton C. Bound and Gagged. New York: A. S. Barnes and Co., 1968.

_____. Continued Next Week: A History of the Motion Picture Serial. Norman: University of Oklahoma Press, 1964.

McBride, Joseph, Editor. Focus on Howard Hawks. Englewood Cliffs: Prentice-Hall, Inc., 1972.

McBride, Joseph and Michael Wilmington. John Ford. New York: Da Capo Press, Inc., 1975.

Madsen, Axel. Billy Wilder. Bloomington and London: Indiana University Press, 1969.

Manvell, Roger. New Cinema in Britain. New York: E. P. Dutton and Co., Inc., 1969.

_____. New Cinema in the USA. New York: E. P. Dutton and Co., Inc., 1968.

Maltin, Leonard, editor. TV Movies. New York: The New American Library, 1982.

Michael, Paul. Humphrey Bogart: The Man and His Films. New York: Bonanza Books, 1965.

Miller, Don. B Movies. New York: Curtiss Books, 1973.

Moolman, Valerie. Women Aloft. Alexandria: Time-Life Books, 1981.

Mosley, Leonard. "Battle of Britain": The Making of a Film. New York: Ballantine Books, 1969.

Movies Unlimited Video Catalog, 1984 Edition. Philadelphia: Movies Unlimited, Inc., 1984.

Munden, Kenneth W., Executive Editor. The American Film Institute Catalog of Motion Pictures Produced in the United States: Feature Films, 1921-1930. New York and London: R. R. Bowker Company, 1971.

Nevin, David. Architects of Air Power. Alexandria: Time-Life Books, 1981.

_____. The Pathfinders. Alexandria: Time-Life Books, 1980.

New York Times Film Reviews, The, 1913-1968 (Vols. 1-6). New York: The New York Times and Arno Press, 1970.

New York Times Film Reviews, The, 1969-1970. New York: The New York Times and Arno Press, 1971.

New York Times Film Reviews, The, 1971-1972. New York: The New York Times and Arno Press, 1973.

New York Times Film Reviews, The, 1973-1974. New York: The New York Times and Arno Press, 1975.

New York Times Film Reviews, The, 1975-1976. New York: The New York Times and Arno Press, 1977.

New York Times Film Reviews, The, 1977-1978. New York: The New York Times and Arno Press, 1979.

New York Times Film Reviews, The, 1979-1980. New York: The New York Times and Arno Press, 1981.

Robinson, David. Hollywood in the Twenties. New York: Paperback Library, 1970.

Ronnie, Art. Locklear: The Man Who Walked on Wings. New York: A. S. Barnes and Co., 1973.

Saunders, John Monk. Wings. New York: Grosset & Dunlap, 1927.

Seagrave, Sterling. Soldiers of Fortune. Alexandria: Time-Life Books, 1981.

Skogsberg, Bertil. Wings on the Screen: A Pictorial History of Air Movies. New York: A. S. Barnes and Co., 1981.

Smith, Julian. Looking Away: Hollywood and Vietnam. New York: Scribner, 1975.

Stedman, Raymond William. The Serials: Suspense and Drama by Installment. Norman: University of Oklahoma Press, 1971.

Suid, Lawrence H. Guts & Glory. Reading: Addison-Wesley Publishing Co., 1978.

Thomas, Bob. King Cohn. New York: Bantam Books, 1968.

_____. Selznick. New York: Pocket Books, 1972.

Whitehouse, Arch. Legion of the Lafayette. New York: Modern Literary Editions Publishing Co., 1962.

Wood, Robin. Howard Hawks. New York: Doubleday & Company, Inc., 1968.

Zicree, Marc Scott. The Twilight Zone Companion. New York: Bantam Books, 1982.

Zierold, Norman. The Moguls. New York: Avon Books,
1972.